THE LEGO® IDEAS BOOK

WRITTEN BY HANNAH DOLAN, SIMON HUGO, TORI KOSARA,
JULIA MARCH, AND CATHERINE SAUNDERS

CONTENTS

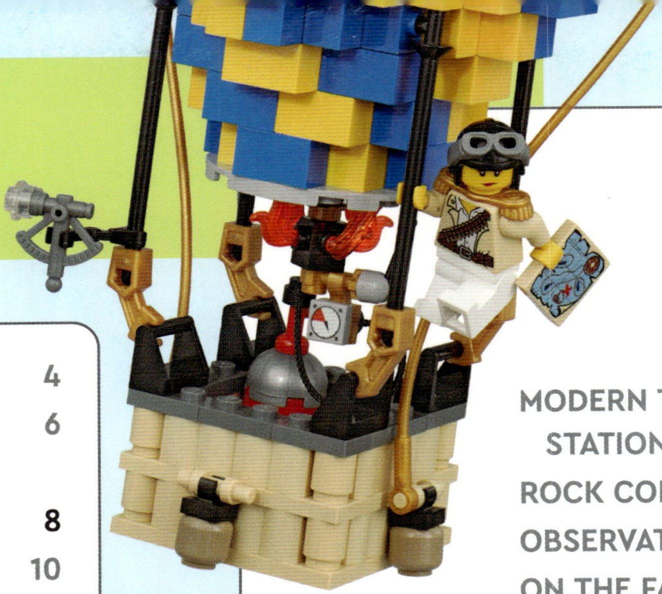

Fly up, up, and away in a hot-air balloon on page 61

Observe the stars on page 44

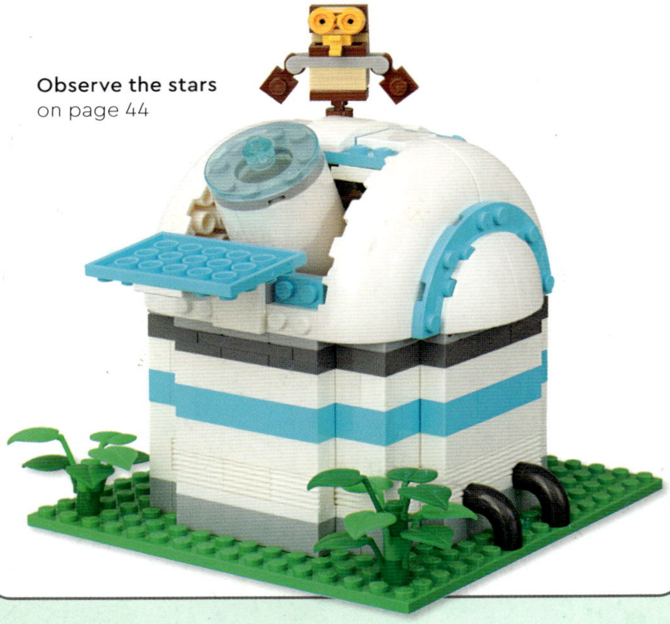

Make a pet dog on page 105

Do a loop the loop in a stunt plane on page 155

INTRODUCTION

With a pile of LEGO® pieces and a dash of creativity, you can build almost anything you can imagine! In this book, you'll find hundreds of ideas to inspire you to make awesome models with your own LEGO collection. Here are some things to think about before you begin building.

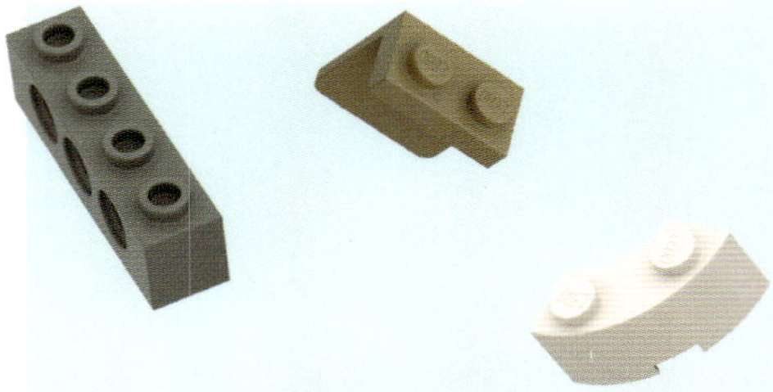

PIECE BY PIECE

There are thousands of different LEGO pieces and they come in many colors. You can find out more about piece types on the Brick Types and Useful Pieces pages at the back of this book.

GATHER YOUR PIECES

There's one thing you'll definitely need before you can build: LEGO pieces! Don't worry about the size of your collection or how new it is. The original LEGO System of Play elements, made in 1958, still fit perfectly with those made today. You can also buy secondhand LEGO pieces at thrift stores, share with friends and neighbors, or play with them at schools and libraries.

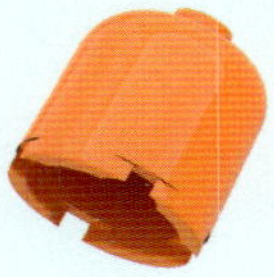

IDEAS

Inspiration can strike anywhere. Use the builds in this book to spark your imagination, then create lots of models of your own. You might get other ideas along the way by looking at the world around you, or from books, TV shows, movies, or games.

MAKE IT YOUR OWN

The models in this book are here to inspire you, but you don't have to copy them exactly. Get creative and personalize your builds. You might build something completely different to what's on the page in front of you—and that's great!

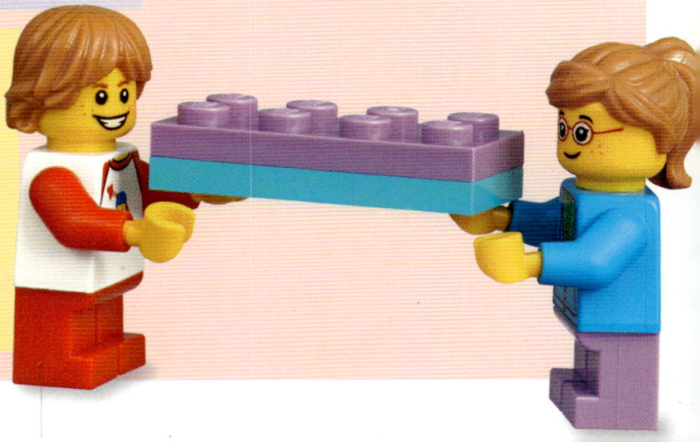

READY, STEADY, BUILD

Once you have your pieces, you can build whatever you like. With so many amazing LEGO pieces and inspiring model ideas, you might be stuck on exactly how to begin. Try out some of these ideas!

PICK A TECHNIQUE

Some of the pictures on the pages that follow show you how the models are connected and focus on some useful building techniques. If you want to try something out, go for it and see where it leads you.

WRITE IT DOWN

Look at some of the models in the book and write down what you like about them and what you don't. This might fire up your imagination so you can start building.

DECIDE ON AN IDEA

Is your head full of things you want to build? List out all the model ideas you'd like to make. Then choose just one idea and begin building it.

JUST BUILD

Start clicking some LEGO pieces together and see what happens. Look at the shape you've made and think about what it can become as you build.

PLAN AHEAD

You could draw your model before you begin building, or you might find that you're the sort of builder who just likes to start building without sketching first.

LOOK AT YOUR PIECES

Grab a handful of pieces and spread them out so you can see what you're working with. Can you create your own version of a model in this book using some of them?

BRICK TIPS

Once you're ready to build, you'll need to start thinking like a builder. Here are some tips to get you started. You might want to keep some of these in mind when you're making your models, or you might have your own way of doing things. The most important thing is to have fun!

SORT IT OUT

Organize some of your LEGO collection into element types and colors before you get started. This will save you time searching for pieces as you build.

THINK BIG . . . OR SMALL

Decide what scale you want your model to be before you start so you have the right amount of LEGO pieces. If you're building something that minifigures can sit, play, or live inside, that's minifigure scale. Anything smaller than that is microscale. You may also want to build something bigger than minifigure scale, like the baby below—this model's size is called "Miniland" scale.

MICROSCALE

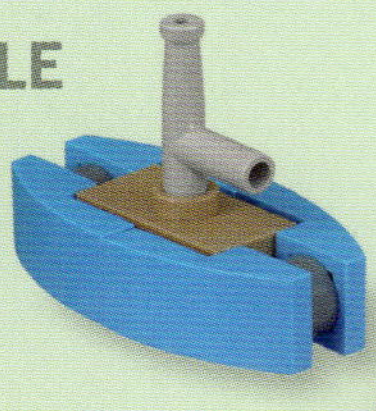

MINIFIGURE SCALE

MINILAND SCALE

DON'T WOBBLE

Build your models on a sturdy base and add in plates between your stacks of bricks to make them stable. This will keep them from toppling over.

MAKE SPACE

It's easiest to build on a flat surface with plenty of room for your pieces and models. Try building at a table or in a clear space on the floor.

MEASURE YOUR MINIFIGURES

If you want minifigures to fit inside your build, think about how much height and arm and leg room is necessary so you can invite them in.

CHANGE IT UP

Don't worry if you don't have the perfect piece. Get creative with what you do have and think about other elements you can use instead.

MAKE IT STABLE

Press your bricks together well to give your builds stability. You can also keep pieces in place by overlapping them with other pieces. Making your models stable will mean you can play with them again and again.

BUILD TOGETHER

Sometimes, it's more fun to create models with family and friends. Why not share ideas and the joy of building?

FLYING COLORS

Who says all pirate ships need to be brown? If you want to make a pink boat for your pirate crew, go for it. Use whatever colors you like when you're building.

DON'T WORRY!

If your model doesn't turn out the way you wanted it to, you can start again. Or you could even change it into something else. There is no right or wrong way to build.

KEEP GOING

Whatever happens, don't give up! The fun is in the building, so just keep connecting your bricks until things click for you.

Look closely at the buildings, nature, vehicles, and people you see every day. What amazing details haven't you noticed before and how could you re-create them with LEGO® pieces? Try building exactly what you see, or add fun elements to create something unique.

BUILDING BRIEF

Objective: Build a museum
Use: Displaying interesting objects
Features: Rooms, exhibits, display cases, visitors
Extras: Gift shop, café, interactive features

1×8 plate links two 1×5×4 half arches to make one wide arch
Decorative stonework runs around the middle of the walls
SOMEONE'S STOLEN THE LIZARD.

MUSEUM OF UNUSUAL THINGS

Museums have lots of ancient, important, and unusual things to look at and learn about. What will you put in your museum? Perhaps it could be nature-themed, an art gallery, or a science center. Whatever you think is fascinating will attract visitors.

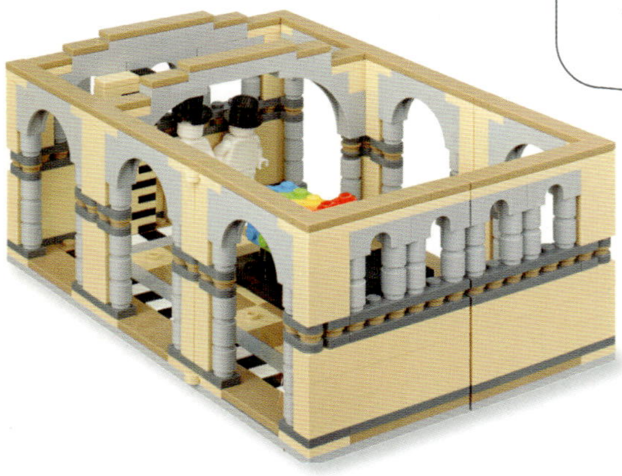

CLOSED SIDES

This doorway becomes two when the room is folded shut

Doorways are topped by 1×6×2 arches

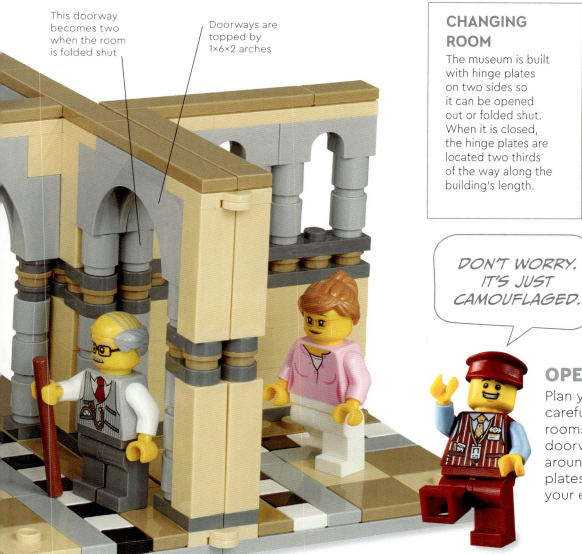

CHANGING ROOM

The museum is built with hinge plates on two sides so it can be opened out or folded shut. When it is closed, the hinge plates are located two thirds of the way along the building's length.

Hinge plates are added at the top of the walls

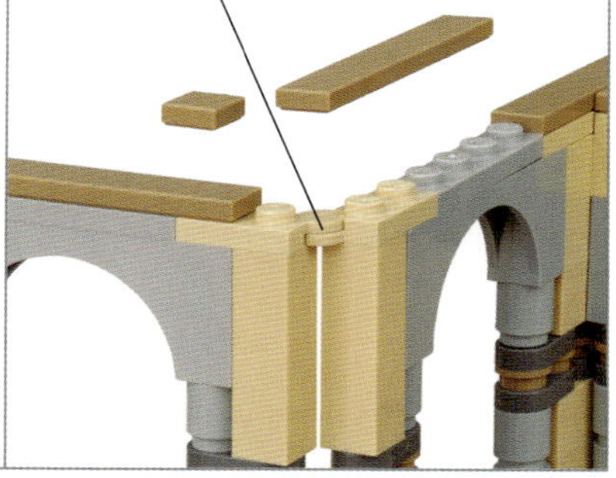

DON'T WORRY. IT'S JUST CAMOUFLAGED.

OPEN PLAN

Plan your museum layout carefully. You'll need different rooms connected by wide, open doorways so visitors can move around easily. Use lots of jumper plates on the floor to attach your eye-catching exhibits to.

EXHIBITS

Minifigures will flock to your museum to see things that they can't find anywhere else. This museum features a dazzling rainbow sheep statue and record-breaking wonders like the world's tallest LEGO top hat and amazing camouflaging lizard (er, where did it go?).

Colorful plates attach sideways

RAINBOW SHEEP STATUE

This plate and tile measuring scale highlights the hat's height

Hat is a LEGO® Technic cylinder on a round jumper plate

TALLEST TOP HAT

"Information board" is built onto a bracket plate

CAMOUFLAGING LIZARD

ROOFTOP GARDEN

Take your LEGO house-building to the next level with colorful details and creative uses of everyday spaces. The thriving rooftop garden at the top of this two-story apartment bulding is a relaxing place where minifigures can connect with nature.

BUILDING BRIEF

Objective:	Build a minifigure home with creative outdoor spaces
Use:	Gardening, relaxation
Features:	Roof terrace, plants, flowers
Extras:	Seating, stepping stones, water features

A low wall around the roof garden keeps minifigures safe

SIDE VIEW

I COULD REALLY PUT DOWN ROOTS HERE.
Experiment with unusual window positioning
Green base plates give the whole build a garden feel

1×1 half circle tile
1×1 quarter circle tile
2×6 plate matches the color of the wall

SIDE PANELS

This colorful building is made even more eye-catching by the tiled patterns on its sides. Each decorative panel is made from 12 small tiles on a 2×6 plate. They fit sideways onto bracket plates built into the walls.

BRIGHT BLOCK

Use vibrant bricks, plates, and tiles to make the architecture of your apartment building stand out. You could also add unusual details and patterns to the corners with small pieces. What furniture could you build inside?

This vine "grows" out of a brick with four side studs
I ALREADY HAVE!
Use transparent 1×6×5 bricks to make big windows— or just leave empty spaces

SMALL SPACE, BIG IDEAS

Think about your favorite outdoor spaces. What parts of them could you add to your rooftop garden? How about a water feature, a rock garden, or a barbecue area? Or maybe a DJ booth and disco lights!

LEVEL UP

Make your eco-home even greener by adding a "living wall" of climbing plants on one side. Build them on using pieces with side studs or clips.

GROW WILD

Lots of LEGO pieces are designed to look like plants. But when you start to combine those pieces with others in your collection, the number of bushes and blooms you can create grows and grows!

Green feather pieces fit onto tiles with clips

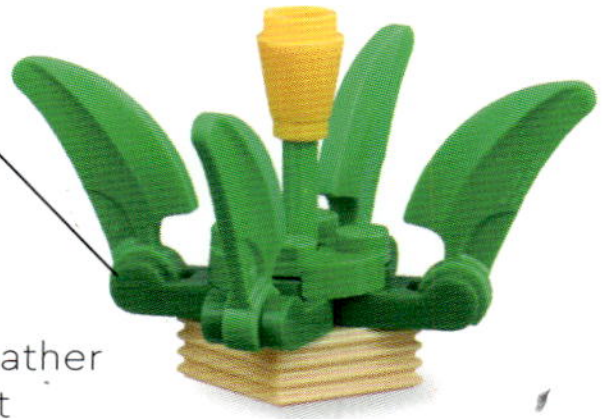
Leaves clip onto four 1×1 plates with bars

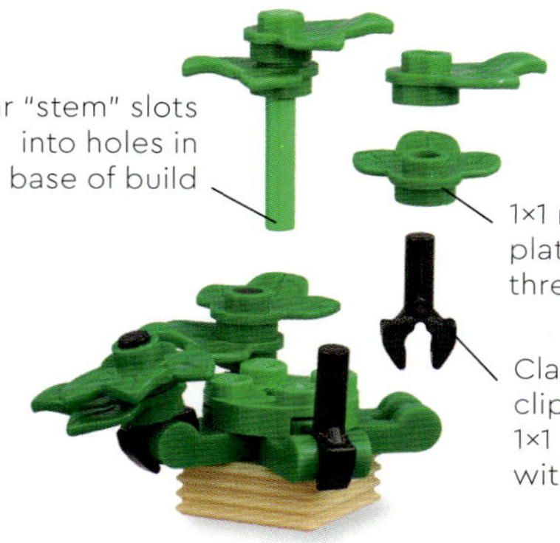
Bar "stem" slots into holes in base of build
1×1 round plate with three leaves
Claw piece clips onto 1×1 plate with bar

HAUNTED HOUSE

Boo! This house definitely looks haunted, but there's no need to be scared of a building challenge like this. It's all about the details, from the creepy tree lurking next to the unwelcoming house, to the gruesome gate with clanking chains. Only the bravest minifigure would dare enter!

WHY IS EVERYTHING UPSIDE DOWN?
Brown half arch pieces make good tree branches
Hanging weeds have overgrown this once-mighty tree
This half arch piece is smaller than the other two

THIS PLACE IS TOO CREEPY, EVEN FOR ME!
Who is hiding behind this door?

Each gate piece swings on two 1×1 bricks with clips
"Keep out" sign is a printed tile
KEEP OUT

EERIE EXTERIOR

When building the walls of your haunted house, use LEGO pieces in dark or muted colors and think about textures. Adding textured bricks that have "exposed" brickwork among smooth pieces gives the walls a shabby, rundown look.

BUILDING BRIEF

Objective: Build a hair-raising home
Use: Scaring your minifigure friends—and perhaps your human ones, too!
Features: Boarded-up windows, old-fashioned features
Extras: Haunted tree, creaking gate, scary residents

Golden spire is a minifigure ski pole!
Brickwork-textured parts suggest a crumbling facade
Pale green details for weeds, mold, and general gunkiness
This cobweb piece clips onto bricks with bars

RAISING THE ROOF

The tallest part of the roof is made from six slope bricks in a triangle shape. They are supported by an arch brick and two decorative scroll bricks underneath, and held together by a row of jumper plates on top.

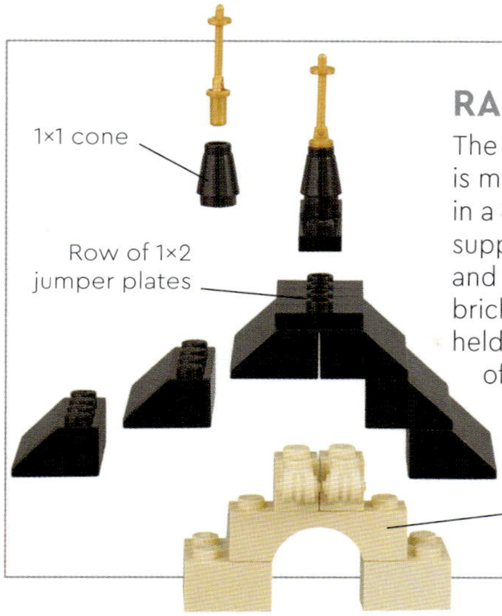

1×1 cone
Row of 1×2 jumper plates
1×4 arch brick

HOME SHRIEK HOME

Inside, the house is divided into three spine-chilling spaces. A ghost haunts the attic, while a vampire stalks the downstairs room. The resident spider and mouse seem cute and friendly by comparison.

1×1 bricks with scrolls add realistic architectural details
Leaf piece attaches to a side stud at ground level

SIDE VIEW

Who left this cheese in the attic?!
Did you know that most LEGO ghosts glow in the dark?

AAARGH, I'VE JUST SEEN A SPIDER!

INTERIOR VIEW

BUILDING BRIEF

Objective: Build mini monster trucks and a rally course
Use: Sports entertainment, racing
Features: Trucks, race track, obstacles
Extras: Stadium seating, fire, hoops

MONSTER TRUCK RALLY

With their massive tires and awesome modifications, monster trucks are tough. Try building a set of them in microscale, then make a rally track for your trucks to power around. Monster trucks often have funny names or humorous features, such as spots, shark teeth, or a dog tail. How will you make yours stand out?

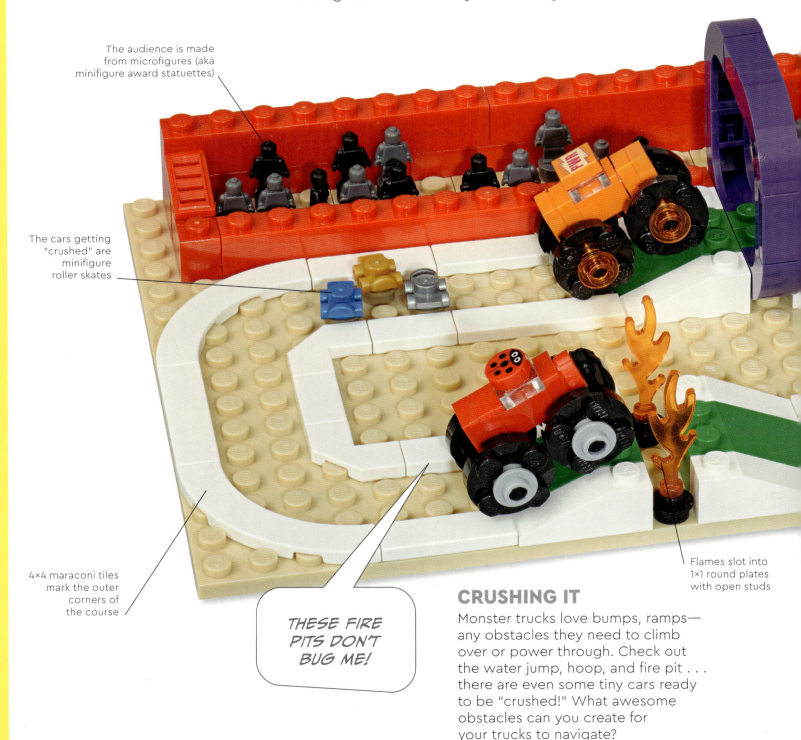

The audience is made from microfigures (aka minifigure award statuettes)
The cars getting "crushed" are minifigure roller skates
4×4 maraconi tiles mark the outer corners of the course
THESE FIRE PITS DON'T BUG ME!
Flames slot into 1×1 round plates with open studs
PWR

CRUSHING IT

Monster trucks love bumps, ramps—any obstacles they need to climb over or power through. Check out the water jump, hoop, and fire pit . . . there are even some tiny cars ready to be "crushed!" What awesome obstacles can you create for your trucks to navigate?

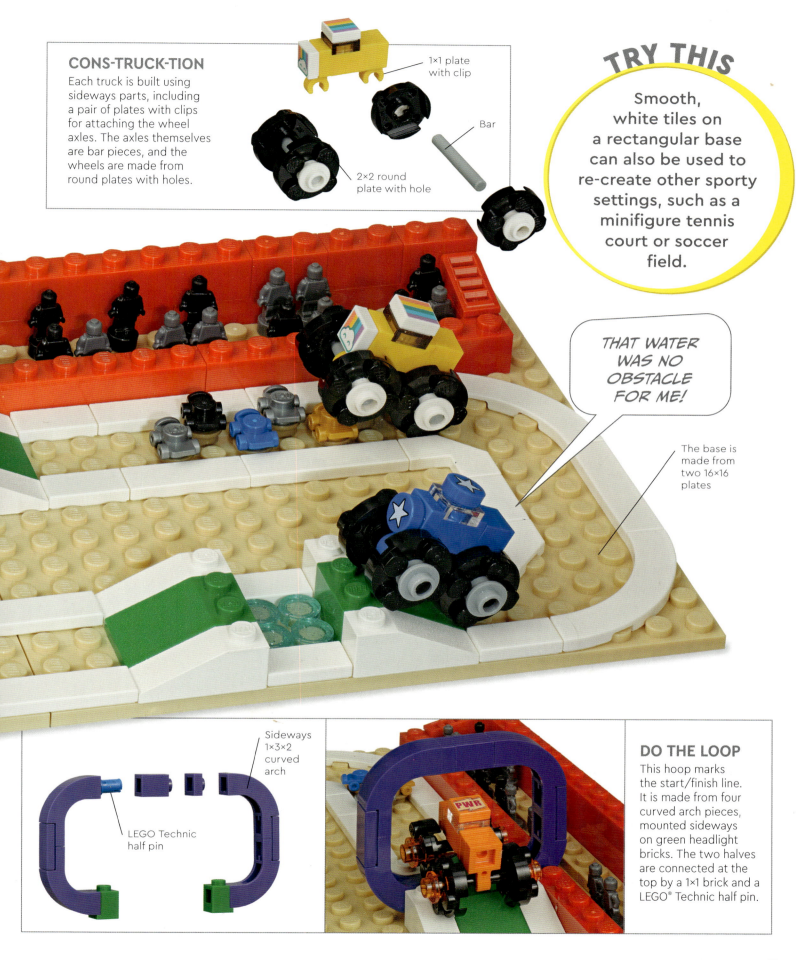

CONS-TRUCK-TION

Each truck is built using sideways parts, including a pair of plates with clips for attaching the wheel axles. The axles themselves are bar pieces, and the wheels are made from round plates with holes.

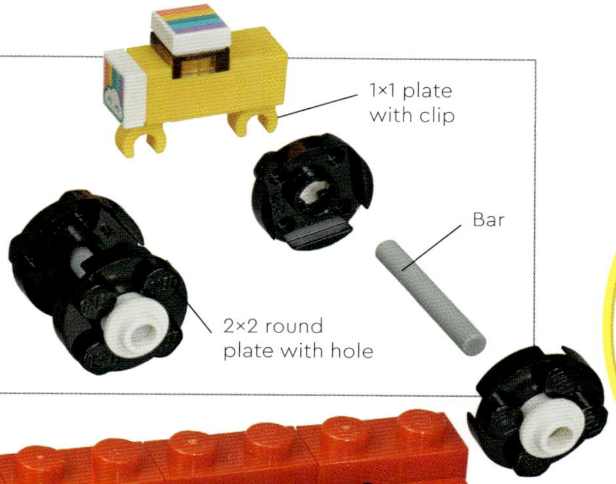

1×1 plate with clip
Bar
2×2 round plate with hole

TRY THIS

Smooth, white tiles on a rectangular base can also be used to re-create other sporty settings, such as a minifigure tennis court or soccer field.

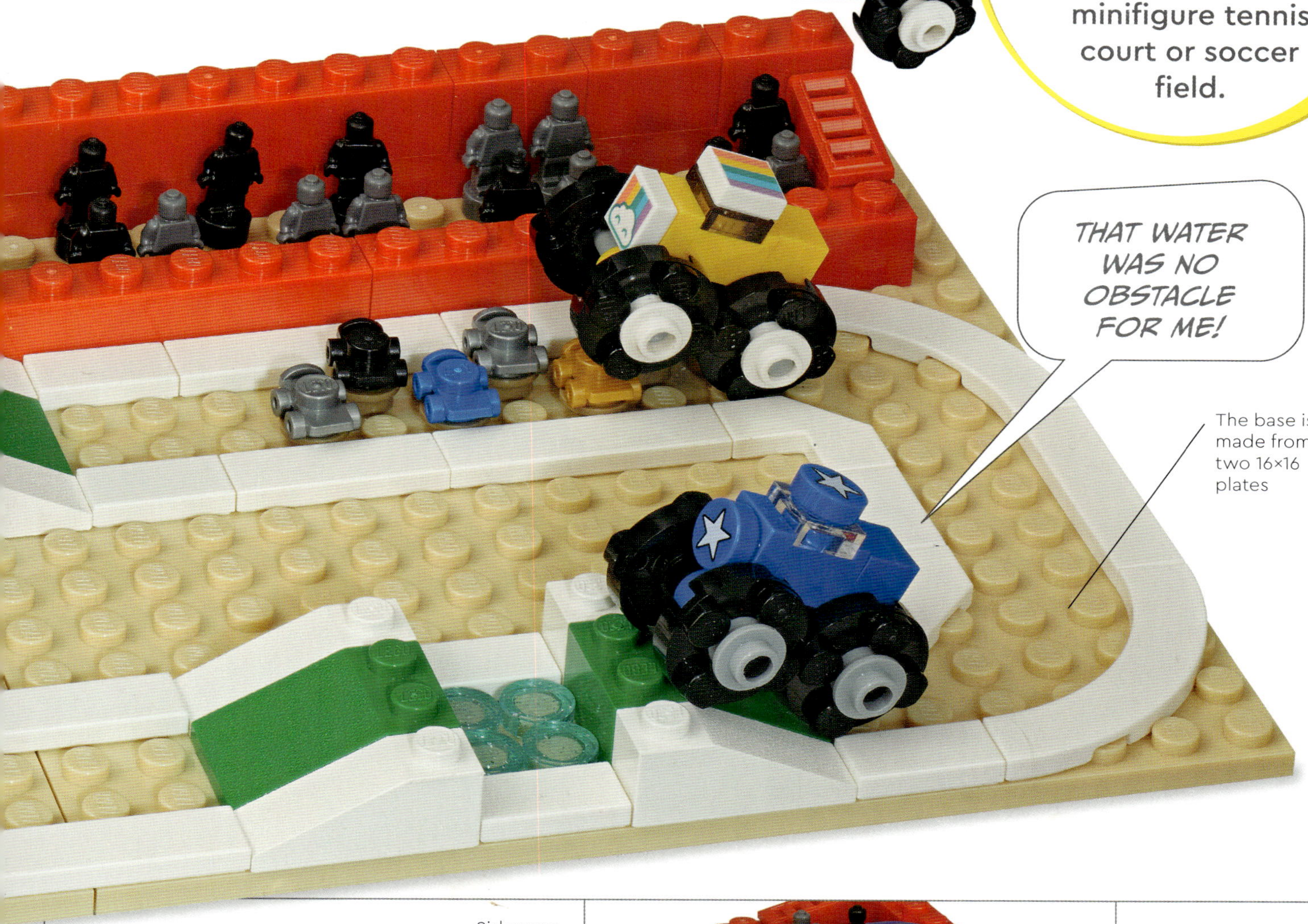

THAT WATER WAS NO OBSTACLE FOR ME!
The base is made from two 16×16 plates

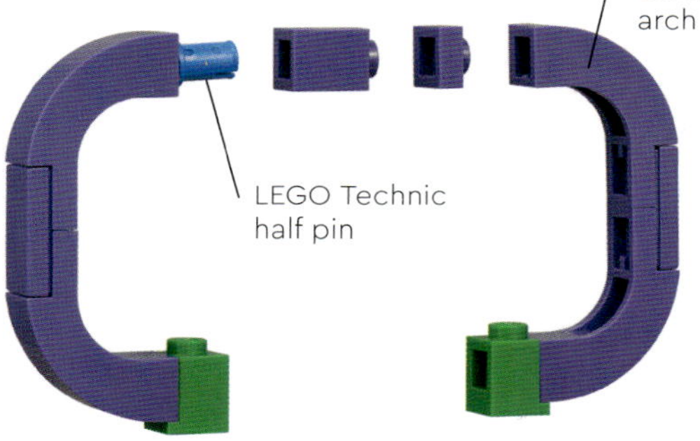

Sideways 1×3×2 curved arch
LEGO Technic half pin

PWR

DO THE LOOP

This hoop marks the start/finish line. It is made from four curved arch pieces, mounted sideways on green headlight bricks. The two halves are connected at the top by a 1×1 brick and a LEGO® Technic half pin.

BUILDING BRIEF

Objective:	Build a lighthouse
Use:	Guiding ships to or from land
Features:	Tower, lantern, jetty
Extras:	Land, fishing equipment, pulley, sea creatures

2×2 round plate with octagonal bar

BRIGHT LIGHT

The most important part of a lighthouse is its lantern, which warns passing ships away from land. This one has two bright bulbs made from 2×2 slide plates inside radar dishes.

Transparent minifigure heads can be backup bulbs

SPARE BULBS

KEEP IT REAL

To make this flashy-looking building, stack up sections of red and white bricks (or whatever colors you like) on top of plates. You can make it as tall as you like. You could even connect a house for the lighthouse keeper.

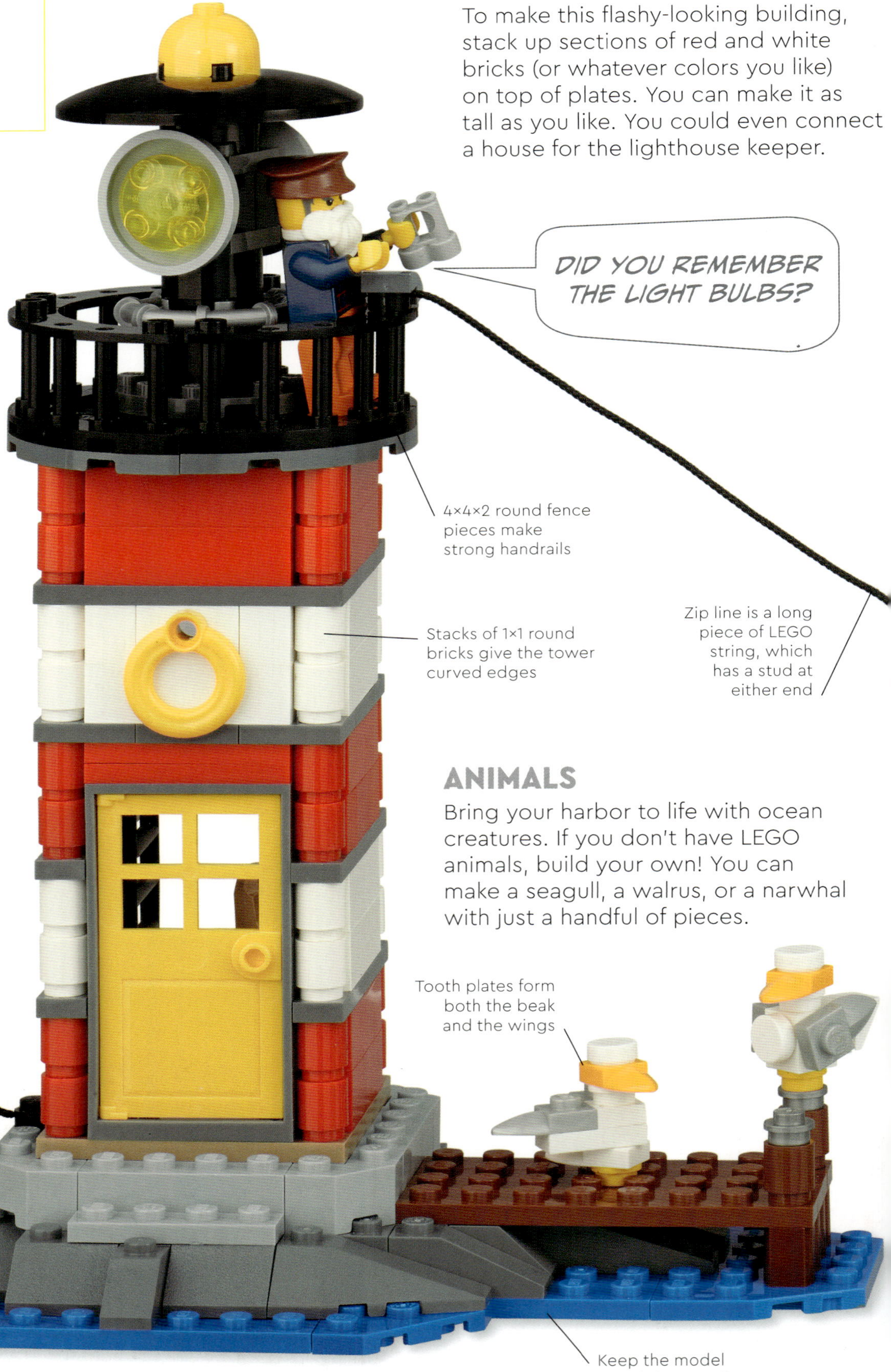
DID YOU REMEMBER THE LIGHT BULBS?
4×4×2 round fence pieces make strong handrails
Stacks of 1×1 round bricks give the tower curved edges
Zip line is a long piece of LEGO string, which has a stud at either end
Tooth plates form both the beak and the wings
Keep the model steady by securing it to base plates
MMMM . . . COOKIE!

ANIMALS

Bring your harbor to life with ocean creatures. If you don't have LEGO animals, build your own! You can make a seagull, a walrus, or a narwhal with just a handful of pieces.

WALRUS

LIGHTHOUSE

Themed models like this make great team projects. Sharing ideas, building tips, and LEGO pieces with your friends or family is a fun way to build and play. This coastal construction has a central lighthouse structure, plus a little spit of land and several small, seafaring animals. You could each choose a different part of the scene to build.

COME ON IN

Decorate the inside of your model, too. This lighthouse keeper has a fireplace to keep him warm, personal treasures on the mantelpiece, and a handy map on the wall.

TRY THIS

This lighthouse has a classic red-and-white stripe design but you can make yours any color or pattern. It just has to be easy for ships to spot, so go wild!

OOPS! I KNEW I'D FORGOTTEN SOMETHING.

This steering wheel makes the telescope look realistic

LAND AHOY

This small section of a cliff is made from gray and green bricks and slopes. Add a telescope for spotting ships on the horizon and a pulley for delivering essentials to the lighthouse keeper.

One rock panel piece forms the main structure of this spit of land

If you don't have this crate piece, you could build one from small bricks and plates

Half pin fits onto the paint roller piece

1×1 cone

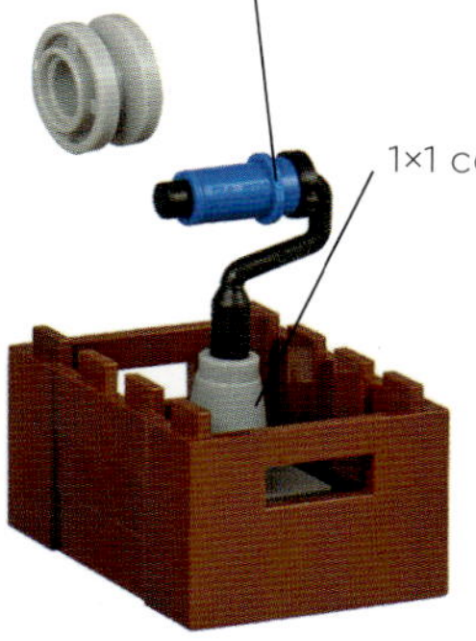

PULLEY SYSTEM

A simple pulley on a zip line delivers vital supplies, such as pizza, to the lighthouse. A small wheel, attached to a paint roller accessory and pin on the box, glides along the rope.

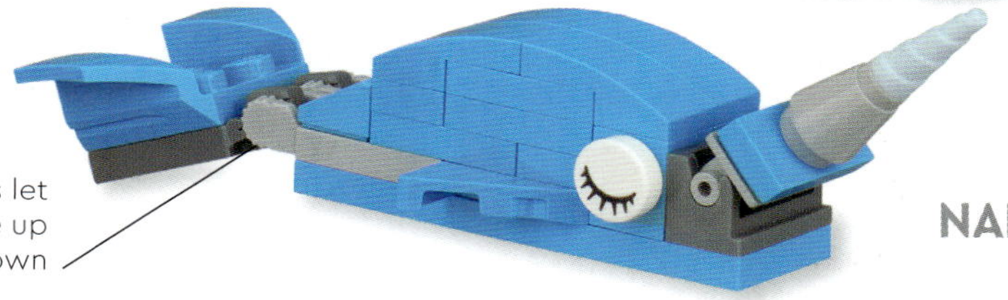

Click hinges let the tail move up and down

NARWHAL

BUILDING BRIEF

Objective: Build an underground world
Use: Carrying minifigures' water, services, and sewage
Features: Pipes, ladder, pavement, sewer
Extras: Wheelbarrow, tools, signs, cones

UNDER THE STREETS

Have you ever thought about what might be under your feet? In a city, you may find networks of pipes and cables carrying water, electricity, gas, and sewage (well, it's got to go somewhere . . .). There are so many possibilities for an underground build—unusual creatures, escape tunnels, or even buried treasure.

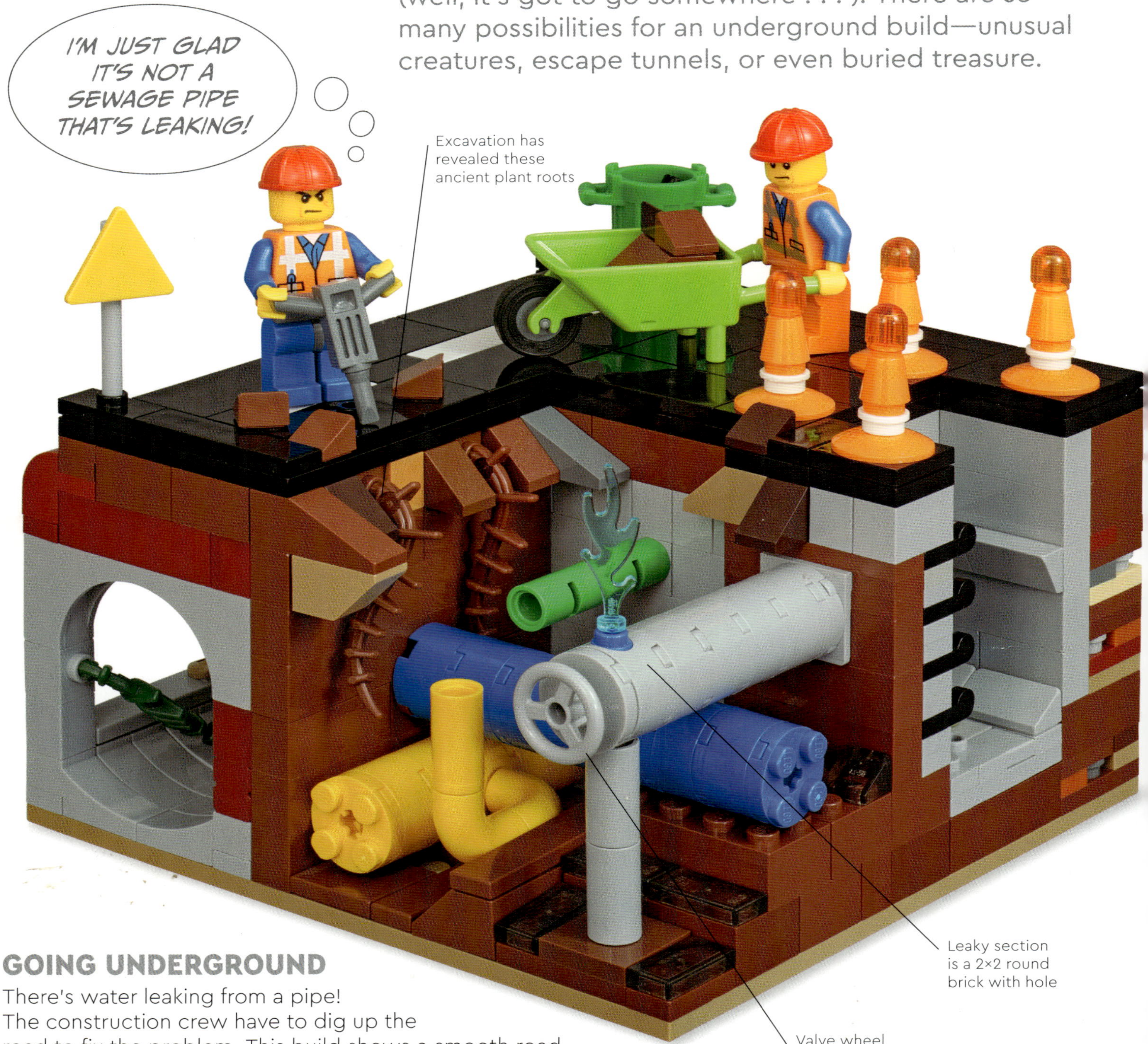
I'M JUST GLAD IT'S NOT A SEWAGE PIPE THAT'S LEAKING!
Excavation has revealed these ancient plant roots
Leaky section is a 2×2 round brick with hole
Valve wheel attaches to a sideways round jumper plate

GOING UNDERGROUND

There's water leaking from a pipe! The construction crew have to dig up the road to fix the problem. This build shows a smooth road surface as well as the pipe network and sewers below it. How many levels will your build have? How will your underground scenes connect to the world above?

BUILD TIP

Though it looks entirely smooth, the top of this build has several carefully placed studs to secure the minifigures, trash can, cones, and rubble.

SIDE VIEW

The slimmer pipes are made from LEGO Technic cylinders

Plates with bars make a ladder down this shaft

SIDE VIEW

HEY, WHERE DID YOU GET THAT LOVELY SOUP FROM?
DOWNSTAIRS!

SEWER VIEW

Rat is secured onto a jumper plate

GOING UNDERGROUND

The small side tunnel is perfectly suited to rats! The junction where the tunnels meet is finished with a 4×4 round plate with hole, with four macaroni tiles on top.

UNDER THE EARTH

Deep underground, there's a treasure trove of rocks and minerals. Miners dig vertical tunnels called shafts to find gold, tin, copper, and other useful resources. This build is another two-part challenge—as well as a dark, earthy underground part, you also need to create the landscape on the surface.

BUILDING BRIEF

Objective:	Build a gold mine
Use:	Mining for valuable rocks and minerals
Features:	Entrance, mine cart, tracks, tools, rocks, lanterns
Extras:	Gold store, plants, dynamite

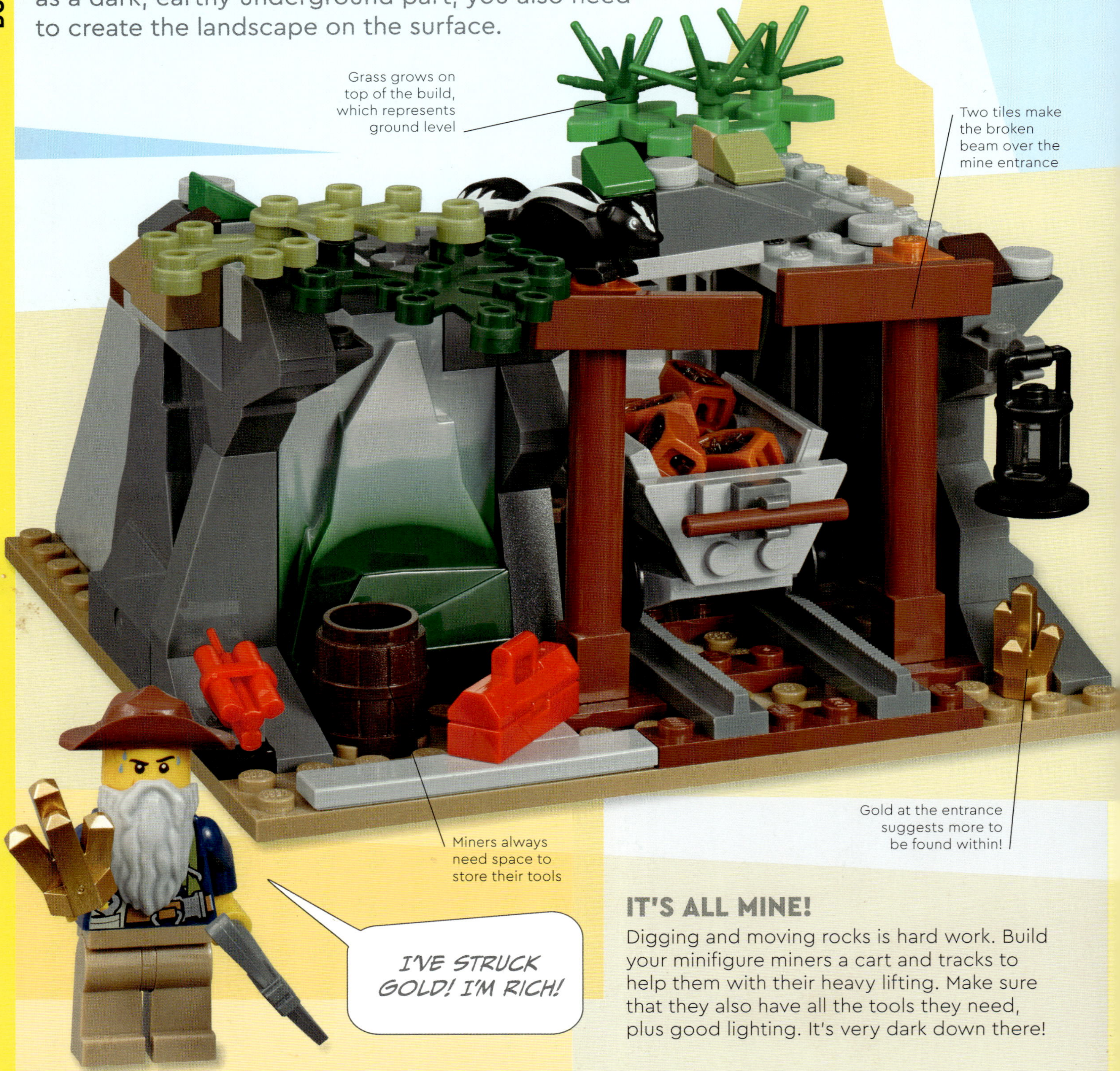
Grass grows on top of the build, which represents ground level
Two tiles make the broken beam over the mine entrance
Gold at the entrance suggests more to be found within!
Miners always need space to store their tools
I'VE STRUCK GOLD! I'M RICH!

IT'S ALL MINE!

Digging and moving rocks is hard work. Build your minifigure miners a cart and tracks to help them with their heavy lifting. Make sure that they also have all the tools they need, plus good lighting. It's very dark down there!

TODAY, ALL I'VE FOUND IS THIS STRANGE GEM.

Hanging lanterns are needed to light the underground cave

Rails found mostly in LEGO City train sets

INSIDE VIEW

TRY THIS

Underground rails aren't just for miners! You could also build a modern subway system with shiny trains and stations for LEGO® City commuters.

Jagged walls made from 2×4×6 rock panels

SIDE VIEW

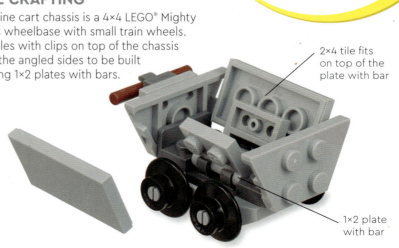

MINE CRAFTING

The mine cart chassis is a 4×4 LEGO® Mighty Micros wheelbase with small train wheels. Four tiles with clips on top of the chassis allow the angled sides to be built on using 1×2 plates with bars.

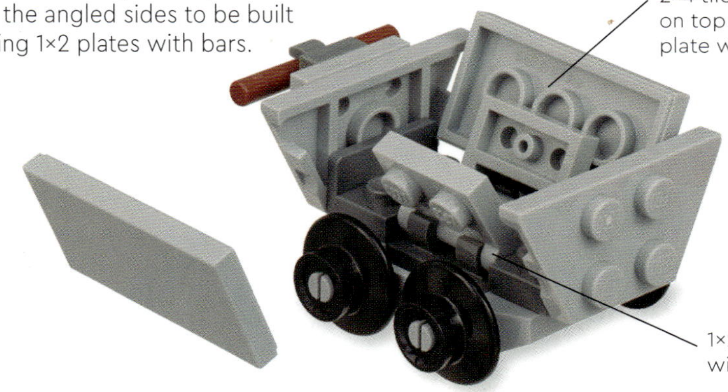

2×4 tile fits on top of the plate with bar

1×2 plate with bar

MICROSCALE CITY

Microscale buildings are very small, but building them can be a big challenge. With clever planning and a creative use of pieces, your microscale models can be just as impressive as anything larger. This cityscape is also modular, which means you can move buildings around to redesign your city.

URBAN PLANNING

Your color choices are a simple way of making it obvious what microscale buildings represent. Here, it's red for a fire station, white for a hospital, and tan for an apartment building. Simple microscale vehicles, including a fire engine, also bring the microscale city to life.

Cars are built onto 1×1 plates in the road

Diving board ladder is a sideways grille slope

CHANGE IT

Your microscale city doesn't have to be modular. Several small builds can look just as impressive gathered together without being combined on a single base.

BUILDING BRIEF

Objective: Build a microscale city
Use: City planning, microbuilding
Features: Fire station, hospital, housing
Extras: Vehicles, trees, recreation areas

All the buildings have tiled tops for a more realistic look

Exposed studs make the green areas look more natural

SIDE VIEW

1×1 round bricks are water storage tanks

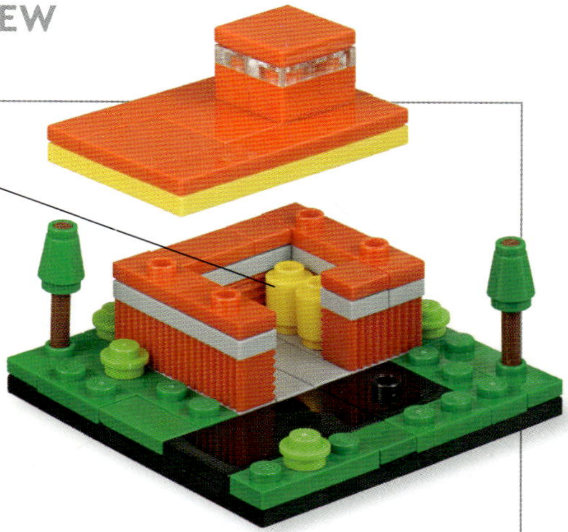

FIRE STATION

Windows are headlight bricks facing inward

APARTMENT BLOCK

SPACES FOR BASES

Each area of the city is a standalone build that can be moved around to make different layouts. They are attached to the main base using jumper plates, so they stay in place but they are easy to remove as well.

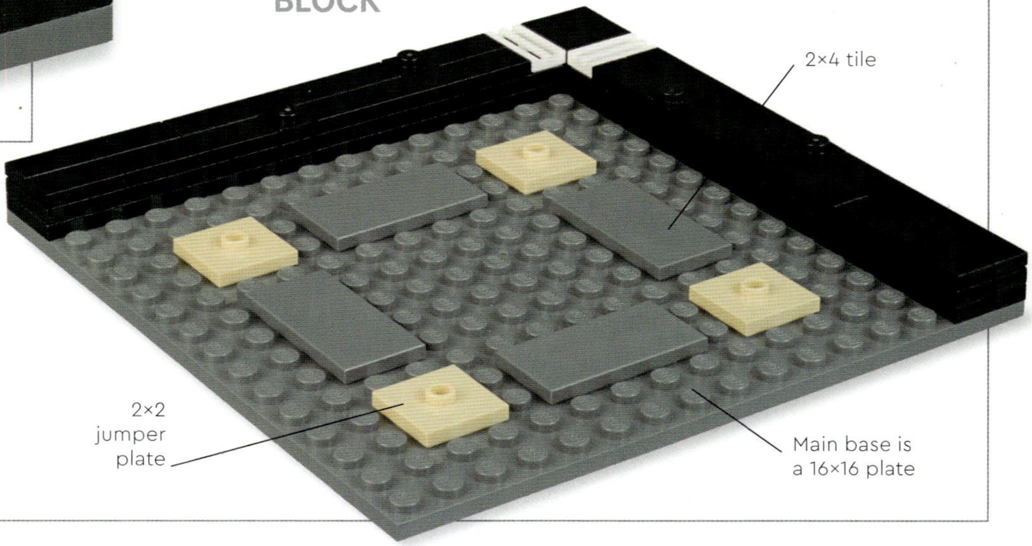

2×4 tile

2×2 jumper plate

Main base is a 16×16 plate

WATERFRONT SKYLINE

Welcome to the big city! Cities such as London, New York, Sydney, and Dubai have famous skylines. You could use them for inspiration or dream up your own imaginary cityscape. Get creative with your choice of colors, the shapes of the roofs, and the style of the windows.

BUILDING BRIEF

Objective: Build a waterfront skyline
Use: A place to work, rest, play, and shop
Features: Tall buildings with different architectural features
Extras: Trees, water, walls

CITY PLANNING

In a city, the building possibilities are endless. Add a short, wide building, or make one of your skyscrapers twice as tall as the rest. A single row of transparent blue tiles creates a glistening waterfront for this skyline. You could add more water, a jetty, and even some boats.

MADE OF LOGS

One side of this L-shaped building is a stack of gently curved log bricks. The other side alternates blue and transparent 1×1 plates most of the way up.

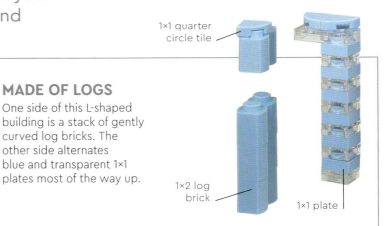

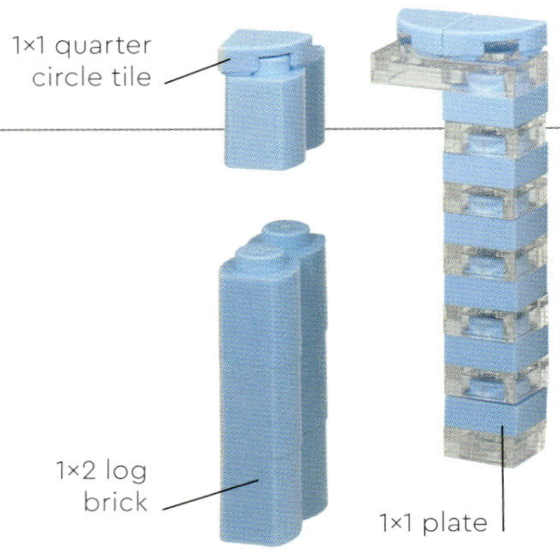
1×1 quarter circle tile
1×2 log brick
1×1 plate

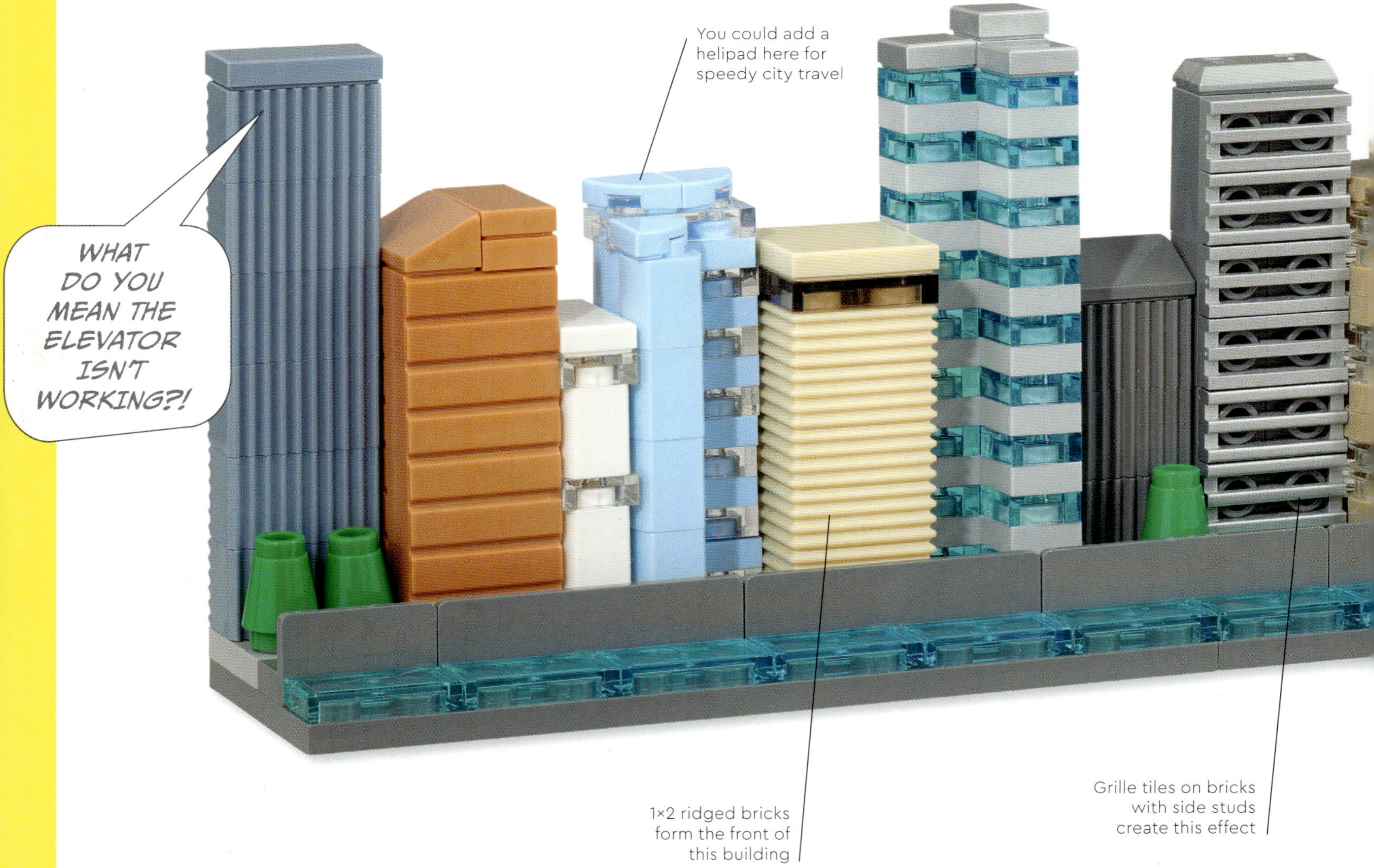
WHAT DO YOU MEAN THE ELEVATOR ISN'T WORKING?!
You could add a helipad here for speedy city travel
1×2 ridged bricks form the front of this building
Grille tiles on bricks with side studs create this effect

BUILD TIP

Think about what goes on in your buildings as you design them. Are they office buildings, hotels, apartments, or high-rise police headquarters?

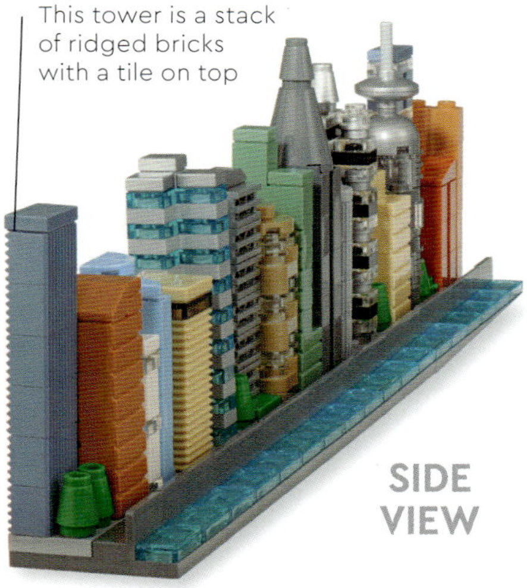

This tower is a stack of ridged bricks with a tile on top

SIDE VIEW

ALL ROUND

This shimmering skyscraper is made entirely from round pieces, including 1×1 round bricks, 2×2 round plates, and a 2×2 dome. Its saucer-shaped observation deck is made from two small radar dishes slotted onto a bar.

Bar piece

Stack of 1×1 round plates

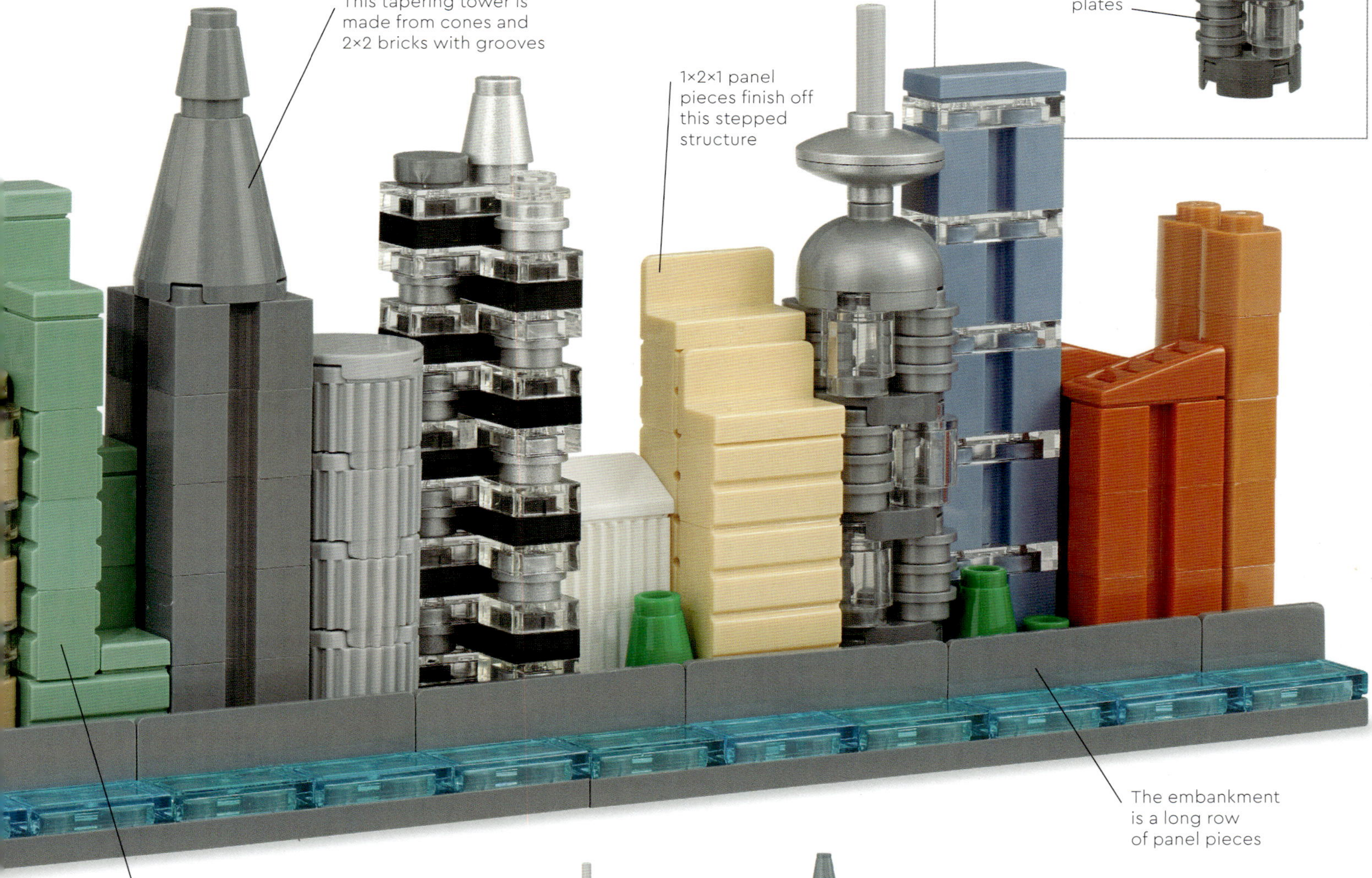

This tapering tower is made from cones and 2×2 bricks with grooves

1×2×1 panel pieces finish off this stepped structure

The embankment is a long row of panel pieces

Side-on textured pieces have a look all of their own

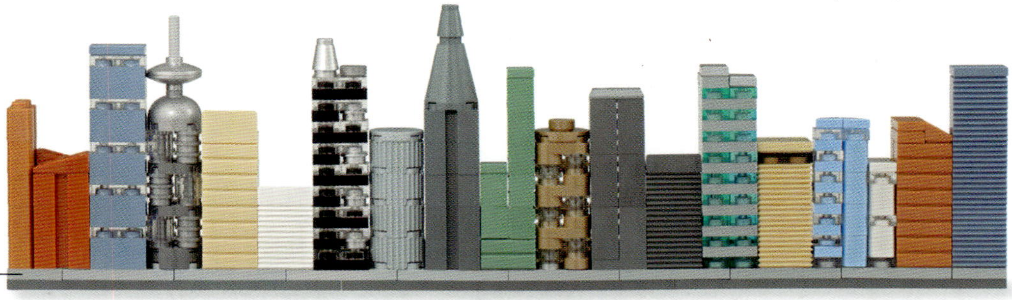

The buildings sit on two layers of plates

REAR VIEW

MICRO HARBOR

A harbor is a bustling and busy place, with cargo ships and pleasure boats moving in and out regularly. Whether you're building in microscale or minifigure scale, the details are everything. This model fits so much on just a 16×16 base plate. There's a crane ready to lift cargo on and off the container ship, a factory, and even a stylish apartment building.

BUILDING BRIEF

Objective: Build a microscale harbor
Use: A place to work and play
Features: Jetties, boats, crane, water
Extras: Factory, apartments, road, greenery, cars

Ridged bricks give this factory front an industrial look
Plant shoots become palm trees in a microscale world
Yacht masts are minifigure hose nozzles
Piers are 1×6 tiles built onto 1×1 round plates

LEVEL UP

Extend your harbor scene to the left to include a beach with beach huts, and to the right to include lots of colorful shipping containers.

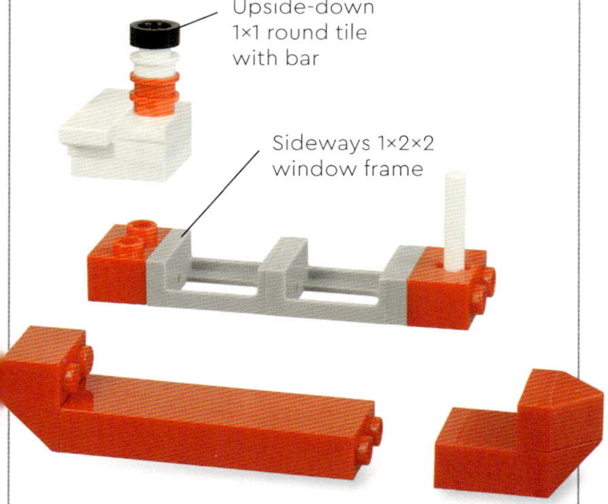
Upside-down 1×1 round tile with bar
Sideways 1×2×2 window frame

SHIPBUILDING

The hull of this ship is built sideways, with window frame pieces suggesting realistic cargo storage spaces. The ship's control tower is built upright from various plates and attached to a brick with side studs.

These small boats are upside-down tooth plates

FRONT VIEW

WORK AND PLEASURE

This harbor is an industrial area, where ships load and unload goods, but it's also a fashionable spot to be. Smaller boats can launch from the wooden jetties and residents of the apartment building can enjoy stunning views out to sea.

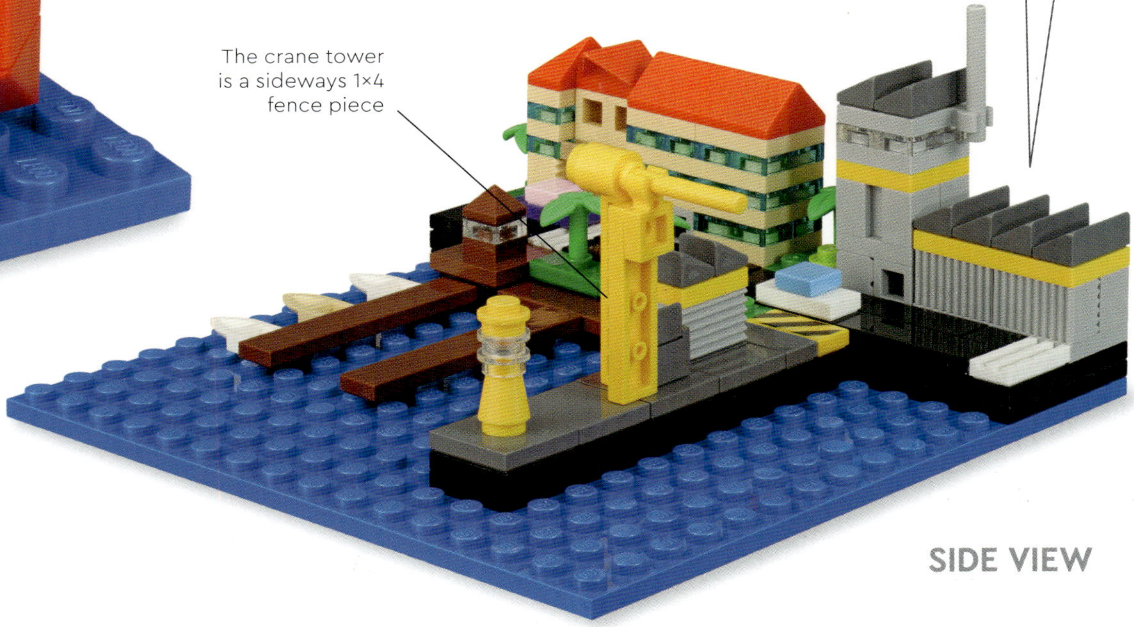
NOW, WHERE DID I DOCK MY SHIP?
The crane tower is a sideways 1×4 fence piece

SIDE VIEW

A lighthouse helps ships navigate at night

BUILDING BRIEF

Objective: Build a store
Use: A place for minifigures to browse
Features: Large windows, colorful exterior, goods on display
Extras: Sidewalk, ATM, balcony

TEMPTING TREATS

It's not only the wide windows that attract customers to this store: the colorful walls, window and door frames, and awnings really make it stand out. There needs to be space inside your store for minifigures to move around, a cash register, and, of course, lots of TOYS!

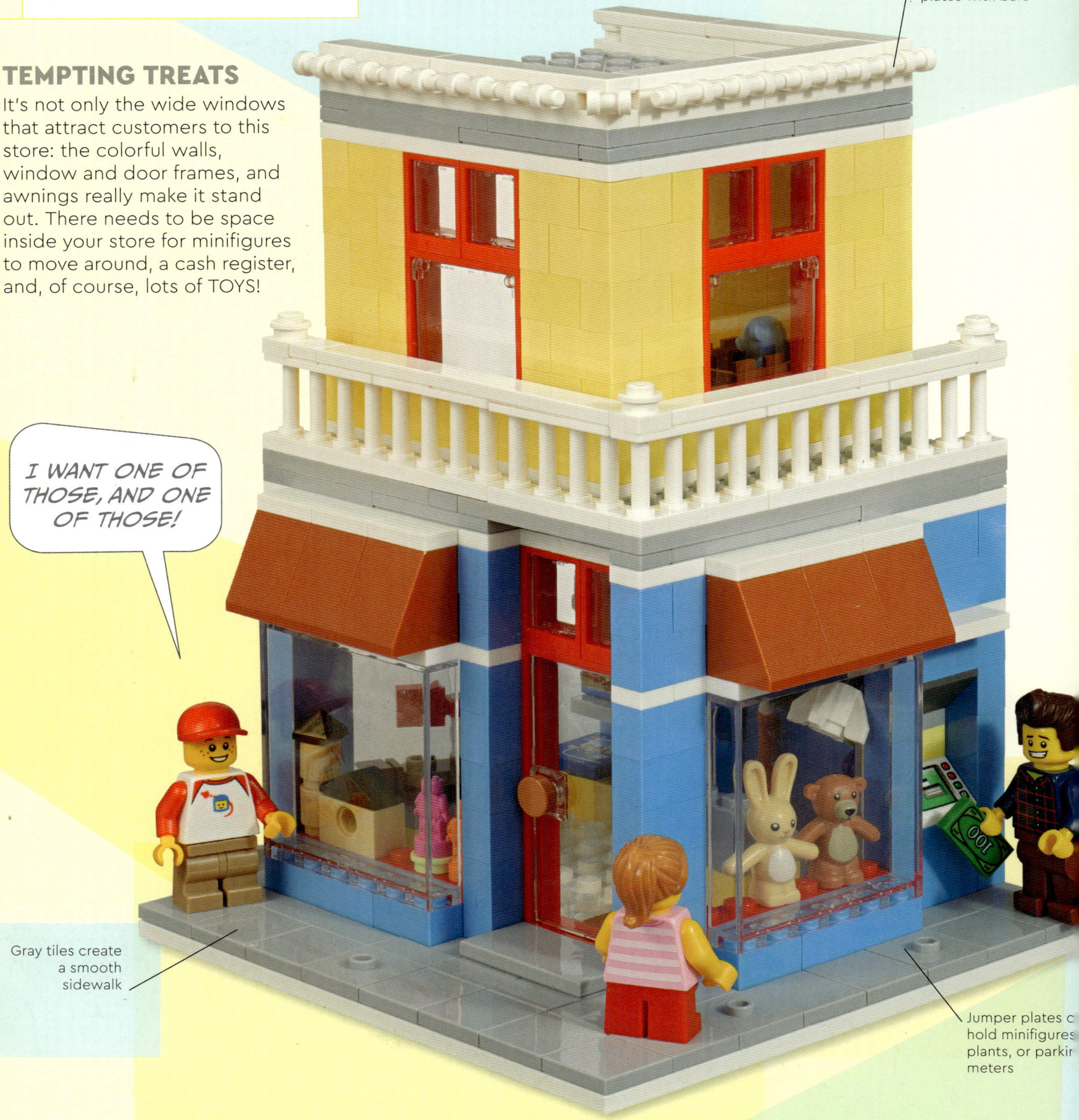
I WANT ONE OF THOSE, AND ONE OF THOSE!
100

Decorative cornice built out of 1×2 plates with bars

Gray tiles create a smooth sidewalk

Jumper plates c hold minifigures plants, or parkir meters

TOY STORE

On any LEGO® Main Street, the highlight has to be the toy store! The most important feature of the exterior is its windows—they need to be big enough to show off the store's fun products. The window displays can be cute, comical, or festive, but they must be irresistible, so that any passing minifigures simply have to stop and look.

BUILD TIP

Make multi-story buildings with easily detachable sections by topping each level with smooth tiles and the occasional 1×4 plate with two studs.

Roof is a 10×10 plate

Spare teddy bears are stored in this crate upstairs in the storeroom

Rocket stand made from 1×1 tile with clip and plate with bar

These tiles are printed to look like tiny LEGO sets

EXPLODED VIEW

Window made from one large and two small frames

Display windows are 1×6×5 transparent wall pieces

SIDE VIEW

CASH BACK

The back of the cash machine build extends into the store, so it's designed to double as an in-store display area. Colorful 1×1 round plates make it look like a LEGO Store-style "Pick a Brick" wall!

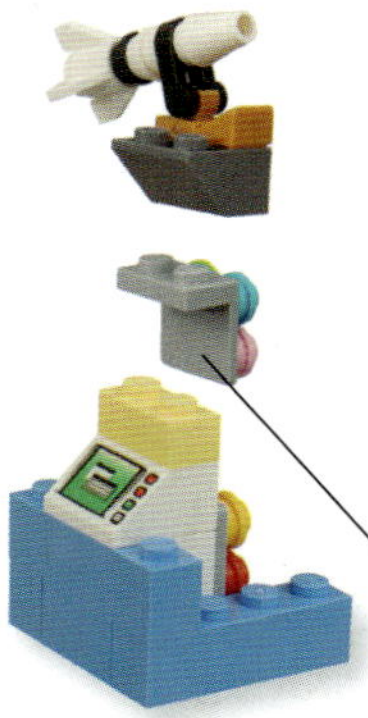

1×2/2×2 bracket plate has four side studs

CONSTRUCTION SITE

There can hardly be a better place to practice your building skills than on a LEGO construction site. Who cares if the structure your minifigures are making never actually gets built? It can remain a work in progress! Think about which hardworking vehicles you will need for your building project, too.

BUILDING BRIEF

Objective: Build a construction site
Use: Constructing buildings, lifting and digging
Features: Buildings in progress, scaffolding, construction vehicles
Extras: Safety barriers, various tools, and vehicle attachments

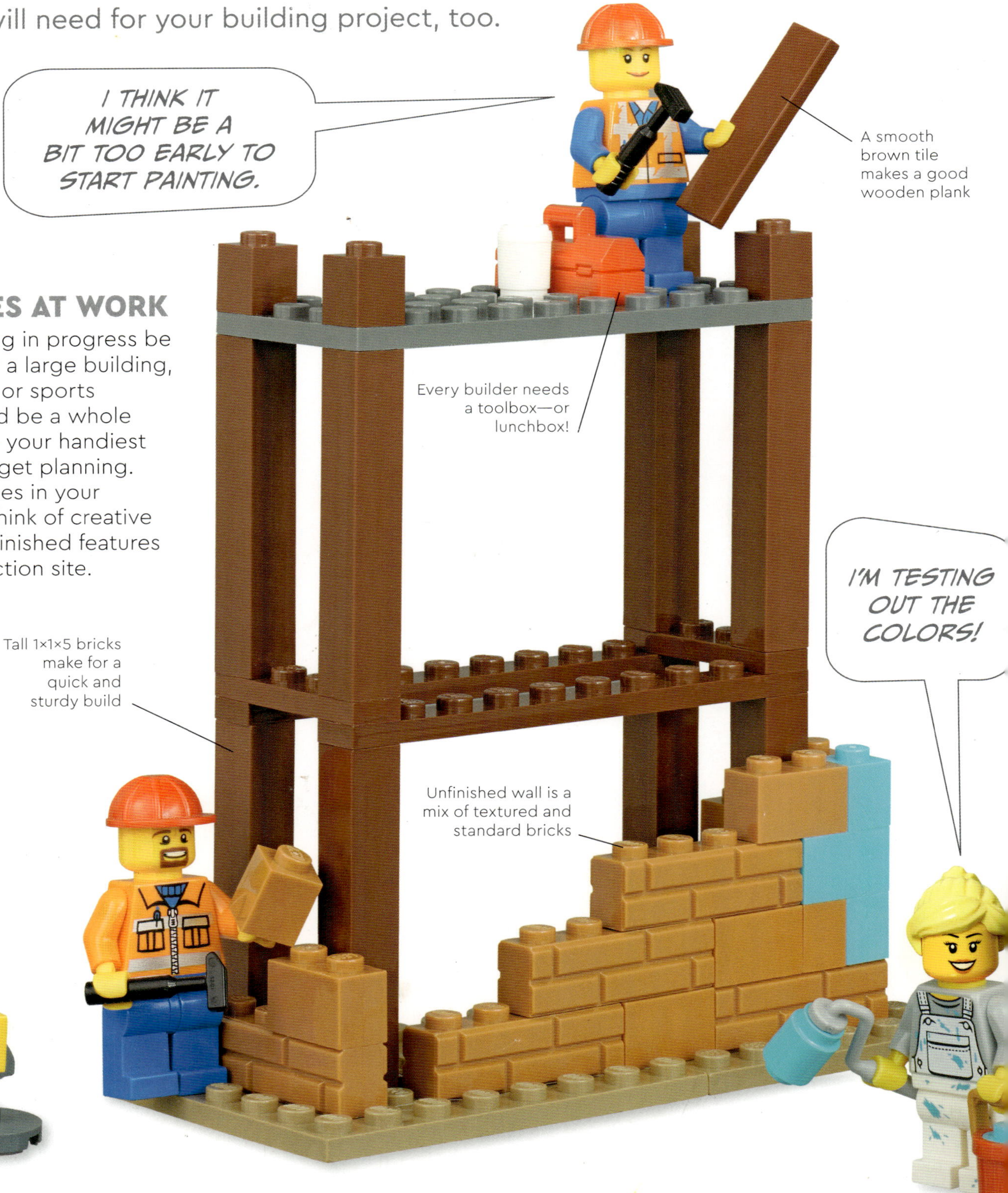
I THINK IT MIGHT BE A BIT TOO EARLY TO START PAINTING.
A smooth brown tile makes a good wooden plank
Every builder needs a toolbox—or lunchbox!
Tall 1×1×5 bricks make for a quick and sturdy build
Unfinished wall is a mix of textured and standard bricks
I'M TESTING OUT THE COLORS!

MINIFIGURES AT WORK

Will your building in progress be a small house or a large building, such as a castle or sports stadium? It could be a whole town! Assemble your handiest minifigures and get planning. Look at the pieces in your collection and think of creative ways to add unfinished features to your construction site.

Barrier base is a claw in a round jumper plate

Crane hook fits into a plate with a ball socket
Large rollcage piece protects the minifigure driver
Rollcage fits onto a pair of tiles with clips
Headlight is a 1×1 plate with ring and 1×1 round tile
Chunky tires for rough terrain

HELPING HAND

Minifigures can't do everything alone—they need construction vehicles like this one to help them clear, dig, and lift things around the site. You could even work with friends to build a whole fleet of them.

LEVEL UP

Bring in the whole construction crew! What other vehicles and machines would be handy to have on your site? Think about the jobs they'll be doing.

Crane arm joints made from plates with bars and plates with clips
Trailer has room to carry the pallet of bricks
REAR VIEW
Plate with angled bar allows the trailer to attach
2×3 curved plate with hole
TRAILER

WIND FARM

Wind farms like this are usually in breezy locations, by the sea or on top of hills. The wind turns the blades on the turbines, which then spin generators to create electricity.

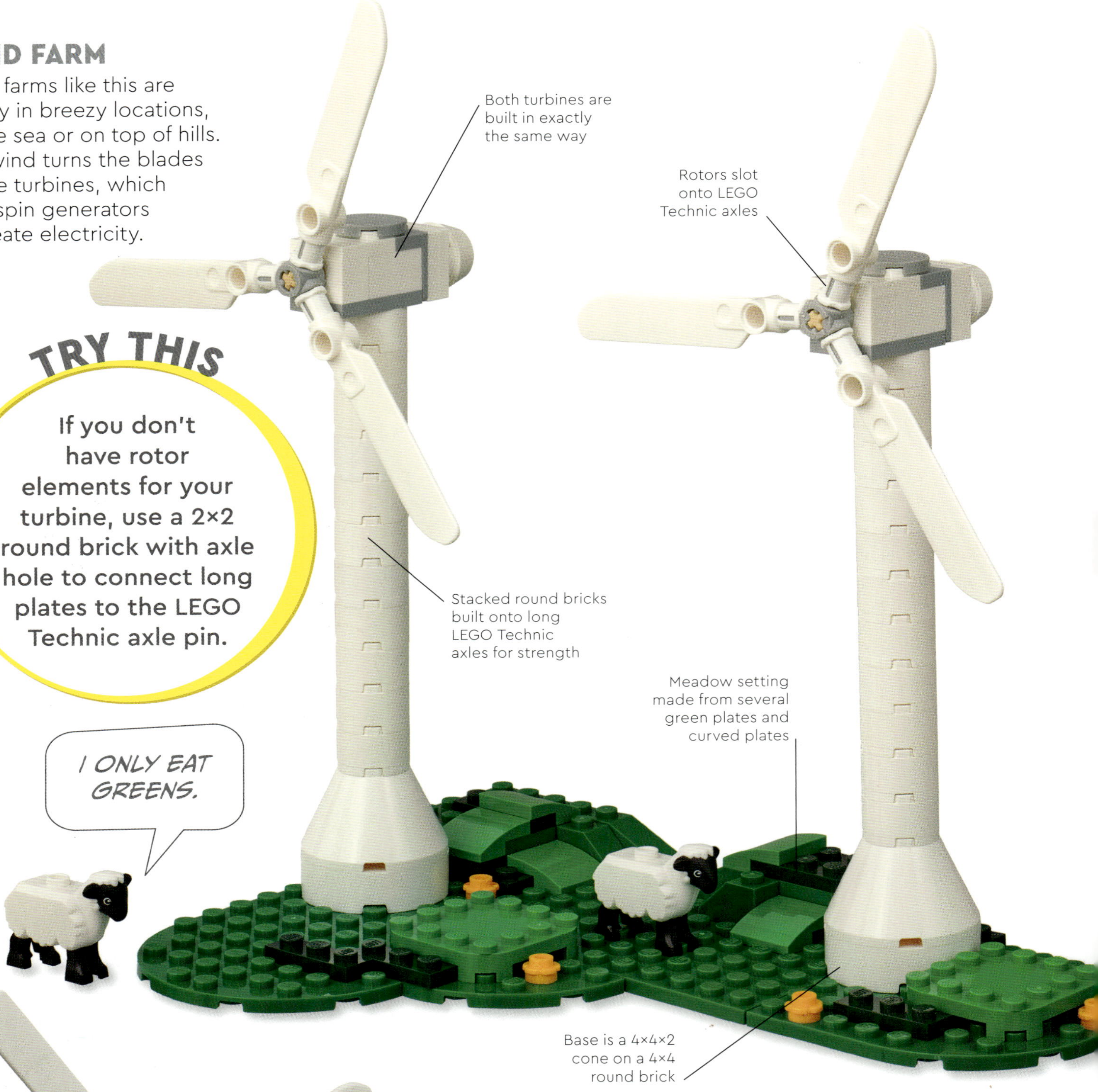
Both turbines are built in exactly the same way
Rotors slot onto LEGO Technic axles
Stacked round bricks built onto long LEGO Technic axles for strength
Meadow setting made from several green plates and curved plates
I ONLY EAT GREENS.
Base is a 4×4×2 cone on a 4×4 round brick

TRY THIS

If you don't have rotor elements for your turbine, use a 2×2 round brick with axle hole to connect long plates to the LEGO Technic axle pin.

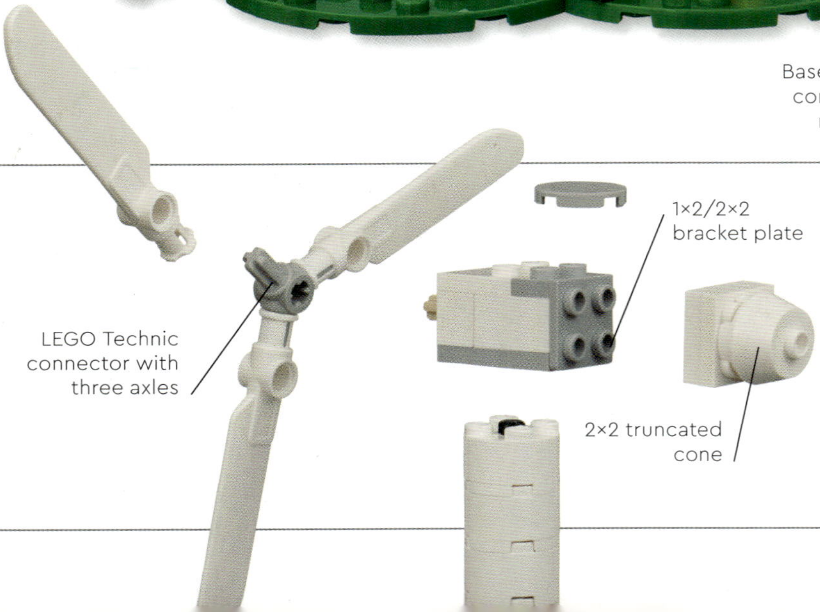
1×2/2×2 bracket plate
LEGO Technic connector with three axles
2×2 truncated cone

ROTARY CONNECTION

The horizontal top section of a wind turbine is called the nacelle. In this build, the nacelles' length helps balance the weight of the rotors, which spin freely on a LEGO Technic axle pin inside a brick with axle hole.

RENEWABLE ENERGY

Energy is what powers people's cars and homes. Renewable energy comes from things that won't run out, such as wind, water, and the sun. Try creating some energy-themed builds, from wind farms to solar panels to hydropower dams. You could even invent a new way to create or use renewable energy!

BUILDING BRIEF

Objective:	Build renewable energy models and ideas
Use:	To produce renewable energy
Features:	Blades, generators, power source
Extras:	Windy location, solar panels

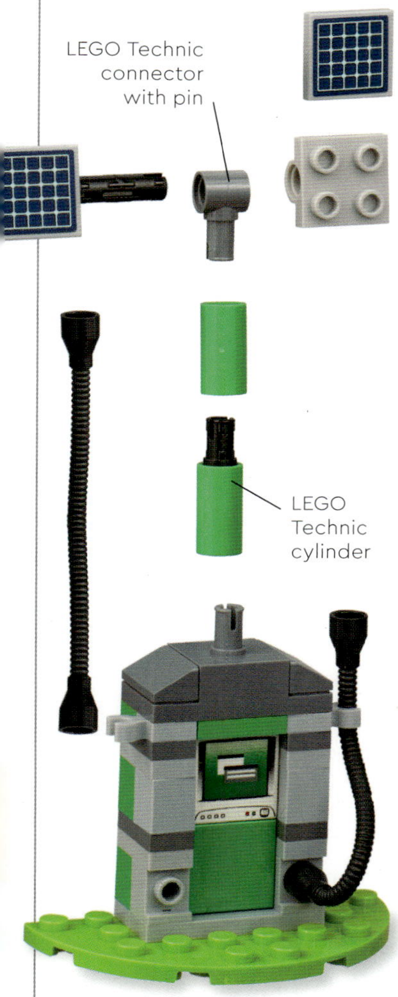
LEGO Technic connector with pin
LEGO Technic cylinder

CHARGING STATION

Electric cars don't need gas to run—they are powered by electricity. This LEGO electric car "recharges" by plugging into the electricity charging station via a hose piece.

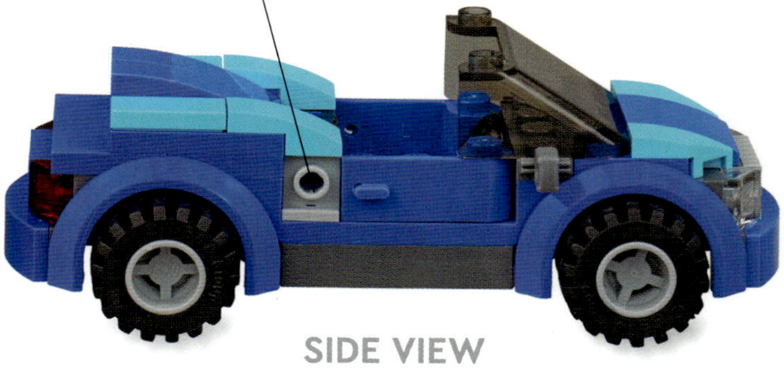
Headlight brick serves as the charging socket

SIDE VIEW

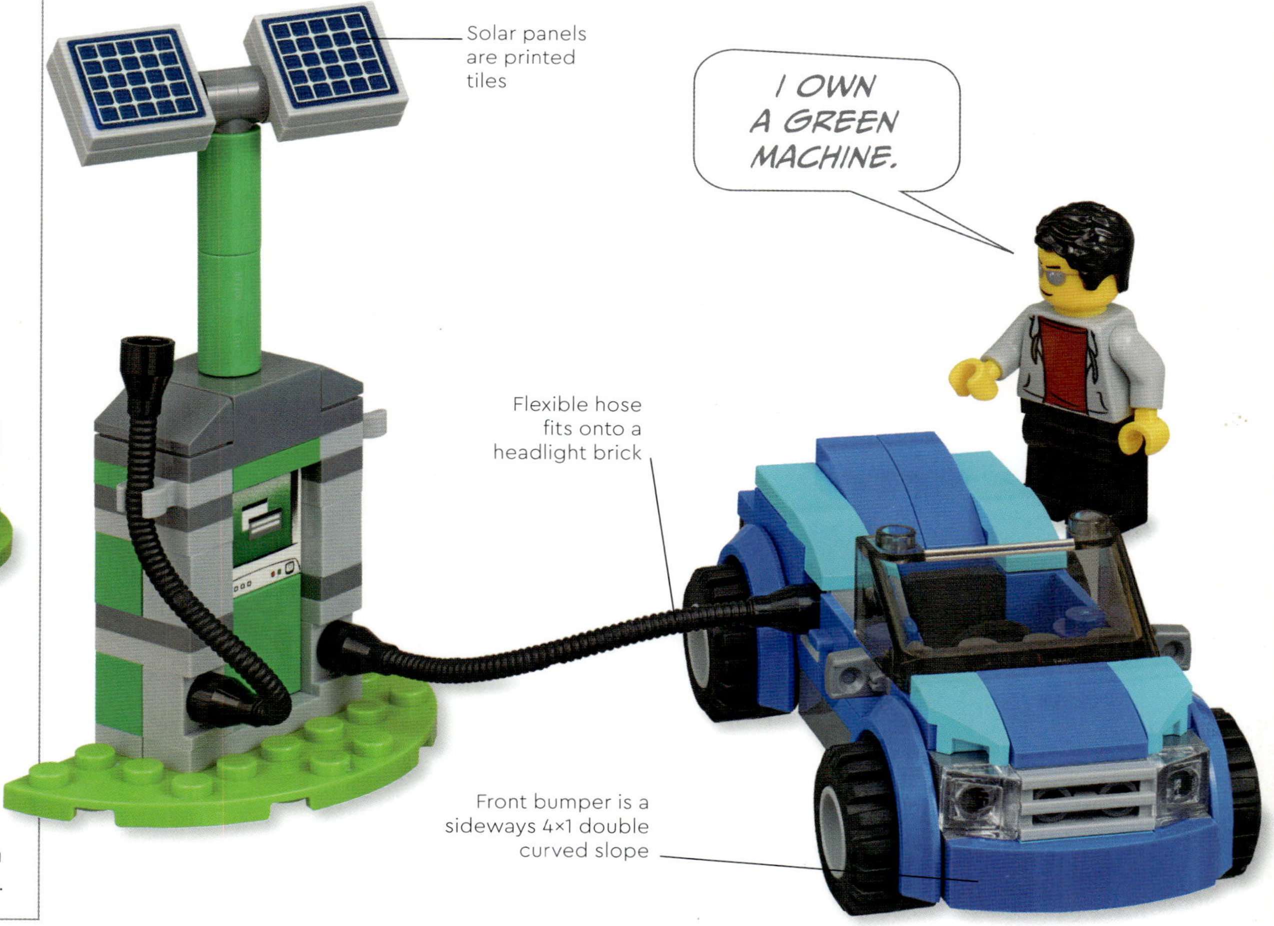
Solar panels are printed tiles
I OWN A GREEN MACHINE.
Flexible hose fits onto a headlight brick
Front bumper is a sideways 4×1 double curved slope

CHASE THE SUN

The solar panels on top of the charging station can be tilted and turned to face the sun throughout the day. They are mounted on 2×2 plates with rings beneath, which fit onto a long LEGO Technic friction pin.

BUILDING BRIEF

Objective:	Build a botanical garden
Use:	Designing beautiful landscapes, building unusual plants
Features:	Lots of plants and flowers, paths, fences, greenhouse
Extras:	Ornaments, statues, lights, water features, benches

BOTANICAL GARDENS

Beautiful botanical gardens are filled with plants from all around the world. Visitors can journey through tropical and desert areas and look at striking flowers they might not usually see. For your own botanical garden, you can re-create real plants or cultivate fantastic flora that only exist in your imagination.

TRY THIS

Flowers come in many different shapes and sizes. Look for eye-catching ones in your local area or online to get inspiration for your botanical builds.

GARDEN DESIGN

Planning is important when building a botanical garden. As well as thinking about what will grow where, you also need to make sure there are plenty of paths for your minifigure visitors to meander along. Will your garden have any statues, water features, or benches to rest on?

This plant's pistil is made from a mini doll's crown
Path area is made from a single 16×16 road plate
SHHHHH!

SIDE VIEW

HOTHOUSE

You can grow plants from tropical climates in a greenhouses. Use LEGO window pieces to create a transparent structure that will keep tropical plants warm all year round.

Roof is made from five sloped window pieces

Yellow crystals are usually used to make minifigure French fries

HEY! YOU'RE NOT ALLOWED TO PICK THE FLOWERS!

A red pumpkin piece makes for an extra-bulbous bud

GARDEN LIGHTING

Add some atmosphere to your botanical garden by building lighting for evening visitors. This classic lamppost has a brick with side studs in the middle that the four lanterns hang from.

Each lamp is built onto a minifigure paint roller

Stacking different leaf plates creates a natural effect

SIDE VIEW

FLOATING VILLAGE

Sometimes you'll want to build historical locations as accurately as possible, but other times you could combine realism with fantasy to create something extraordinary and different. Choosing which buildings to feature and planning the layout of a medieval village is already an interesting project, but why not make it a village on water?

BUILDING BRIEF

Objective: Build a medieval floating village
Use: A historical and unusual place to live
Features: Houses, inn, important buildings
Extras: Rafts, stores, bridges

Hanging inn sign is a 2×3 tile with clips

SIDE VIEW

Green elements suggest moss growth on the roof

Arch bricks fit perfectly around the curved windows

Visitors can tie their boats to the wooden boardwalk

Overlapping blue plates look like wavy water

MEDIEVAL INN

Black exterior beams and latticed windows give this village its medieval look. Build a place for your minifigures to meet up and drink some ye olde tea. What other meeting places might your village need? How about a market with food stands?

TRY THIS

The floating villagers rely on boats for any food that isn't fish. So why not build them a grocer's barge with a sail and a sale on?

RAFT

The middle of the raft is a 1×2×2 brick with side studs

Flat rooftop is made from two semi-studded 4×6 plates
I SPY A STRANGER IN THESE PARTS.
Every house in the village has a life buoy hanging outside

MAYOR'S HOUSE

This house belongs to the village VIP. It could be for the medieval mayor, or just your favorite minifigure. This one has gold LEGO flags around the entrance. How will you make yours stand out from the rest of the houses?

Most medieval homes are bigger upstairs than downstairs!

REAR VIEW

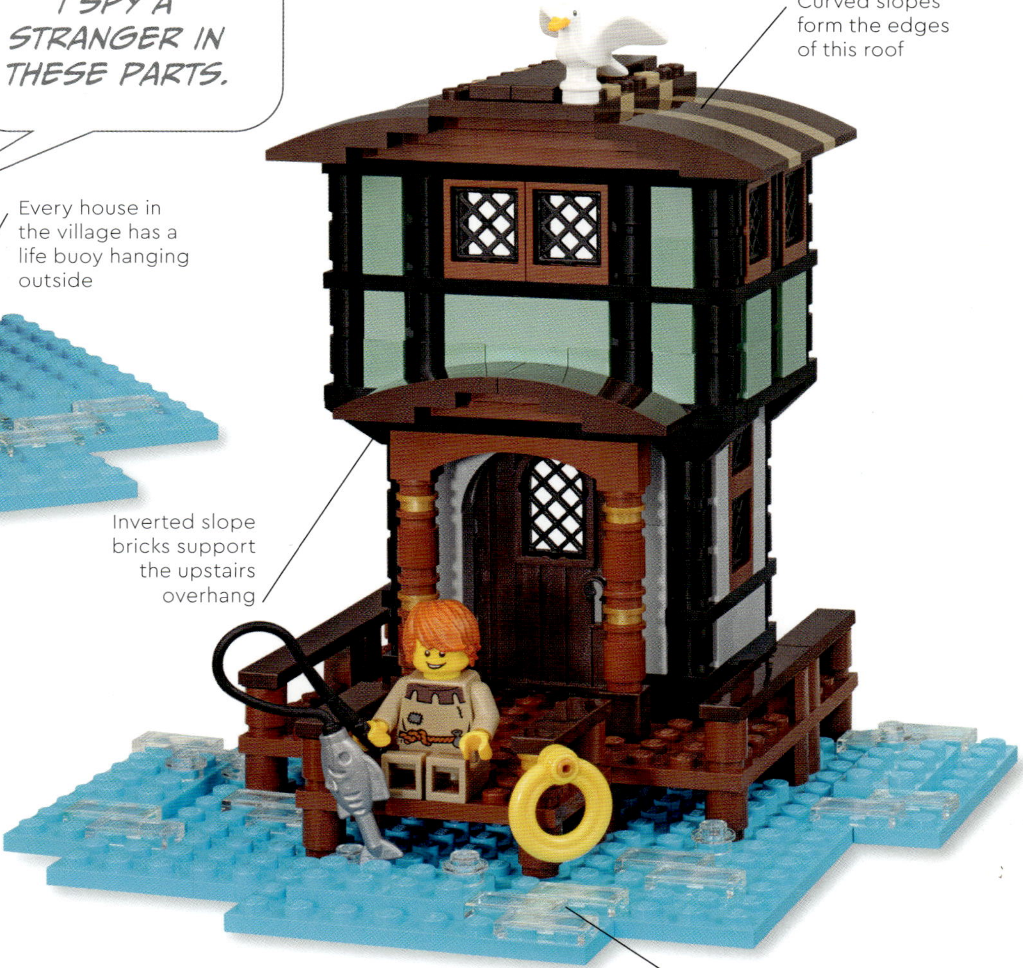
Curved slopes form the edges of this roof
Inverted slope bricks support the upstairs overhang
Small transparent pieces add sparkle to the water surface

WATER WAY TO LIVE

The whole village is built on stilts so waves can pass underneath the homes, rather than crashing into the walls. Use large plates to build sturdy platforms onto the stilts, and smaller ones to add jetties and bridges.

4×6 plate makes a jetty at the front
Main platform is a 10×12 plate

HOMES ON THE WATER

All the houses are built on stilts to keep them well above the water. Instead of yards, the houses have jetties where minifigures can fish for their dinner and moor their boats. You could try connecting all the buildings by creating bridges.

MODERN TRAIN STATION

Some of the most iconic buildings in the world are train stations. They come in all sizes and styles, from ornate, historical buildings to sleek, modern masterpieces. Curved and transparent pieces give this microscale station a minimalist modern look.

BUILDING BRIEF

Objective: Build a train station
Use: For trains to arrive and depart from
Features: Station building, tracks, trains
Extras: Trees, garden, ticket office

Transparent 1×4×3 curved slopes are used for the upper windows
Each side of the roof is made from four large curved arches
Train tracks are rows of 1×2 grille tiles
Stacked flower plates work as bushes at this scale
Foliage is made from randomly stacked jumper plates
I HOPE MY LUGGAGE FITS ON THE TRAIN!

MAKING IT CLEAR

The cavernous station concourse is made entirely from transparent panel pieces. The ones at the front and back have their panelled sides facing out, while the ones on the sides are facing in. This avoids any gaps in the corners.

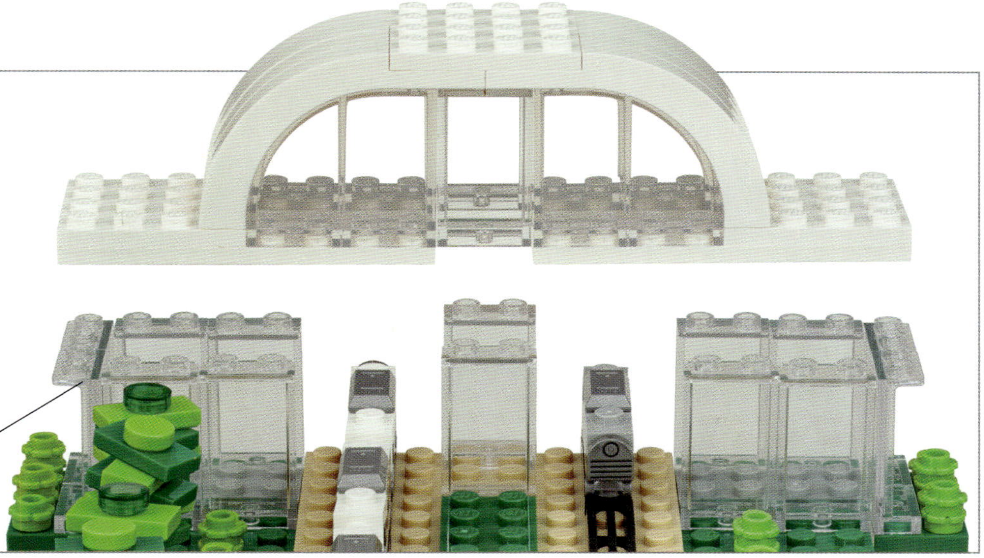

1×2×3 transparent panel piece facing inward

INSIDE AND OUT

Lots of curved and rectangular transparent pieces make floor-to-ceiling windows, which create a light and bright interior for the station. The green spaces on the exterior provide a calm contrast to the hustle and bustle of the station.

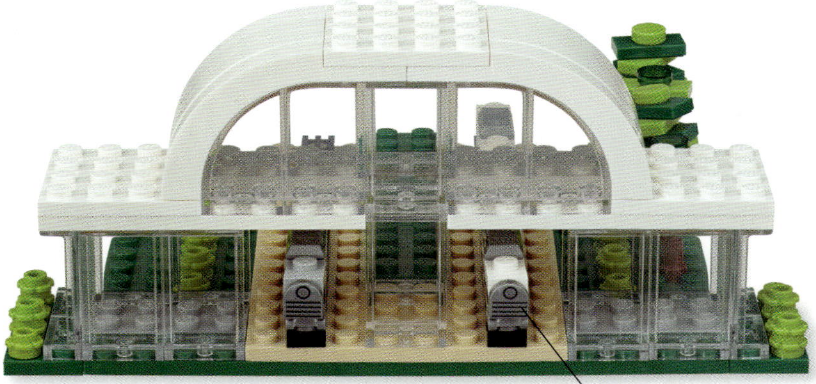

REAR VIEW

The front of each train is a printed curved tile

CHANGE IT

This station has two trains of the same kind, but yours could also be visited by an ultra-sleek bullet train, or an old-fashioned steam engine.

1×1/1×1 bracket plates enclose the windows at both ends

Train wheels are minifigure roller skates

TRAIN CAR

The train cars are not really connected to each other

FRONT VIEW

BUILDING BRIEF

Objective:	Build a concert or arts venue
Use:	A place for minifigures to perform
Features:	Stage, lights, speakers, DJ decks, microphones
Extras:	Dance floor, audience seats

Each lamp is a minifigure megaphone
Bar holders with clips hold the microphones

SIDE VIEW

SETTING THE STAGE

Decide what kind of stage you're building and make sure there's enough space for all the lights, speakers, and performers. How many minifigures will have musical instruments? Make sure everyone has room to shine.

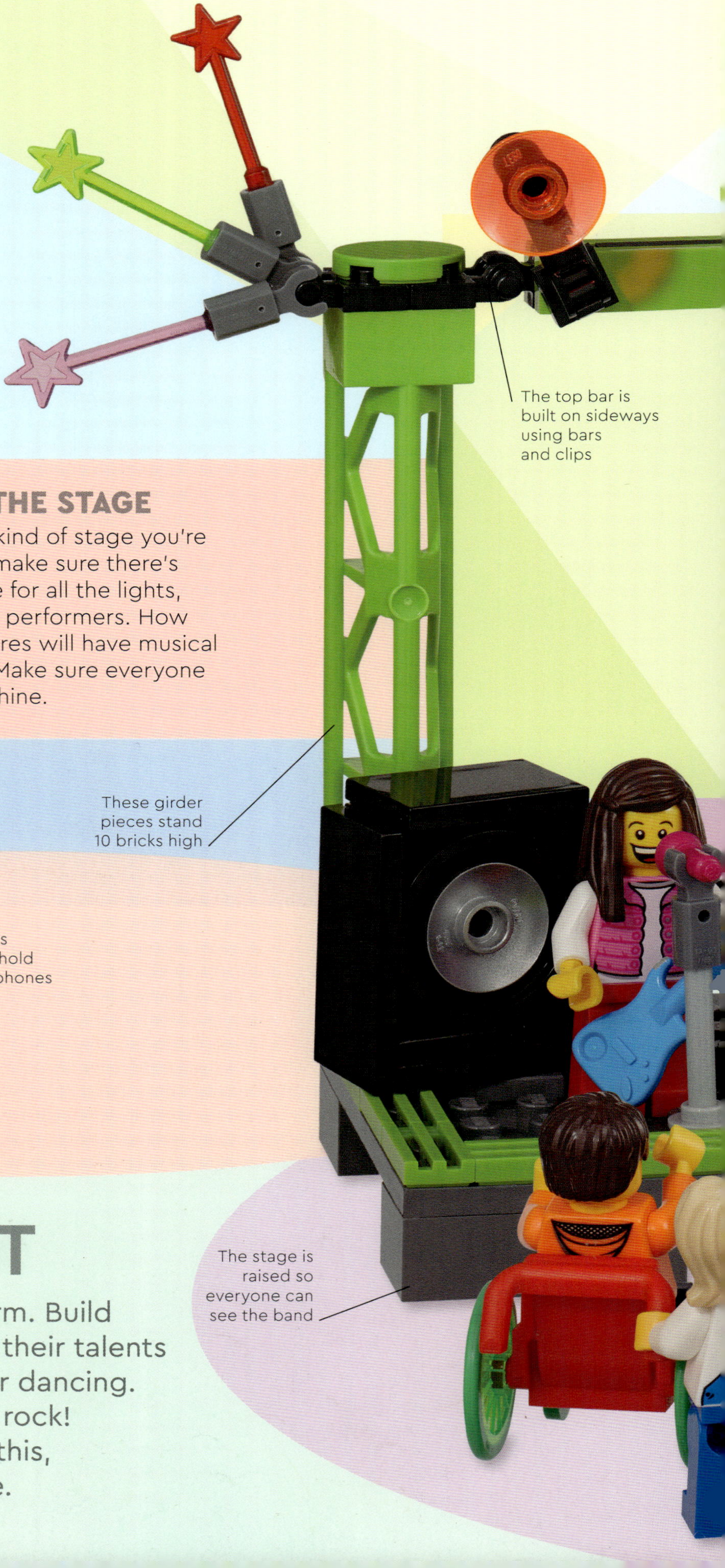
The top bar is built on sideways using bars and clips
These girder pieces stand 10 bricks high
The stage is raised so everyone can see the band

ROCK CONCERT

Some minifigures just love to perform. Build them a place where they can share their talents for making music, singing, acting, or dancing. This minifigure band looks ready to rock! You could build a simple stage like this, a theater, or a whole stadium venue.

This lighting rig has lamps in lots of different colors
LET ME HEAR SOME NOISE!
DID SHE SAY SHE WANTS TO HEAR MY NOSE?

CHANGE IT

What other live music events will you build? A dance contest, a musical theater performance, or maybe even a classical concert with orchestra!

MAKE IT LOUD

The speaker cone is made from a pair of radar dishes. These fit onto the back of a headlight brick in the rear of the speaker box. The box sides are tiles built onto bricks with side studs.

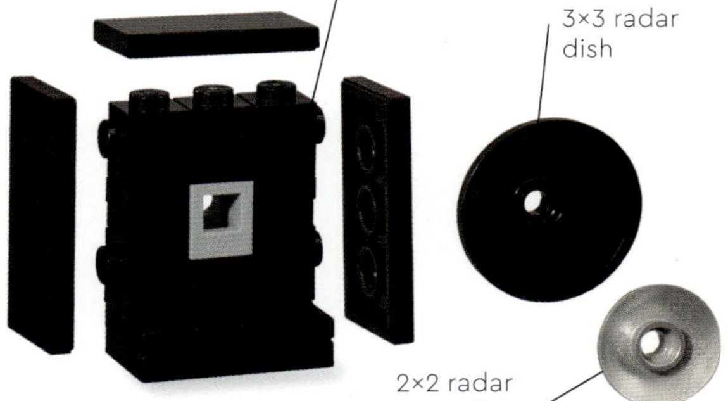
1×1 brick with side stud
3×3 radar dish
2×2 radar dish

BUILDING BRIEF

Objective: Build an observatory and telescopes
Use: Observing the night sky
Features: Domed roof, hatch, movable telescope
Extras: Smaller telescope, garden, nocturnal creatures

This owl is mostly made from upside-down plates

A transparent 4×4 radar dish serves as the scope's objective lens

Base is a 16×16 plate

LEVEL UP

Give your moon-gazing minifigures an even better view by mounting your observatory on a turntable. Then they can spy the night sky in every direction!

A GOOD SPOT

The best place for an observatory is away from artificial light so that you can see the night sky clearly. This model sits on a green base plate, but yours could be built high on a hill. What sort of environment will you create around yours?

OBSERVATORY

The sky's the limit with LEGO building! Curious minifigures can study the night sky from this awesome observatory. A powerful telescope sits under the domed roof, ready to be raised through the hatch and pointed at the stars. Telescopes don't need to be huge, though. Why not build a smaller one for stargazing in the backyard?

These pipes are attached to the base, not the wall

SIDE VIEW

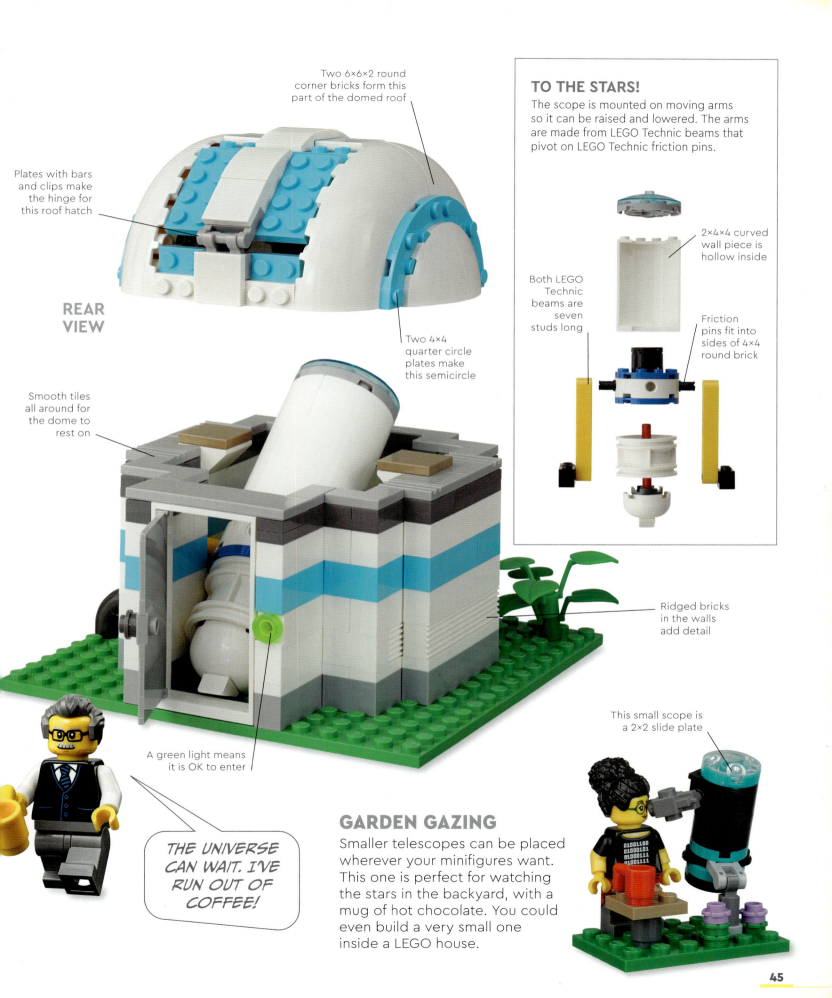

Two 6×6×2 round corner bricks form this part of the domed roof
Plates with bars and clips make the hinge for this roof hatch
Two 4×4 quarter circle plates make this semicircle

REAR VIEW

TO THE STARS!

The scope is mounted on moving arms so it can be raised and lowered. The arms are made from LEGO Technic beams that pivot on LEGO Technic friction pins.

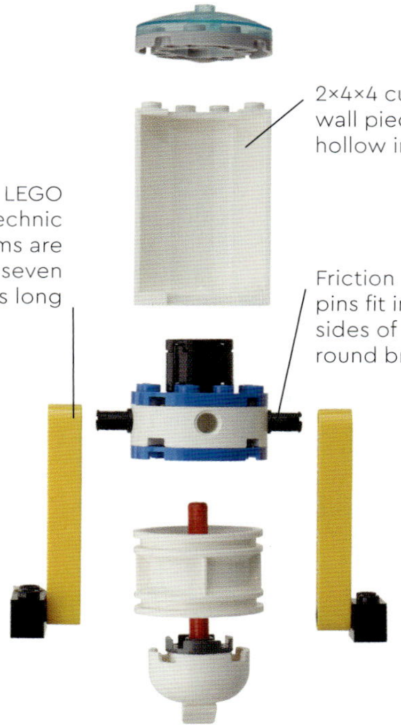
2×4×4 curved wall piece is hollow inside
Both LEGO Technic beams are seven studs long
Friction pins fit into sides of 4×4 round brick

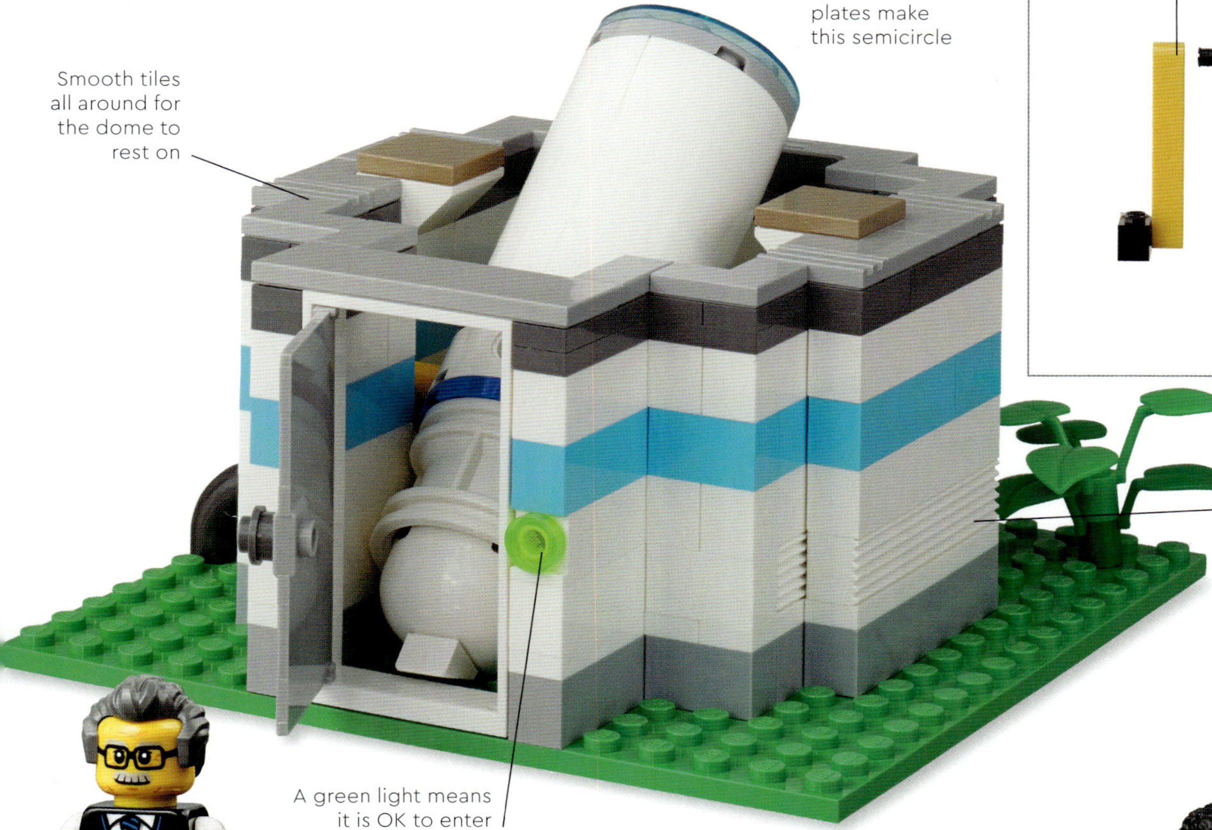
Smooth tiles all around for the dome to rest on
Ridged bricks in the walls add detail
A green light means it is OK to enter

THE UNIVERSE CAN WAIT. I'VE RUN OUT OF COFFEE!

GARDEN GAZING

Smaller telescopes can be placed wherever your minifigures want. This one is perfect for watching the stars in the backyard, with a mug of hot chocolate. You could even build a very small one inside a LEGO house.

This small scope is a 2×2 slide plate

BUILDING BRIEF

Objective:	Build a farm
Use:	Taking care of animals, growing crops
Features:	Animal homes, muddy earth, crops
Extras:	Plants, fencing, scarecrow

ON THE FARM

Get back to nature down on the farm. Think about what you love most about farms. You could plan a big building, such as a farmhouse, or create several smaller models, like these. The henhouse, cornfield, and pig pen could be combined with your friends' or family's farm models for a team build.

The back of the roof is topped with smooth tiles

BACK VIEW

HAPPY HOMES

Houses for farm animals are really fun to create. They can be simple shelters or more elaborate models with unusual features. Maybe these chickens would like a roof terrace or a pool for their henhouse? Or a high fence to keep out foxes . . .

EGG BOX

This traditional clapboard coop is made by building smooth tiles on to bricks with side studs. Inside, a small roosting perch is built into the back wall. Right now, it is occupied by a hen that hasn't hatched yet!

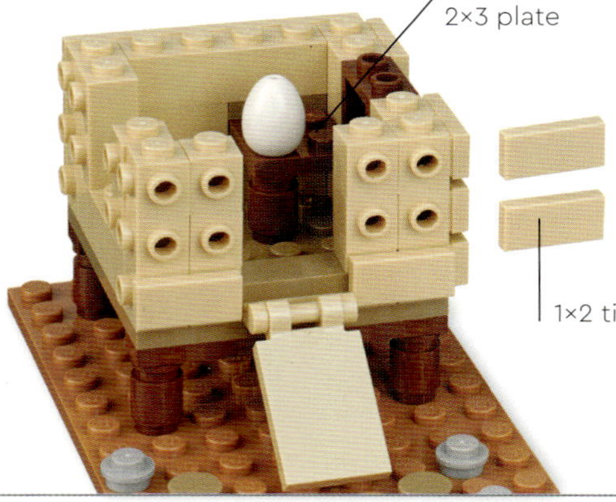
Perch is a 2×3 plate
1×2 tile

Latticed window looks like chicken wire
Sloped part of the roof is a single 6×8 slope piece
MAYBE THIS ISN'T THE BEST DISGUISE FOR STEALING CHICKENS!
The door folds down to make an exit ramp
Stilts help keep the hen house warm and dry
Pale brown base plate makes uneven muddy earth

Arm is a black carrot top piece

BACK VIEW

KEEP AWAY!

Keep your crops safe from hungry birds with a scarecrow. Make it look as terrifying as you can. What other ways can you think of to protect your fields? How about some guard cats patrolling the fence, or an army of scarecrows?

Scarecrow body is a 1×1 brick with four side studs
Each corncob is a minifigure brush element
The fence is made from tiles and 1×1 bricks with side studs

FENCE POSTS

The fences that keep these pigs penned in are made from bars and bar holders with clips. The bars attach to the base of the build by slotting into parts with hollow studs.

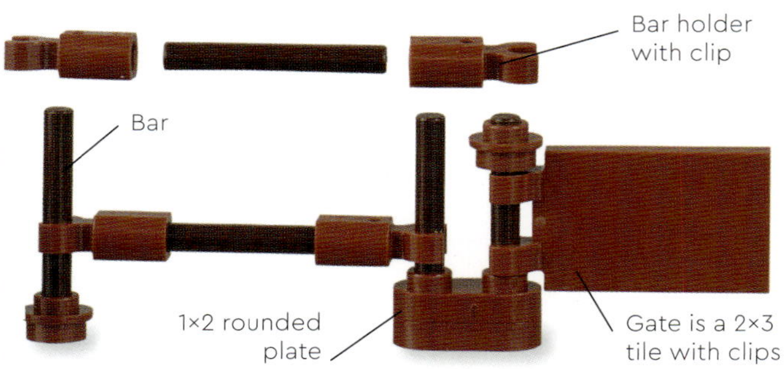
Bar holder with clip
Bar
1×2 rounded plate
Gate is a 2×3 tile with clips

HOW DO THESE PIGS KEEP ESCAPING?

TRY THIS

How many different farm animals can you build from bricks? What is the smallest number of pieces you can use to make a recognizable duck?

GLORIOUS MUD

These pigs have food, water, and plenty of mud to cool off in. What more could pigs need? You could also add a sty for them to sleep in, or a horse to keep them company.

Dark brown plates are well-trodden mud
1×1 round tiles make good pebbles

TRACTOR

There's always so much work to do on a LEGO farm, from growing crops to taking care of animals, and few machines work harder than a LEGO tractor. This vital vehicle transports the farmer and animals around the farm and helps to plant and harvest crops. What attachments could you build?

BUILDING BRIEF

Objective: Build a tractor
Use: Lifting, pulling, planting, harvesting
Features: Chunky tires, steering wheel, driver's seat, big engine
Extras: Trailers, tools, extra machinery

Hand brake is topped with a minifigure microphone

SIDE VIEW

Front wheels fit onto a 2×4 plate with pins

UNDERNEATH VIEW

OFF-ROADING

A tractor needs to be tough enough to cope with bumpy and muddy ground, so sturdy tires are a must. The rest is up to you! You can experiment with colors and special features. What could your tractor pull or what work will it do?

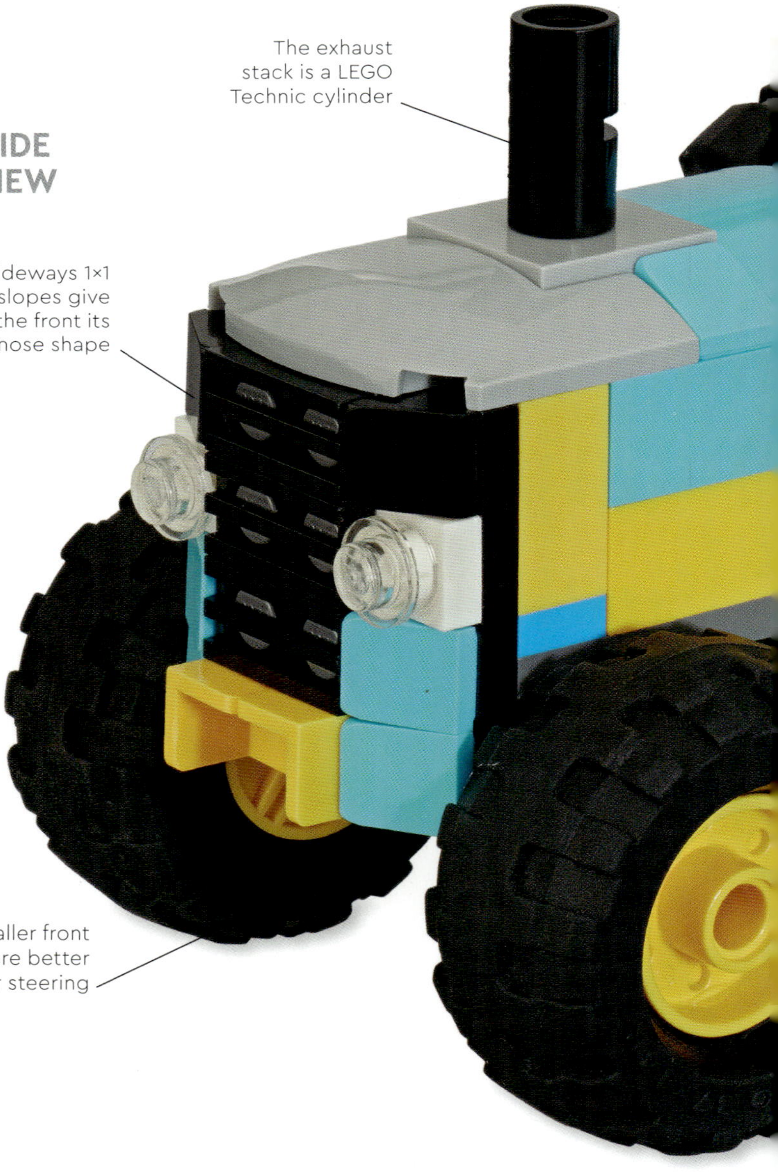
The exhaust stack is a LEGO Technic cylinder
Sideways 1×1 slopes give the front its bullnose shape
Smaller front wheels are better for steering

TRY THIS

Tractors aren't the only cool things you find on farms! Why not build a combine harvester, a seed-planting plane, or even a horse-drawn plow?

Brick with side studs
2×2 hinge plate
1×6×3 curved arch

BIT-PART TRACTOR

The front and back sections of the tractor are built separately and then added to the main build. The back section attaches to two hinge plates and includes large curved arches to make realistic-looking mudguards.

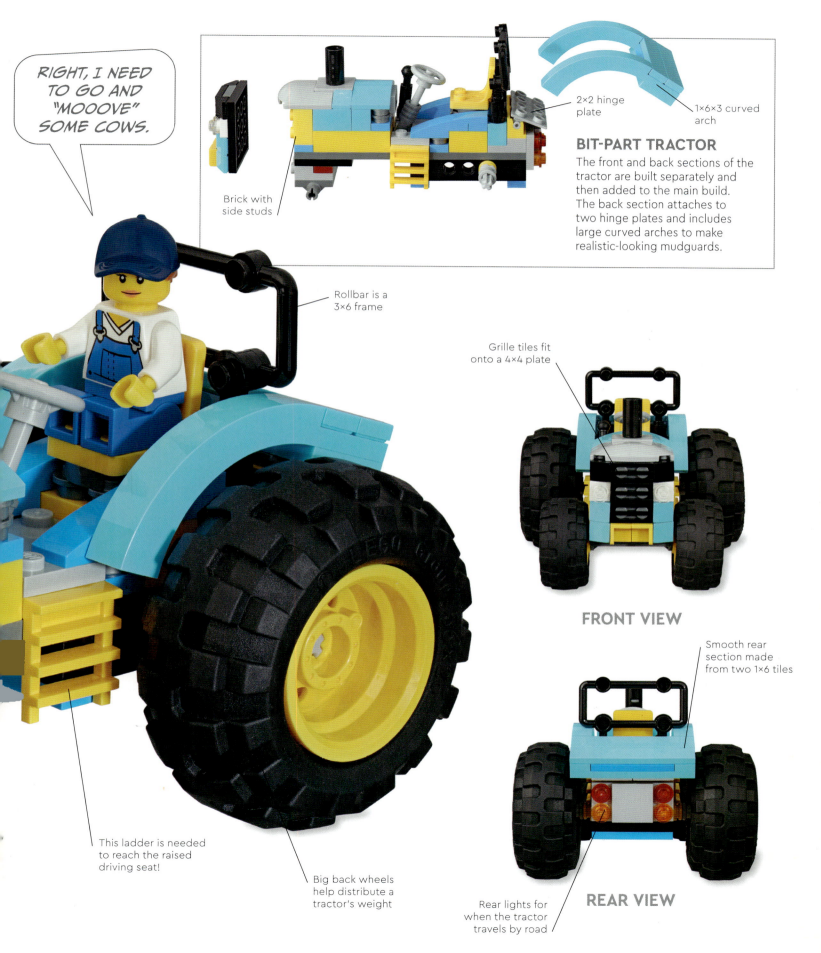

RIGHT, I NEED TO GO AND "MOOOVE" SOME COWS.
Rollbar is a 3×6 frame
This ladder is needed to reach the raised driving seat!
Big back wheels help distribute a tractor's weight

Grille tiles fit onto a 4×4 plate

FRONT VIEW

Smooth rear section made from two 1×6 tiles
Rear lights for when the tractor travels by road

REAR VIEW

BUILDING BRIEF

Objective: Build a talent-show stage
Use: Showing off special talents
Features: Stage, lights, judges' desk
Extras: TV cameras, buzzers

I HOPE THIS PANS OUT!

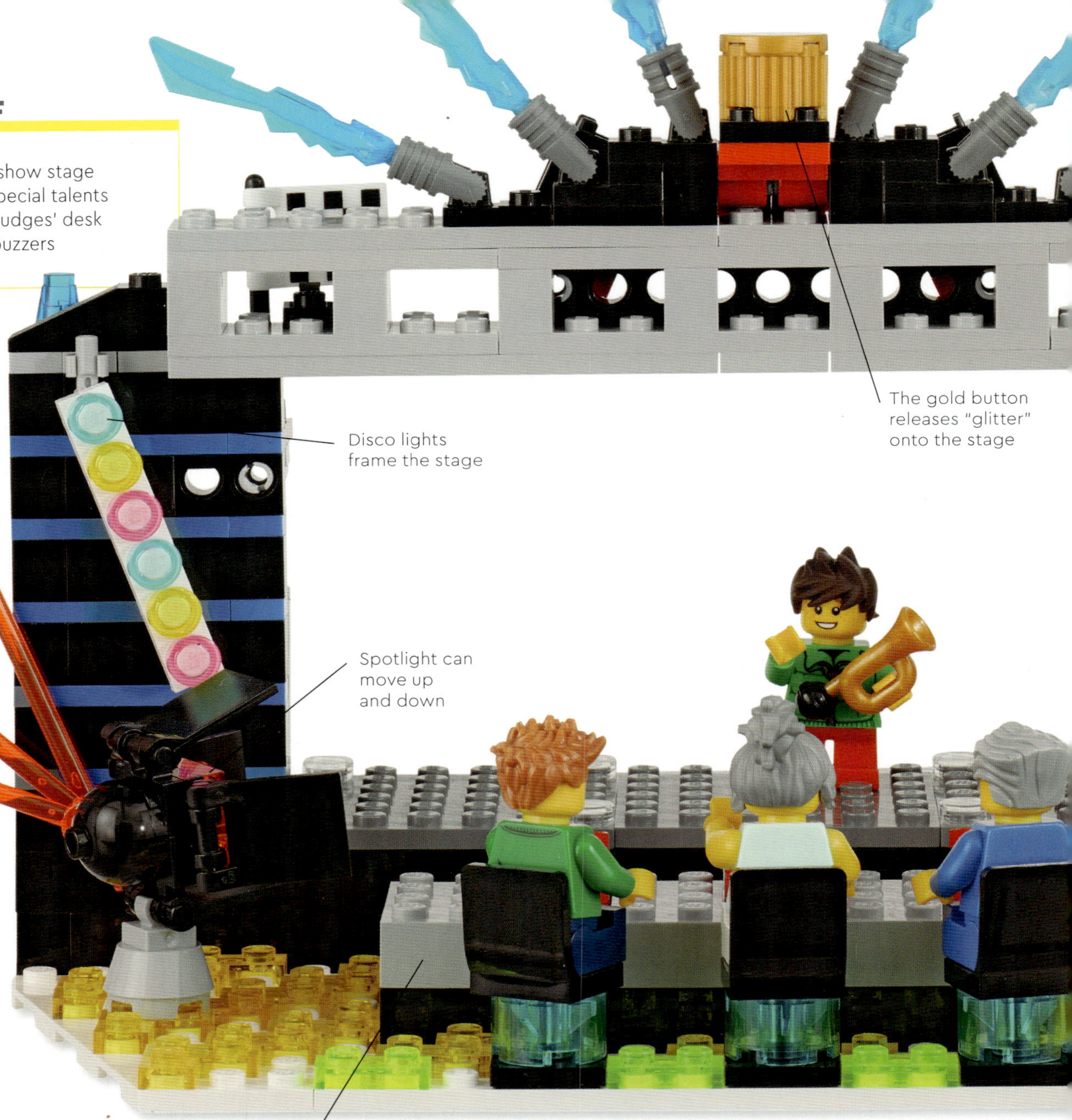
The gold button releases "glitter" onto the stage
Disco lights frame the stage
Spotlight can move up and down
Three judges sit behind an imposing desk

TALENT SHOW

There's much more to this talent show stage than meets the eye. When the judges press their big red buttons, they can open a trapdoor, fly a flag of surrender, or even pelt the performers with falling fish! Happily, there is also a gold button, used to shower the truly talented in glittery glory.

BUTTON IT!

Each red button is built onto a hidden seesaw mechanism. A seesaw in the middle pushes up the central trapdoor. The seesaws on either side connect to L-shaped "prods" that can tip the flag and the bucket of fish over.

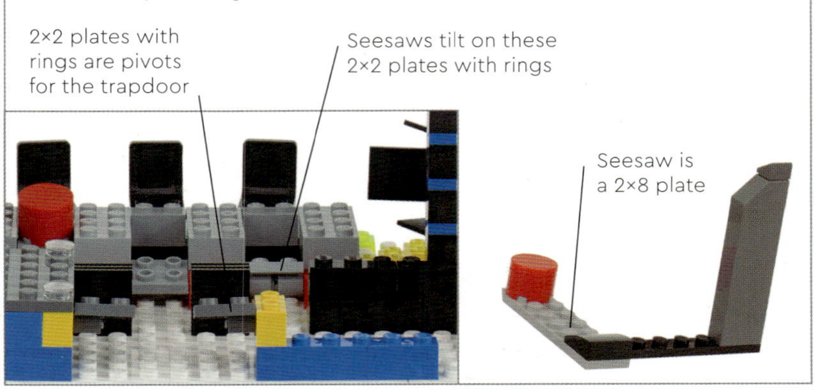
2×2 plates with rings are pivots for the trapdoor
Seesaws tilt on these 2×2 plates with rings
Seesaw is a 2×8 plate

SORRY . . . NEXT!

EXIT STAGE UP

When the middle judge presses her big red button, a trapdoor launches the unlucky performer right off the stage! The trapdoor is a 6×6 plate that blends in perfectly with the stage when closed, so contestants better tread carefully . . .

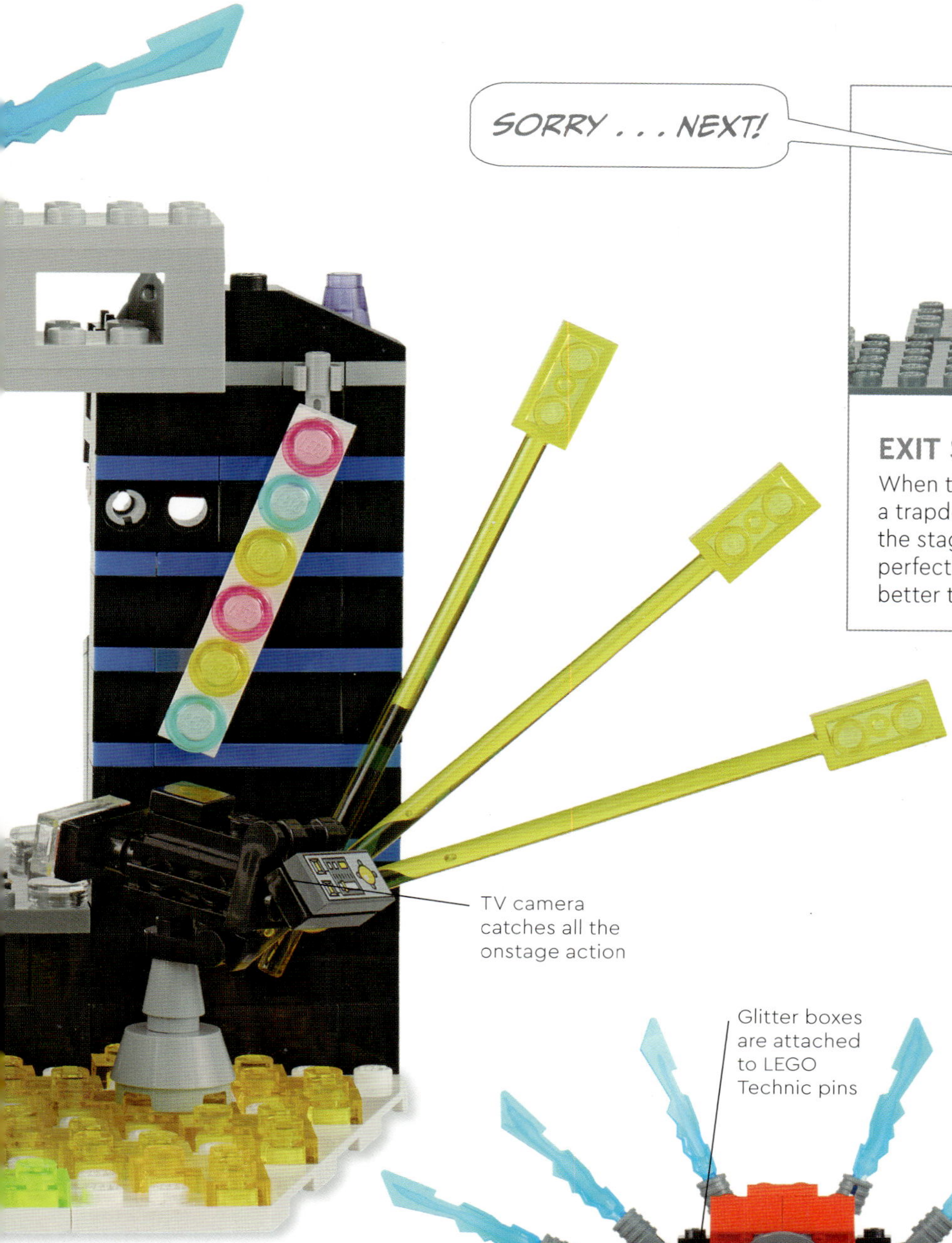
TV camera catches all the onstage action

IT'S SHOWTIME

The camera by the stage is rolling and the supersize spotlight has found its target—it's time to turn your model into a prime-time TV talent show! Do your minifigures have what it takes? Gather up your favorites and think about what their top talents might be.

Glitter boxes are attached to LEGO Technic pins
These fish fly when the bucket tips
Flag pivots on a plate with a ring beneath
This prod lifts up when the first judge hits his button
This prod rises when the third judge presses his button
Trapdoor is under the minifigure's feet!

REAR VIEW

GO EXPLORE

Take off on a journey of discovery and meet animals, aliens, mythical beasts, Vikings, and more. You'll see the wonders of the ancient world, ride old-fashioned vehicles, visit cities and natural habitats, and land on other planets. What are you waiting for? Pack up your LEGO® pieces—and go explore!

BUILDING BRIEF

Objective: Create microscale buildings
Use: Display, travel, mini adventures
Features: Details at a small scale
Extras: Souvenirs, vehicles, tiny people

WORLD LANDMARKS

All you need is a handful of pieces and a little imagination to make incredible microbuilds of famous buildings and landmarks. These models are small, but they are big on wow factor! Display your tiny buildings in your bedroom so you and your friends can travel the world without ever leaving home.

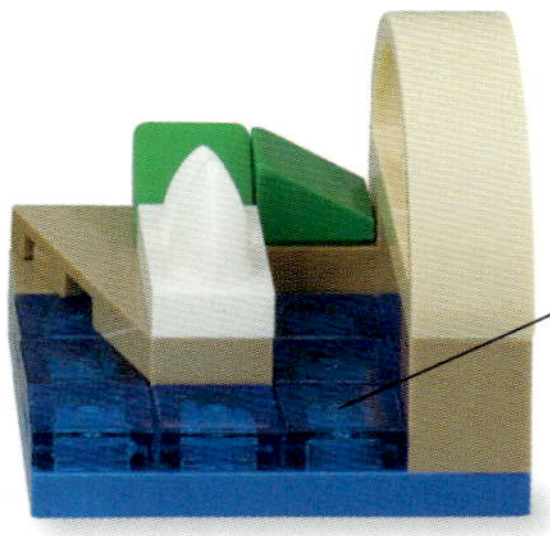
Make water using transparent blue tiles on top of a blue plate

SIDE VIEW

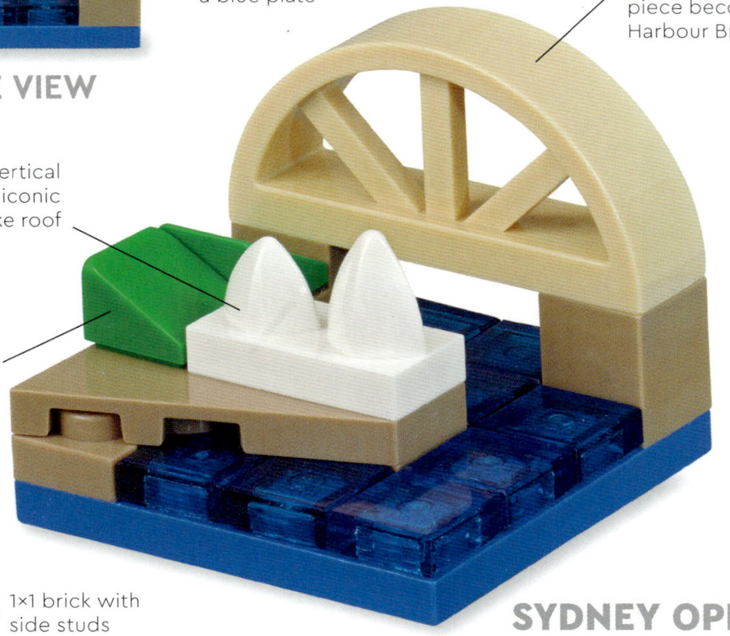
Rounded window piece becomes Sydney Harbour Bridge
Tile with vertical teeth is the iconic shell-like roof
1×1 slope bricks are greenery at the harbor

BUILD TIP

Look at photos of real buildings or landmarks and then pick out the details that make them easy to identify. Which pieces in your collection can you use to re-create them?

SYDNEY OPERA HOUSE

A single LEGO piece gives this microscale building its sail-like shape, which makes it instantly recognizable. Why not build the whole harbor with a few more types of pieces?

1×1 brick with side studs
Attach grille tiles after the base is complete
Jumper plates hold the building on the base

GOING UP

Build your skyscraper a wide, stable base to make it sturdy, then build up the rest of the structure in layers. The grille tiles and some plates attach sideways.

EMPIRE STATE BUILDING

You'll only need to use a fraction of the 10 million bricks used to build the real-world version of this skyscraper. Stacked-up bricks with side studs make a tall, sturdy structure and allow you to add details to the sides.

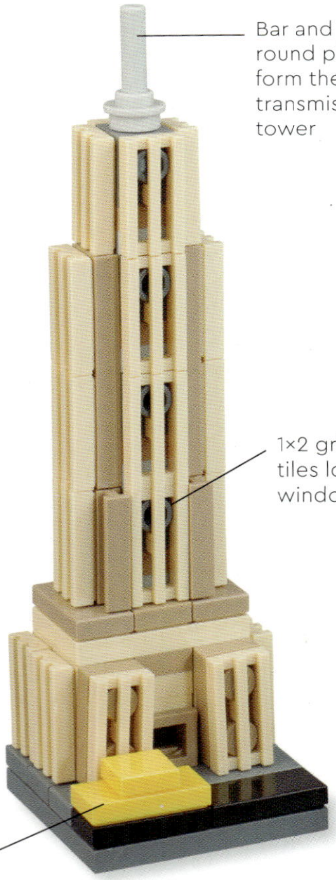
Bar and 1×1 round plate form the transmission tower
1×2 grille tiles look like windows
Just two pieces make an iconic yellow taxi

TAJ MAHAL

The Taj Mahal in Agra, India, is built symmetrically, just like this microbuild. It took 16 years to build the real Taj Mahal, but making a mini version shouldn't take quite as long!

2×2 dome piece forms the central "onion" dome

Arched doorway is the back of a tooth plate

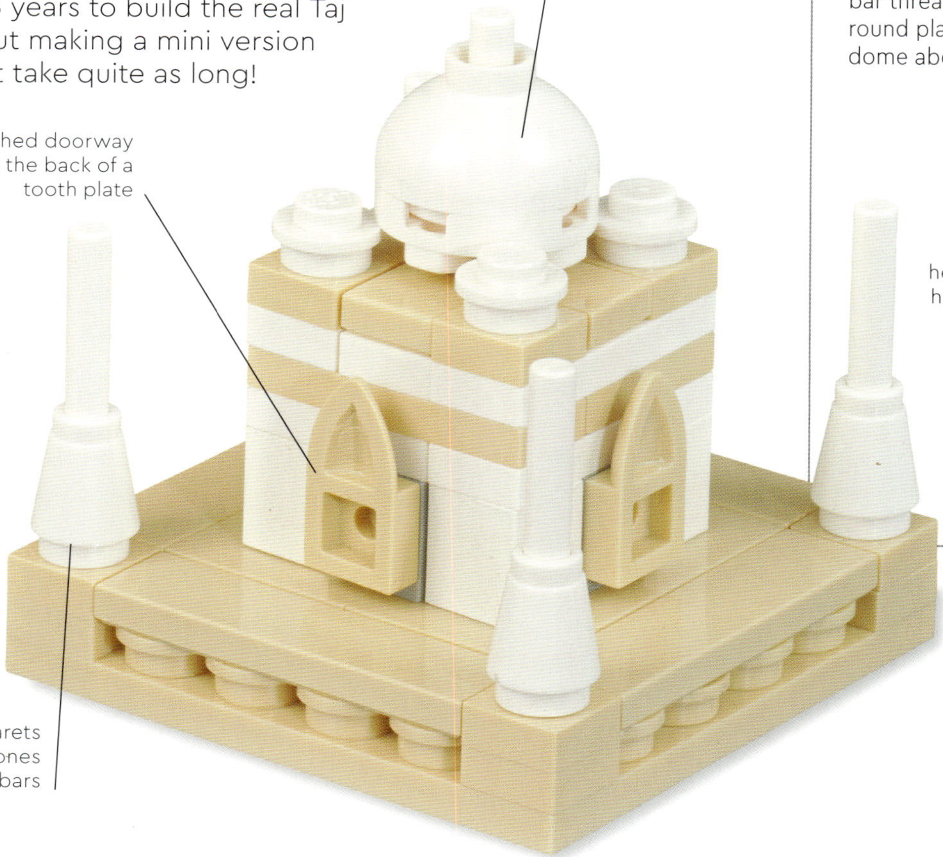

Make minarets with 1×1 cones and bars

POLE POSITION

Hidden inside this microbuild is a gold 1×1 round plate that attaches to a bar piece. The bar threads through a 2×2 round plate with hole and the dome above to secure the roof.

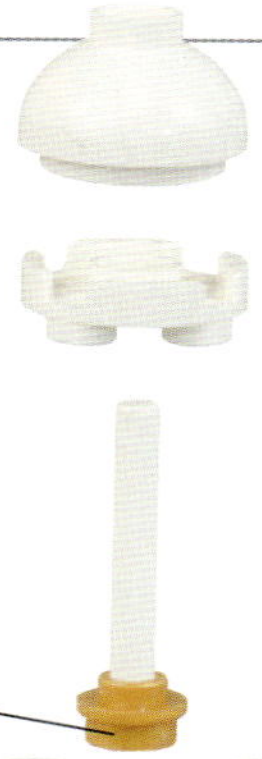

1×1 round plate with open stud

The back of a headlight brick holds the door

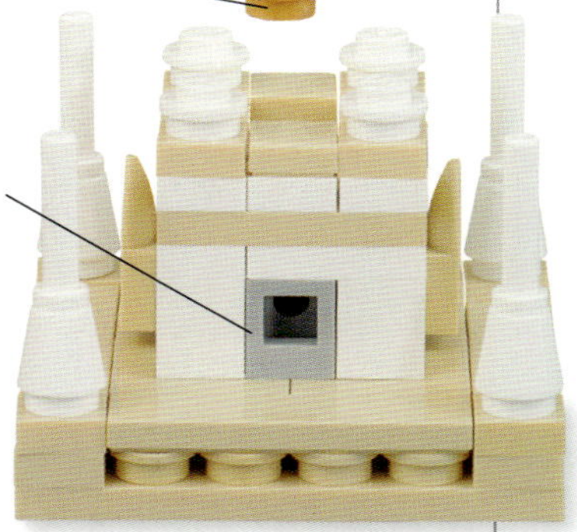

EIFFEL TOWER

This building has a distinctive shape that's easy to re-create with a handful of LEGO pieces. You could build the tower on its own or secure it to the Gardens of the Trocadero.

French flag made from two 1×1 plates and a tile with clip

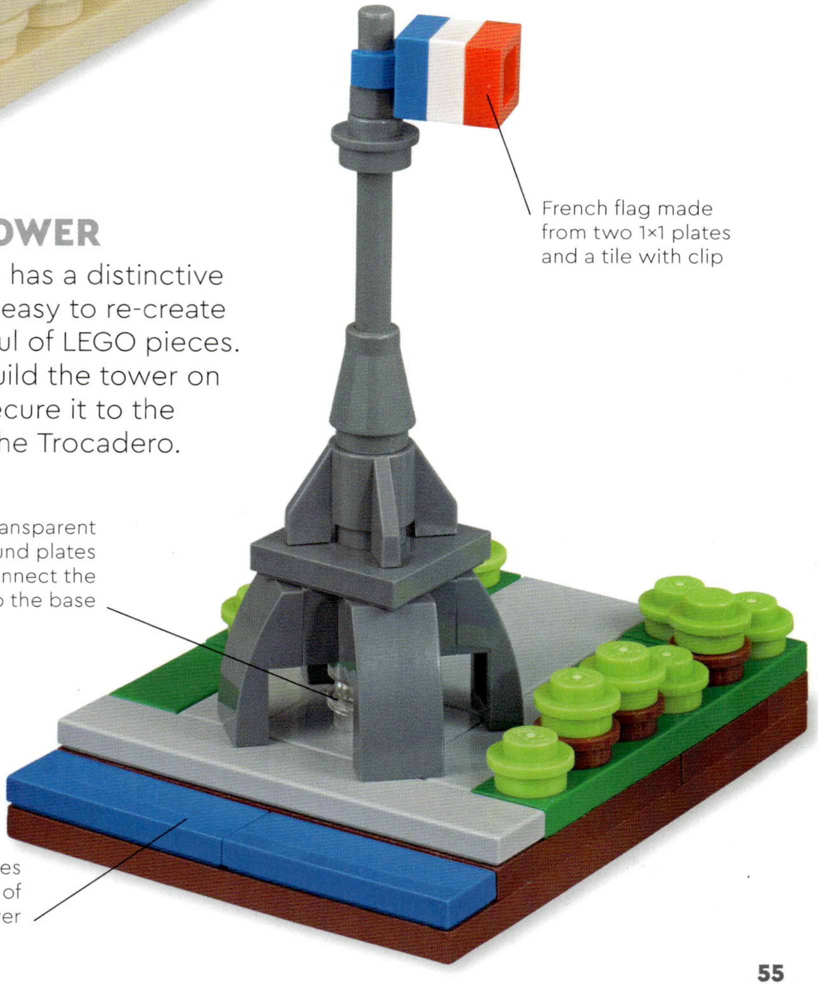

1×1 round bricks for trees and shrubs

REAR VIEW

MAGNIFIQUE!

Two transparent 1×1 round plates connect the tower to the base

Two 1×3 tiles create a hint of the Seine River

DINOSAUR COMMITTEE

An asteroid is about to hit Earth! Can the dinosaurs save themselves? This committee of five desperate dinos has gathered around a table to explore ideas. You only need a few models—dinosaurs, a table, a tree, the asteroid—to create a fun scene like this. Why not tweak some other historical events?

BUILDING BRIEF

Objective:	Reimagine a scene from history
Use:	Problem-solving and play
Features:	Dinosaurs, meeting table
Extras:	Asteroid, prehistoric landscapes

TRY THIS

Try building models of machines or equipment that could capture or deflect the incoming asteroid. What incredible contraptions can you come up with?

2×2 round brick with spikes makes a leafy layer

TREE

GET THINKING, FRIENDS, OR WE'RE HISTORY!

Is this bar a pencil, a pointer, or a magic wand for whooshing away asteroids?

2×2 round brick for sturdy legs

Plate with three teeth makes sharp claws

T. REX

A red T. rex is furiously jotting down ideas. Its little hands are tiles with clips, which help it to grip onto things.

STEGOSAURUS

Steggy has big feet, a big body, and big armor plates, but only a little brain. Its big idea is to bat the asteroid away with its swishy tail.

1×2 slope makes a bony plate

1×1 pyramid slope for a spiky tail

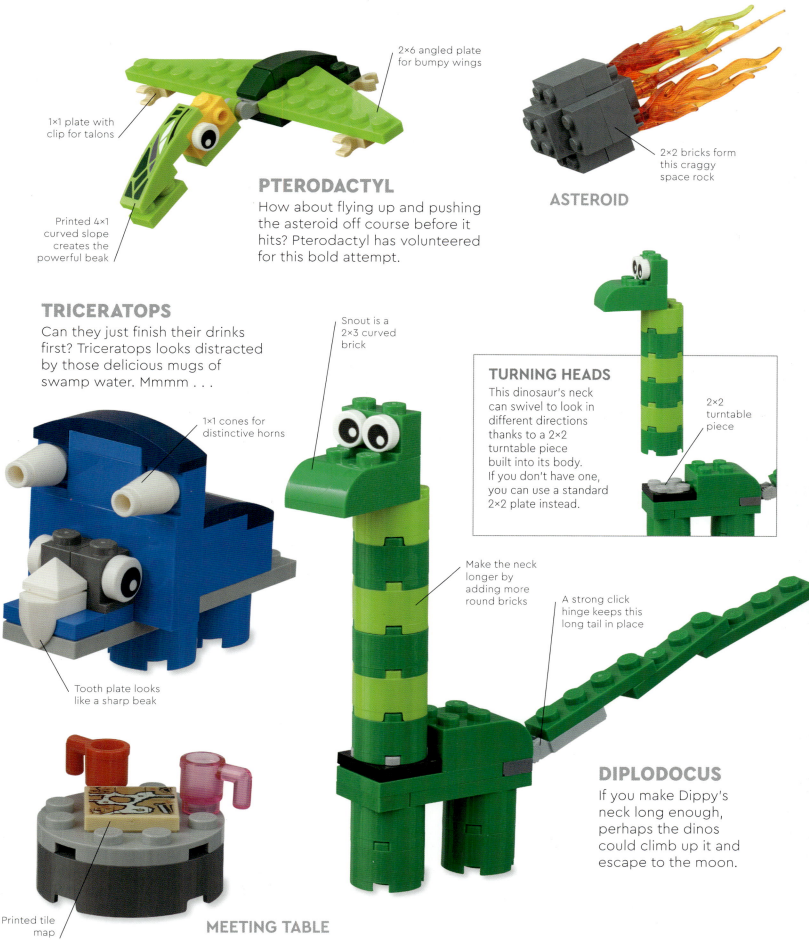

2×6 angled plate for bumpy wings
1×1 plate with clip for talons
Printed 4×1 curved slope creates the powerful beak

PTERODACTYL

How about flying up and pushing the asteroid off course before it hits? Pterodactyl has volunteered for this bold attempt.

2×2 bricks form this craggy space rock

ASTEROID

TRICERATOPS

Can they just finish their drinks first? Triceratops looks distracted by those delicious mugs of swamp water. Mmmm . . .

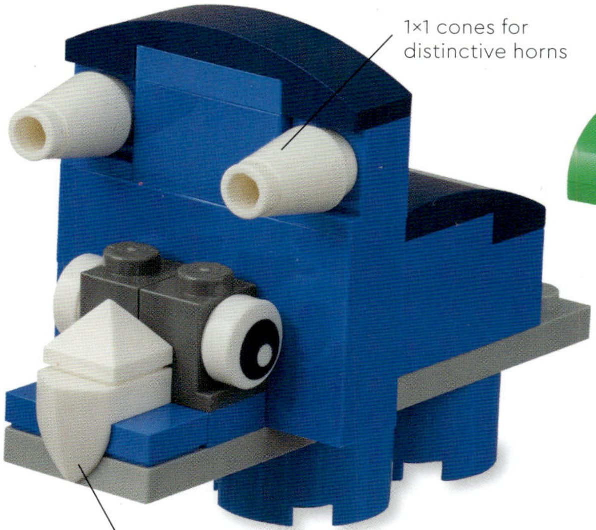

1×1 cones for distinctive horns
Tooth plate looks like a sharp beak

TURNING HEADS

This dinosaur's neck can swivel to look in different directions thanks to a 2×2 turntable piece built into its body. If you don't have one, you can use a standard 2×2 plate instead.

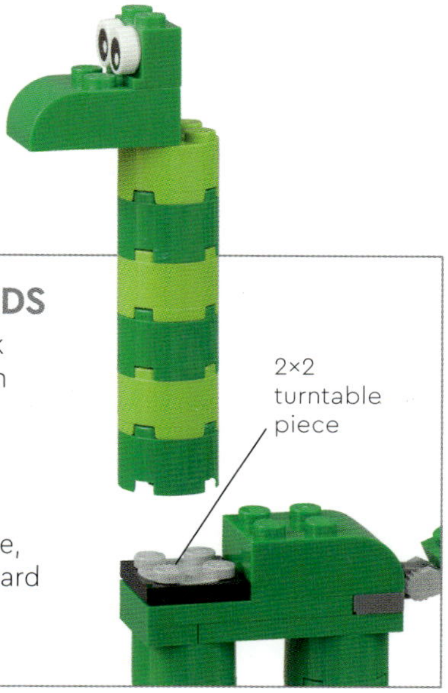

2×2 turntable piece

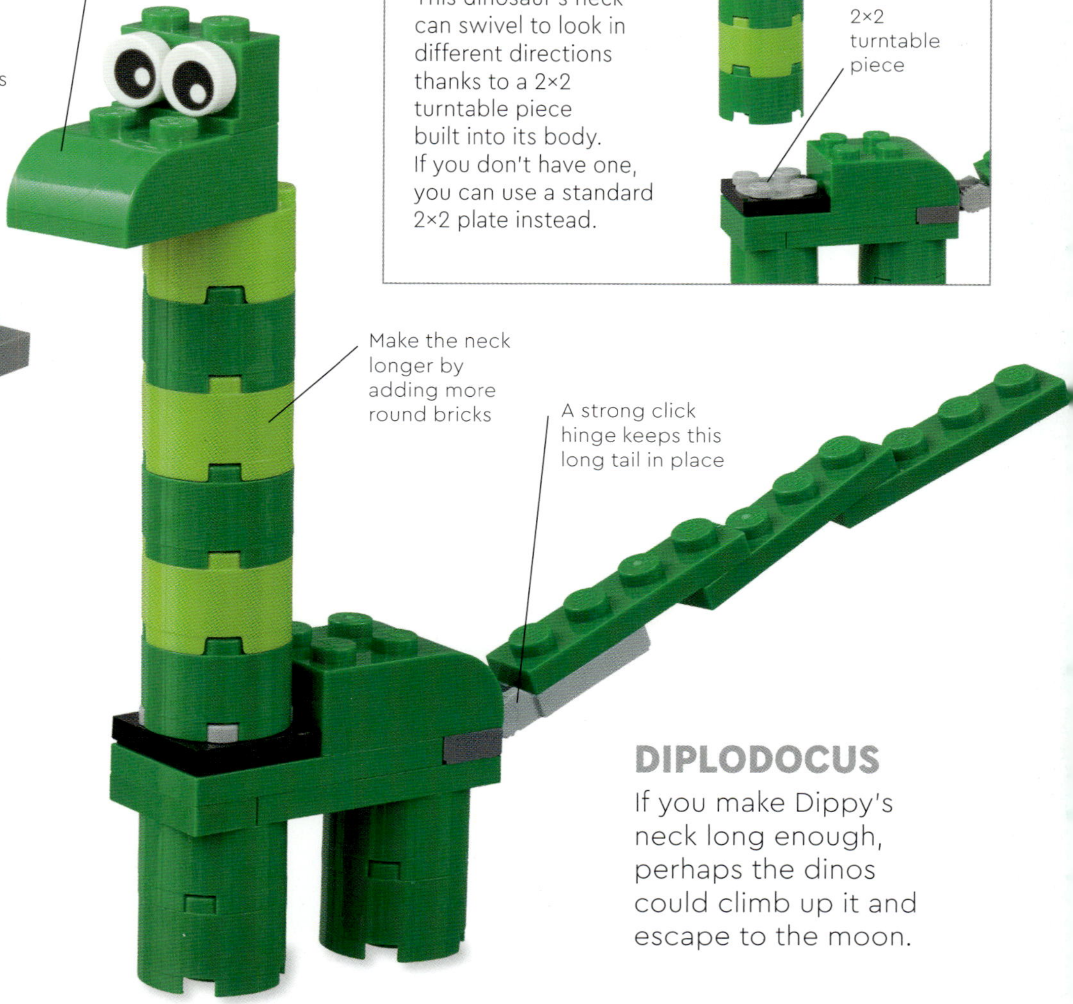

Snout is a 2×3 curved brick
Make the neck longer by adding more round bricks
A strong click hinge keeps this long tail in place

DIPLODOCUS

If you make Dippy's neck long enough, perhaps the dinos could climb up it and escape to the moon.

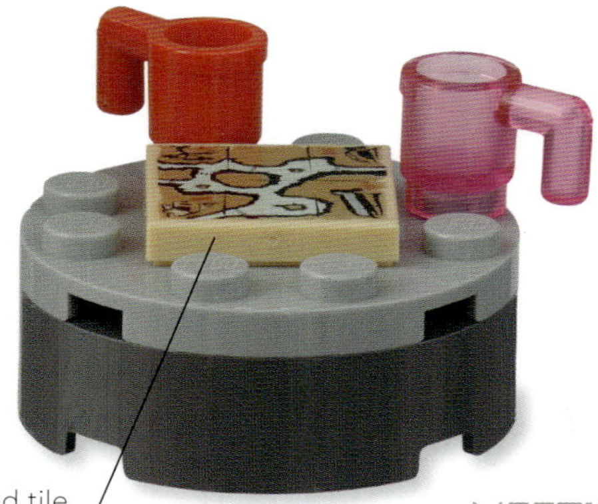

Printed tile map

MEETING TABLE

BUILDING BRIEF

Objective:	Build ancient Egypt in microscale
Use:	Exploring the ancient world
Features:	Sphinx, temple with columns, Nile riverfront
Extras:	Vegetation, boats

ANCIENT EGYPT

The Sphinx watched thousands of years of ancient Egyptian history roll by. Imagine what this famous statue saw! The Nile River, for sure. Palm trees, definitely. Pyramids, of course. This microscale scene also features boats and a jetty leading to a riverside temple. Will yours be as peaceful as this one, or will a rampaging mummy come along to cause chaos?

NILE RIVERFRONT

In a micro build like this, tiny three-leaf plant pieces look like lofty palm trees and a single tile makes a long jetty. Add more pyramids if you like, all in different sizes.

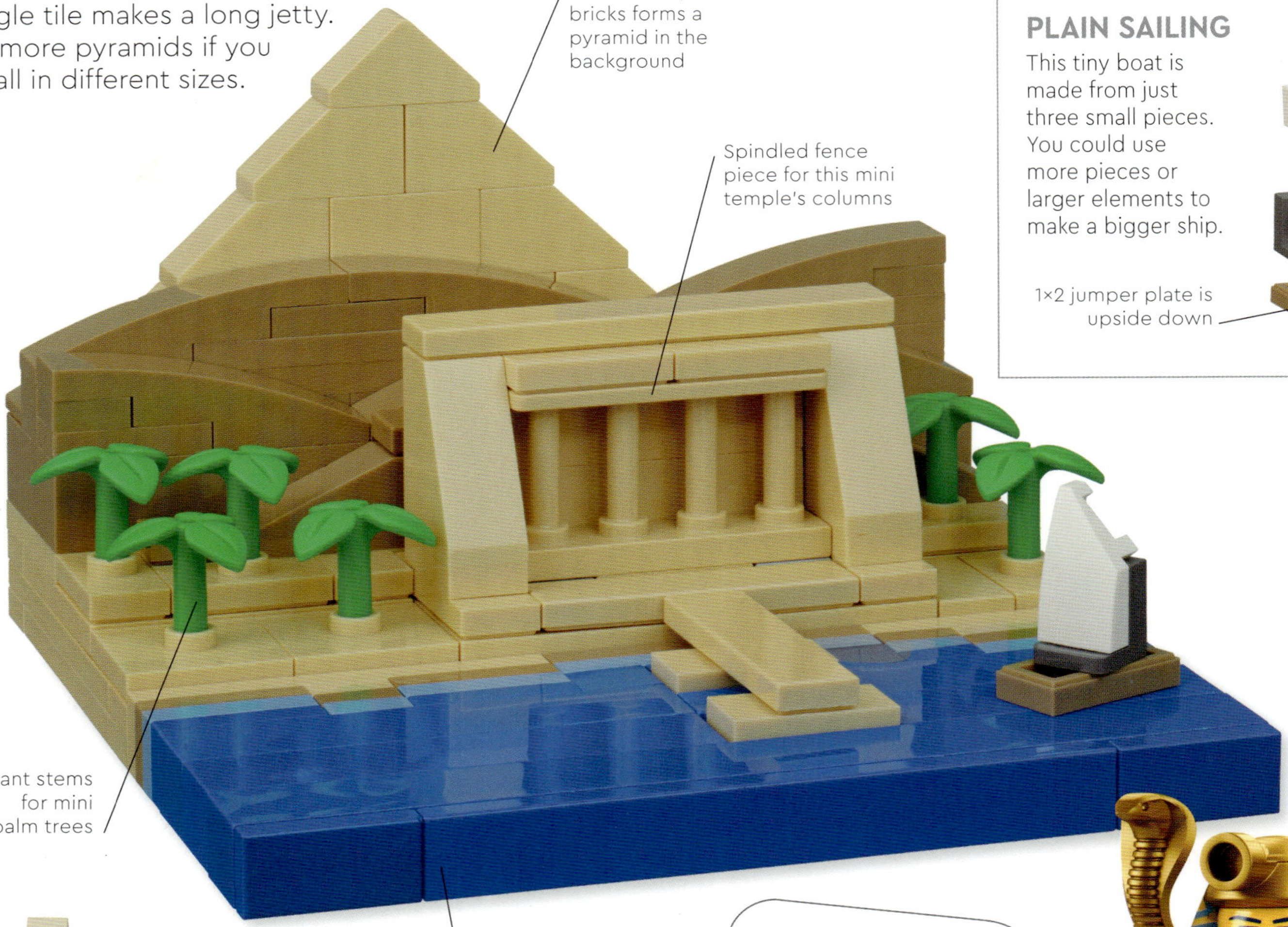

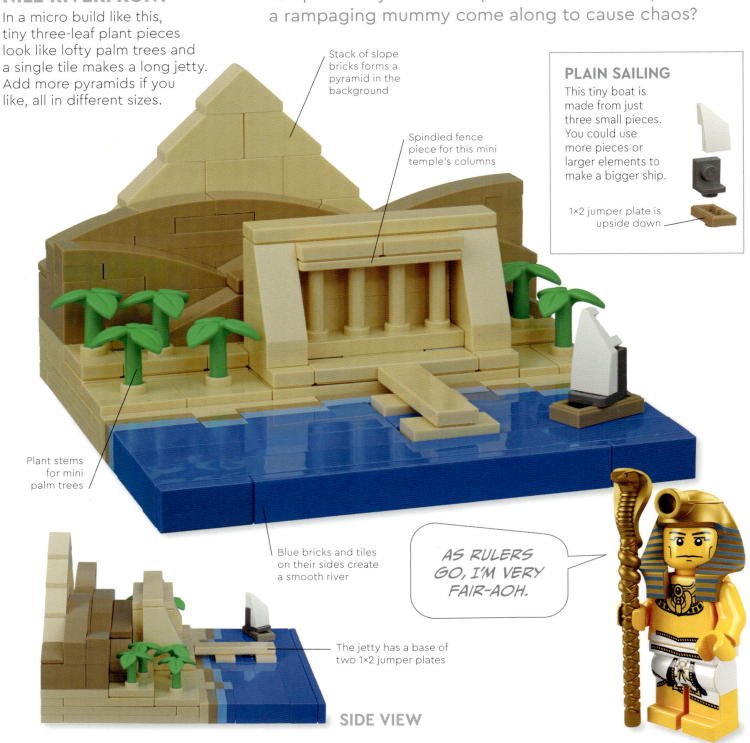

Stack of slope bricks forms a pyramid in the background

Spindled fence piece for this mini temple's columns

Plant stems for mini palm trees

Blue bricks and tiles on their sides create a smooth river

PLAIN SAILING

This tiny boat is made from just three small pieces. You could use more pieces or larger elements to make a bigger ship.

1×2 jumper plate is upside down

The jetty has a base of two 1×2 jumper plates

SIDE VIEW

AS RULERS GO, I'M VERY FAIR-AOH.

SIDE VIEW

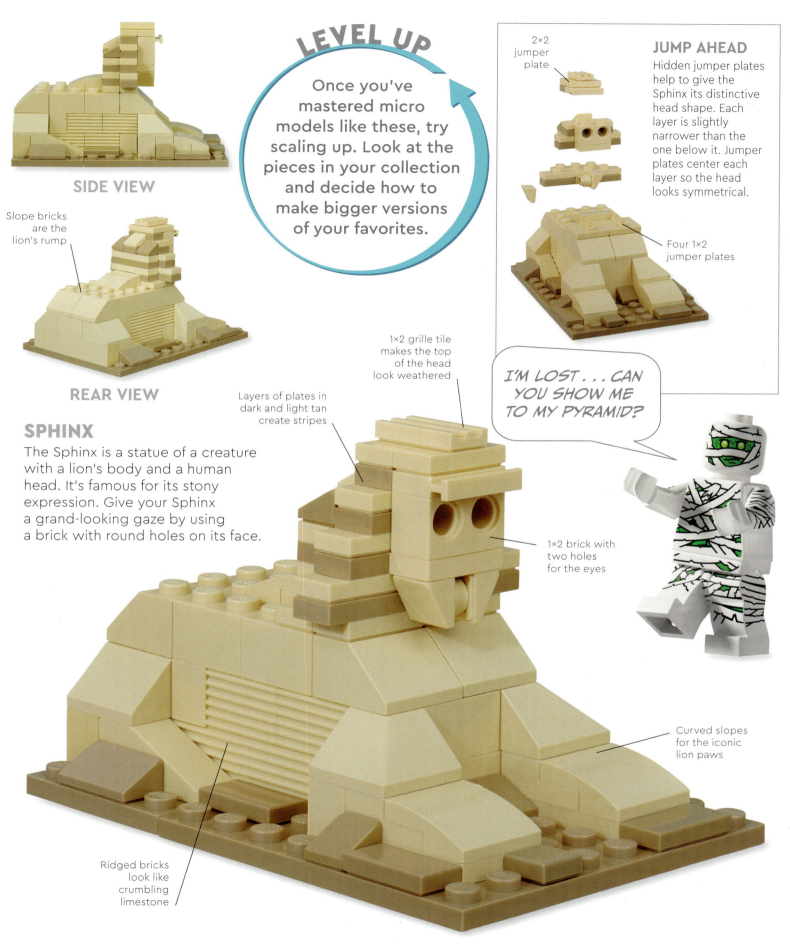

Slope bricks are the lion's rump

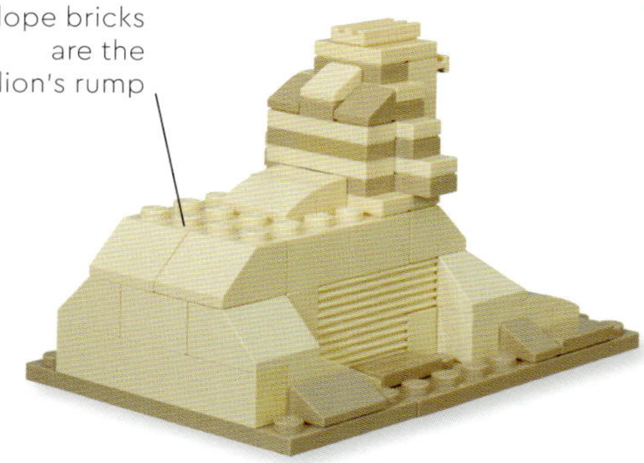

REAR VIEW

LEVEL UP

Once you've mastered micro models like these, try scaling up. Look at the pieces in your collection and decide how to make bigger versions of your favorites.

JUMP AHEAD

Hidden jumper plates help to give the Sphinx its distinctive head shape. Each layer is slightly narrower than the one below it. Jumper plates center each layer so the head looks symmetrical.

2×2 jumper plate

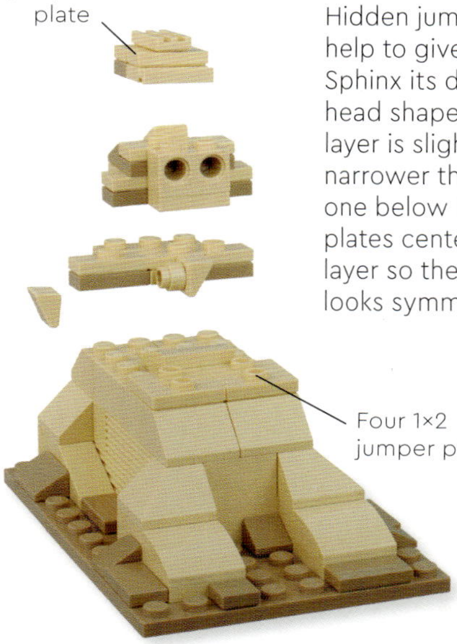

Four 1×2 jumper plates

SPHINX

The Sphinx is a statue of a creature with a lion's body and a human head. It's famous for its stony expression. Give your Sphinx a grand-looking gaze by using a brick with round holes on its face.

1×2 grille tile makes the top of the head look weathered

Layers of plates in dark and light tan create stripes

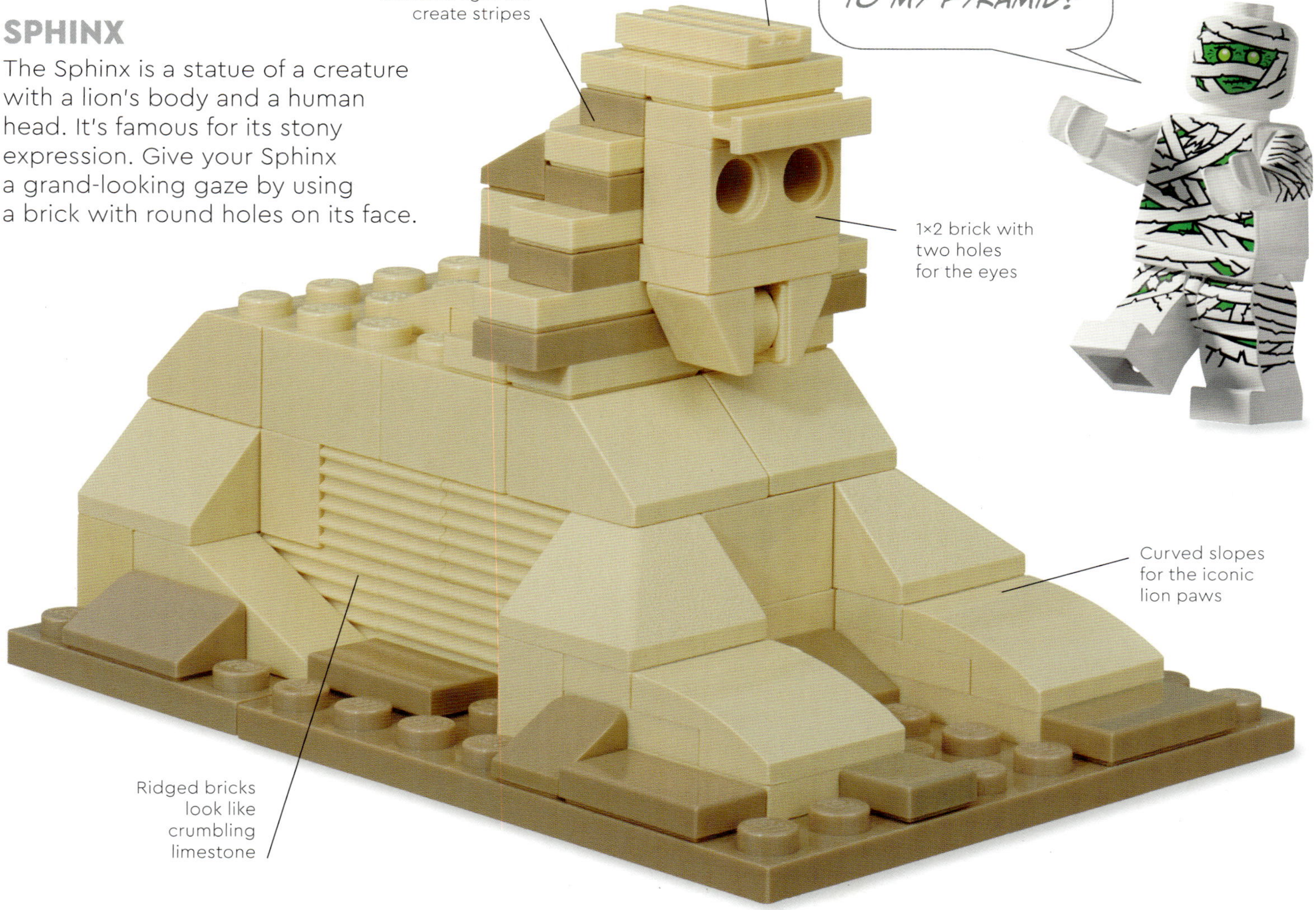
I'M LOST . . . CAN YOU SHOW ME TO MY PYRAMID?

1×2 brick with two holes for the eyes

Curved slopes for the iconic lion paws

Ridged bricks look like crumbling limestone

BUILDING BRIEF

Objective: Build old-fashioned vehicles
Use: Getting around in times gone by
Features: Seats, steering mechanism, power source
Extras: Wheels, luggage, lighting

OLD TIMEY TRANSIT

Travel back to days of old in style! Before engines, vehicles were powered by animals, hot air, steam, or wind. Consider building a horse-drawn stagecoach or a hot-air balloon like these, or try making a ship with sails or a steam-powered car. Look up pictures of old-fashioned transportation and let them inspire your classic creations.

MAKE A SEAT

Stagecoaches could transport several passengers at a time, so include plenty of space inside for seats and leg room. Drinks and snacks are optional!

Curly gold plant stem for the luggage rail end

STAGECOACH

This horse-pulled carriage is built to travel down old dirt roads and over bumpy cobblestones. It has a driver's seat and comfortable facilities inside. There's also room on top for luggage—and dramatic highway robbery scenes!

GIVE ME THAT JEWEL OR WE MUST DUEL!
Use gold pieces to add fancy-looking features
Connect small bricks, jumper plates, and tooth plates to make luggage
This 1×2 brick secures the horse's reins
1×2 plate with bar is a step to get into the carriage

HOT-AIR BALLOON

The balloon part of this aircraft is called an envelope. This one is made from lots of bricks, with thinner plates at the top. To get the shape right, stack up bricks from the bottom, making each layer a little wider than the one below.

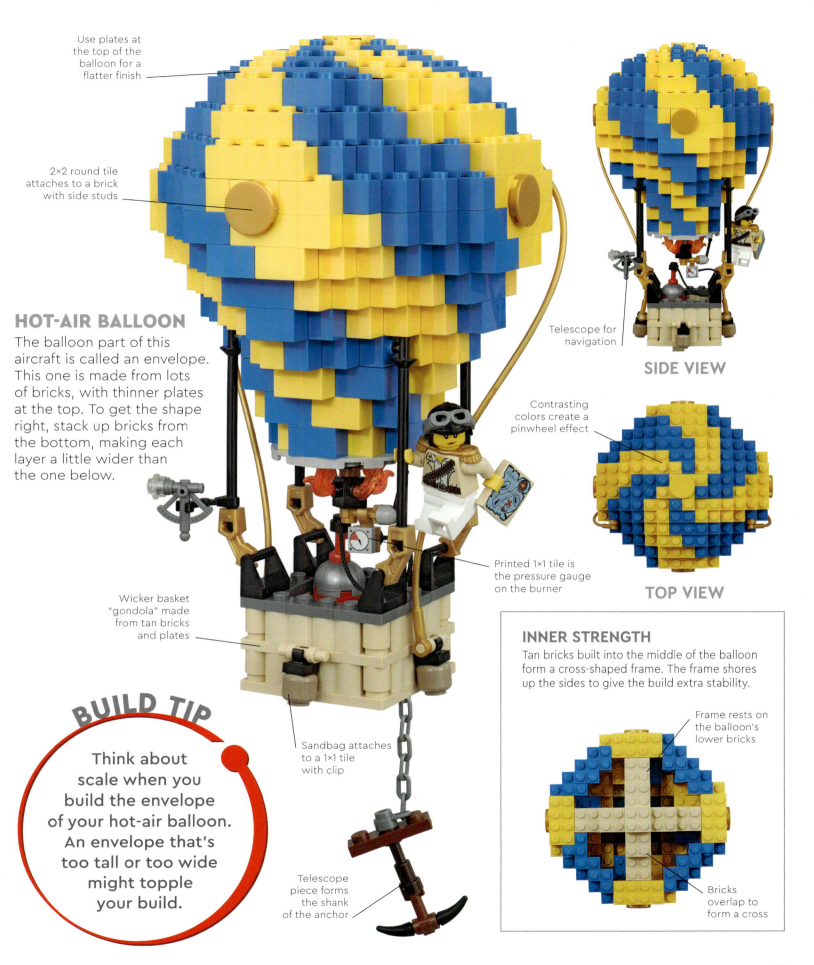

Use plates at the top of the balloon for a flatter finish
2×2 round tile attaches to a brick with side studs
Wicker basket "gondola" made from tan bricks and plates
Printed 1×1 tile is the pressure gauge on the burner
Sandbag attaches to a 1×1 tile with clip
Telescope piece forms the shank of the anchor

Telescope for navigation

SIDE VIEW

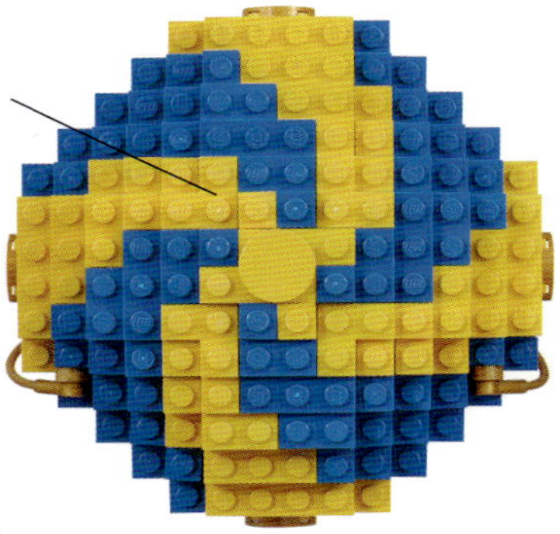

Contrasting colors create a pinwheel effect

TOP VIEW

BUILD TIP

Think about scale when you build the envelope of your hot-air balloon. An envelope that's too tall or too wide might topple your build.

INNER STRENGTH

Tan bricks built into the middle of the balloon form a cross-shaped frame. The frame shores up the sides to give the build extra stability.

Frame rests on the balloon's lower bricks
Bricks overlap to form a cross

FANTASTICAL BEASTS

There's a magical secret to the way these colorful creatures are constructed: their bodies are built in a similar way. Build the square torso then add the unique features each beast has. A unicorn needs a horn and a dragon might breathe fire. What characteristics do a Pegasus or mermaid have?

BUILDING BRIEF

Objective:	Build magical creatures
Use:	Populating enchanted lands
Features:	Horns, tails, eyes
Extras:	Rainbows, fire, spikes

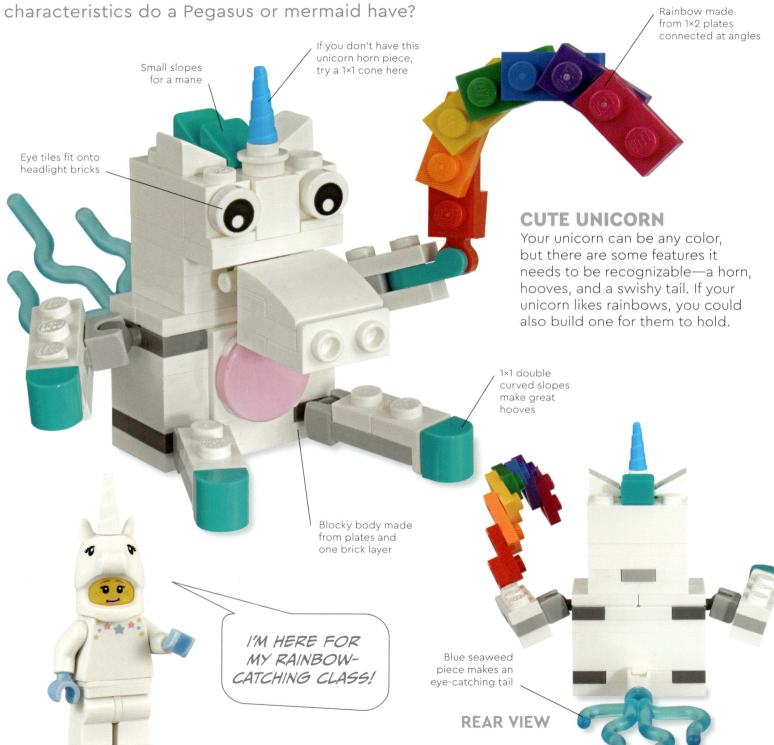

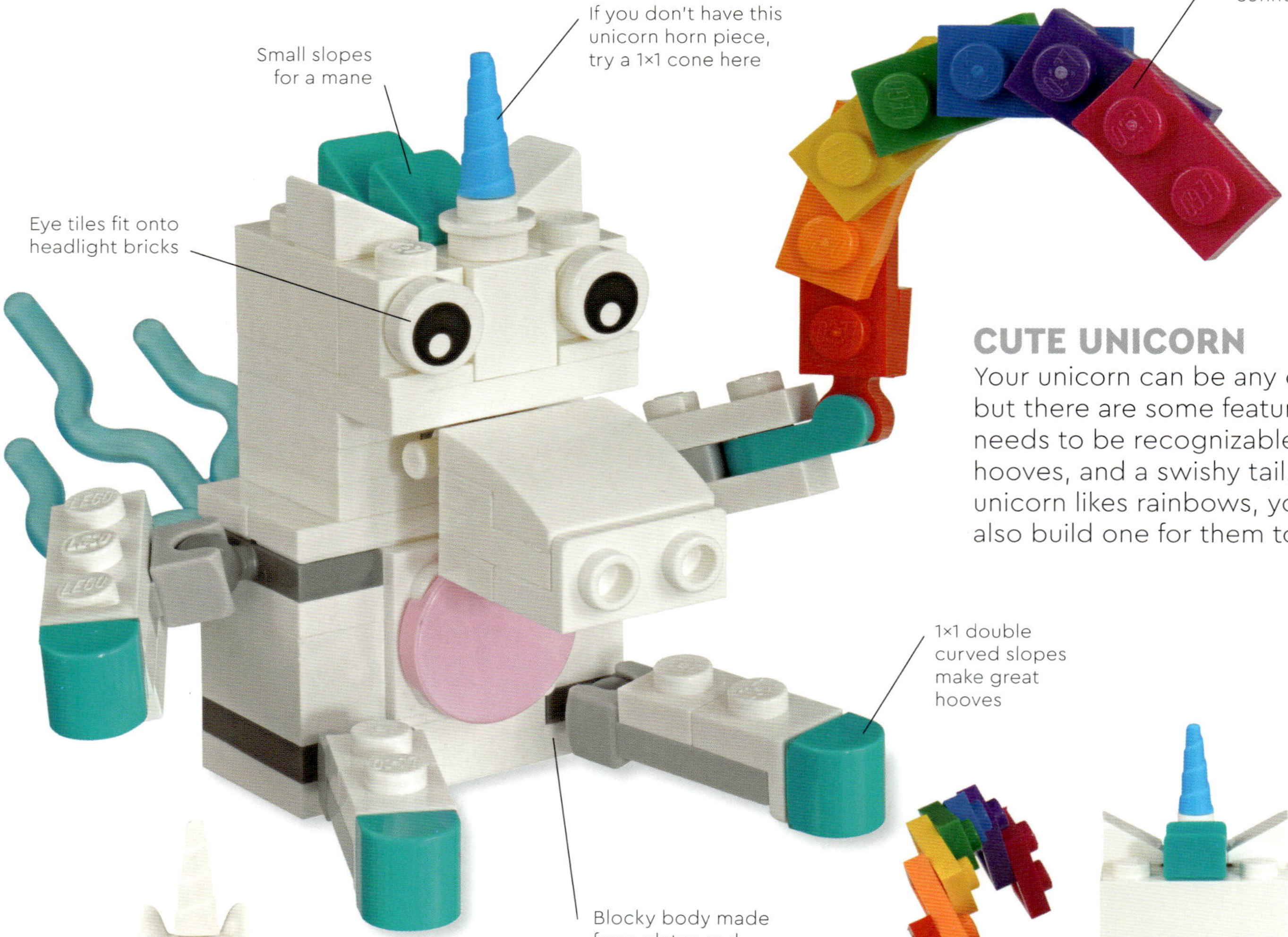
Rainbow made from 1×2 plates connected at angles
If you don't have this unicorn horn piece, try a 1×1 cone here
Small slopes for a mane
Eye tiles fit onto headlight bricks
1×1 double curved slopes make great hooves
Blocky body made from plates and one brick layer

CUTE UNICORN

Your unicorn can be any color, but there are some features it needs to be recognizable—a horn, hooves, and a swishy tail. If your unicorn likes rainbows, you could also build one for them to hold.

I'M HERE FOR MY RAINBOW-CATCHING CLASS!

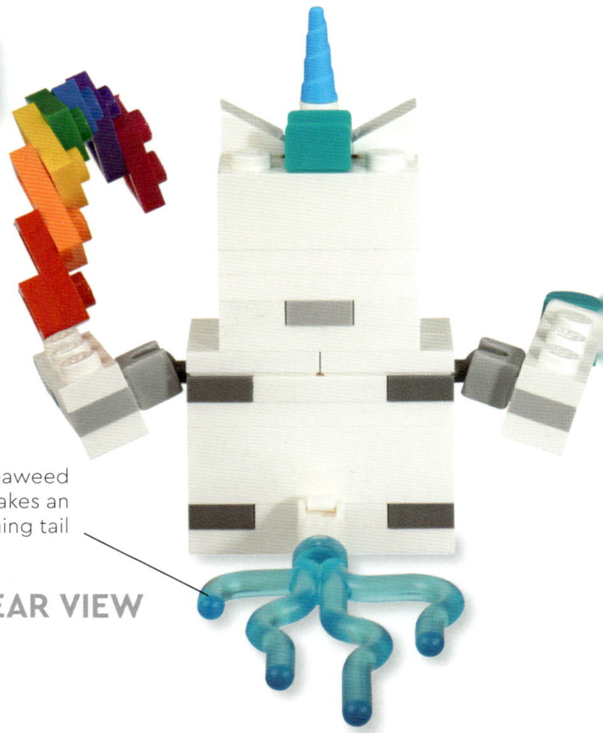
Blue seaweed piece makes an eye-catching tail

REAR VIEW

FIERY DRAGON

This fierce fire-breather has a scaly tail and sharp horns, but you might give your dragon smooth skin or even feathery wings. Let your imagination run wild when making mythical creatures!

1×1 round plates make the horns look longer
1×1 tile with clip makes a claw
Tan ingot pieces form armor-like skin
Long foot is a curved slope attached to a plate with socket

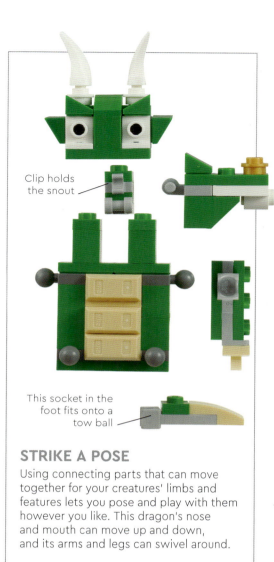

Clip holds the snout
This socket in the foot fits onto a tow ball

STRIKE A POSE

Using connecting parts that can move together for your creatures' limbs and features lets you pose and play with them however you like. This dragon's nose and mouth can move up and down, and its arms and legs can swivel around.

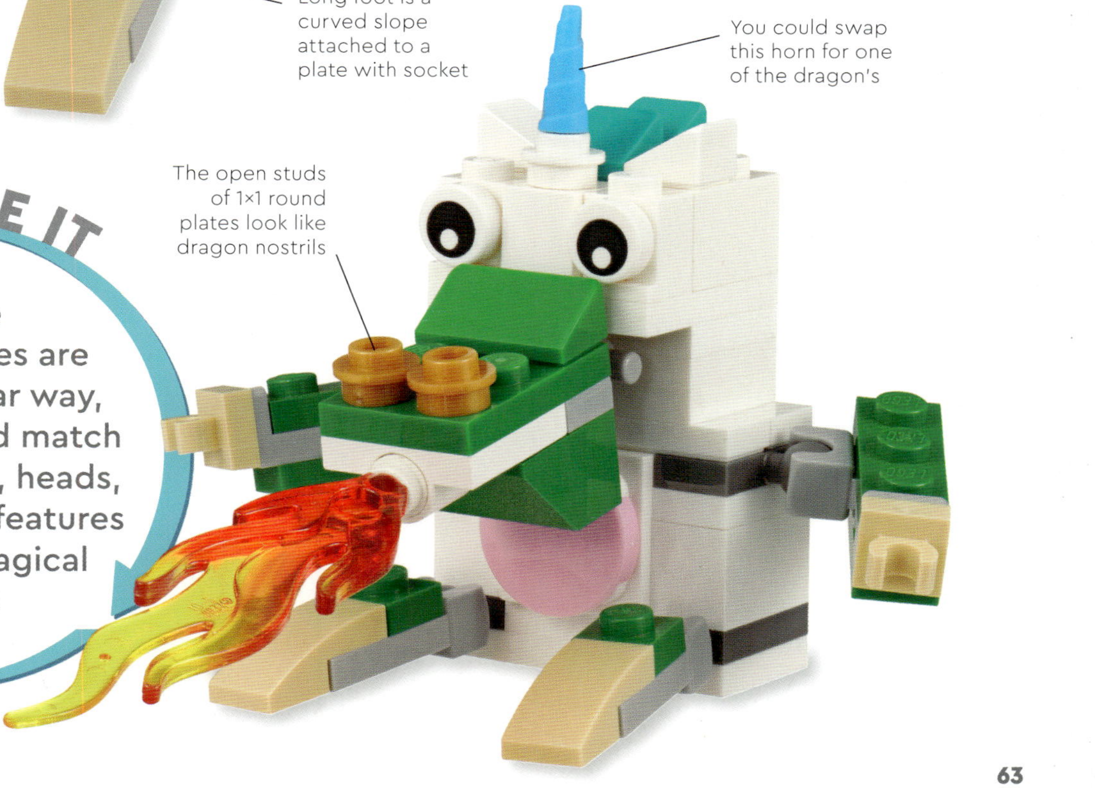
You could swap this horn for one of the dragon's
The open studs of 1×1 round plates look like dragon nostrils

CHANGE IT

Because these creatures are built in a similar way, you can mix and match their arms, legs, heads, tails, and other features to create a magical mashup!

SPACE RACE

This isn't just a racetrack—it's a spacetrack! Three tiny spaceships race around the LEGO nebula (in other words, your home), flying through hoops as they go. In case your pilots get lost, point the way with little arrows that seem to float in space. There are a few ways of making the hoops, so be creative. And let's hope they really are hoops, and not black holes!

BUILDING BRIEF

Objective: Build microscale spaceships and a racing track
Use: Flying around in space
Features: Wings, thrusters
Extras: Hoops, lights, direction markers

HEY!
YOU JUMPED
THE LIGHTS!

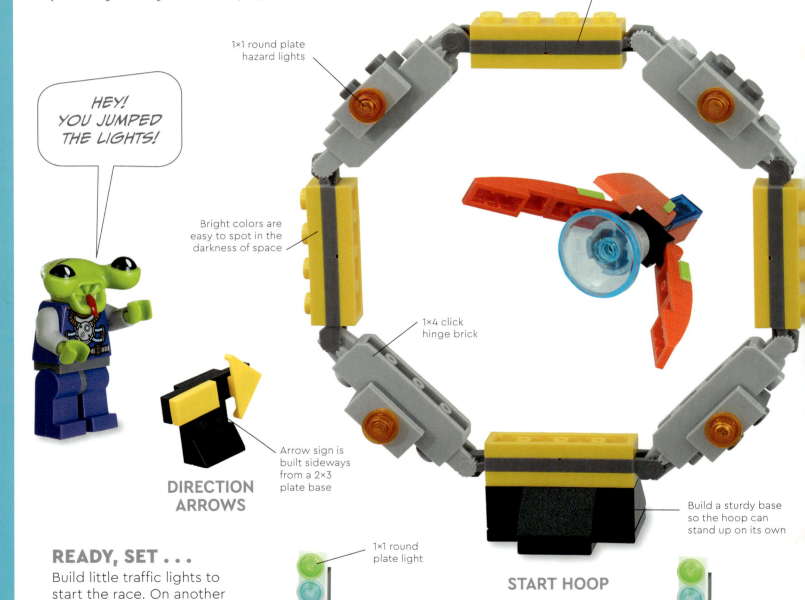

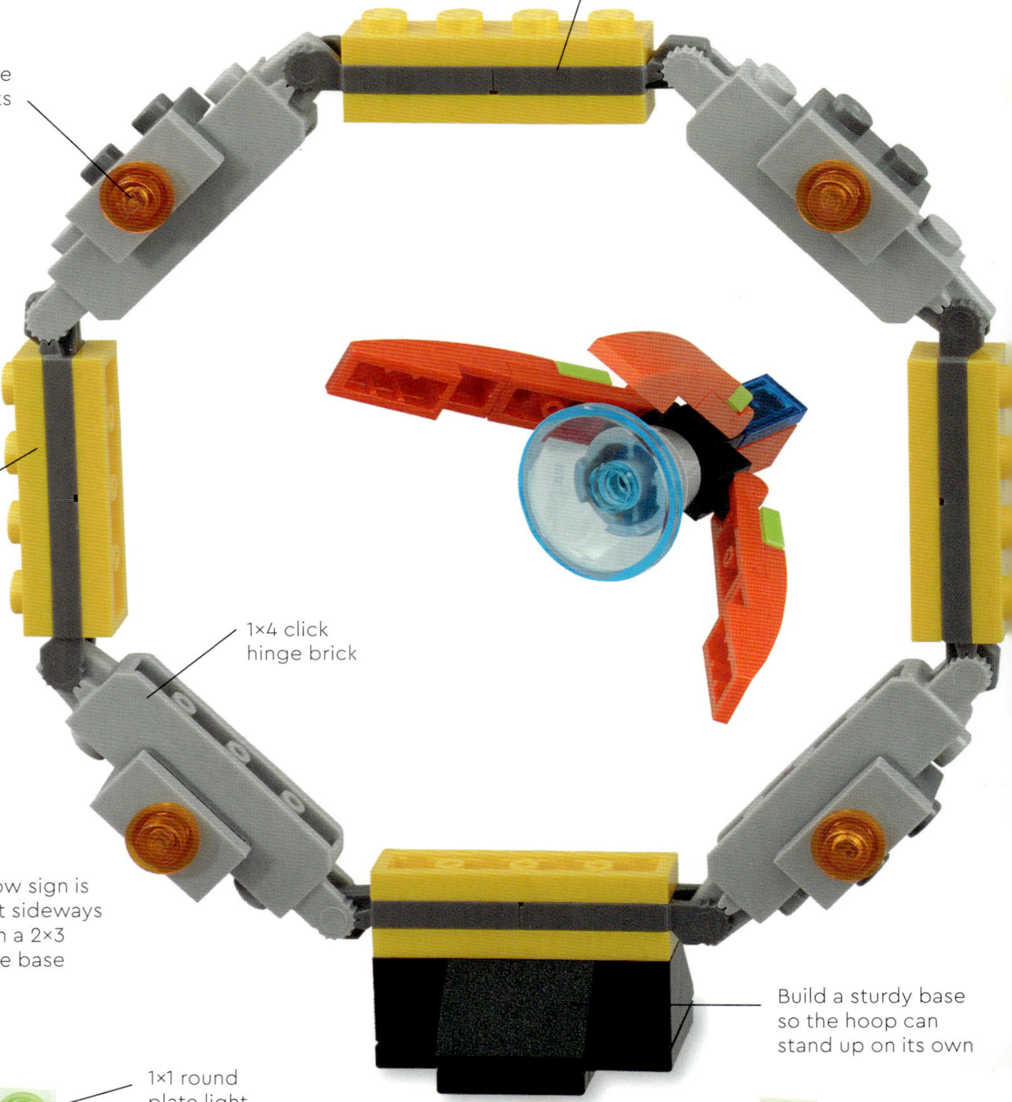
Will you make hoops, squares, or a completely different type of obstacle, such as hurdles, for your racers?
1×1 round plate hazard lights
Bright colors are easy to spot in the darkness of space
1×4 click hinge brick
Build a sturdy base so the hoop can stand up on its own

START HOOP

Arrow sign is built sideways from a 2×3 plate base

DIRECTION ARROWS

READY, SET . . .

Build little traffic lights to start the race. On another planet, you can use any colors to tell racers to stop, go, and slow down! You could also create some arrow markers for your racers to follow around the track.

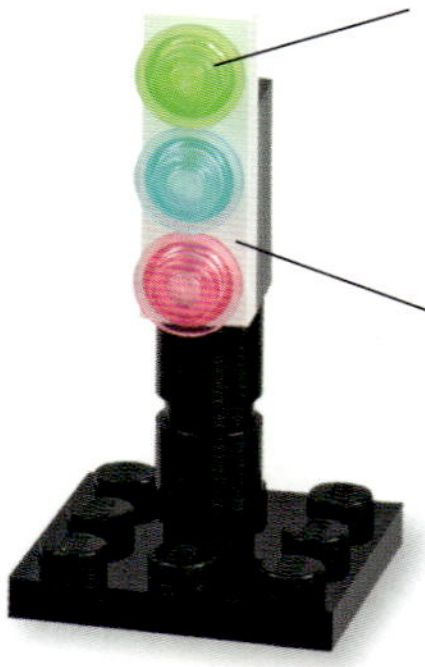
1×1 round plate light
1×3 plate attaches to a brick with side studs

3×3 plate base

STARTING LIGHTS

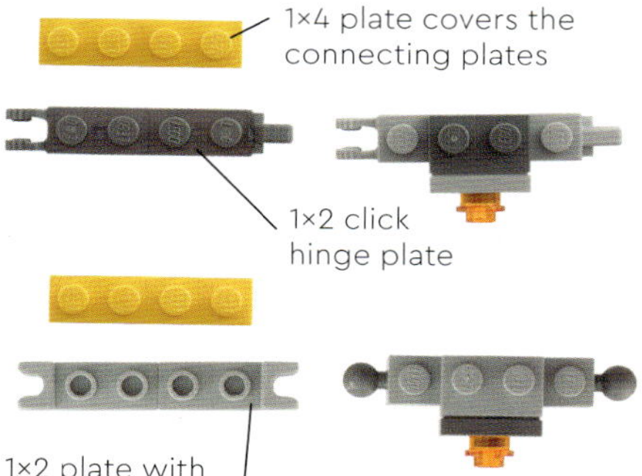
1×4 plate covers the connecting plates
1×2 click hinge plate
1×2 plate with tow ball socket

TWO TECHNIQUES

The two hoops on the racetrack look very similar, but they're built using different connecting pieces. The first hoop uses click hinge pieces, while the second uses tow ball—or ball and socket—connections. Both techniques allow the pieces to curve into a circular shape.

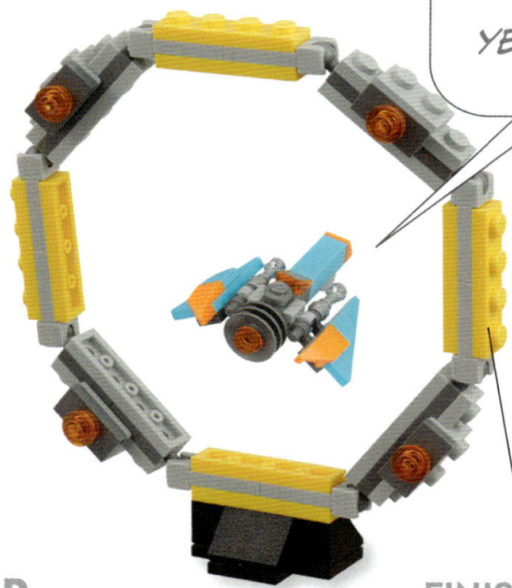
I'M LIGHT YEARS AHEAD!
Extra plates make the hoop stronger

FINISH HOOP

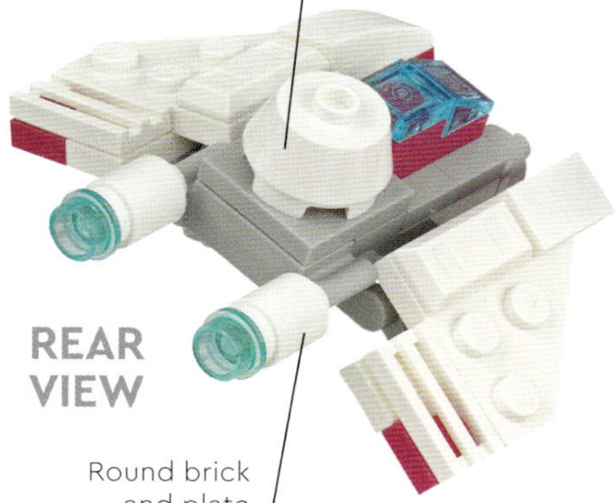
2×2 truncated cone could be a command center or escape pod
REAR VIEW
Round brick and plate thrusters

HOOP THE HOOP

In this race, the first ship to make it through both hoops is the winner. If flying through hoops is too easy, you could add some extra hazards for your pilots to dodge. How about an asteroid or an angry alien?

LEVEL UP

Build a full space racecourse including stadium seating and a podium to crown the winner. Set a timer and race against your friends' ships to see whose is the fastest.

The wings can move up and down
1×2 grille tile air vent
Use transparent pieces for windshields

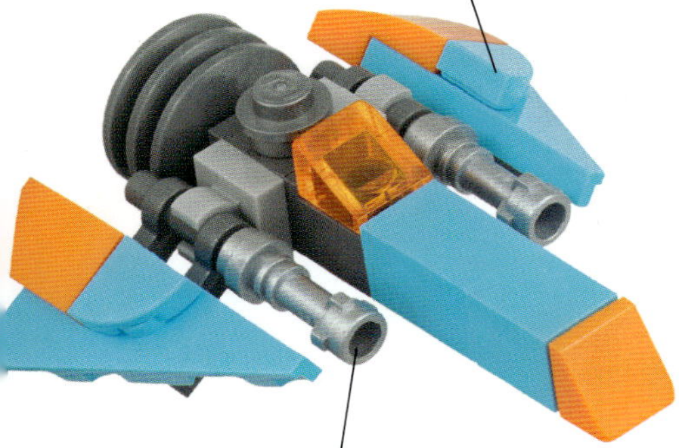
Smooth tiles create a sleek look
Telescope pieces could be asteroid blasters!

MINI SPACESHIPS

You need only a handful of bricks to make a microscale spaceship. Go for a roughly triangular shape, with a wing on either side and perhaps a pointy nose cone.

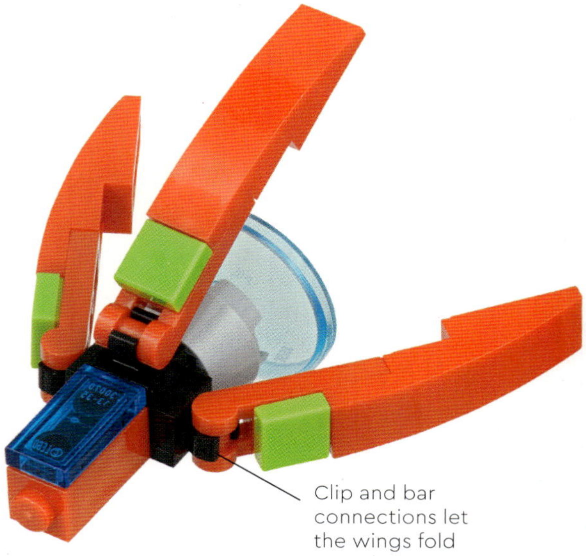
Clip and bar connections let the wings fold in and out

SPACE EXPLORERS

Blast off on a moon-size mission to find new LEGO planets! They could be rocky or smooth, big or small. You'll definitely need a spacecraft and equipment, such as a mech suit and a science lab, to help you explore these exciting places. What galactic secrets are waiting to be discovered?

BUILDING BRIEF

Objective:	Build imaginary planet surfaces
Use:	Space travel, intergalactic adventures, scientific research
Features:	Planet surface, mech walker, research station, spacecraft
Extras:	Excavation equipment, space gems

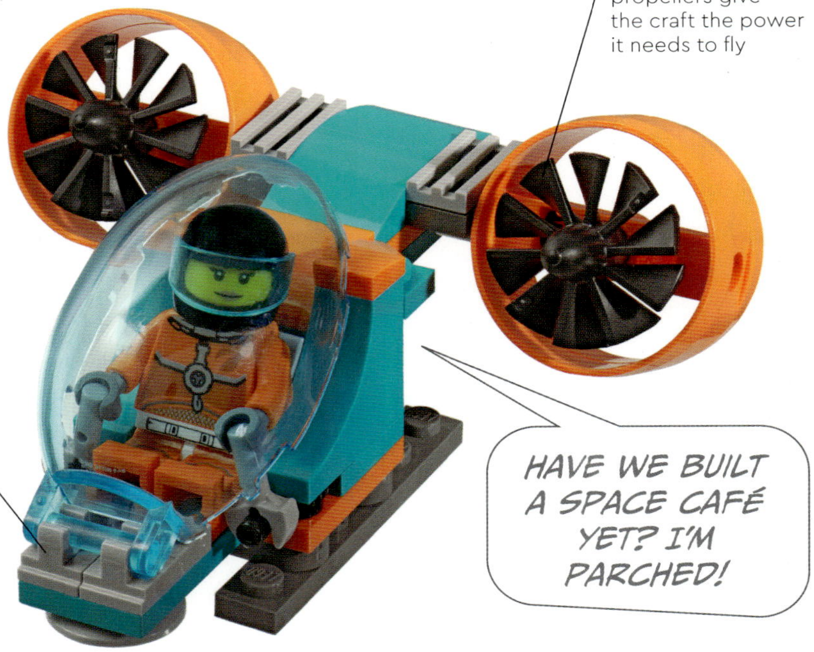
Two large propellers give the craft the power it needs to fly
Tiles with clips hold the cockpit windshield in place
HAVE WE BUILT A SPACE CAFÉ YET? I'M PARCHED!

IDENTIFIED FLYING OBJECT

How will you zoom around your new planet? Whatever shape you make your ship, leave room for a minifigure or two to take the controls in the cockpit. This craft has landing skids made from plates but yours could have wheels or legs.

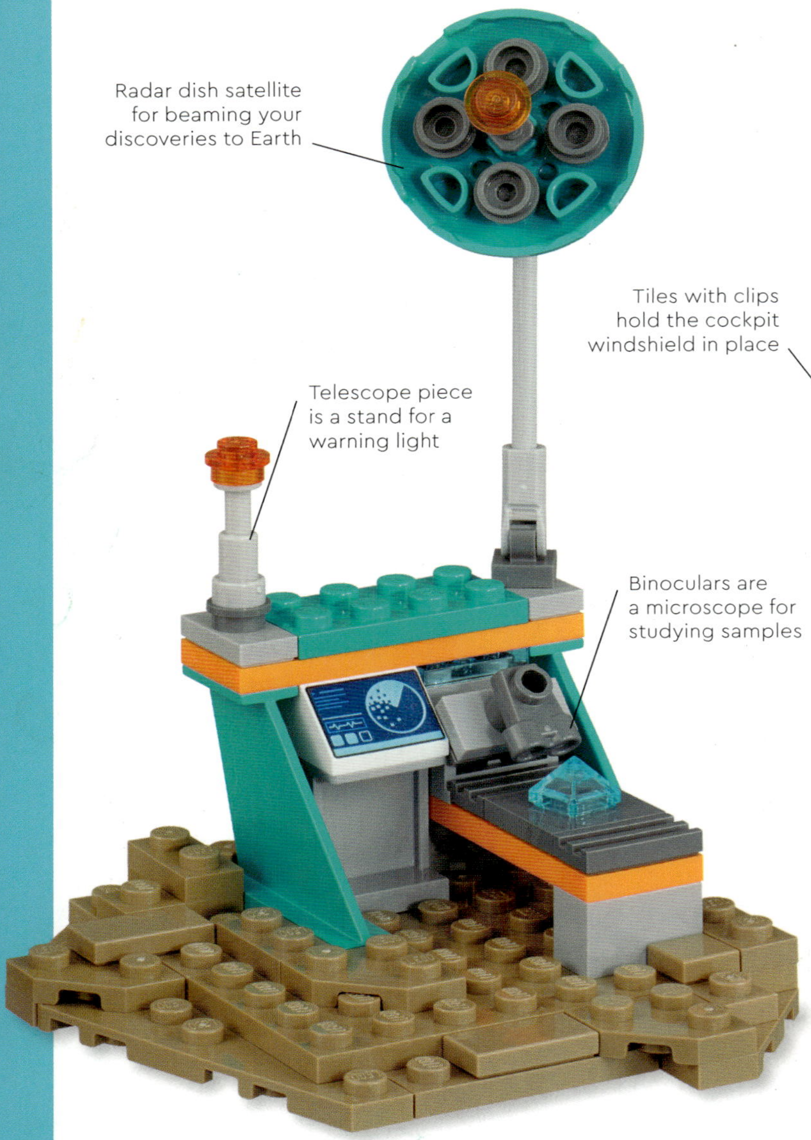
Radar dish satellite for beaming your discoveries to Earth
Telescope piece is a stand for a warning light
Binoculars are a microscope for studying samples

RESEARCH STATION

Build a scientific laboratory to help you learn about your planet. Include some technology and a place to study space specimens. You can build a small station, like this one, or make a whole building.

TRY THIS

Why not try building a larger planet surface with a friend or two? Create your own small builds and then connect them to create a whole new world!

Find or make excavation equipment
1×1 bricks and pyramid slopes make space gems
Slope bricks create a rocky surface

PLANET SURFACE

Your planet could be made of anything from rocks and water to cookie dough or cheese. Use your transparent LEGO pieces to add some special features to be excavated, such as gems or space rocks.

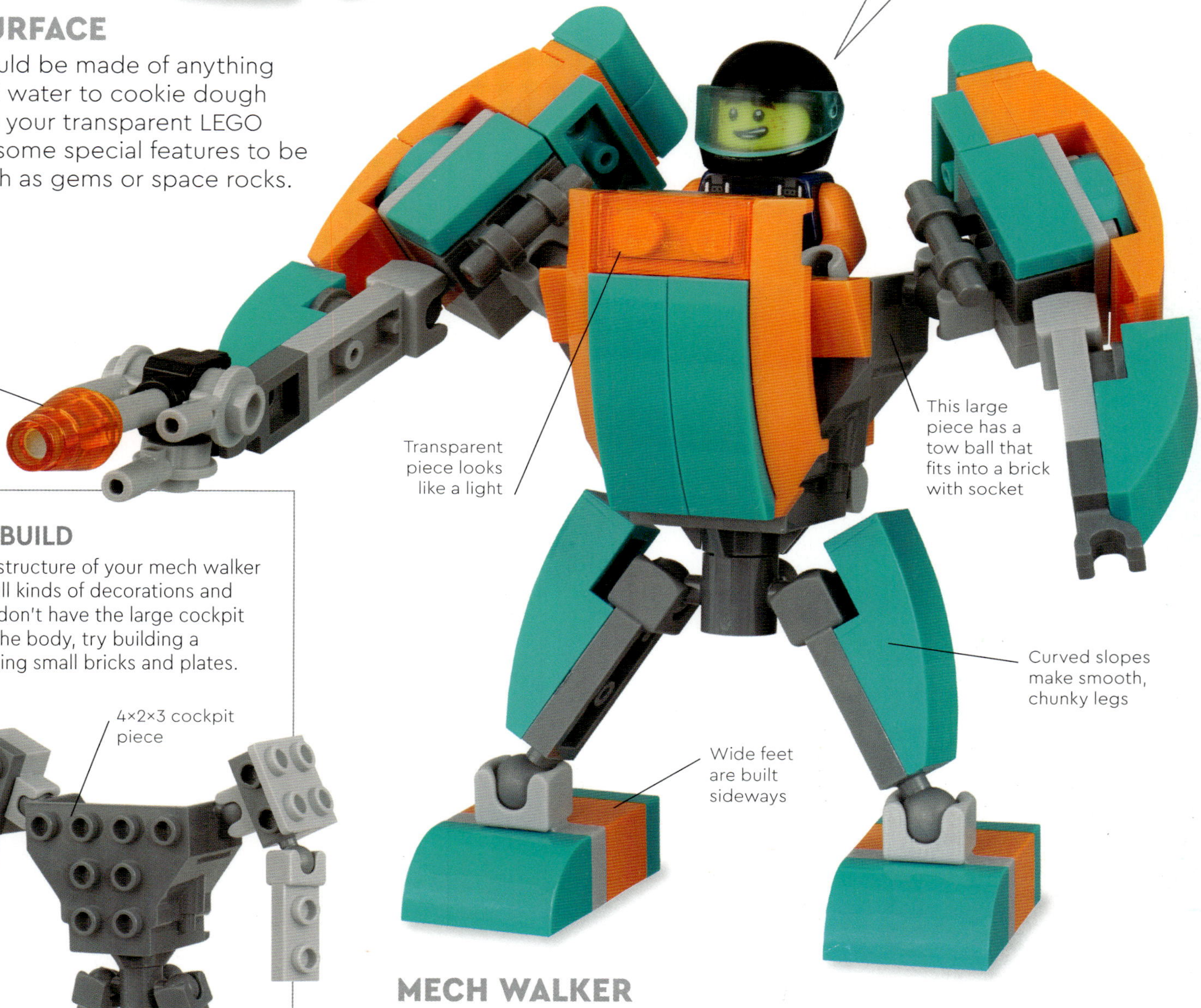
NO, BUT MY MECH WALKER HAS AN IN-BUILT COFFEE MACHINE!
Customize your suit with added gear such as a metal detector
Transparent piece looks like a light
This large piece has a tow ball that fits into a brick with socket
Curved slopes make smooth, chunky legs
Wide feet are built sideways

SKELETON BUILD

Build the basic structure of your mech walker before adding all kinds of decorations and features. If you don't have the large cockpit piece used for the body, try building a similar shape using small bricks and plates.

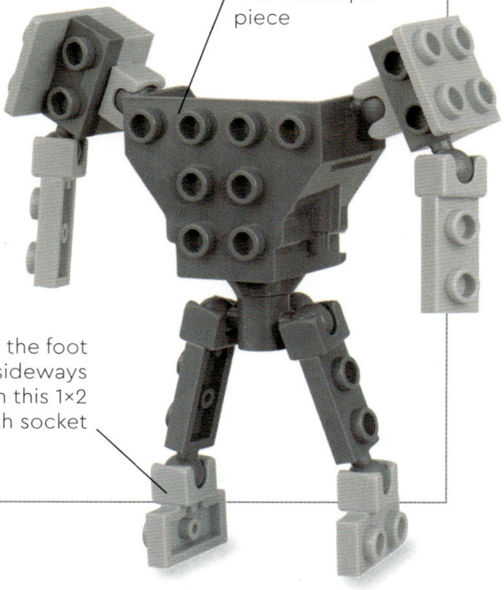
4×2×3 cockpit piece
Build the foot out sideways from this 1×2 plate with socket

MECH WALKER

Your minifigures may need special gear for exploring unfamiliar terrain. This mech walker uses tow ball and socket connections to give the suit posable arms and legs. If you don't have those LEGO elements, try out other connecting pieces like clips and bars or click hinges.

VIKING LONGSHIP

If your minifigures long for adventure, build them a longship and set sail on a Viking voyage! Think about where they'll go and what they might see. Perhaps they'll journey to a Viking village made for feasting and festivities—but look out! Danger could be lurking beneath the waves . . .

BUILDING BRIEF

Objective: Build a Viking adventure
Use: Transportation, exploration
Features: Viking longship, mast, sail
Extras: Figurehead, sea serpents, shields

SETTING SAIL

Your ship can go faster and farther with a sail like this one, which is made by connecting rows of plates. Make sure the sail isn't too long or there won't be room underneath for your crew!

Brown plates keep the red and white plates in place
2×8 plate
3×2 wedge plate adds shape

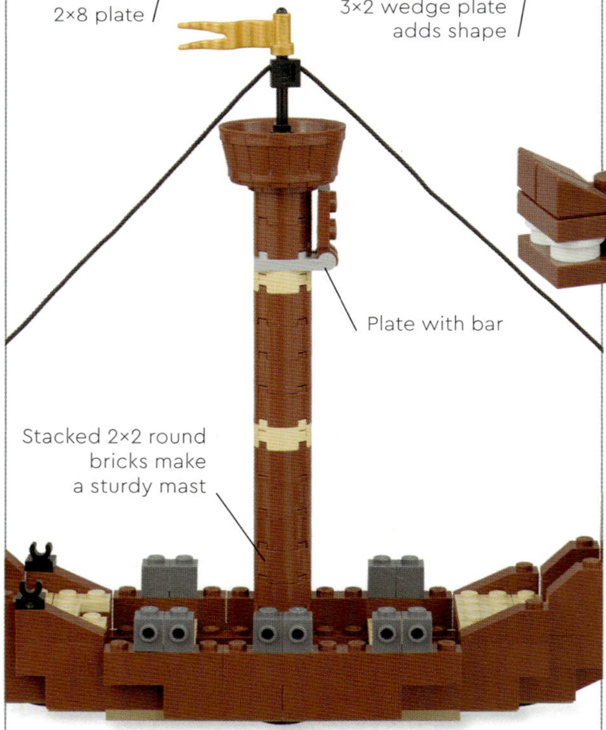
Plate with bar
Stacked 2×2 round bricks make a sturdy mast

LONG RIDE

The key to building a Viking longship is in the name—it should be longer than it is wide. Vessels like these were made out of wood and had cloth sails. This one has a carved dragon on the bow (front). What will yours have as a figurehead?

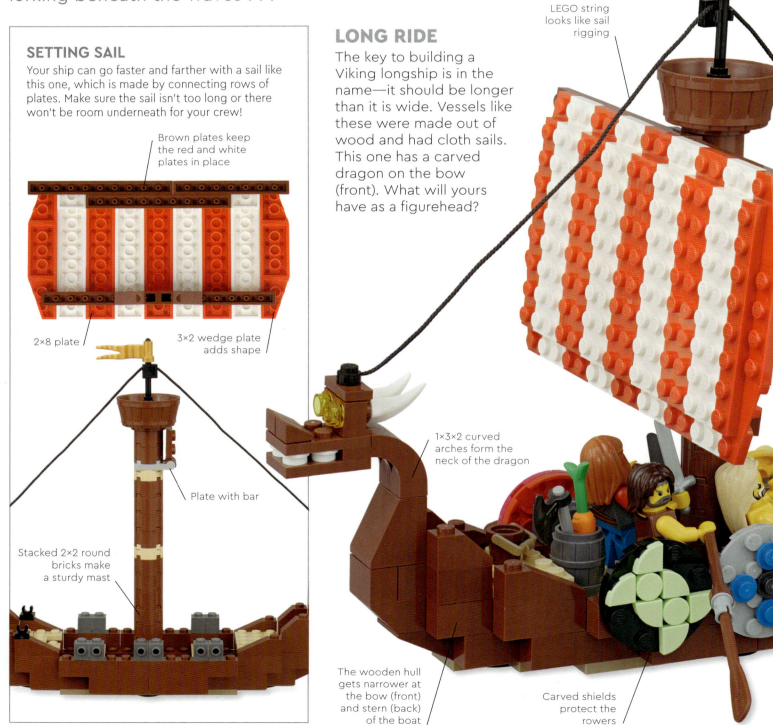

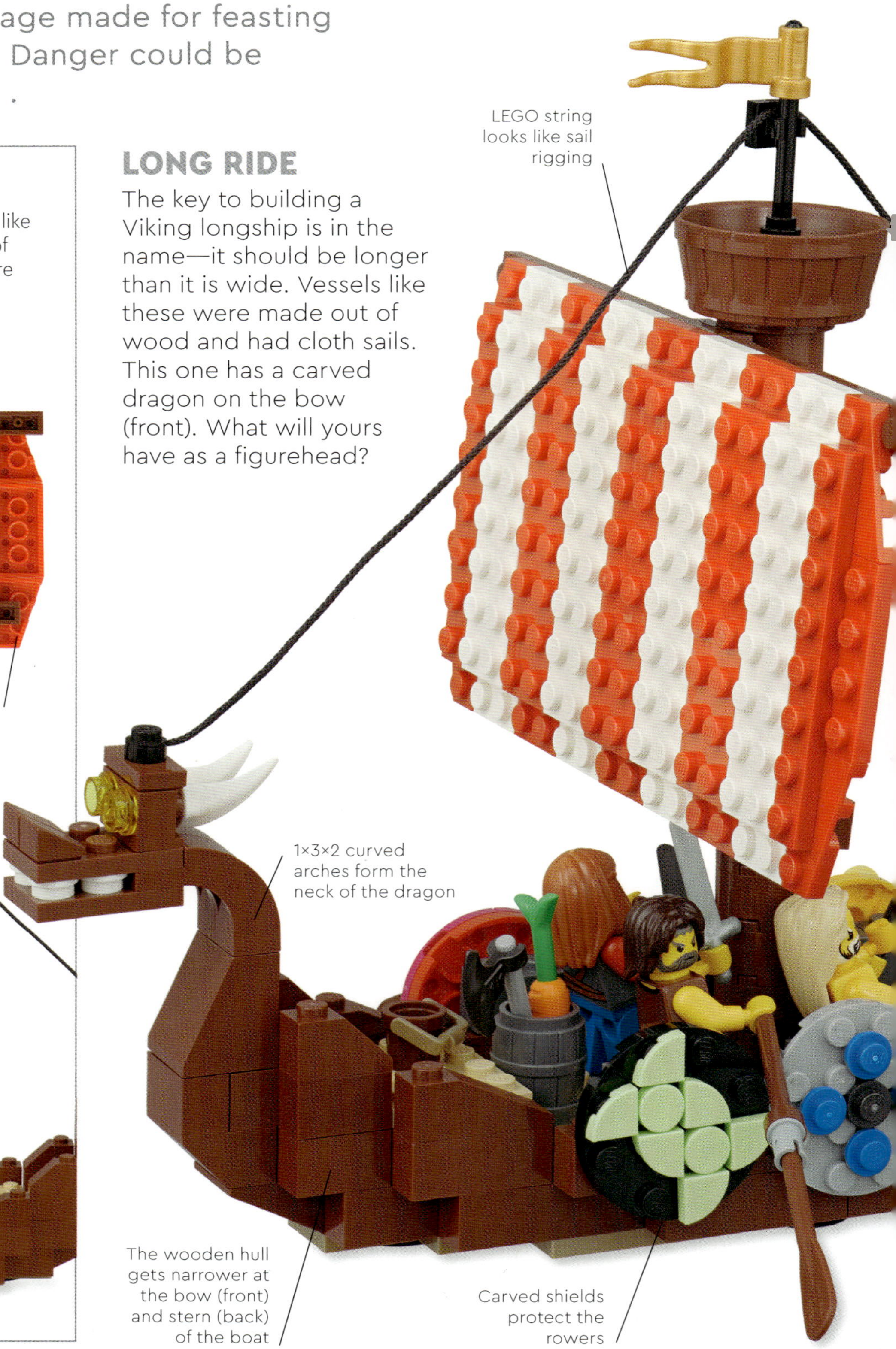
LEGO string looks like sail rigging
1×3×2 curved arches form the neck of the dragon
The wooden hull gets narrower at the bow (front) and stern (back) of the boat
Carved shields protect the rowers

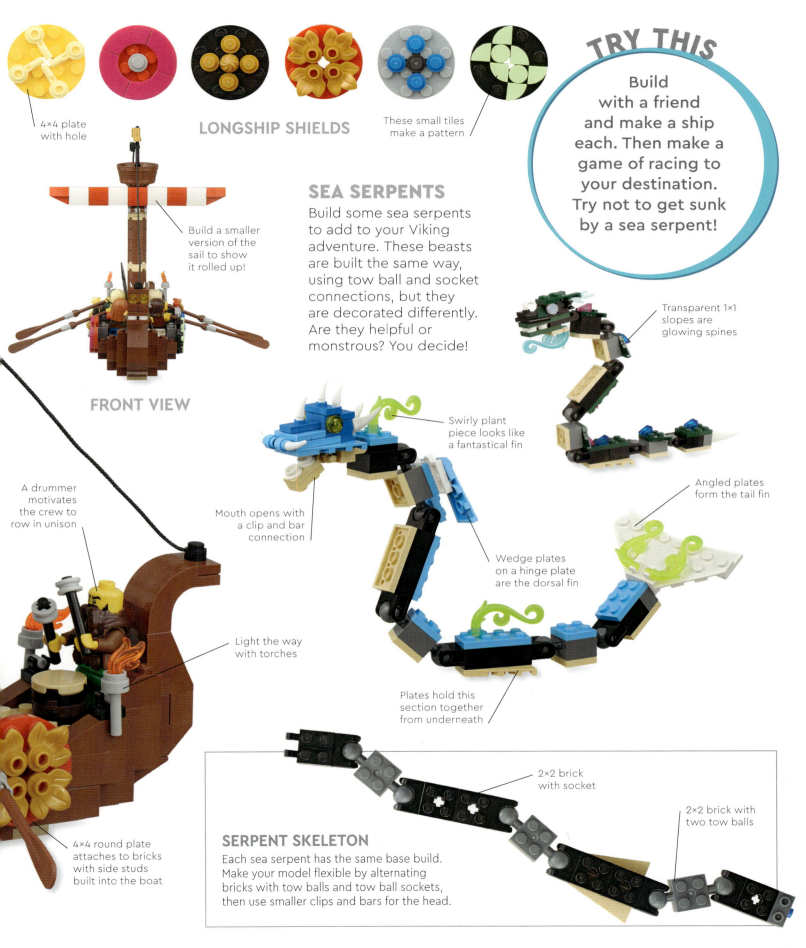

4×4 plate with hole

LONGSHIP SHIELDS

These small tiles make a pattern

TRY THIS

Build with a friend and make a ship each. Then make a game of racing to your destination. Try not to get sunk by a sea serpent!

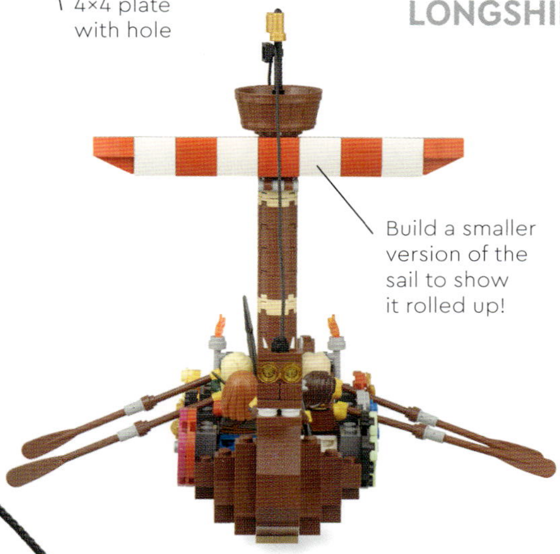

Build a smaller version of the sail to show it rolled up!

FRONT VIEW

SEA SERPENTS

Build some sea serpents to add to your Viking adventure. These beasts are built the same way, using tow ball and socket connections, but they are decorated differently. Are they helpful or monstrous? You decide!

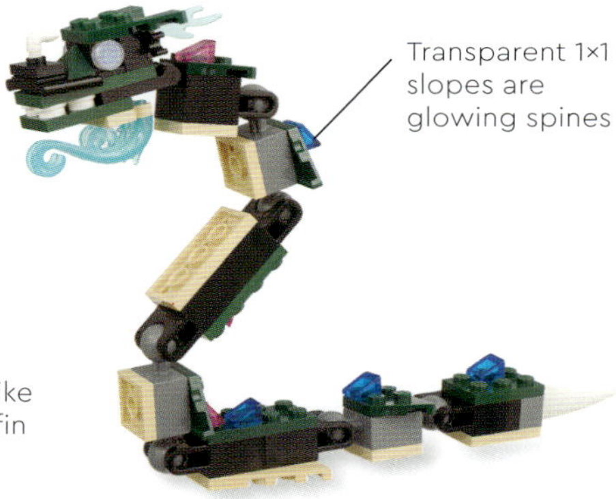

Transparent 1×1 slopes are glowing spines

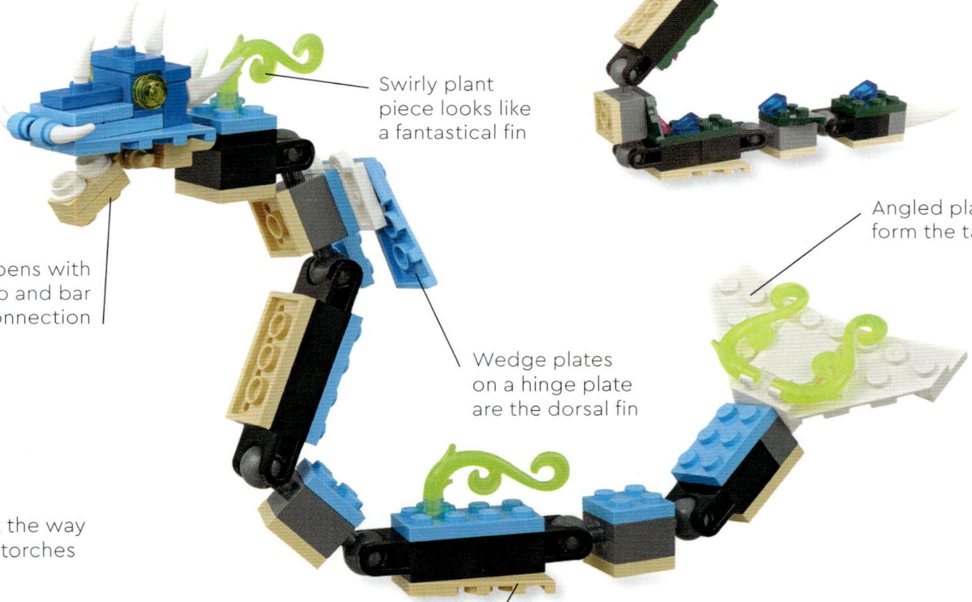

Swirly plant piece looks like a fantastical fin

Mouth opens with a clip and bar connection

Angled plates form the tail fin

Wedge plates on a hinge plate are the dorsal fin

Plates hold this section together from underneath

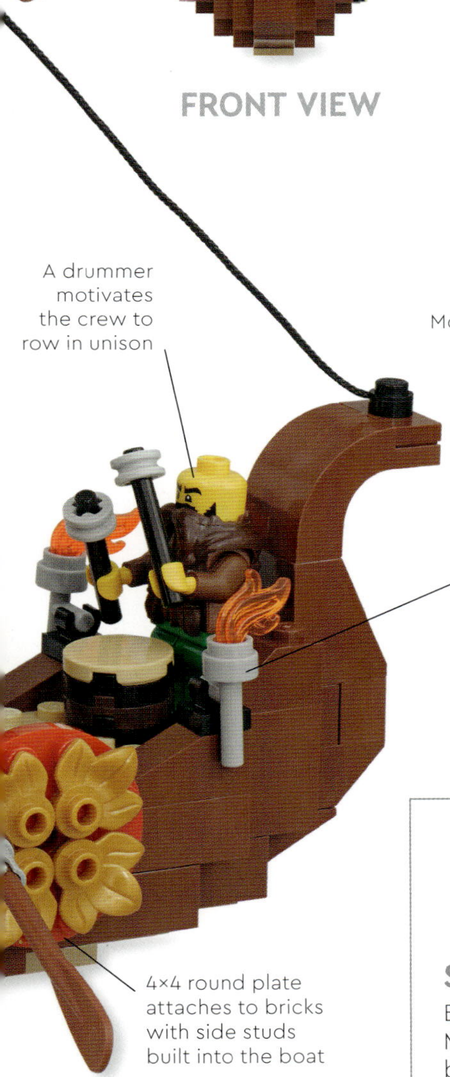

A drummer motivates the crew to row in unison

Light the way with torches

4×4 round plate attaches to bricks with side studs built into the boat

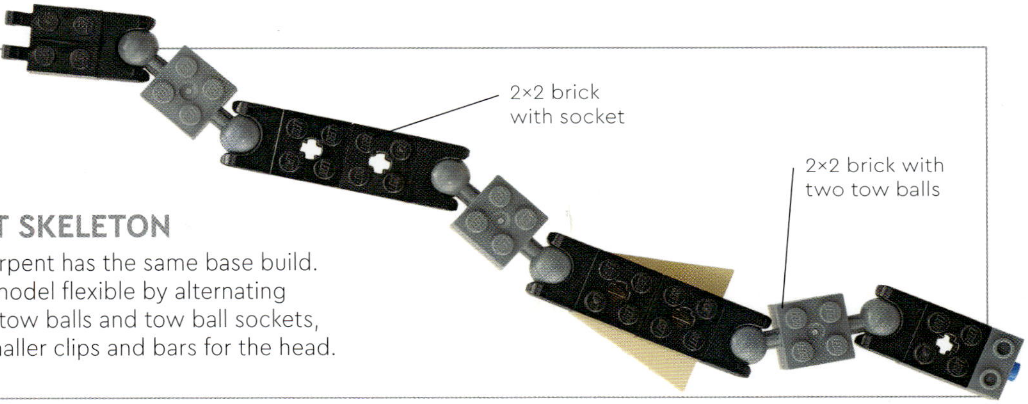

2×2 brick with socket

2×2 brick with two tow balls

SERPENT SKELETON

Each sea serpent has the same base build. Make your model flexible by alternating bricks with tow balls and tow ball sockets, then use smaller clips and bars for the head.

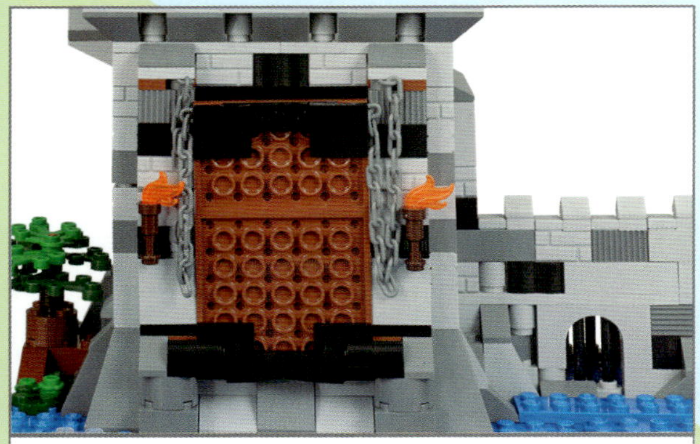

DRAWBRIDGE

This drawbridge door rests on LEGO® Technic plates with rings. The plates rotate on pins so the door can be raised and lowered. Make sure your drawbridge is large enough to cover the entrance when it's raised, to keep the castle safe.

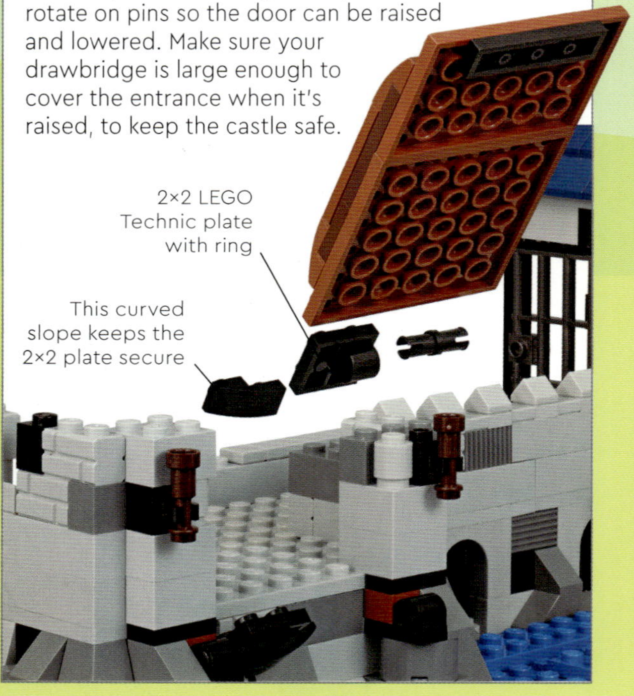
2×2 LEGO Technic plate with ring
This curved slope keeps the 2×2 plate secure

ANCIENT CASTLE

Halt . . . who goes there? The towers, turrets, and battlements on this ancient castle are great for spying approaching enemies. Just remember not to leave the drawbridge down when your minifigure knights are off at a joust! For a personal touch, you could fly flags in your favorite colors, or in those of the sports team you support.

Slope bricks in a mixture of sizes create a pointy roof
I'M JUST WATCHING OUT FOR MY PIZZA DELIVERY!
If barred windows feel too unfriendly, use transparent pieces instead
Use different shades of gray and black for a natural, weathered look
Textured 1×2 bricks for stone walls
Layer up blue plates for a choppy-looking moat

BUILDING BRIEF

Objective:	Build a castle
Use:	A home for knights, epic battles
Features:	Towers, turrets, large entrance
Extras:	Drawbridge, moat, dungeon, rampart, battlements

DEFENSIVE DESIGN

Castles are all about defenses. This ancient fortress has thick stone walls, a moat, a drawbridge, and bars on the windows. There's even a dark dungeon to throw adversaries into in case any manage to make it inside!

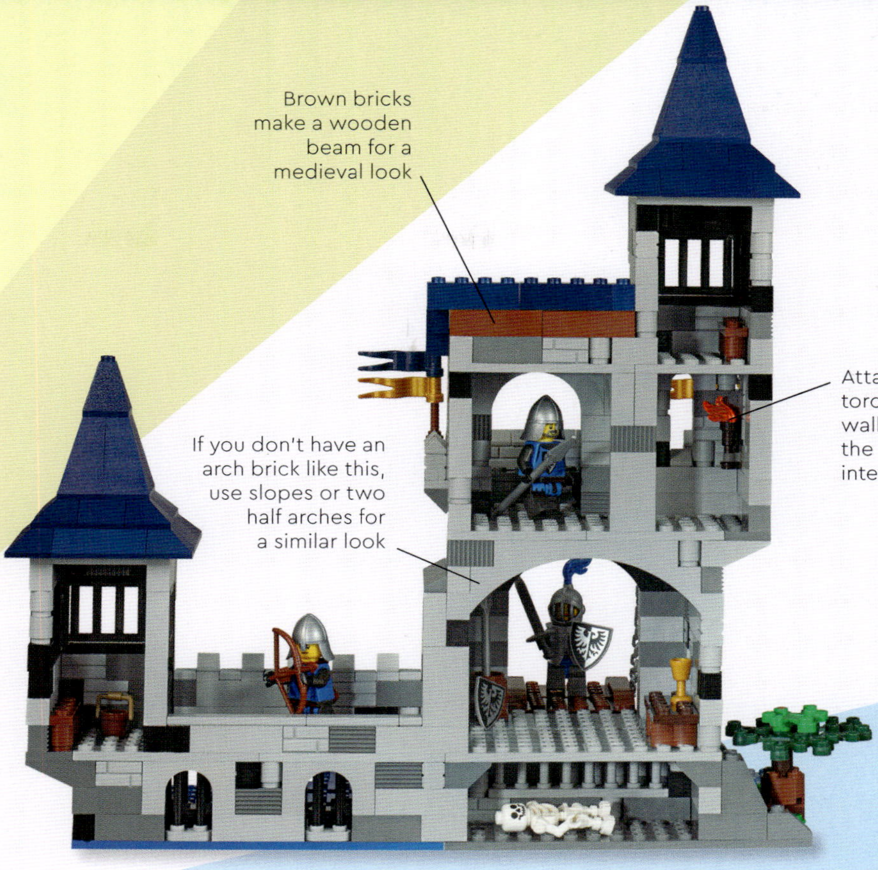

Brown bricks make a wooden beam for a medieval look

If you don't have an arch brick like this, use slopes or two half arches for a similar look

Attach flaming torches to the walls to light the castle's interior

REAR VIEW

...ttlements are ...eature of many ...cient castles

This castle is so ancient, a tree is growing out of it!

Build stone steps or a platform for your drawbridge to rest on

CHANGE IT

Give this castle a very different look by building it in other colors. Use tan and brown bricks for a wooden castle, or bright colors for a fairy-tale one.

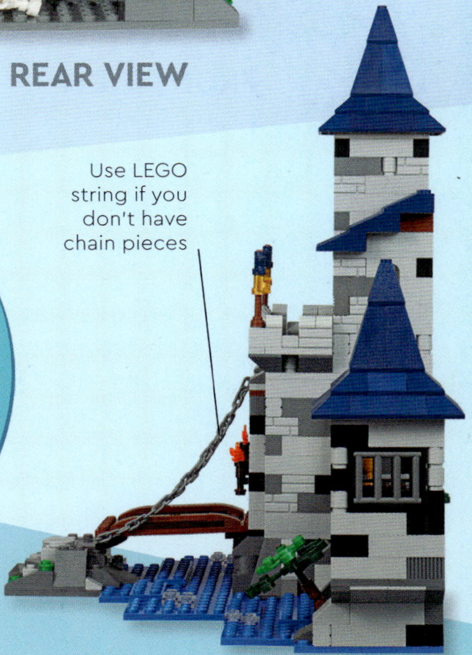

Use LEGO string if you don't have chain pieces

SIDE VIEW

DOWN BELOW

Deep in the basement is this hidden dungeon. Is the skeleton here a long-forgotten former minifigure, or are they taking a nap? Perhaps ask the mouse! If you don't want a prison cell, you could give your castle a modern upgrade with a stone bathroom.

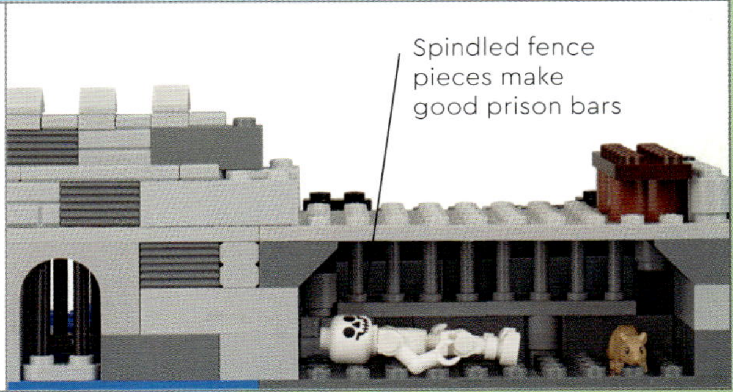

Spindled fence pieces make good prison bars

ANCIENT WONDERS

You don't need a time machine to visit the past! Do some research and use your LEGO collection to build some of the ancient wonders of the world, either as they would have looked newly built or in ruins. What wonders will you create? How about the Colosseum in Rome, or even the Great Wall of China?

BUILDING BRIEF

Objective: Build ancient monuments
Use: Exploring the past
Features: Crumbling ruins, columns, waterfalls, plants
Extras: Surroundings, statues

Two 1×2 grille slopes form the temple's "pediment"

FRONT VIEW

FLIP IT

The bottom of this microscale acropolis is built upside down. Three 2×4 tiles form the base and four plates fit into the tiles, stud-sides down. Columns slot into the stud spaces on each 1×4 plate, connecting the top and bottom of the building.

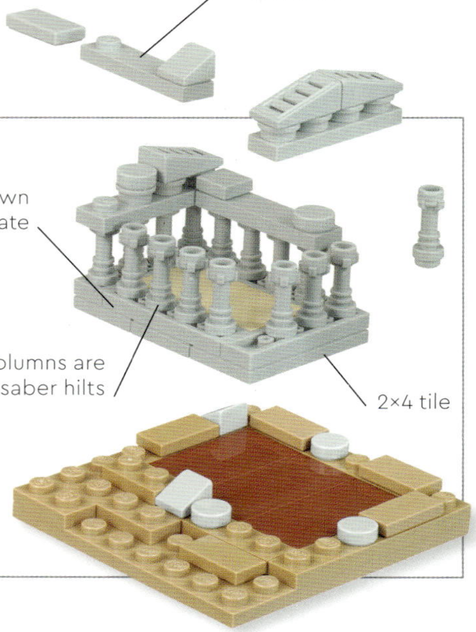

1×4 plate with two studs
Upside-down 1×4 plate
Columns are lightsaber hilts
2×4 tile

PARTHENON

Ancient Greeks built this magnificent marble temple more than 2,000 years ago. In ancient times, it was filled with beautiful statues and sculptures. On the ruin that stands today, only part of the roof remains but the columns around the edges are still intact.

Small tiles and slopes are all that remain of the roof
Stack of plates forms a hill of rocky terrain

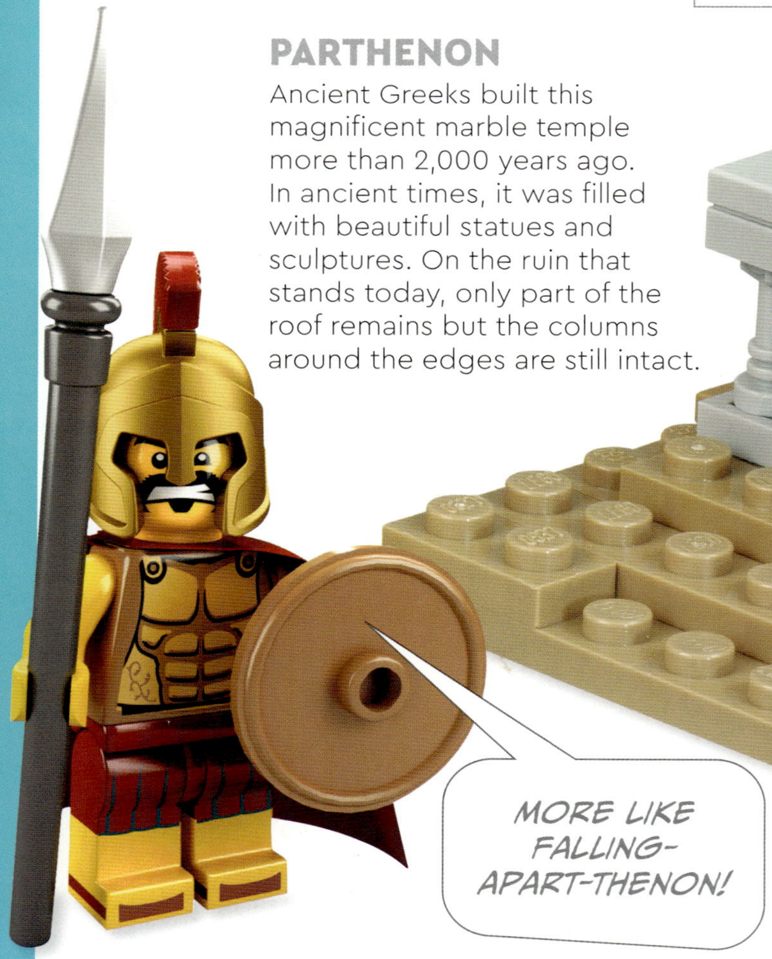

MORE LIKE FALLING-APART-THENON!

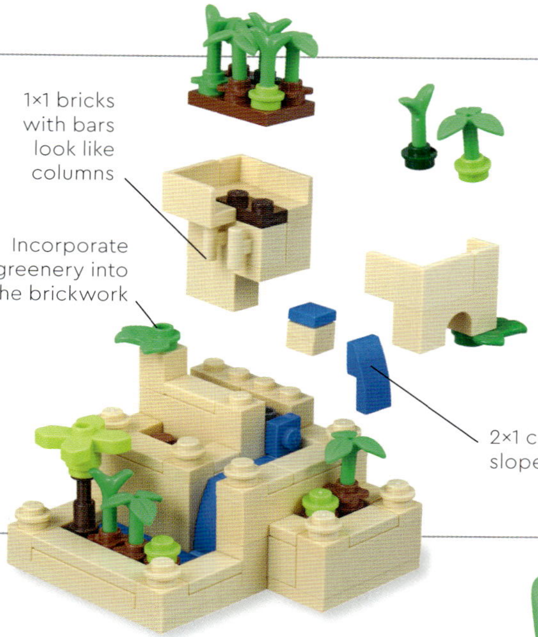

1×1 bricks with bars look like columns

Incorporate greenery into the brickwork

2×1 curved slope

FLOWING WATER

Blue plates and curved slopes attach to bricks with side studs hidden inside the building to form cascading waterfalls. This makes it look as though water is flowing around the building to keep the plants hydrated.

Corner panel pieces form the smaller top level

SIDE VIEW

HANGING GARDENS OF BABYLON

No one knows exactly what these legendary gardens looked like or where they were located. However, it is believed that the gardens were a ziggurat, which is large structure with raised, stepped levels.

TRY THIS

What are the wonders of your world? Do you have any local landmarks where you live that you could re-create with your LEGO collection?

Waterfall flows through this 1×3 arch brick

Telescope piece is a tree trunk

Tan bricks look like the sun-baked brick walls of a ziggurat

BUILDING BRIEF

Objective: Build a medieval wagon and band
Use: A magical, musical parade
Features: Cart, musical instruments
Extras: Magic wand, animals

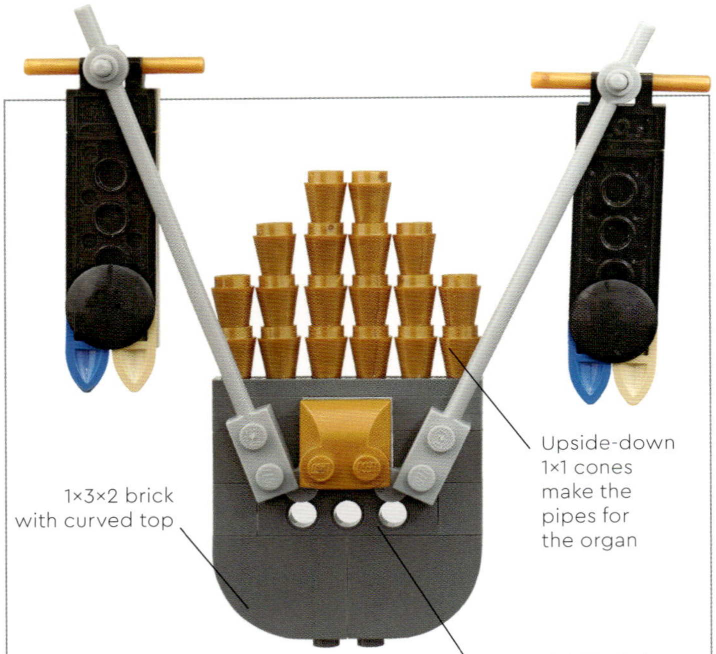
1×3×2 brick with curved top
Upside-down 1×1 cones make the pipes for the organ
1×4 LEGO Technic brick with pin holes

LEGO Technic pin

PINNING THE PIPES

Just a few LEGO Technic pieces connect the pipes of the organ to the rest of the instrument at the back of the cart. Pins in a black brick with pin holes on the organ slot through a gray version of the same brick below the pipes.

1×12 bar has a stud at one end and a 1×2 plate at the other
Long tiles attached sideways are wooden boards

SIDE VIEW

WAGON

In medieval times, many people got around in carts like this one. Build your own rolling wheels using large round bricks with pin holes. And don't forget you'll need an animal like this bull to help move your wagon along.

MEDIEVAL BAND

Are you ready to party like it's 1099? Throw a medieval parade by building a wooden cart with a magical twist, and bring your musical minifigures along for the ride! You could also think about other types of celebrations from long ago. What would a Stone Age party look like? How about a masked carnival in Venice?

Trumpet made from three pieces

THIS IS NOT MOO-SIC!

CHANGE IT

Build music-making carts from other time periods. What features and instruments would your model have if it was from the 1980s or the future?

Wizard's magic wand lights up the Dark Ages
Banners made from narrow plates and tiles with tooth plate ends
BEHOLD MY MEDIEVAL LIGHT SHOW!
Stacks of round bricks, plates, and tiles make drums
This very long horn is supported by a tile with clip on the bull's back
IS IT TRADITION FOR PEOPLE TO THROW OLD TOMATOES AT US?
4×4 round bricks with pin holes make wide wagon wheels
Bar for the neck of the lute

ALIEN LIFE

Take a look at the night sky—there are too many stars to count. Now imagine the many aliens that might live on their surrounding planets. They can't all look like the little green creatures you see in old movies! Yours might look like snakes, or crabs, or just be eyes on tentacles that pop up out of holes in the ground. Will they walk, slither, fly, or whiz around on vehicles?

BUILDING BRIEF

Objective: Build alien species
Use: Intergalactic adventures
Features: Tails, teeth, eyes, legs, tentacles
Extras: Vehicles, homes, landscapes

SCOOTER ALIEN

This cool blue alien lives on a red-hot planet, so it prefers to skim over the surface on its skyscooter. Think about the weather conditions on your alien's planet, then give it a helpful accessory or two.

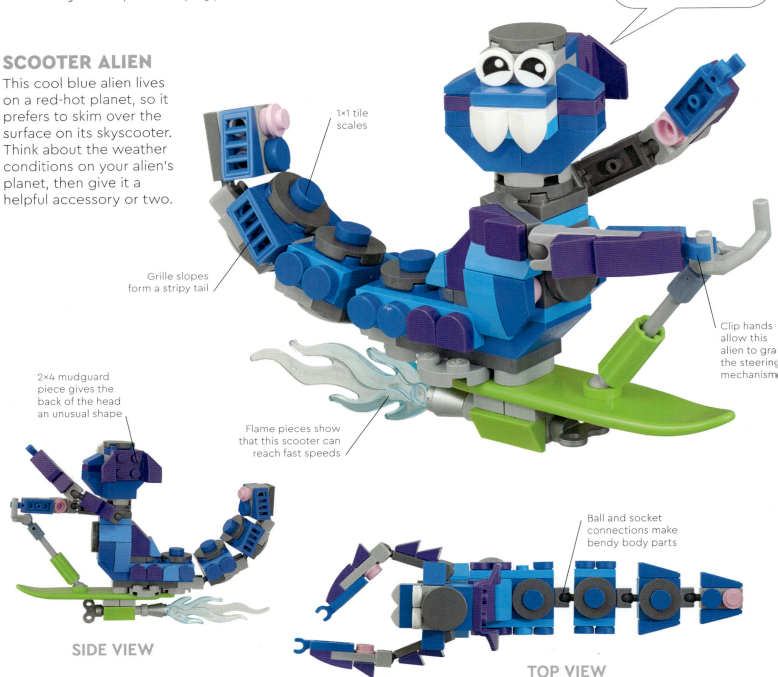

GOT TO FIND THE NEAREST PARKING METEOR!
1×1 tile scales
Grille slopes form a stripy tail
Clip hands allow this alien to gra the steering mechanism
Flame pieces show that this scooter can reach fast speeds

2×4 mudguard piece gives the back of the head an unusual shape

SIDE VIEW

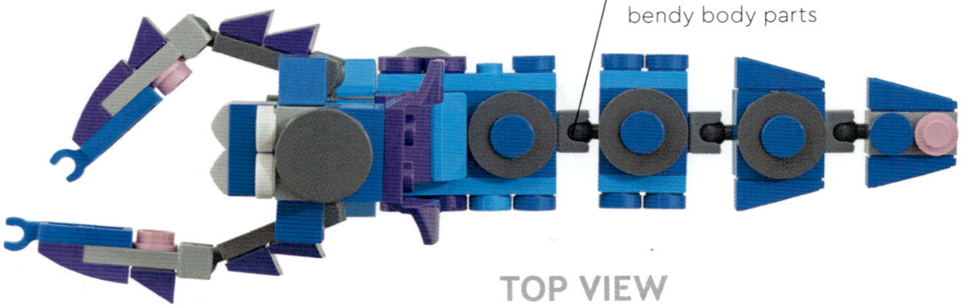
Ball and socket connections make bendy body parts

TOP VIEW

GOGGLY ALIEN

Alien species can be any shape, color, or size, and as extraordinary as you like. Just ask this swivel-eyed, three-legged green space dweller! Let your imagination zoom off in any direction.

Plate with three teeth for toe claws

REAR VIEW

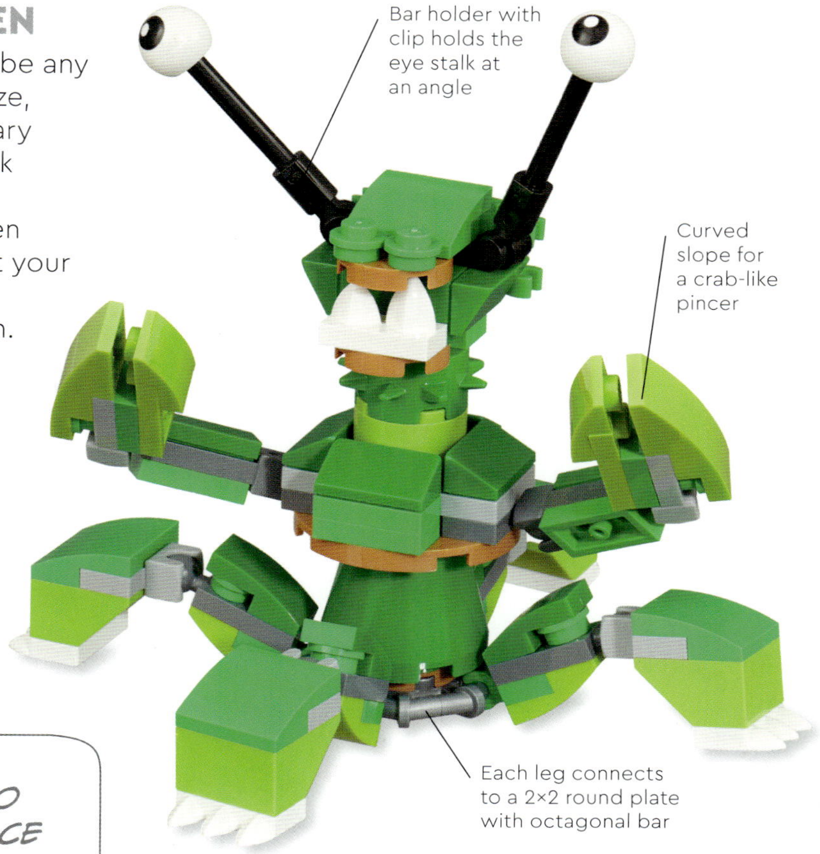

Bar holder with clip holds the eye stalk at an angle
Curved slope for a crab-like pincer
Each leg connects to a 2×2 round plate with octagonal bar

CRATER SQUID

If you want your alien to have tentacles, like this crater squid, try using lots of dinosaur tail pieces. Hide the ends of them behind a crater and people can imagine what lies beneath!

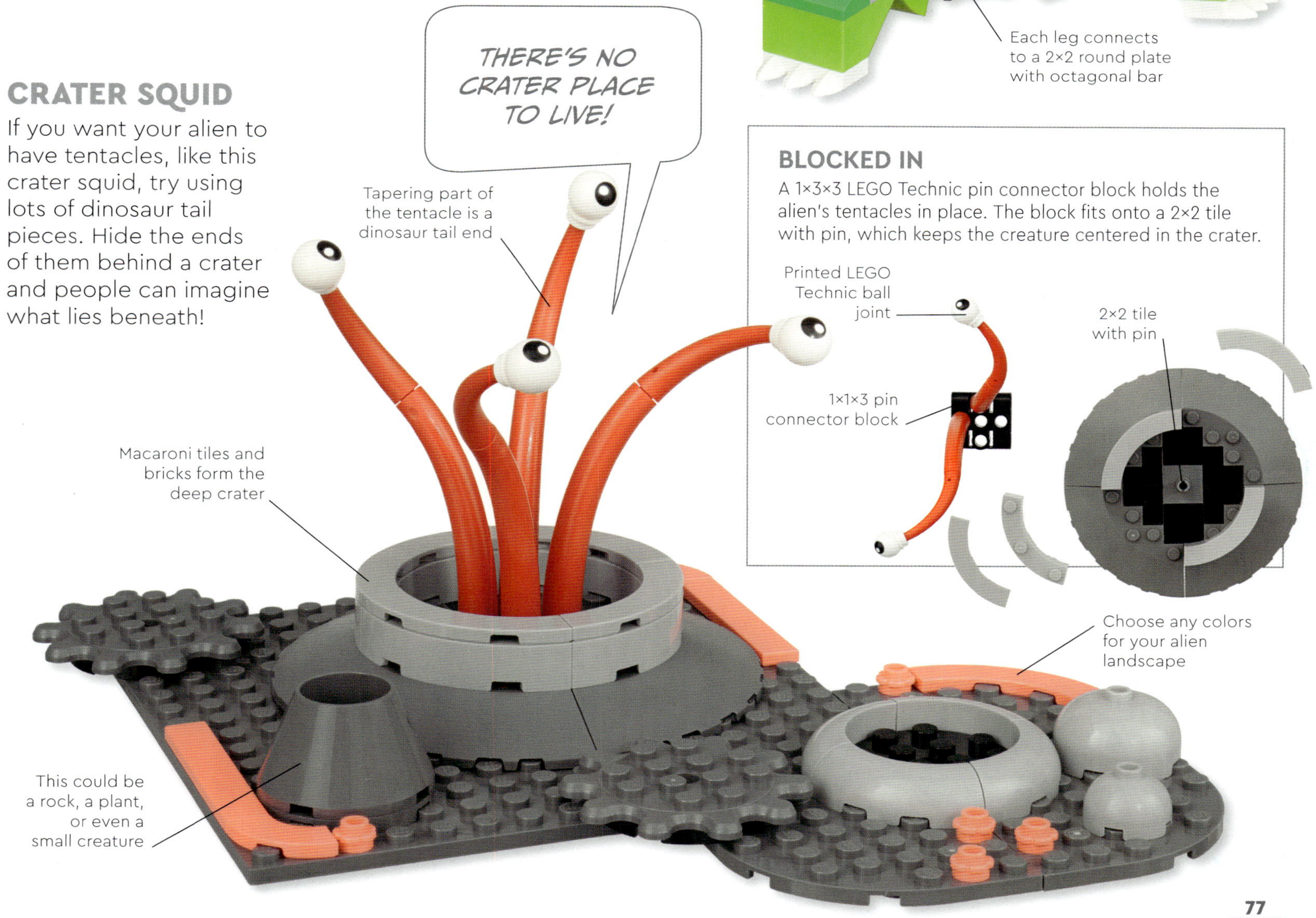

THERE'S NO CRATER PLACE TO LIVE!
Tapering part of the tentacle is a dinosaur tail end
Macaroni tiles and bricks form the deep crater
This could be a rock, a plant, or even a small creature
Choose any colors for your alien landscape

BLOCKED IN

A 1×3×3 LEGO Technic pin connector block holds the alien's tentacles in place. The block fits onto a 2×2 tile with pin, which keeps the creature centered in the crater.

Printed LEGO Technic ball joint
2×2 tile with pin
1×1×3 pin connector block

GALACTIC GYM

Even aliens need a place to get fit. Design an out-of-this-world extraterrestrial exercise center for aliens to work out in. Think about how your alien fitness fans will want to use the space—they might want to bulk up their muscles with weights, climb on an indoor wall, or pound some tiles on a treadmill.

BUILDING BRIEF

Objective: Build an alien fitness center
Use: Extraterrestrial workouts
Features: Gym building, equipment, aliens
Extras: Lockers, sign, shower room

FITNESS CENTER

The gym is created in sections, then connected with hinge plates at the top and bottom. Add as many walls as you like and build in whatever fitness features your gym-goers need.

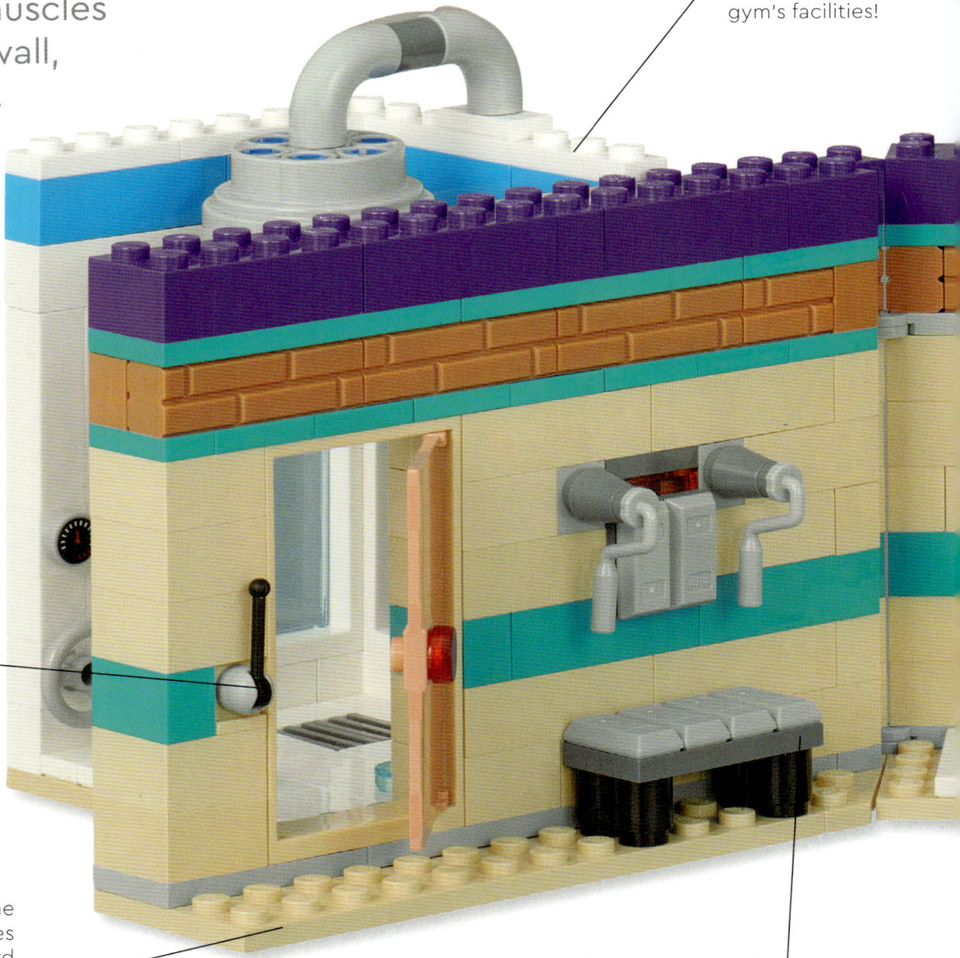

Turn the page to see the gym's facilities!

Joystick holds the door closed when the shower room is in use

The sides of the gym have bases made from standard and angled plates

Aliens can sit on this bench and work out their arms or tentacles using the handles above

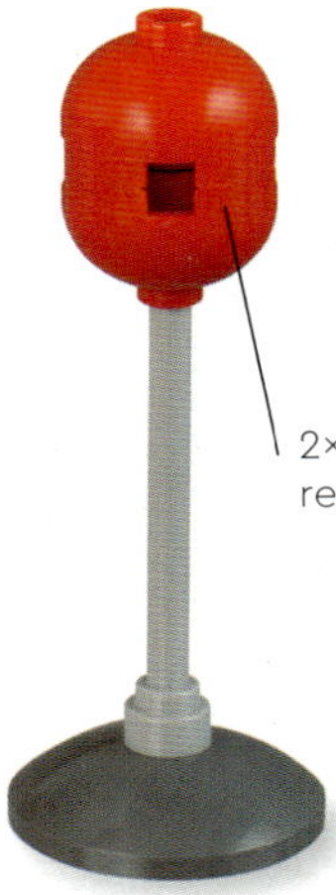

2×2 inverted and regular domes

PUNCHBAG

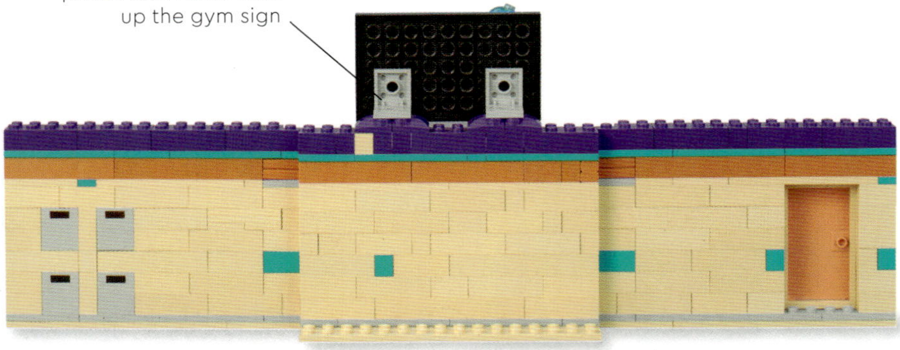

Two 2×2/2×2 bracket plates with holes hold up the gym sign

FLAT REAR VIEW

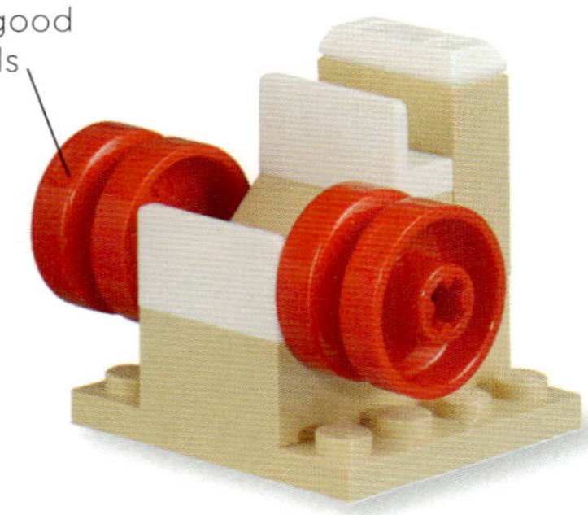

Wheel trims make good barbells

WEIGHT STAND

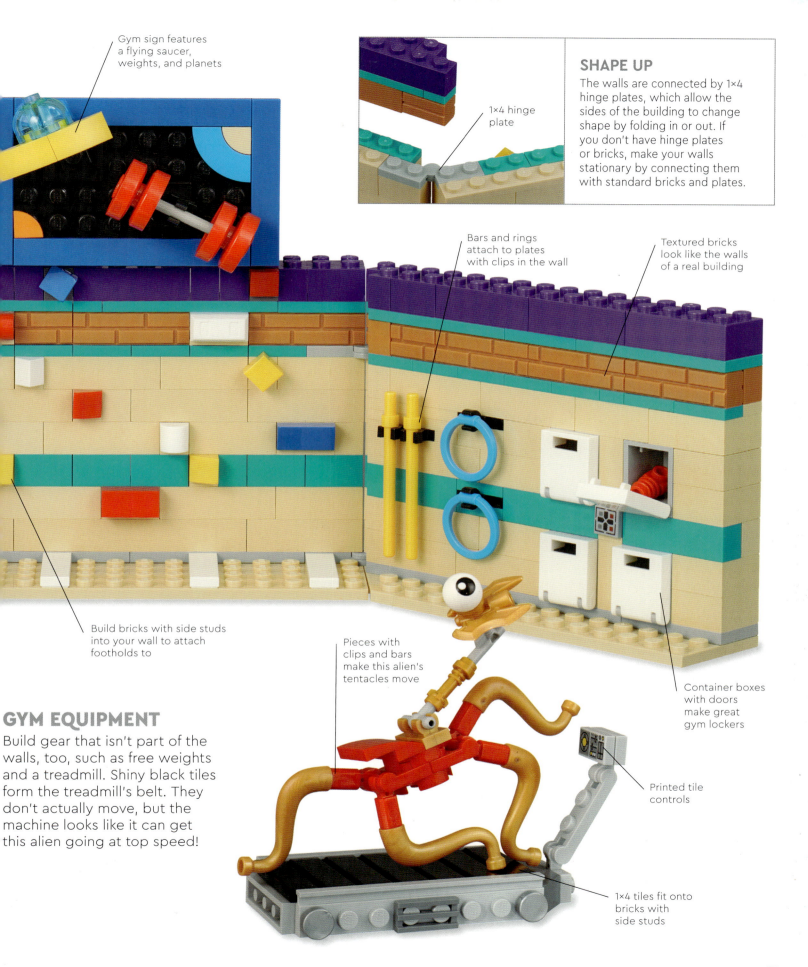

Gym sign features a flying saucer, weights, and planets

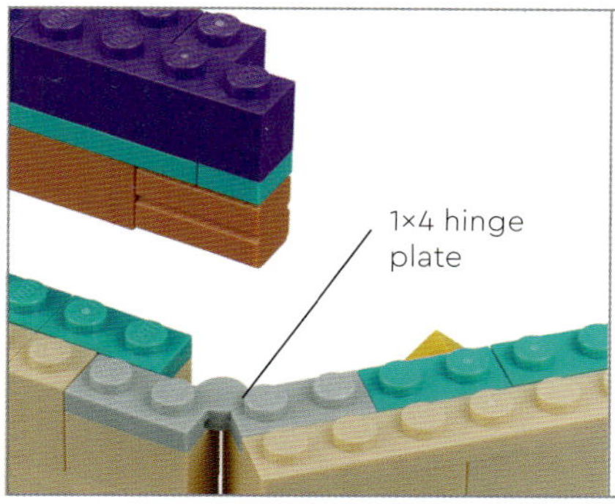

1×4 hinge plate

SHAPE UP

The walls are connected by 1×4 hinge plates, which allow the sides of the building to change shape by folding in or out. If you don't have hinge plates or bricks, make your walls stationary by connecting them with standard bricks and plates.

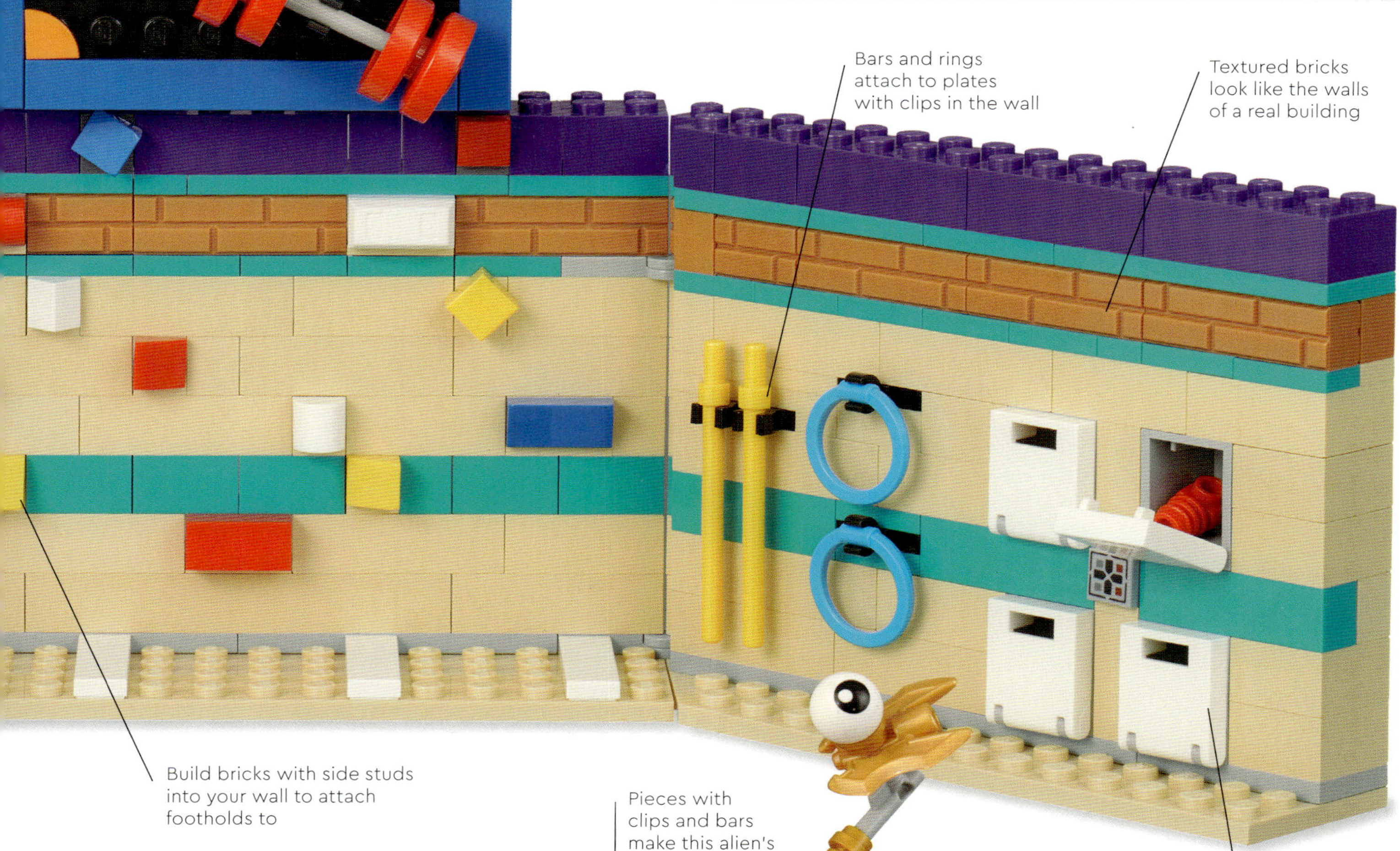

Bars and rings attach to plates with clips in the wall

Textured bricks look like the walls of a real building

Build bricks with side studs into your wall to attach footholds to

Pieces with clips and bars make this alien's tentacles move

Container boxes with doors make great gym lockers

GYM EQUIPMENT

Build gear that isn't part of the walls, too, such as free weights and a treadmill. Shiny black tiles form the treadmill's belt. They don't actually move, but the machine looks like it can get this alien going at top speed!

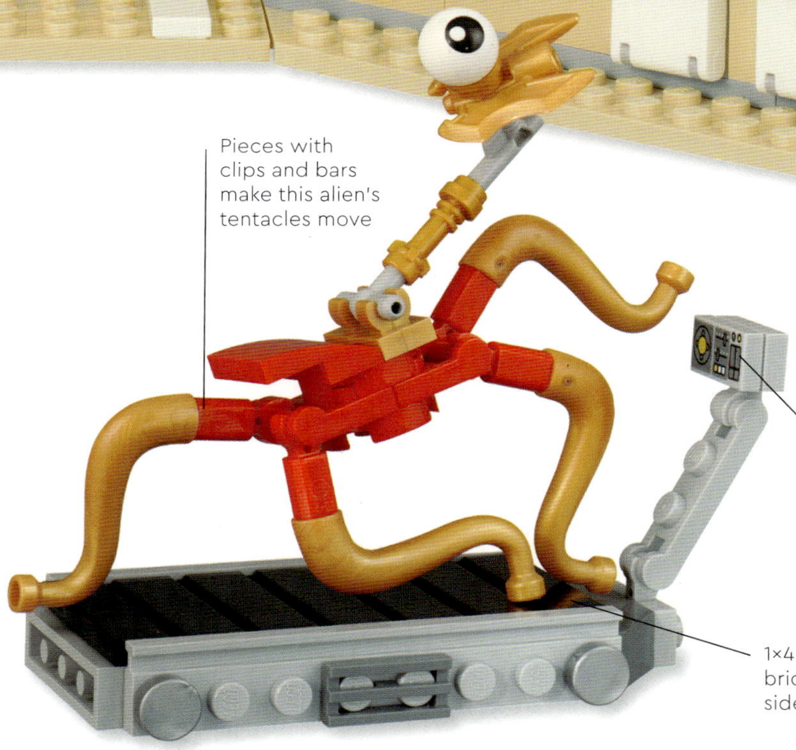

Printed tile controls

1×4 tiles fit onto bricks with side studs

BUILDING BRIEF

Objective: Build alien gym facilities
Use: Extraterrestrial wellbeing
Features: Shower area, vending machine
Extras: Toiletries, food

GYM FACILITIES

Expand your galactic gym by building some useful amenities for your extraterrestrial clients. After a hot and sweaty workout, your gym-goers might want to take a steamy shower or sip a cool drink from a vending machine. Make your facilities accessible to all body shapes and sizes so any alien species can enjoy them.

SHOWER CUBICLE

The calm expression on this spiderlike alien's face shows just how relaxing a long shower can be after exercising. What other bathroom facilities will you add to your gym?

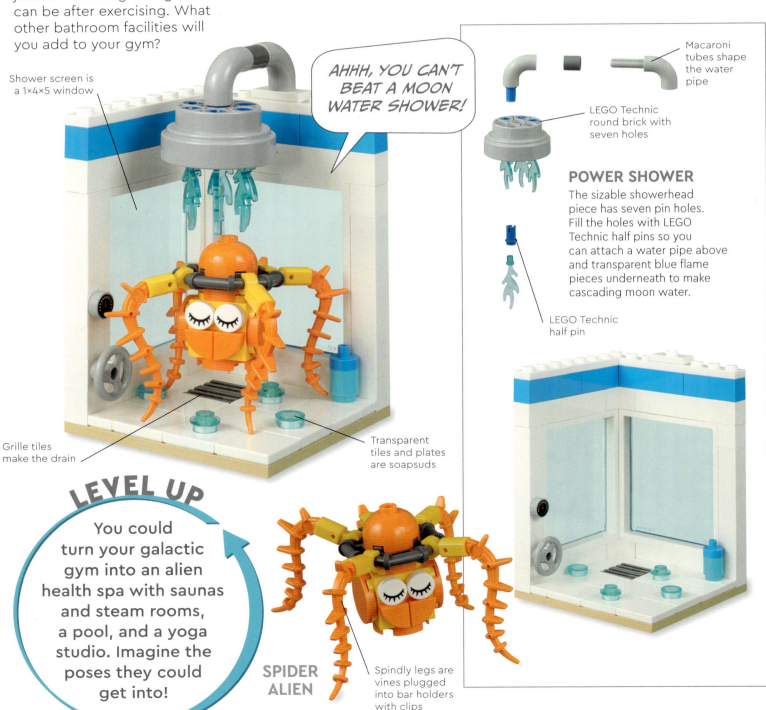

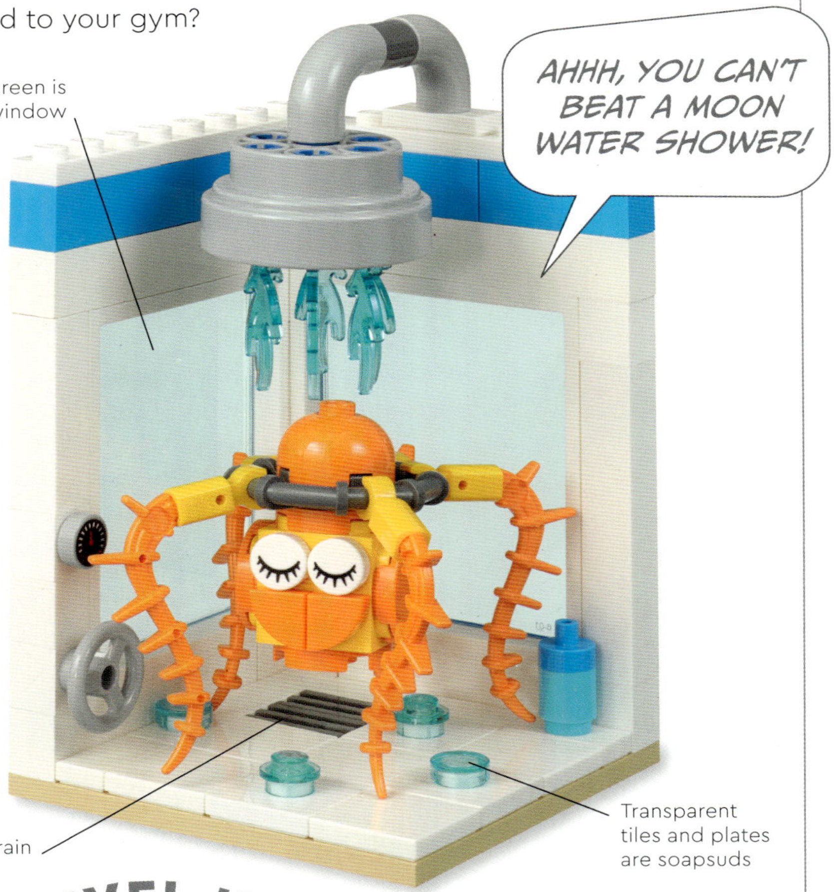
Shower screen is a 1×4×5 window
AHHH, YOU CAN'T BEAT A MOON WATER SHOWER!
Grille tiles make the drain
Transparent tiles and plates are soapsuds

Macaroni tubes shape the water pipe
LEGO Technic round brick with seven holes
LEGO Technic half pin

POWER SHOWER

The sizable showerhead piece has seven pin holes. Fill the holes with LEGO Technic half pins so you can attach a water pipe above and transparent blue flame pieces underneath to make cascading moon water.

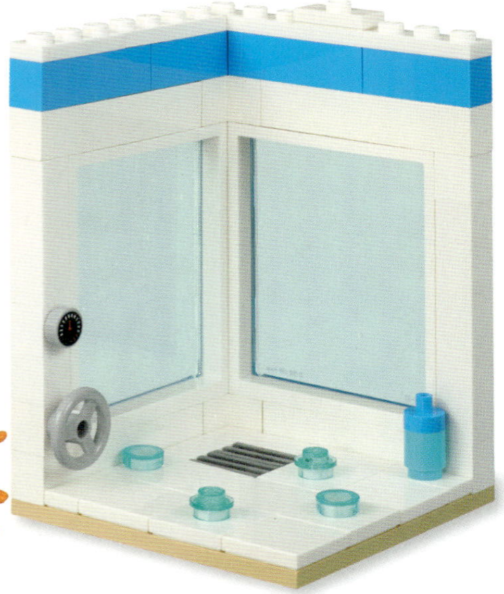

LEVEL UP

You could turn your galactic gym into an alien health spa with saunas and steam rooms, a pool, and a yoga studio. Imagine the poses they could get into!

Spindly legs are vines plugged into bar holders with clips

SPIDER ALIEN

VENDING MACHINE

Insert some cosmic coins and press the right buttons on this drink-dispensing vending machine and you'll be rewarded with a refreshing can of space soda. Your vending machine can dispense anything you like. How about some space-themed snacks like planet popcorn and comet crisps?

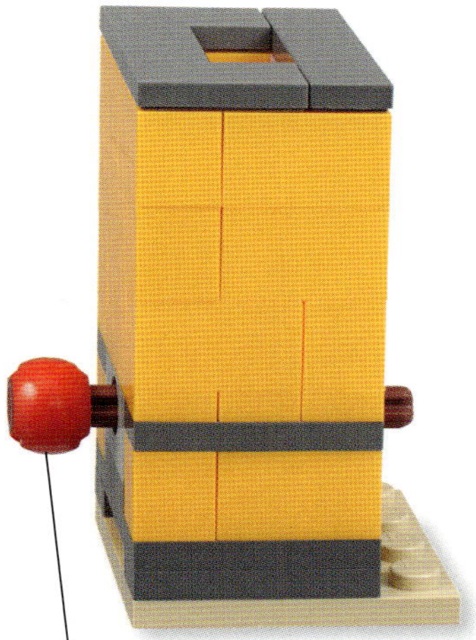

SIDE VIEW

LEGO Technic ball joint with axle hole makes a handle for the mechanism

Refill the vending machine through this gap

Drink can is a 1×1 tile and 1×1 round brick

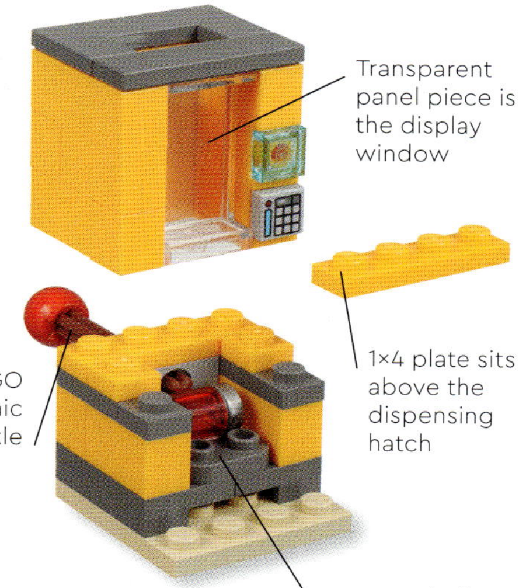

Transparent panel piece is the display window

LEGO Technic axle

1×4 plate sits above the dispensing hatch

1×2 rounded plate holds the can back

DISPENSING DEVICE

A LEGO Technic axle through a hole dispenses one can at a time from the vending machine. The stacked cans drop down into a groove behind a rounded plate until they're ready to be dispensed.

I ONLY COME FOR THE LUNAR-ADE!

VARIED CLIENTELE

What will your alien athletes look like? Will they have tentacles, lots of eyes, or other unique features? They might even lift weights with their teeth!

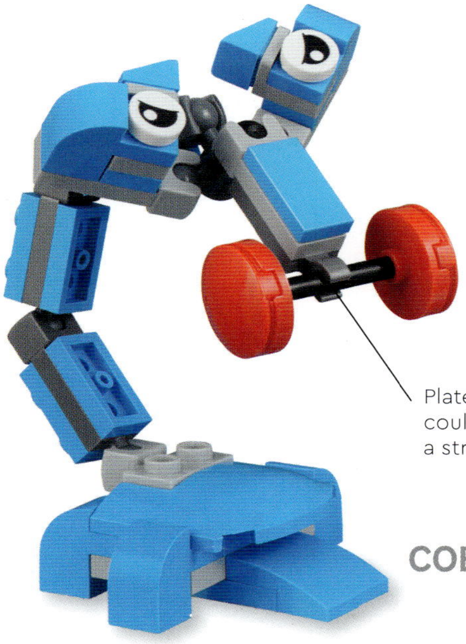

Plate with clip could be teeth or a strange "face arm"

COBRA ALIEN

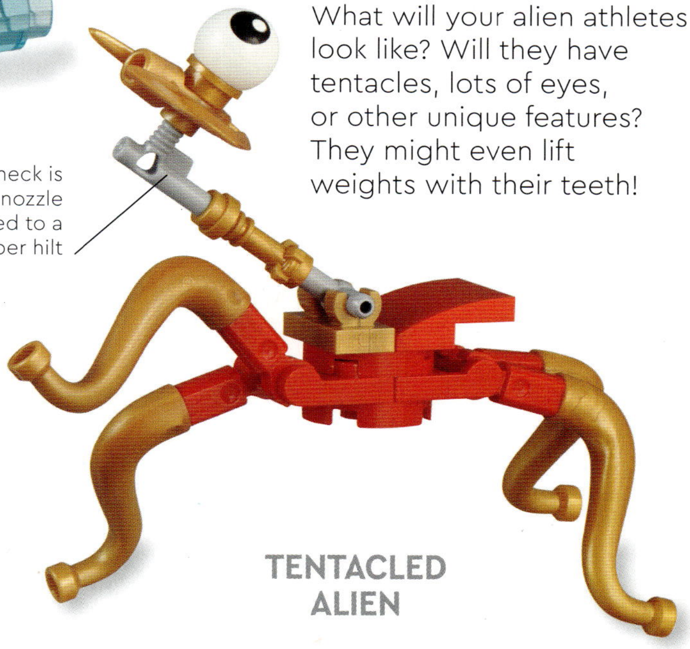

This alien's neck is a hose nozzle attached to a lightsaber hilt

TENTACLED ALIEN

ANCIENT STATUE

Over thousands of years, the paint on Egyptian statues like this one wore away, leaving just the stone that camera-toting tourists see today. Journey through time and create two versions of a landmark: how it might have looked when it was first built and how it appears now.

BUILDING BRIEF

Objective:	Build an ancient and modern version of an object
Use:	Spotting the differences between old and new
Features:	Ancient architecture and design
Extras:	Tourists, plants, building equipment

LOOK BACK

Research an ancient statue to discover how it could have looked long ago. What colors did the builders use? What building materials were available? Including these details will make your build look authentic to the time and place.

Wooden ladder made from spindled fence pieces
Minifigure buckets filled with colorful 1×1 round plates look like paint containers

SIDE VIEW

HE LOOKS JUST LIKE MY DEAR FATHER.

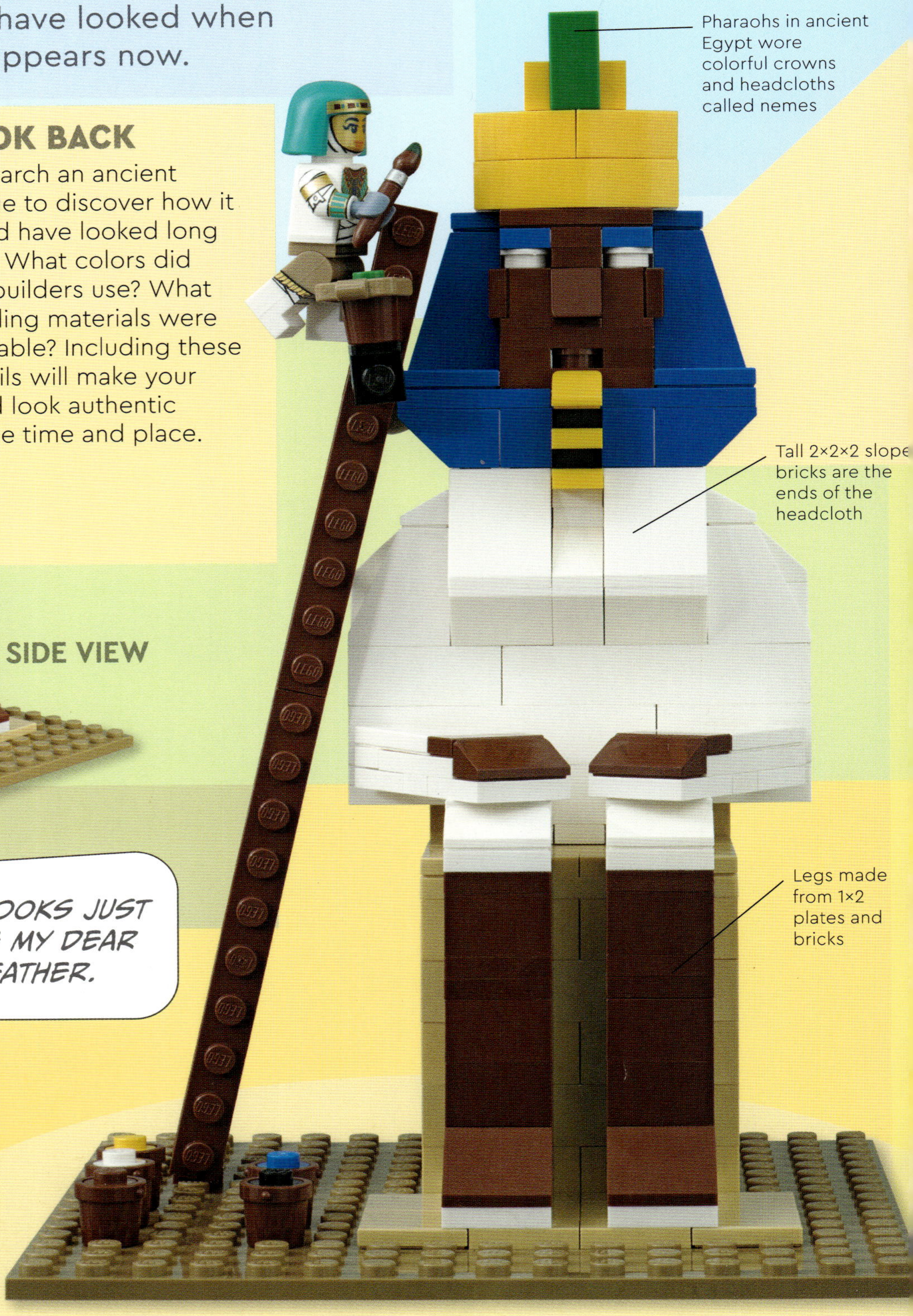
Pharaohs in ancient Egypt wore colorful crowns and headcloths called nemes
Tall 2×2×2 slope bricks are the ends of the headcloth
Legs made from 1×2 plates and bricks

TRY THIS

If you research an ancient object and can't find much information about how it once looked, come up with your own ideas based on what you do know—you might just be right!

ANGLED ARMS

The statue's arms are positioned at an angle thanks to 1×4 hinge plates that are hidden inside the middle of its body build. Tiles fit on top for a smooth, stonelike finish.

This back section is built up from standard bricks

1×4 hinge plate

LOOK NOW

Fast forward to modern times and there is no trace of color left on this ancient, crumbling statue. What pieces can you use to make your weathered wonder look like it's been standing for thousands of years?

WHY DIDN'T THEY MAKE IT MORE COLORFUL?

The colorful headcloth has worn away

Smaller details, such as the nose, have fallen off the statue

Slope instead of a 1×1 brick looks like a chip

Plants have come and gone over the years

Add small pieces of the crumbling statue on the ground

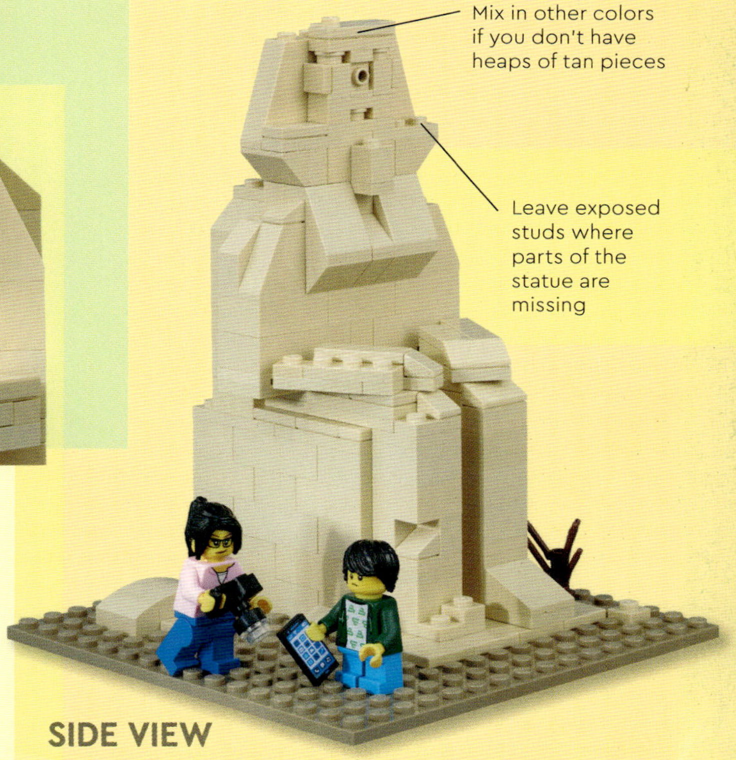

Mix in other colors if you don't have heaps of tan pieces

Leave exposed studs where parts of the statue are missing

SIDE VIEW

NINJA TRAINING

What a serene scene! A Japanese artist in a peaceful spring garden. But this artist has a secret. After dark, she heads off to an all-action martial arts training session! Why not pick a time and place in history and build an adventure of your own?

BUILDING BRIEF

Objective: Create environments for your own adventure story
Use: Building imaginary scenes
Features: Garden, ninja training area
Extras: Lanterns, weapons storage

This flower element has a pin underneath so it fits inside an open stud

You could add little cherries for a summer tree or brown leaves in the fall

Leaf elements can be any color you have or a mix of different colors

Half arch for a tree branch

2×2 radar dish lantern lid

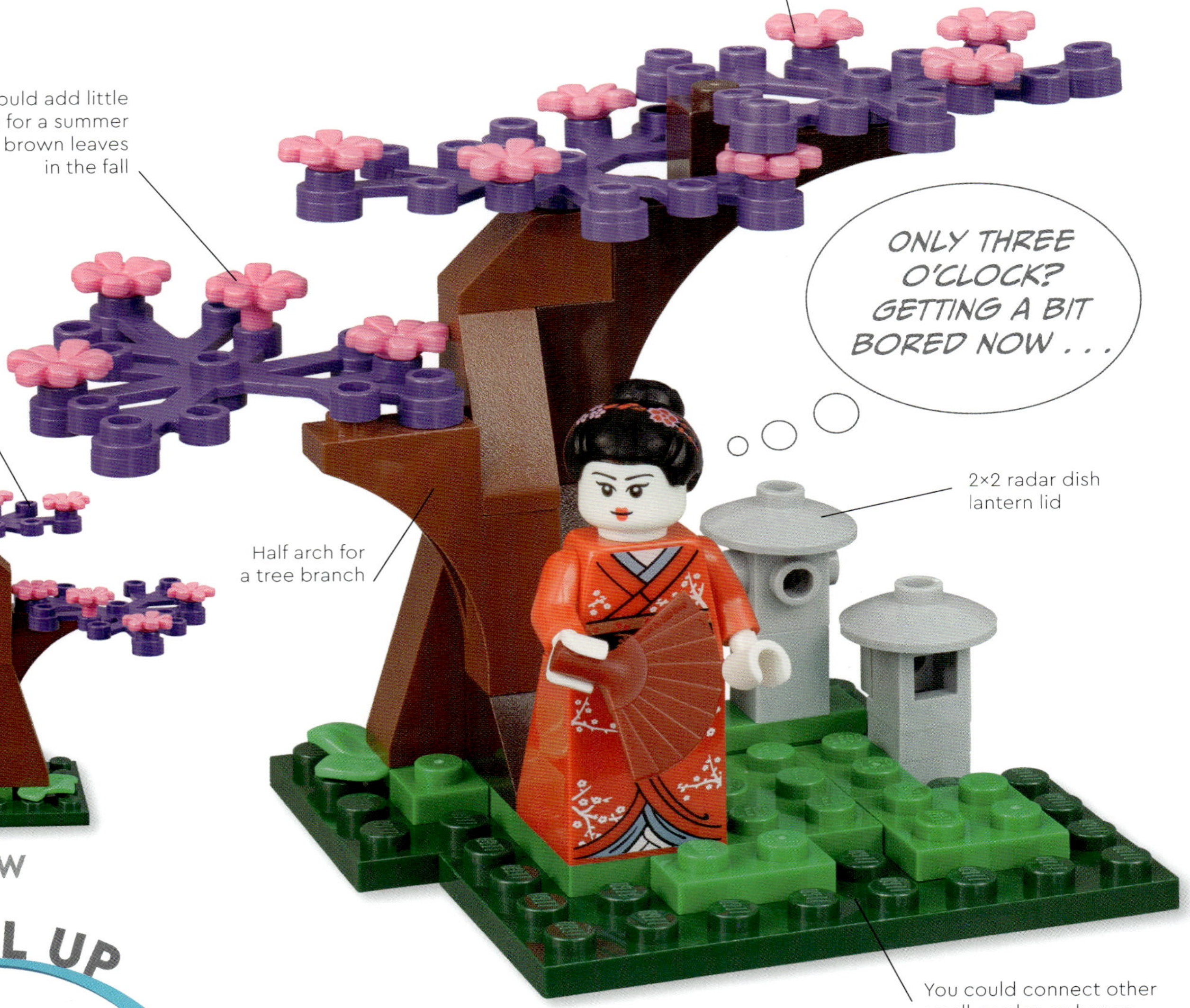
ONLY THREE O'CLOCK? GETTING A BIT BORED NOW . . .

You could connect other small garden or house scenes to these plates

REAR VIEW

LEVEL UP

Once you've figured out your story, add more to the action with extra scenes. Try building some ninja battles or even a hideaway for the villains!

ARTIST BY DAY

This blossom-covered tree will give the artist cooling shade during the day. The lanterns are for when night starts to fall (although she won't be around for long after that!). You only need to build a small section of an environment to create a convincing scene for an imaginary story.

This kind of screen is called a shoji—how will you design yours?

These gold rounded plates with handles add ornate details

龍神
龍神
HMM . . . SHE LOOKS FAMILIAR.

Add jumper plates with single studs so your minifigures can stand on the mat

8×8 plate base

NINJA STORAGE

Every ninja needs a safe place to keep their equipment in good condition. Slide her armor onto a bar and hold it steady with 1×1 round plates.

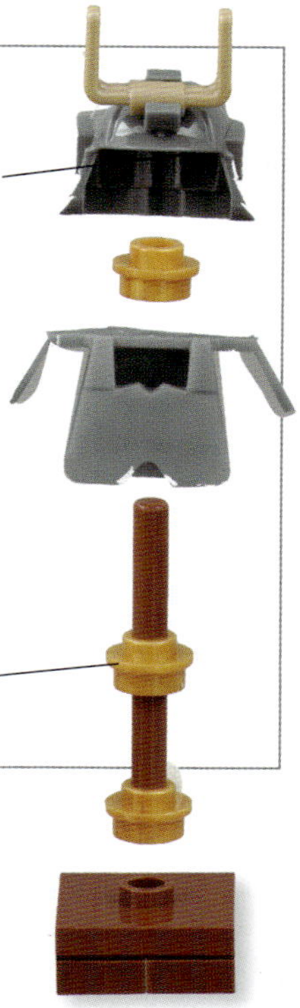

Kendo helmet

1×1 round plate with open stud

What outfits will your adventurer wear?

Keep the sword stand by the mat for easy access

I'M READY!

NINJA BY NIGHT

The training dojo has a square mat with a surface of smooth tiles, and a dragon window built separately behind. Parts of a scene don't need to be connected to look effective. Make sure your ninja has armor and weapons so she's ready to go into battle.

MYTHS AND LEGENDS

Become a legend in your own LEGO time by building a mythical menagerie. Looking into tales from ancient Greece, Rome, or Egypt will give you ideas to explore. Maybe you'll build a one-eyed Cyclops, a snake-haired Medusa, or a Hydra with many heads. Will your models act out their legends or do something unexpected?

BUILDING BRIEF

Objective:	Build characters from ancient stories
Use:	Legendary adventures
Features:	Wings, horns, mystical features
Extras:	Fire, weapons, heroes, villains

Curved slopes make a feathery head plume
This plate with three angled bars makes the wing look splayed
Transparent orange pieces are burning flames and embers

PHOENIX

This mythical bird from ancient Egypt lived for 500 years. When its time was up, it set fire to its nest and died in the flames. Then it rose from the ashes, born anew. And then 500 years later . . .

BUILD TIP

When building the plates with tow balls into the phoenix's body, make sure they are in the same position on both sides. This will ensure the wings and legs line up.

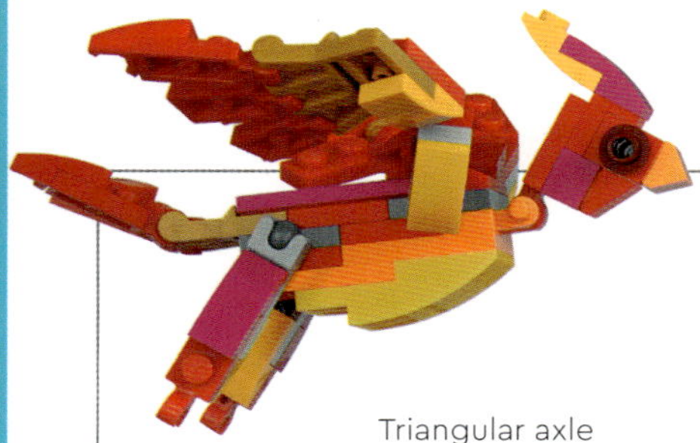

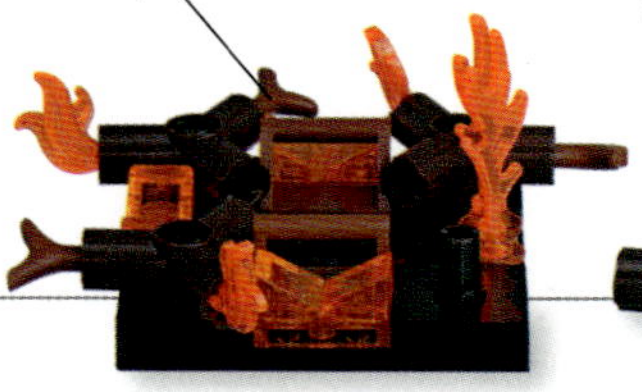
Carrot top
Triangular axle connector

FROM THE ASHES

The burning twigs in the phoenix's nest are made from LEGO Technic triangular axle connectors. Flame pieces and brown carrot tops, which look like smaller twigs, fit into their axle holes. The connectors slide onto 2×2 tiles with pins at each corner of the base plate.

Talons are plates with clips

REAR VIEW

The clips on the legs fit onto a plate with pins
SIDE VIEW

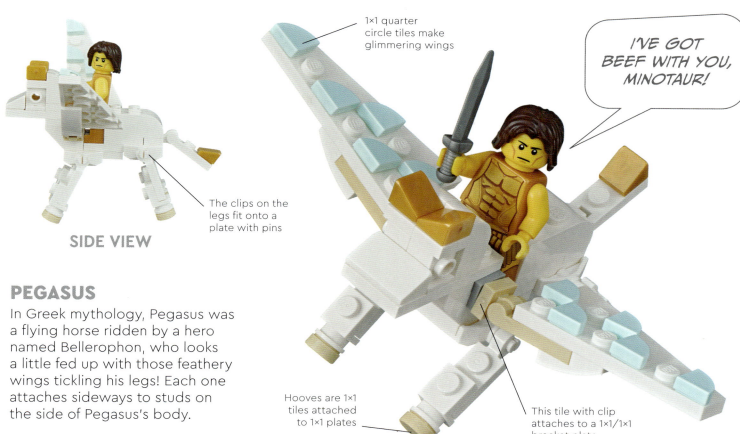

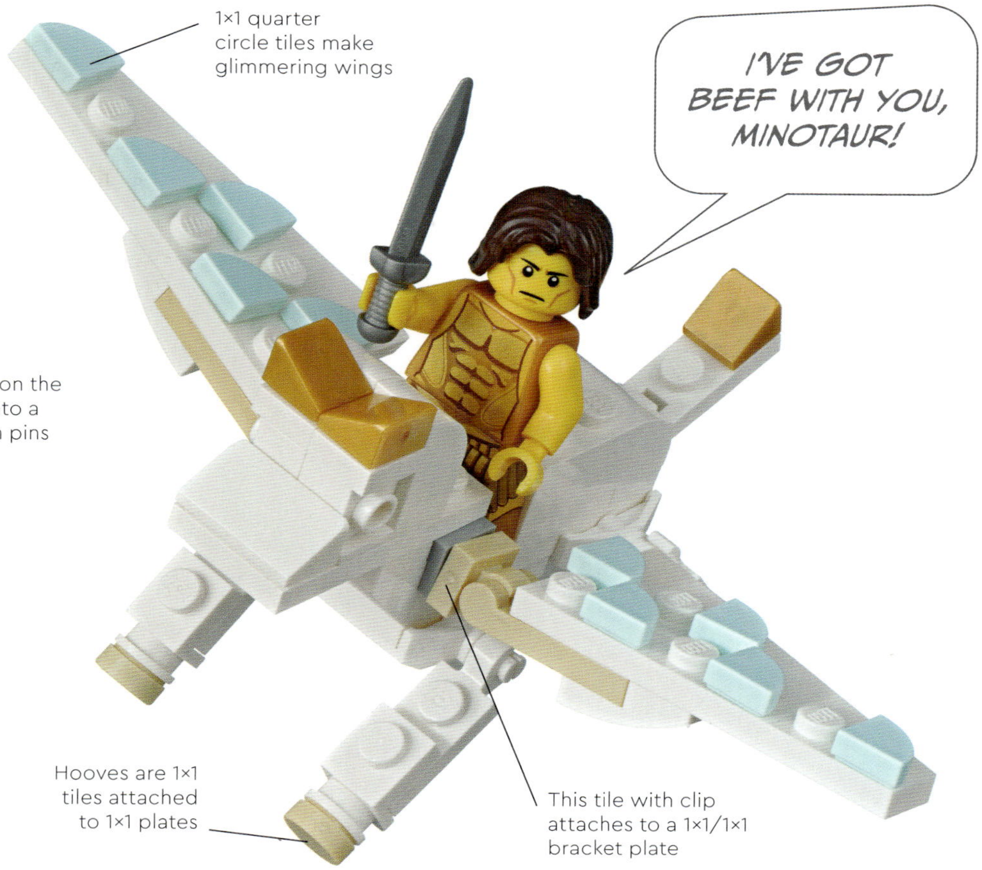
1×1 quarter circle tiles make glimmering wings
I'VE GOT BEEF WITH YOU, MINOTAUR!
Hooves are 1×1 tiles attached to 1×1 plates
This tile with clip attaches to a 1×1/1×1 bracket plate

PEGASUS

In Greek mythology, Pegasus was a flying horse ridden by a hero named Bellerophon, who looks a little fed up with those feathery wings tickling his legs! Each one attaches sideways to studs on the side of Pegasus's body.

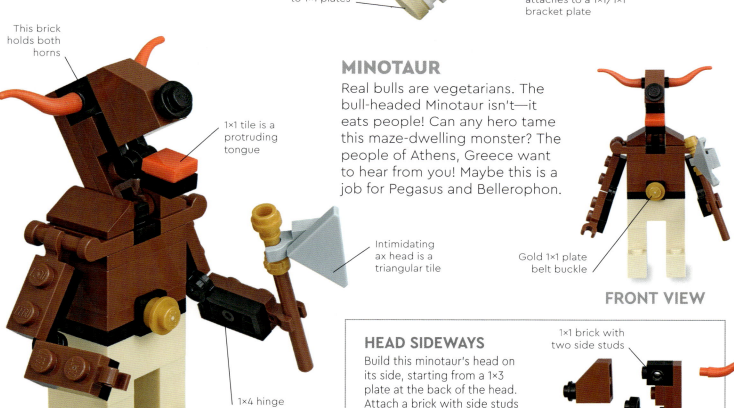

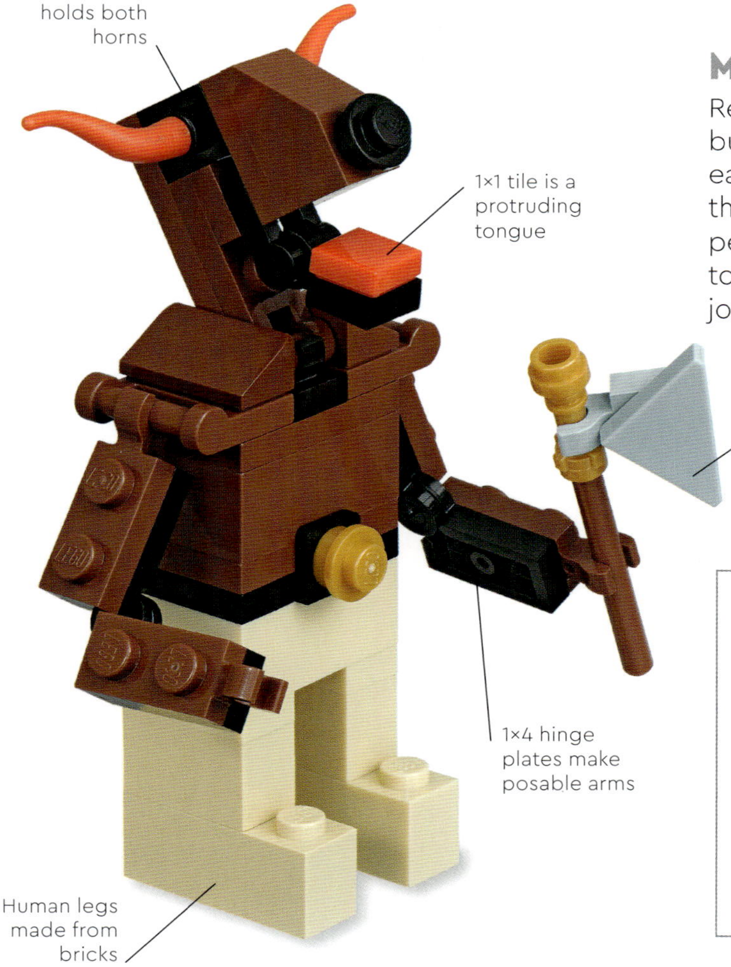
This brick holds both horns
1×1 tile is a protruding tongue
Intimidating ax head is a triangular tile
1×4 hinge plates make posable arms
Human legs made from bricks

MINOTAUR

Real bulls are vegetarians. The bull-headed Minotaur isn't—it eats people! Can any hero tame this maze-dwelling monster? The people of Athens, Greece want to hear from you! Maybe this is a job for Pegasus and Bellerophon.

Gold 1×1 plate belt buckle
FRONT VIEW

HEAD SIDEWAYS

Build this minotaur's head on its side, starting from a 1×3 plate at the back of the head. Attach a brick with side studs on top for the horns to fit onto. Then add a plate with bar for the neck, a slope brick for the snout, and a 1×2 rounded plate with bar for the moving jaw.

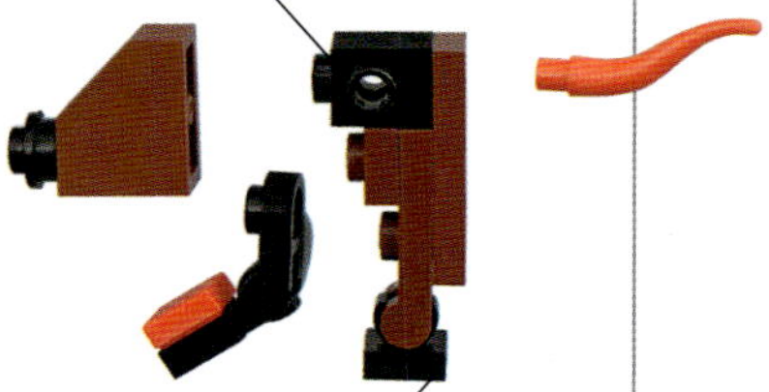
1×1 brick with two side studs
Neck attaches to a 1×1 tile with clip on the body

MINI-MARKET

This LEGO® mini-market on the bustling streets of Old Delhi, India has everything covered. It sells fruits, vegetables, sunshades, and more. Is there anything the storekeeper has forgotten? Maybe sandals for footsore customers! Try expanding the scene with more stores, local wildlife, and even a delivery tuk-tuk to help take goods across the city.

BUILDING BRIEF

Objective:	Create a store
Use:	Restocking supplies, retail therapy
Features:	Storefront, goods, cash register
Extras:	Utility pole, streetlight, storeroom

DESTINATION DETAILS

The tiled roof, arched doorways, palm tree, and colorful awning make this store look like it's in India. Someone has parked their scooter right by the utility pole outside. They've probably dashed into the mini-market to pick up a cooling bottle of mango juice.

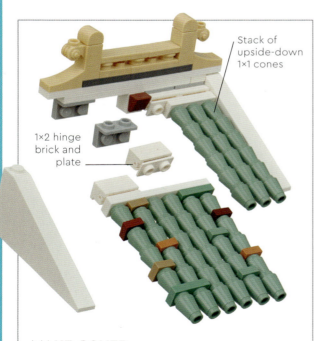

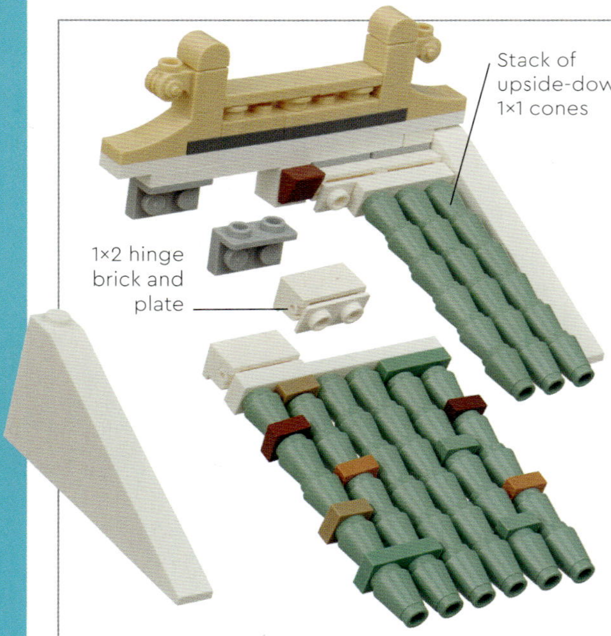
Stack of upside-down 1×1 cones
1×2 hinge brick and plate

MAKE COVER

Stacks of downward-facing cones and plates form the tiles of the roof. They fit onto narrow plates at the top of the roof. Hinge plates and bricks above them allow the roof to lie at an angle, just like a real roof.

1×1 bricks with scrolls add character to the roof
Half arches make pointed entryways

BUILD TIP

If you don't have many LEGO food pieces to stock your store with, build some! Orange cones can be carrots, round plates make good apples, and slopes could be cheese.

LEGO whips look like heavy insulated wiring
LEGO string runs power to the market
Add a streetlight for evening shoppers
Cover plates with tiles to give the roof a smooth finish
Tiny cash register for ringing up items
THAT PESKY BIRD IS AFTER MY FRUIT AGAIN!

1×2×2 brick with side studs

TRANSFORMER

The box at the top of the utility pole is called a transformer. A brick with four side studs at its core allows you to attach gray grille tiles on their sides to make it look like the transformer has metallic cooling fins.

SIDE VIEW

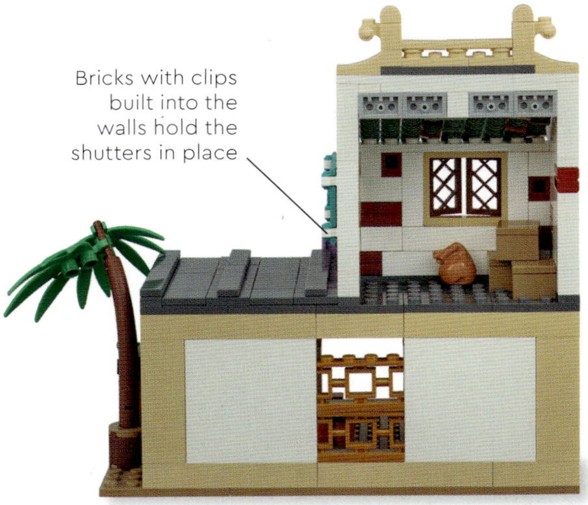

Bricks with clips built into the walls hold the shutters in place

REAR VIEW

CLASSIC FILM SET

This minifigure crew is filming an old-fashioned Western adventure on an Old Hollywood film set. In this scene, a crook has stolen some loot and is escaping across a desert with a vulture in hot pursuit! Can you think of other scenes you could build and direct for this movie? What other filmmaking equipment might the crew need?

BUILDING BRIEF

Objective: Build a film set
Use: Making movies, acting out scenes
Features: Lights, set, camera
Extras: Props, seating, clapboard

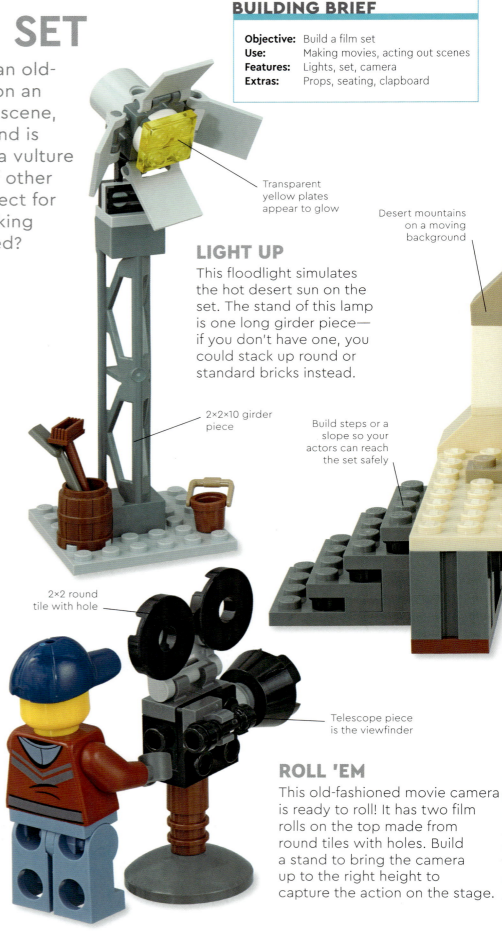

Transparent yellow plates appear to glow
2×2×10 girder piece

LIGHT UP

This floodlight simulates the hot desert sun on the set. The stand of this lamp is one long girder piece—if you don't have one, you could stack up round or standard bricks instead.

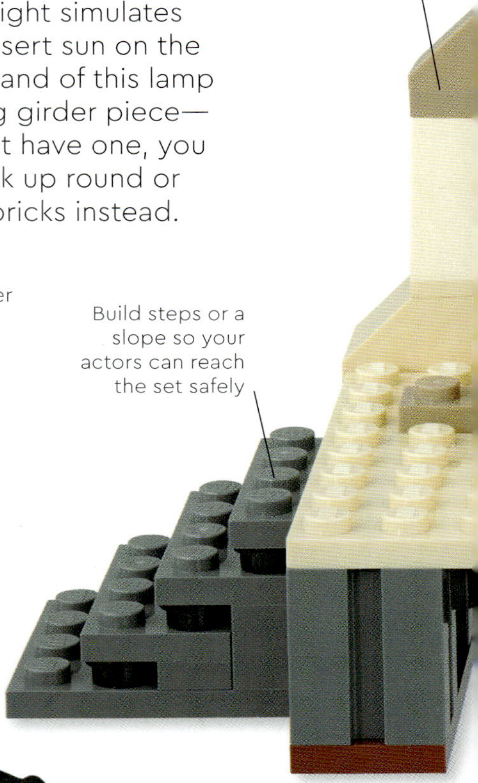

Desert mountains on a moving background
Build steps or a slope so your actors can reach the set safely

Clip and bar connection allows the clapboard to clap

CLAPBOARD

1×2 plate with bar
1×1 brick with one side stud
2×2/1×2 inverted bracket

CAMERA CLOSE-UP

The movie camera is built up and out from an inverted bracket plate. Two small bricks with side studs fit onto the back of it to form the square body of the camera.

2×2 round tile with hole
Telescope piece is the viewfinder

ROLL 'EM

This old-fashioned movie camera is ready to roll! It has two film rolls on the top made from round tiles with holes. Build a stand to bring the camera up to the right height to capture the action on the stage.

TRY THIS

Many movies that were filmed in the past are black and white. Build your scene in only black, white, and gray pieces to create a classic "silver screen" look.

Match the height of the base to the stage

Desert fort is tiny because it's in the distance!

CHANGE OF SCENE

On this film set, different backgrounds can be wheeled into place behind the action to change the look of the scenes. Build the wheel base and top it with any scenery you like.

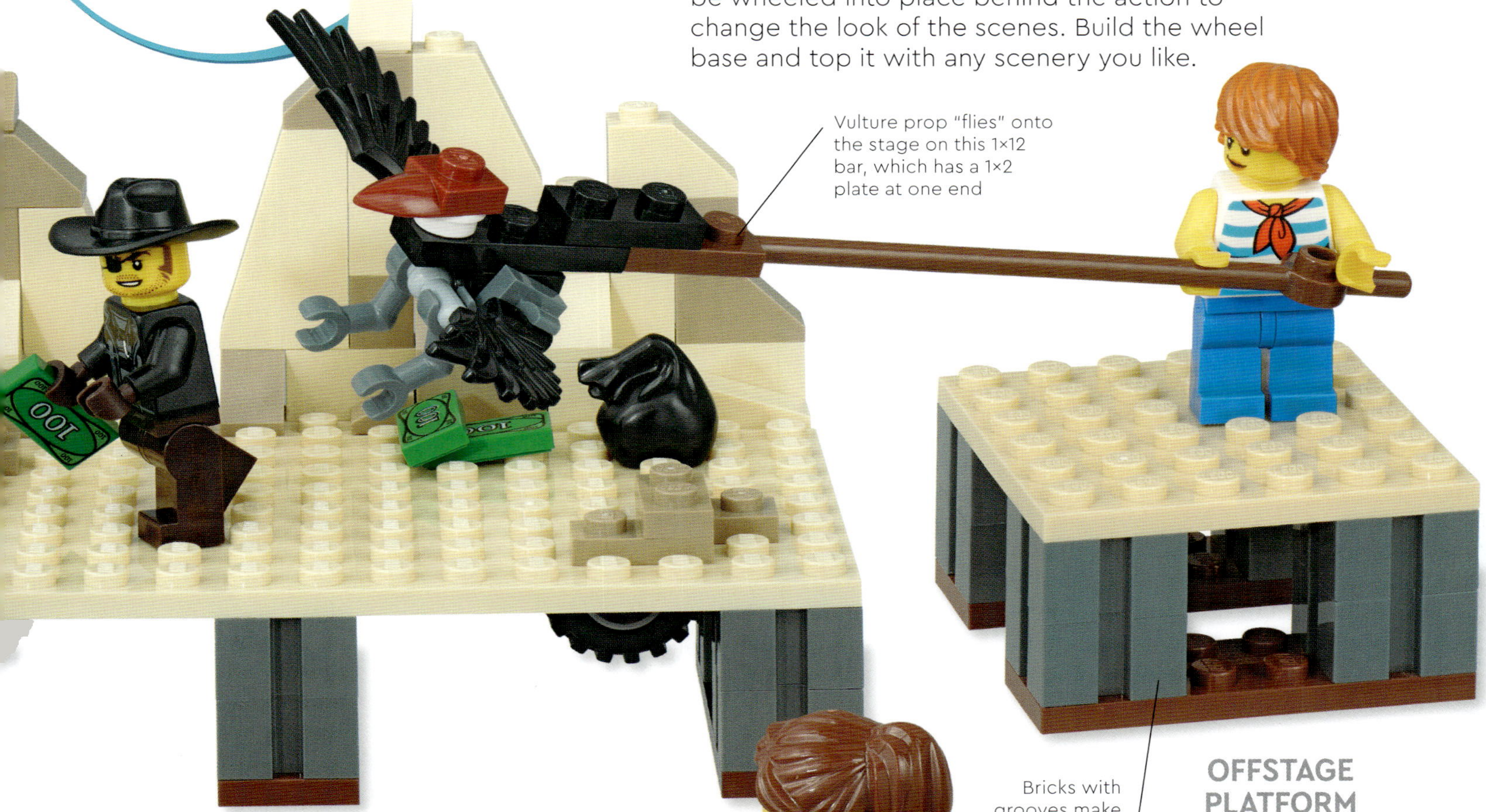

Vulture prop "flies" onto the stage on this 1×12 bar, which has a 1×2 plate at one end

Bricks with grooves make sturdy legs to raise the stage

OFFSTAGE PLATFORM

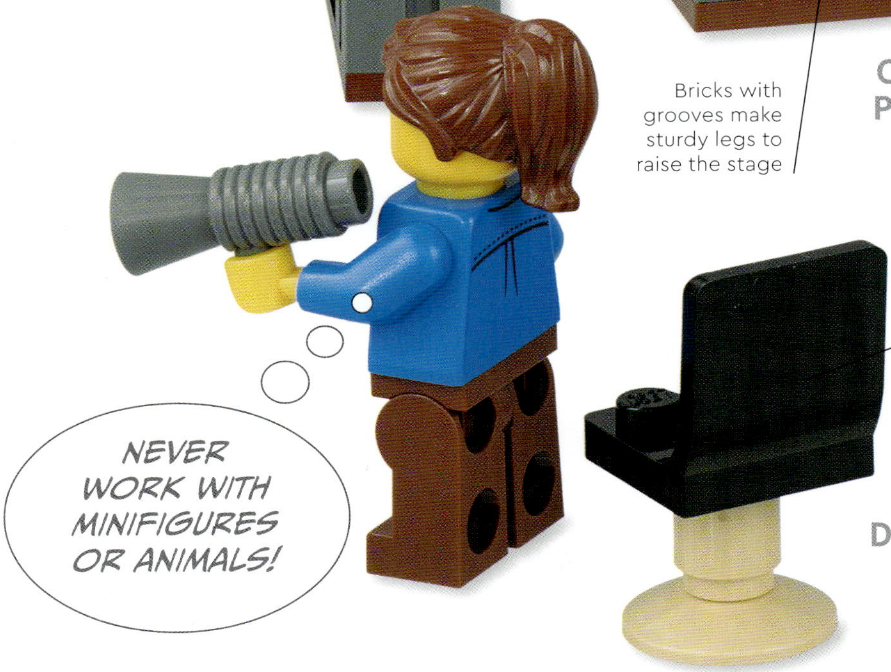
NEVER WORK WITH MINIFIGURES OR ANIMALS!

. . . AND ACTION!

Set the stage so your minifigures can act out the movie's storyline. The base plate on this stage looks like a sandy desert and there's a dramatic backdrop of scorched mountains. Keep the build simple so the stage is strong and has lots of room for actors and props.

2×2 driver's seat piece on a round brick and radar dish

DIRECTOR'S CHAIR

JAPANESE GARDEN

Tea drinking is a very old tradition in Japan. Here, a minifigure is sipping a cup of matcha tea in a wooden tea hut called a *chashitsu*. The tea ritual is a time for peaceful contemplation, so a *chashitsu* is always set within a beautiful garden. Fill your *chashitsu* garden with calming, restful things to look at.

BUILDING BRIEF

Objective:	Build a Japanese tea hut and garden
Use:	A place to relax
Features:	Plants, trees, water feature
Extras:	Lanterns, pagodas, paths, fences

This water lily leaf is a minifigure paint palette

GARDEN VIEW

PEACEFUL PLACE

What will you add to your garden? What makes you feel calm? Your minifigures might love to watch a cherry tree blossom. A little shrine would be good, too, and a pool filled with slow-moving koi carp.

Branches are half arch pieces

If you don't have this ornamental lattice fence, use any fence pieces you have

Round tiles for a natural stone path

Add lanterns for nighttime contemplation

CARP POND

Transparent pieces, including tiles printed with fish, fill this little pond with water and life. If you don't have these pieces, use tiles with clips and connect fish pieces.

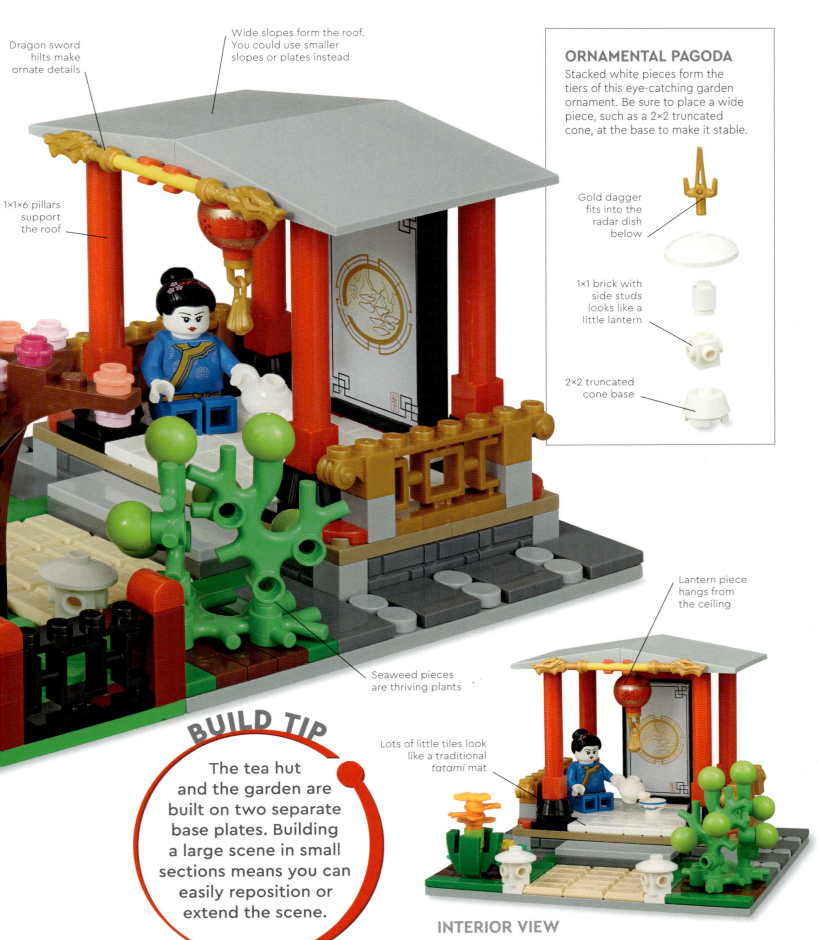

Dragon sword hilts make ornate details
Wide slopes form the roof. You could use smaller slopes or plates instead
1×1×6 pillars support the roof
Seaweed pieces are thriving plants

ORNAMENTAL PAGODA

Stacked white pieces form the tiers of this eye-catching garden ornament. Be sure to place a wide piece, such as a 2×2 truncated cone, at the base to make it stable.

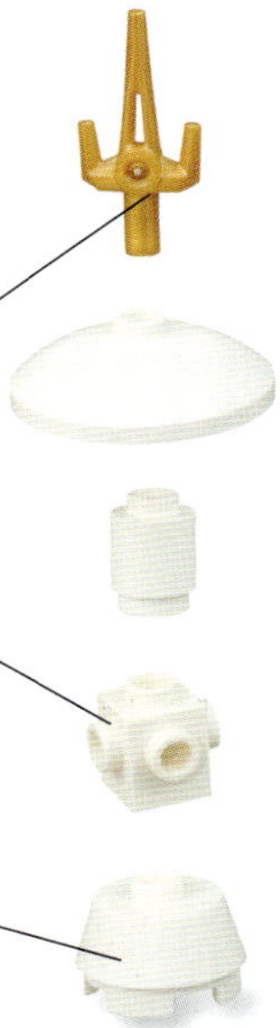
Gold dagger fits into the radar dish below
1×1 brick with side studs looks like a little lantern
2×2 truncated cone base

BUILD TIP

The tea hut and the garden are built on two separate base plates. Building a large scene in small sections means you can easily reposition or extend the scene.

Lantern piece hangs from the ceiling
Lots of little tiles look like a traditional *tatami* mat

INTERIOR VIEW

BUILDING BRIEF

Objective:	Build time machines
Use:	Traveling through time
Features:	Futuristic gadgets, seating or standing areas
Extras:	Power source, laboratory

TIME TRAVEL

What time is it? If you own a time machine, it's up to you—so get building. Will yours be a teleporter? Or a time-hopping vehicle like the one driven by the gent in the top hat? He started out in the 1800s, but who knows whether he's traveling back or forward in time. Bon voyage!

BUILD TIP

To make sure there is room for your minifigure pilot, start with the cockpit of your time machine. Then build upward and outward in whatever style you like.

OH DEAR. I LEFT MY GLOVES IN THE ICE AGE!
Futuristic-looking propeller is a printed 4×4 radar dish
Does this jewel power the machine's magic?
Bumper bar piece is also used at the back of the vehicle

TIME FLIES

This moving time machine is not only useful for traveling to other moments in time—it's also good for getting around when you get there. It has a high-tech mechanical look thanks to its pipes, connectors, and handlebars.

LEGO Technic ball joints make strange contraptions

FRONT VIEW

SMOOTH RIDE

This time machine is ready to land on any terrain thanks to landing skids, which are often used on snow vehicle models. Tiles with clips connect the skids to plates with bars on the body of the vehicle.

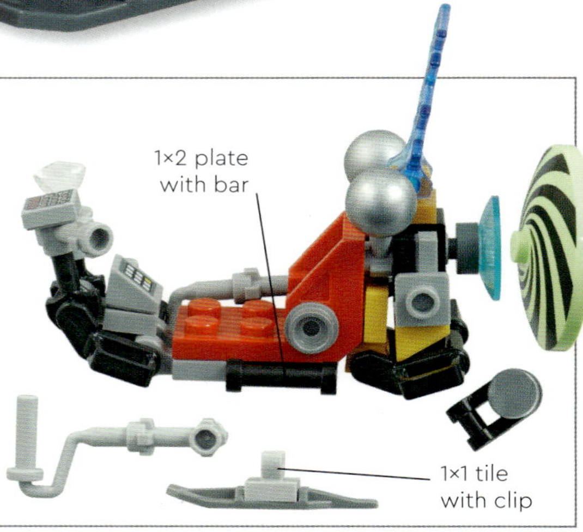
1×2 plate with bar
1×1 tile with clip

SIGNAL STACK

Two sizes of inverted radar dishes give this transmission tower height. A telescope piece extends the tower so that the LEGO Technic ball joint at the top can send or receive tiny LEGO particles when it's switched on.

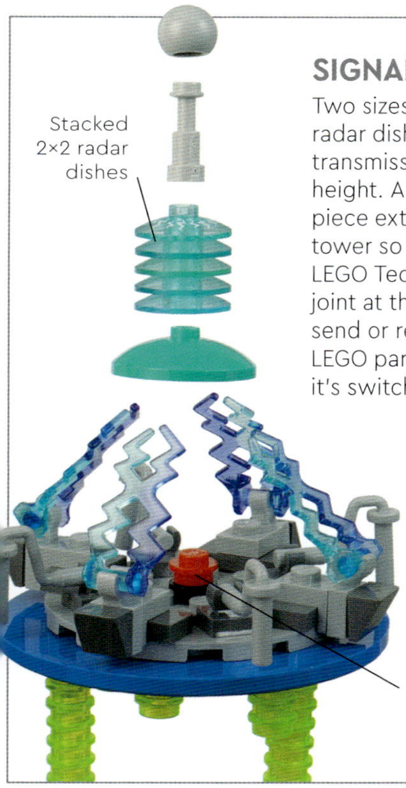

Stacked 2×2 radar dishes
1×1 round plate

TELEPORTER

For instant time travel, a teleporter is a must. You need a chamber for a minifigure to stand or sit in and some complex technology. Then three, two, one . . . where did he go?

Lightning pieces are bolts of electricity
1×1 transparent round plates look like whirring energy
3×6×6 half cylinder covers the rear of the chamber

OOPS . . . I FORGOT TO ADD A BUTTON TO BRING HIM BACK!
2×8 plate with rail holds the back wall together
Transparent bars look like neon strip lights
1×1 round plates with bars are the chair's arm rests

SCIENCE LAB

The teleporter is inside this secret science lab. It has a complicated-looking control panel and a comfy chair so that the inventor can rest once the time traveler is on his way.

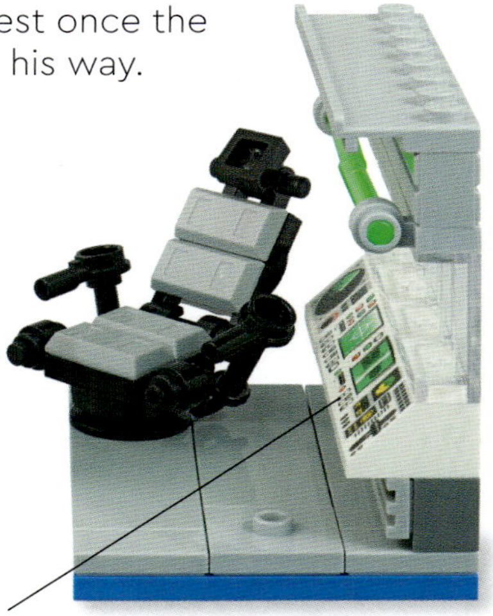

Printed slopes look like screens and controls

SIDE VIEW

BUILDING BRIEF

Objective:	Make a multitude of timepieces
Use:	Timekeeping, time-traveling adventures, souvenirs
Features:	Clock faces, hands, mechanisms
Extras:	Cuckoos, sand, robots

TIMEPIECES

Most people like to bring back souvenirs from their holidays. This time-traveling robot does, too. Every time they teleport, they bring home a clock from a different age. They like to know what made the people of the past tick! What interesting LEGO pieces can you use to make your own LEGO timepieces?

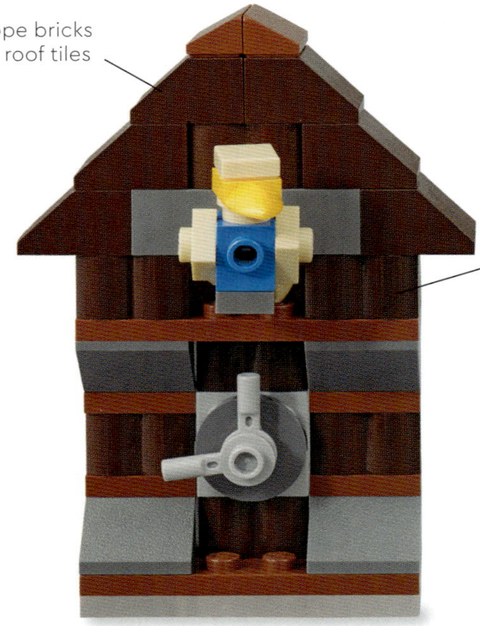
Slope bricks for roof tiles
Brown 1×2 log bricks look like carved wood

CUCKOO CLOCK

Traditional cuckoo clocks are shaped like a house with a tiled, pointed roof. A little bird pops out to announce the hour. What other creatures could you build to pop out of your clock?

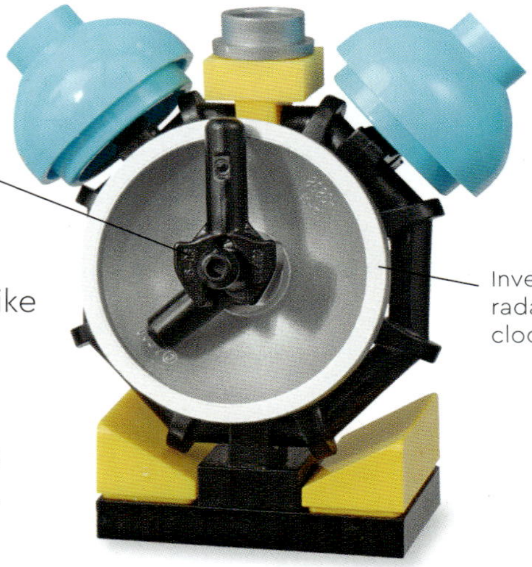
Claw pieces for the hands
Inverted radar dish clock face

ALARM CLOCK

Brrrring! Bell alarm clocks like this have been waking up schoolkids and workers of the world for at least 100 years. The bells on this clock are tiny dome bricks.

SAND TIMER

Before ticking clocks, there were sand timers. When you turn the timer over, sand trickles from one globe to the other. You could flip this build either way to show that more or less time (sand) remains in the top globe.

Bars fit inside red 1×1 cones to make columns
Round plate makes a stable base at both ends of the timer

ILLUSION OF TIME

A tan 2×2 dome makes the top globe look fuller than the bottom. Together with the funnel-shaped tan 1×1 cone inside the transparent dome below, it looks as though sand is actually flowing!

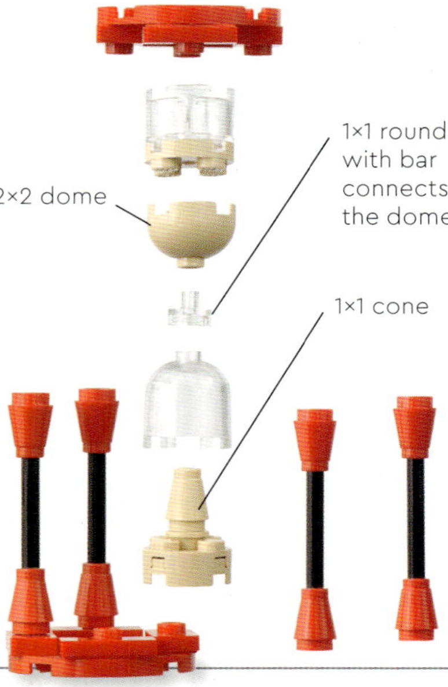
2×2 dome
1×1 round tile with bar connects the domes
1×1 cone

TIME ON YOUR SIDE

Bricks with side studs keep key parts of this build in place. The clock face fits onto a 1×2 brick with side studs, and tiles with clips connect to 1×1 bricks with side studs to hold the pendulum and the weight.

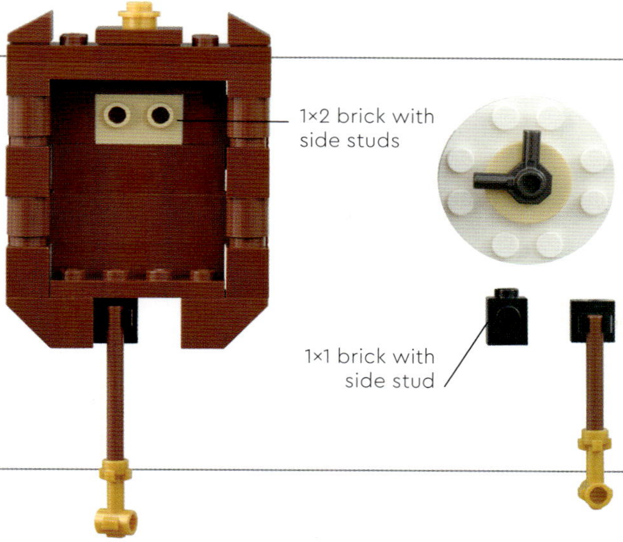
1×2 brick with side studs
1×1 brick with side stud

Studs on the plate are numbers on the clock face

TIME-TRAVELING ROBOT

Antennae and round, metallic eyes are common robot features. But this one is a special time-traveling robot. Add a clock face to its chest to let everyone know!

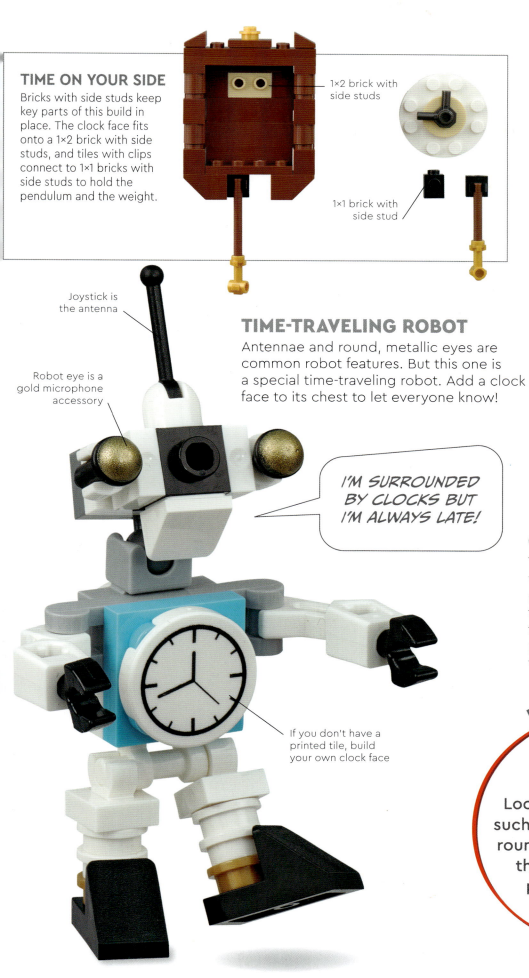

Joystick is the antenna
Robot eye is a gold microphone accessory
I'M SURROUNDED BY CLOCKS BUT I'M ALWAYS LATE!
If you don't have a printed tile, build your own clock face

GRANDFATHER CLOCK

These clocks got their name when a poet wrote about his grandfather's clock in 1876. The two hanging parts underneath the clock face are called the pendulum and the weight—they work together to power the clock.

BUILD TIP

Design the ticking clock face first. Look for round pieces such as radar dishes and round jumper plates for the face, and small pieces with bars for the hands.

EXPRESS YOURSELF

Building with LEGO® pieces is a great way to show off your personality and your own brand of creativity. You can make art, create games, dream up inventions, or direct LEGO movies . . . if you can imagine it, you can probably build it!

WALL ART

Creating with LEGO bricks is not just about building structures—you can also make amazing pictures and portraits to display in your home. Designing artwork with LEGO pieces allows you to use their colors and shapes in completely new ways. You can make art that's quite flat or include lots of 3-D details.

BUILDING BRIEF

Objective: Build LEGO art for your home
Use: Expressing your creativity, decorating walls and surfaces
Features: Base plates, other flat pieces
Extras: Frames, stands, 3-D elements

Bananas serve as long, blond locks of hair
Baked goods make a neatly trimmed beard

Smooth white sides are $1 \times 4 \times \frac{1}{3}$ curved slopes

LANDSCAPES

Many artists are inspired by the outside world. Can you re-create the view from your window or depict your favorite place in LEGO bricks? This simple boat scene is made from just 11 pieces.

PORTRAITS

Try piecing together portraits of your favorite people—including yourself—using your LEGO collection. This one is made from food-themed pieces and minifigure accessories, with lemon tarts for ears and a sausage smile! Find your most interesting or unusual pieces and use them in works of art.

FACE FACTS

Most of the facial features are built onto 1×1 tiles with clips. These can be turned to any angle to change the portrait's mood! Centered features, such as the nose and chin, are aligned using jumper plates.

2×2 round jumper plate

This beveled frame is made from curved slope tiles

ANIMALS

When you draw animals, it can be hard to get the details right. But the details are the fun part when making LEGO animal art! Try out lots of different pieces to get the shapes of your animal's feathers, tails, wings, or teeth just right.

Rounded plates with gears make effective flowers
Grass is made from green minifigure claws

FLOWERS

Paintings of flowers have always been popular with artists. You could build any botanical beauties you see growing in your garden or local park. Go on a nature walk with a friend and make LEGO artwork of anything you spot.

LEGO ART IS MUCH LESS MESSY!
A 2×4 hinge plate supports this frame

STAND

TRY THIS

As well as building pictures into your LEGO frames, why not build some empty frames for displaying your favorite photos or drawings?

ART AND SCULPTURES

Having art on display around the home is a great way to express your personal style. Looking at your favorite artwork, sculptures, and objects every day also makes you feel happy and positive. Share that joy with your LEGO minifigures by filling their homes and public spaces with inspiring 3-D art.

BUILDING BRIEF

Objective:	Build 3-D LEGO art for minifigures
Use:	Decorating minifigure homes, galleries, and parks
Features:	Works of art in all styles, shapes, and sizes
Extras:	Plinths, frames, display cases

TRY THIS

Use microscale building techniques to make a landscape scene for a 3-D "painting"—or to add a display of mini LEGO sets to a minifigure's home.

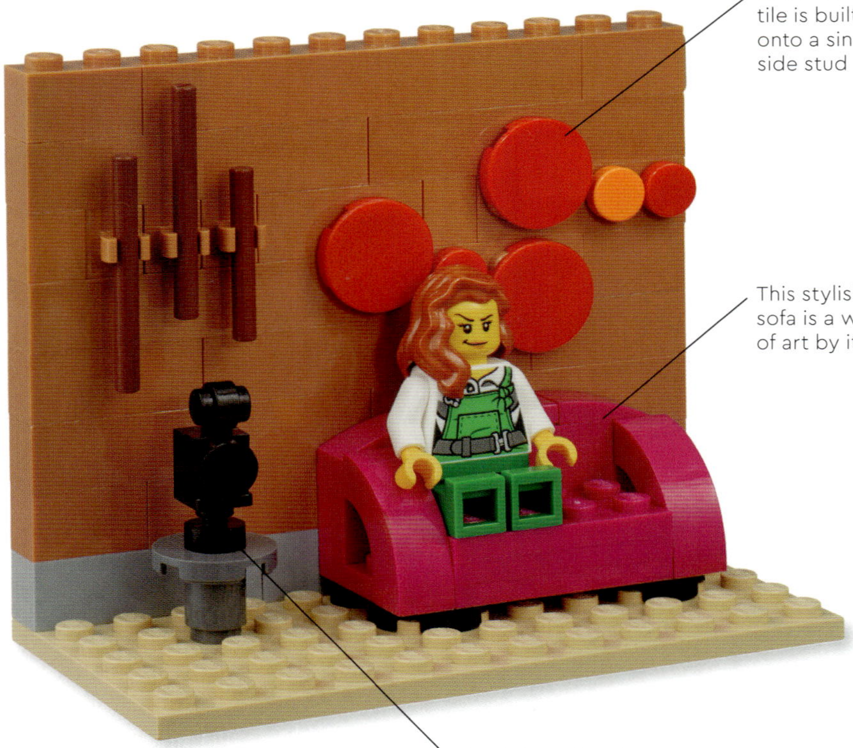

Each round tile is built onto a single side stud

This stylish sofa is a work of art by itself!

Sculpture stands on a jumper plate tabletop

ABSTRACT ART

LEGO art doesn't have to be complicated. The clever use of shapes and colors can create simple abstract wall art. Here, some artfully placed bars on clips and different-size tiles attached sideways to the wall transform this minifigure's living space.

THIS SHELF ROCKS!

This rock crystal piece is a readymade ornament

Trophy is a LEGO® DOTS tile on a plate with a side stud

TREASURED OBJECTS

Having sculptures, ornaments, and mementos on display in a home can reveal a lot about who lives there. Which minifigure might display this musical memorabilia? It looks like they have won an award or two . . .

Fancy frame toppers are gold-colored frog pieces
The "painting" is really a 3-D build set into the wall

HORSING AROUND

The head and body of this posable horse are both just one-stud wide. The four legs make it two-studs wide overall, as these clip side by side onto T-bar pieces that slot into the underside of the body.

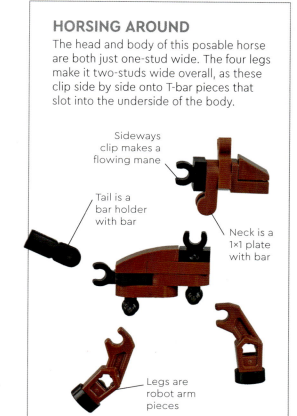

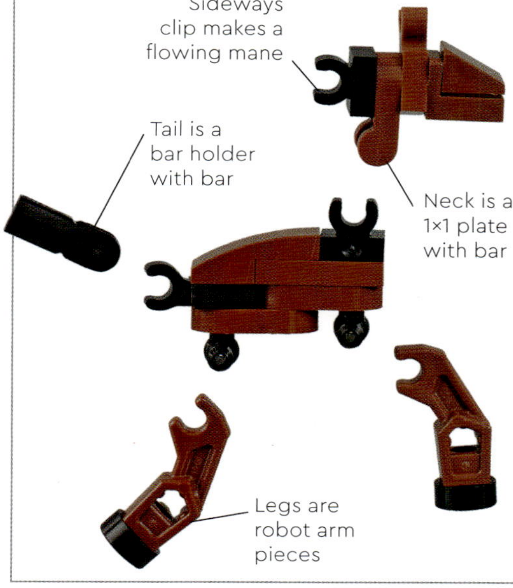
Sideways clip makes a flowing mane
Tail is a bar holder with bar
Neck is a 1×1 plate with bar
Legs are robot arm pieces

GALLERY ART

Take inspiration from famous artists and create a 3-D LEGO art piece fit for a gallery. Edgar Degas painted many racehorses, while Frida Kahlo mostly painted pictures of herself. What would make minifigures stop and stare at your art?

The back of the "painting" is set two studs back from the wall

SIDE VIEW

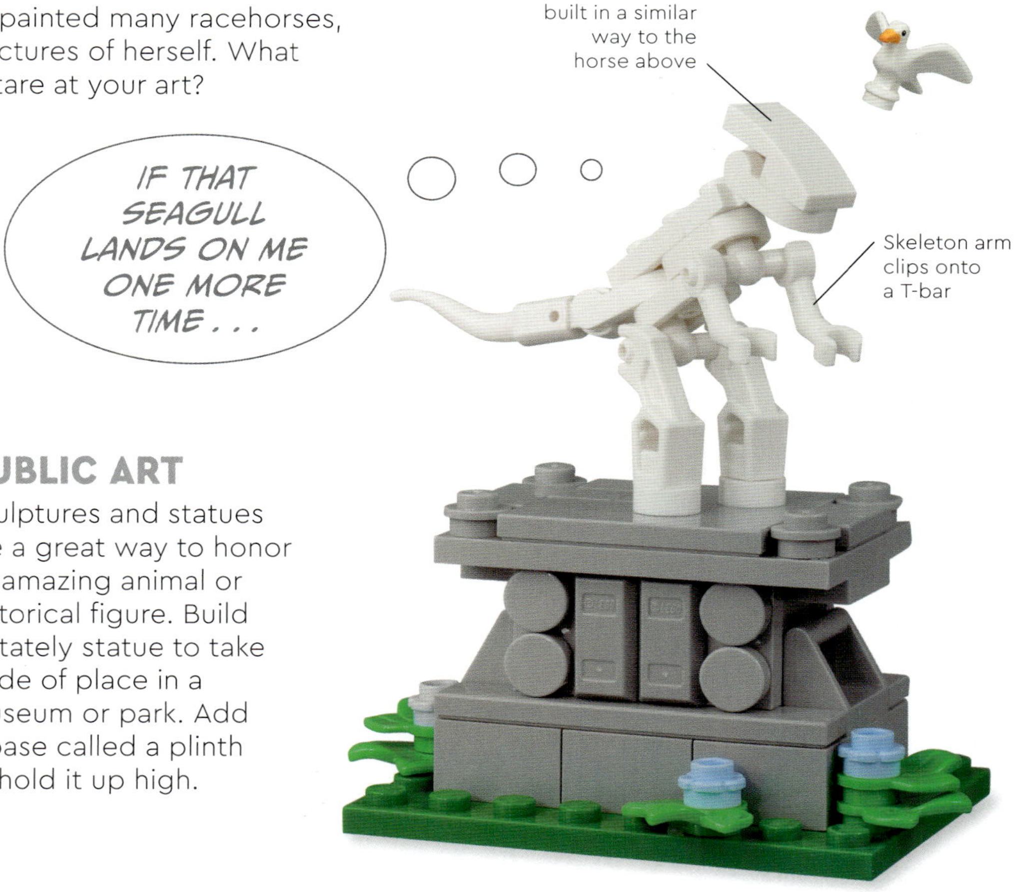
This dinosaur is built in a similar way to the horse above
IF THAT SEAGULL LANDS ON ME ONE MORE TIME . . .
Skeleton arm clips onto a T-bar

PUBLIC ART

Sculptures and statues are a great way to honor an amazing animal or historical figure. Build a stately statue to take pride of place in a museum or park. Add a base called a plinth to hold it up high.

BUILD YOUR FAMILY

Sometimes building inspiration can be right under your nose—or sitting opposite you at the dinner table! Why not create the people you love most in LEGO pieces? Your family could become a permanent display in your house. You might give the family seasonal makeovers, and add new members when they're born.

BUILDING BRIEF

Objective: Build your family in LEGO pieces
Use: Making up or reenacting family stories, decorating your home
Features: Family members including pets
Extras: Special outfits, hairstyles, accessories, moving parts

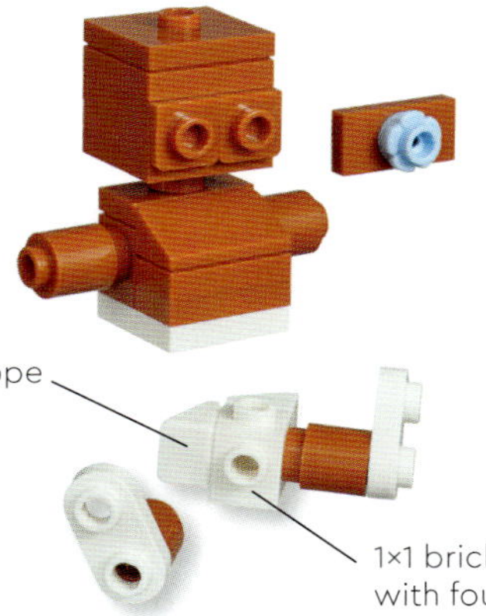
1×1 slope
1×1 brick with four side studs

DIAPER ON

This baby is mostly made out of stacked plates, but her diaper is a brick with four side studs, angled diagonally. Small slopes bulk it out on two sides, while the legs build onto the others.

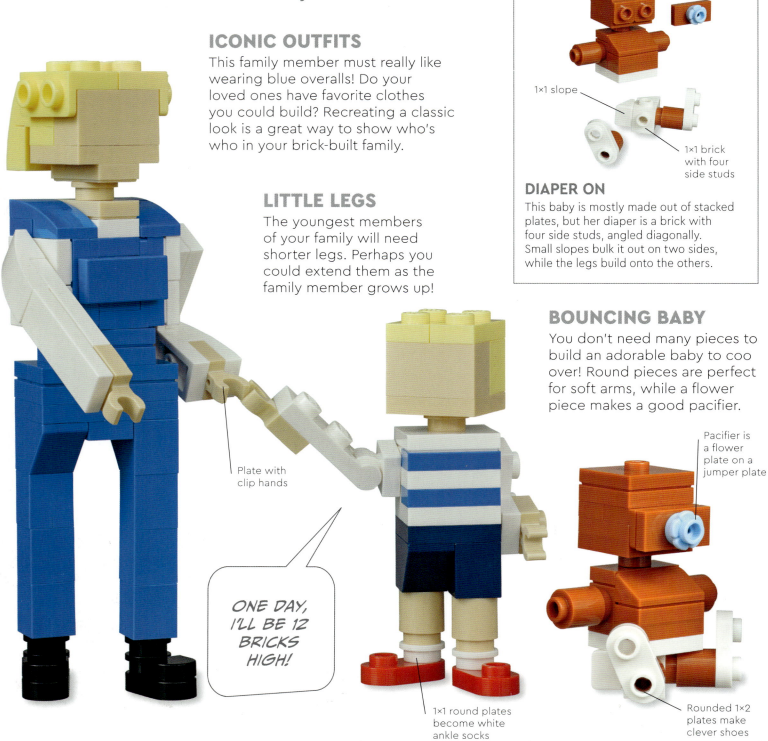

ICONIC OUTFITS

This family member must really like wearing blue overalls! Do your loved ones have favorite clothes you could build? Recreating a classic look is a great way to show who's who in your brick-built family.

LITTLE LEGS

The youngest members of your family will need shorter legs. Perhaps you could extend them as the family member grows up!

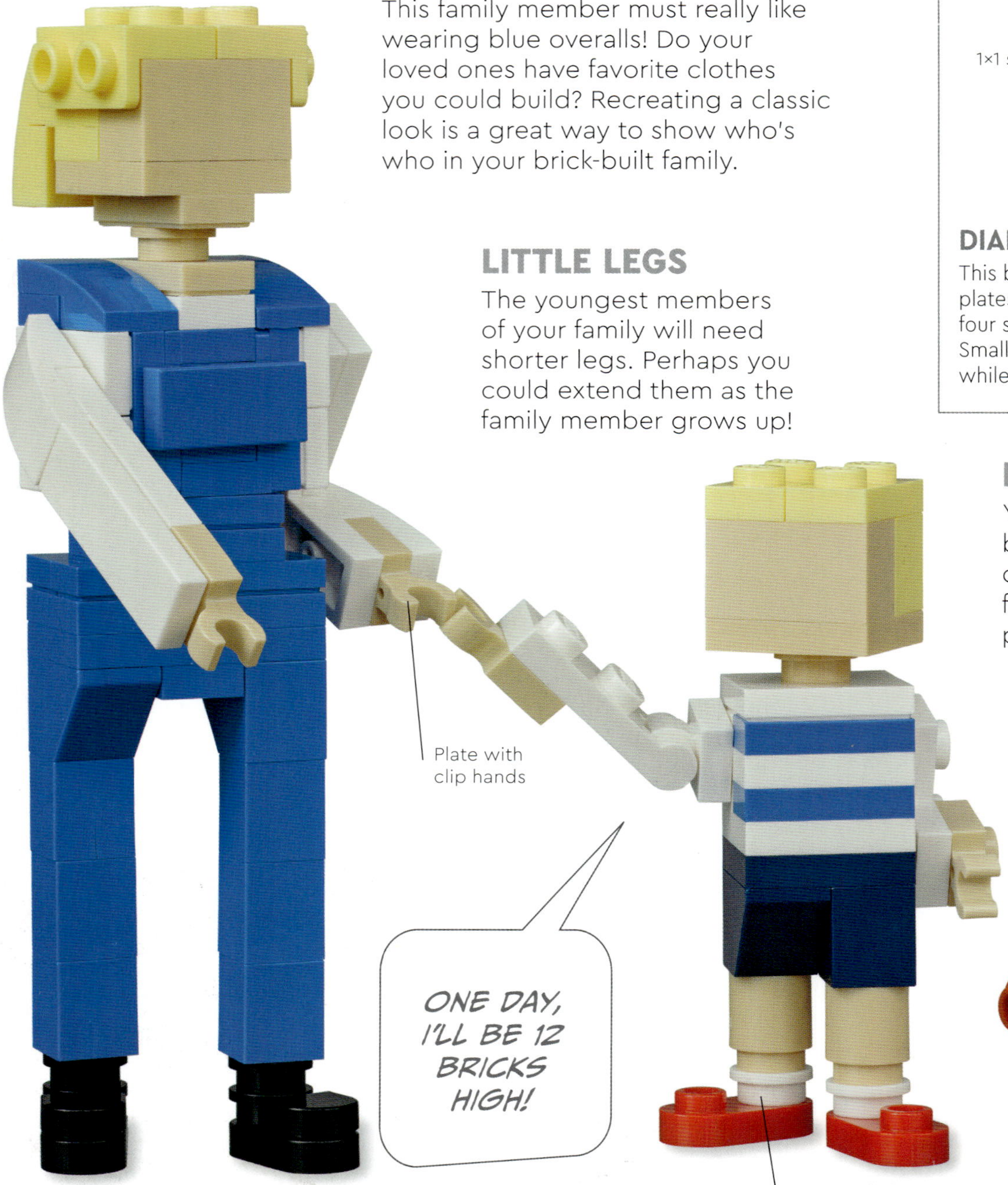
Plate with clip hands
ONE DAY, I'LL BE 12 BRICKS HIGH!
1×1 round plates become white ankle socks

BOUNCING BABY

You don't need many pieces to build an adorable baby to coo over! Round pieces are perfect for soft arms, while a flower piece makes a good pacifier.

Pacifier is a flower plate on a jumper plate
Rounded 1×2 plates make clever shoes

ACCESSORIES

The smallest details can bring lots of character to a figure to make it instantly recognizable. This person's blue hat, glasses, bow tie, and flower boutonniere are clearly inspired by someone with a real sense of style!

Bow tie is a mini doll hair accessory
A model's pose can help to convey who it depicts

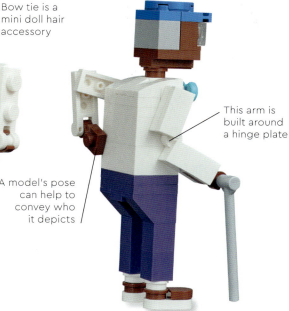

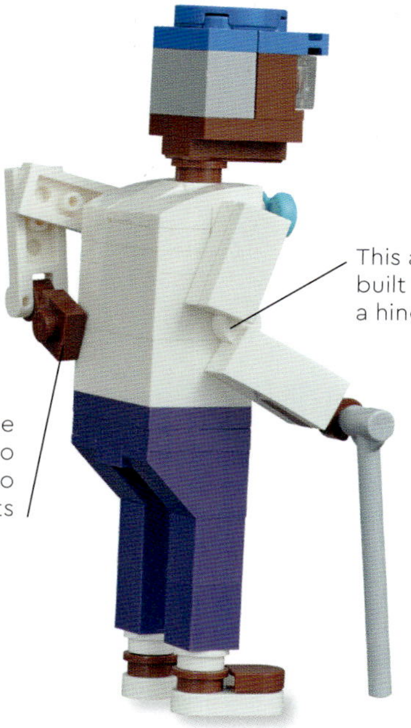
This arm is built around a hinge plate

REAR VIEW

HAIRSTYLES

Recreating hair might seem complicated, but it doesn't have to be. Just a few pieces may be all you need. Here, a sloping piece gives LEGO hair both volume and style.

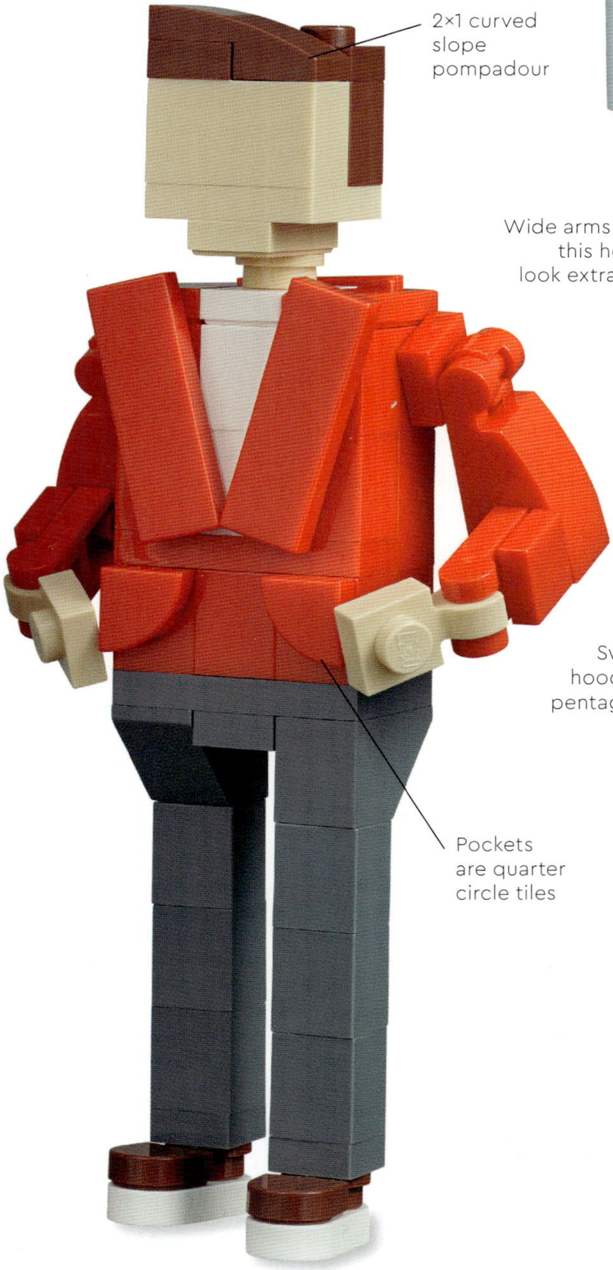
2×1 curved slope pompadour
Pockets are quarter circle tiles

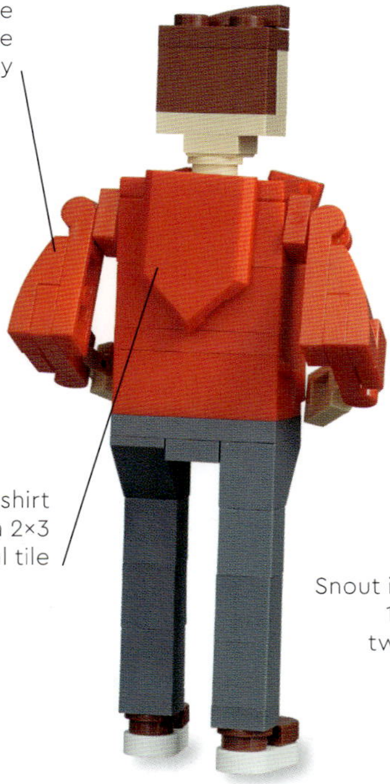
Wide arms make this hoodie look extra cozy
Sweatshirt hood is a 2×3 pentagonal tile

REAR VIEW

TRY THIS

Make a quiz for friends and family by building iconic film, TV, and game characters at this scale and seeing who can identify them fastest.

PETS

If you have pets, they're part of the family, too. From its floppy ears to its perky tail, it's hard to imagine how this dog could be any cuter in real life.

Snout is a sideways 1×1 brick with two side studs

1×2
rounded
plate

COZY NEST

The straw that makes the hen's nest is made from minifigure claw accessories. These are slotted into 1×2 rounded plates, which have hollow studs.

This cogwheel doesn't do anything, but it looks impressive!
Slide made from panel pieces to keep the egg on track
CAN I GET SOME TOAST WITH THAT, PLEASE?
Breakfast utensils attach to jumper plates on the tabletop

TRY THIS

For more invention inspiration, check out the work of classic cartoonists William Heath Robinson and Rube Goldberg in the library or online.

EGG-CELLENT WORK

For this incredible machine, the hen lays the egg, then the egg rolls away to be cracked open and cooked, before falling onto the minifigure's plate. Think about the different stages of your build and how each stage will connect with the next one.

AWESOME INVENTION

How do you like your eggs in the morning? If you like them freshly laid and perfectly cooked, this is the machine for you! Experiment with some inventions of your own that will make your life easier or more fun, and test them out with your LEGO pieces. The more complicated and zany, the better!

BUILDING BRIEF

Objective:	Build an ingenious invention
Use:	Saving time and energy
Features:	Multiple levels, cogs, chutes, levers, flaps, controls
Extras:	Hen's nest, flames, table, plate

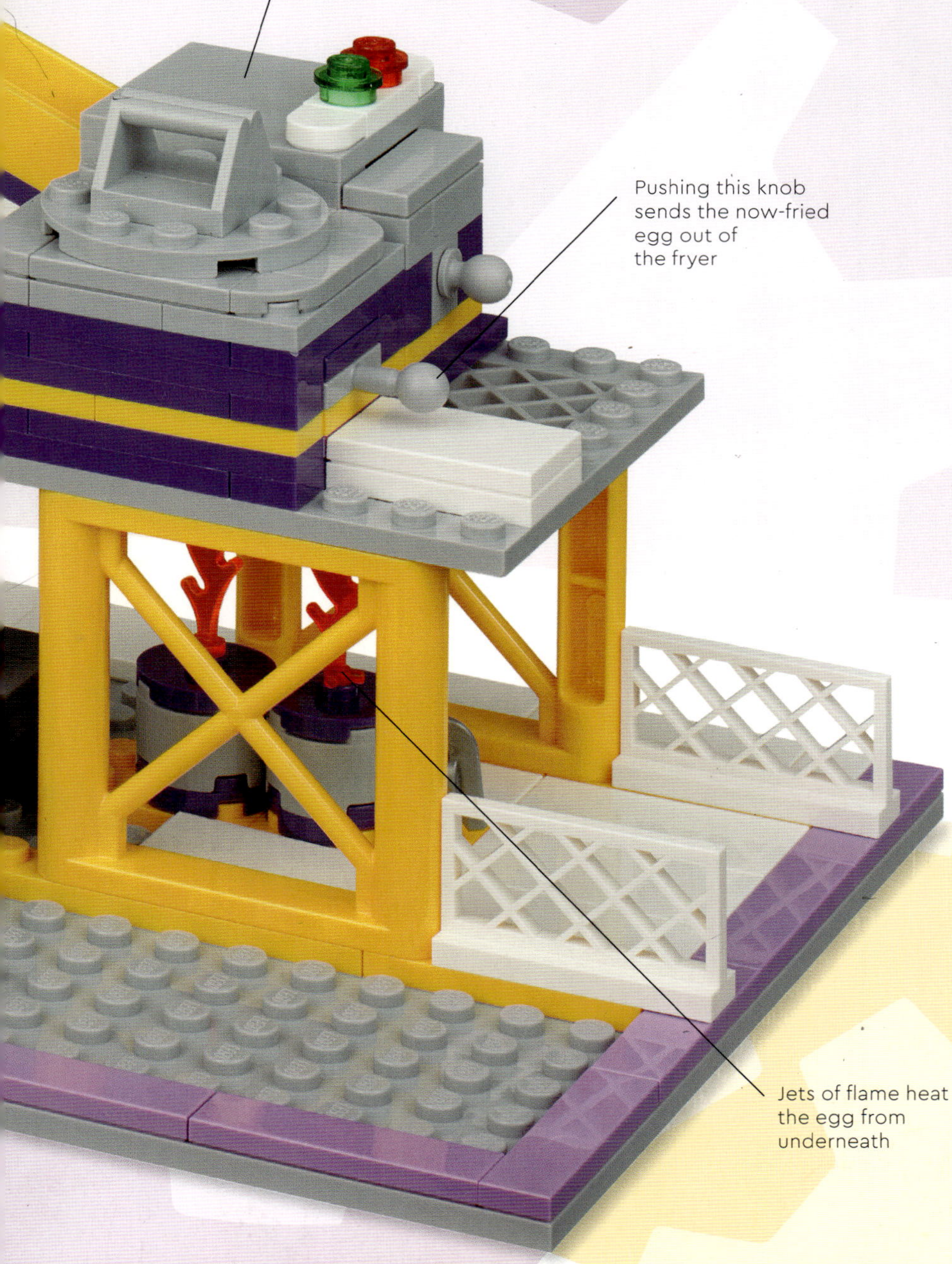

Egg arrives in this compartment for "cracking"
Pushing this knob sends the now-fried egg out of the fryer
Jets of flame heat the egg from underneath

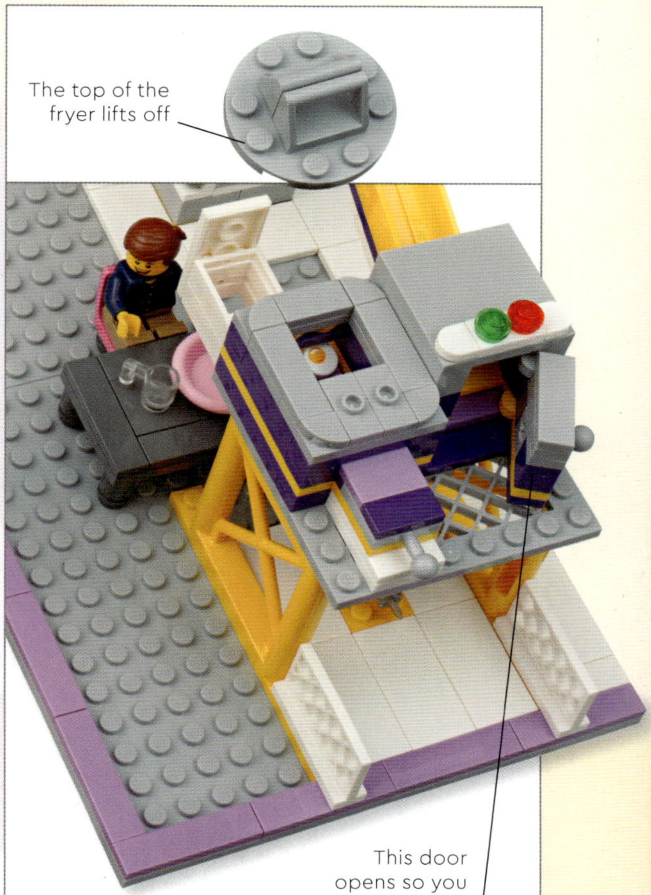

The top of the fryer lifts off
This door opens so you can retrieve the egg

SIMPLE EGG-SPLANATION

The secret to this machine is a quick switch in the cooking area! When the freshly laid egg drops into one side of the fryer, it goes no further. A fried egg tile is already waiting in the other side, ready to be pushed onto the plate.

BUILDING BRIEF

Objective: Build your dream job
Use: Career ideas, funny scenes
Features: Workplaces, equipment, creatures, vehicles
Extras: Tools, wings

DREAM JOB

Can you imagine a profession so fantastically fun that it wouldn't seem like work at all? Maybe that role already exists, or perhaps you need to invent it. Think about all the things you love to do and build your dream job in LEGO pieces.

THIS IS THE BEST TWEET-MENT.
The creature's head is built around a click hinge plate
Shiny, smooth surfaces make for a high-tech, medical look
Leaf plates are used to make the feet
Stool legs are silver cones

SUPER VET

Taking care of animals is an amazing job, but maybe a minifigure vet could specialize in dragons, unicorns, aliens, or even oversize exotic animals, like this one! Build the creatures you'd like to care for, and a place for your LEGO vet to work.

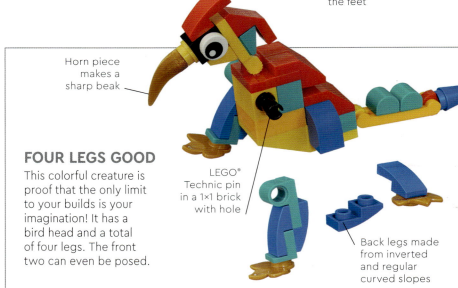

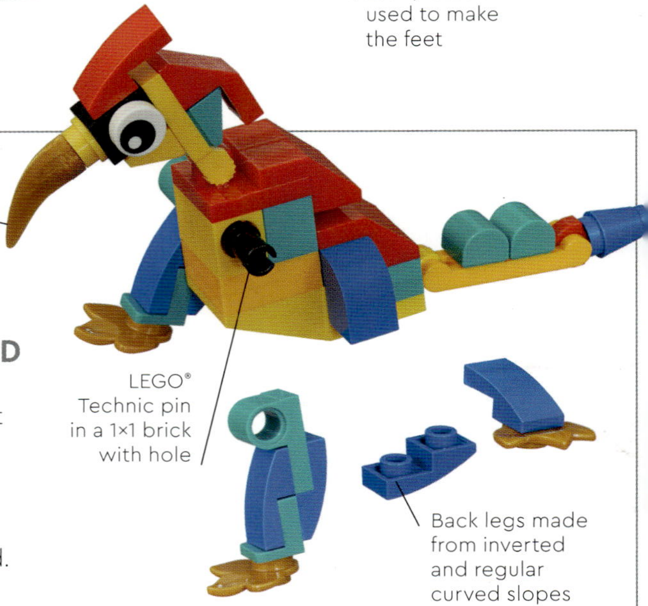
Horn piece makes a sharp beak
LEGO® Technic pin in a 1×1 brick with hole
Back legs made from inverted and regular curved slopes

FOUR LEGS GOOD

This colorful creature is proof that the only limit to your builds is your imagination! It has a bird head and a total of four legs. The front two can even be posed.

Colored tiles make fun wing tips

FRONT VIEW

THIS TRIP WILL FLY BY!

THIS IS MUCH MORE FUN THAN THE BUS!

BUILD TIP

Think about the functions you want a vehicle to have so you can decide how to attach features such as wings, wheels, or sails before you build.

FLYING TAXI DRIVER

This flying taxi has wings, not wheels. It will take your minifigures where they need to go in style, and traffic jams will be a thing of the past! Can you think of other ways to change existing jobs to make them better or more fun?

Passengers get plenty of room—and a great view

The front still looks like a car rather than a plane

Windshield keeps flies out of the happy pilot's teeth!

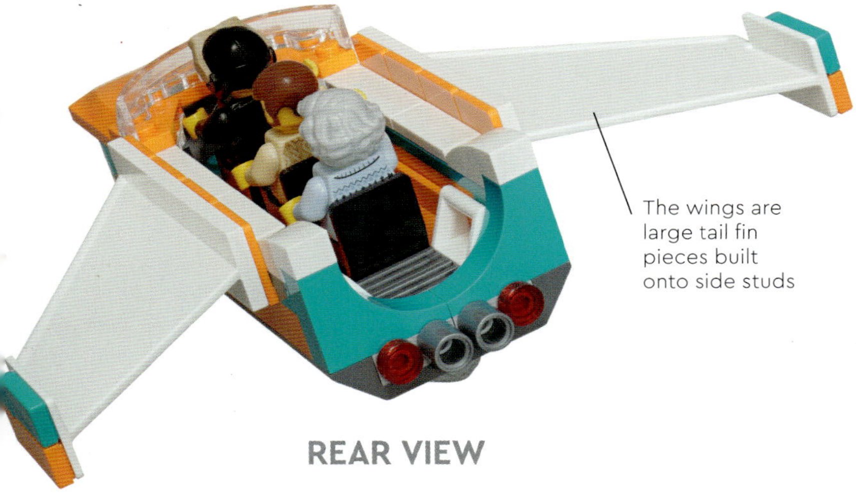

The wings are large tail fin pieces built onto side studs

REAR VIEW

WINGING IT

The gray base of this build is made from parts usually used to make boat hulls and helicopter fuselages. The large wing pieces fit onto bracket plates with side studs, built securely into the sides of the craft.

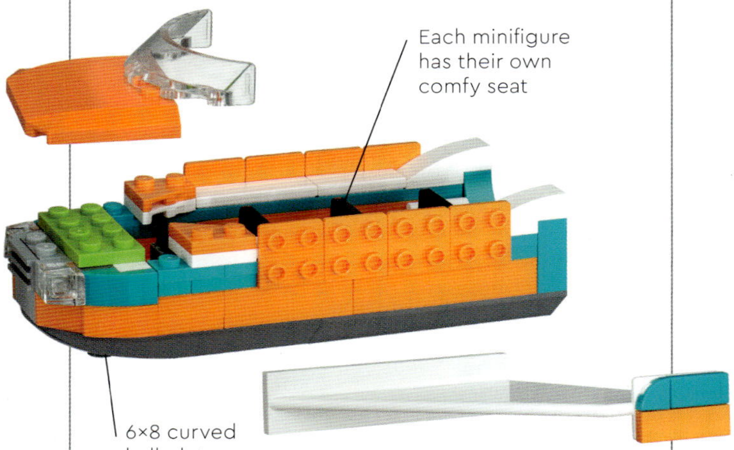

Each minifigure has their own comfy seat

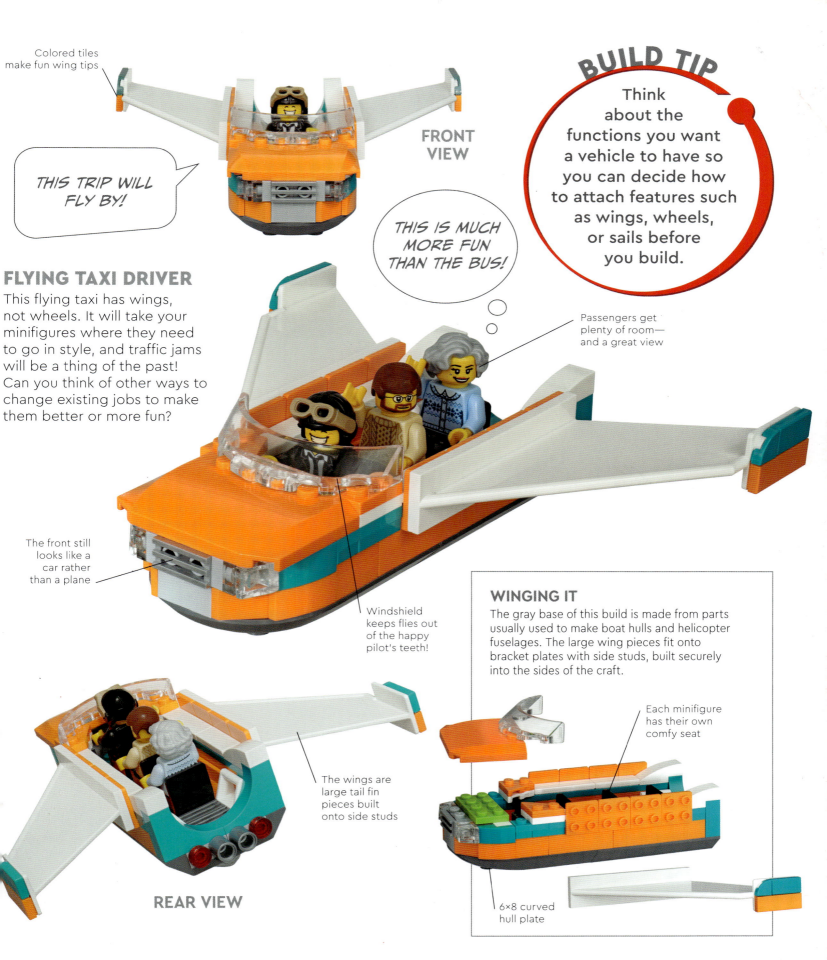

6×8 curved hull plate

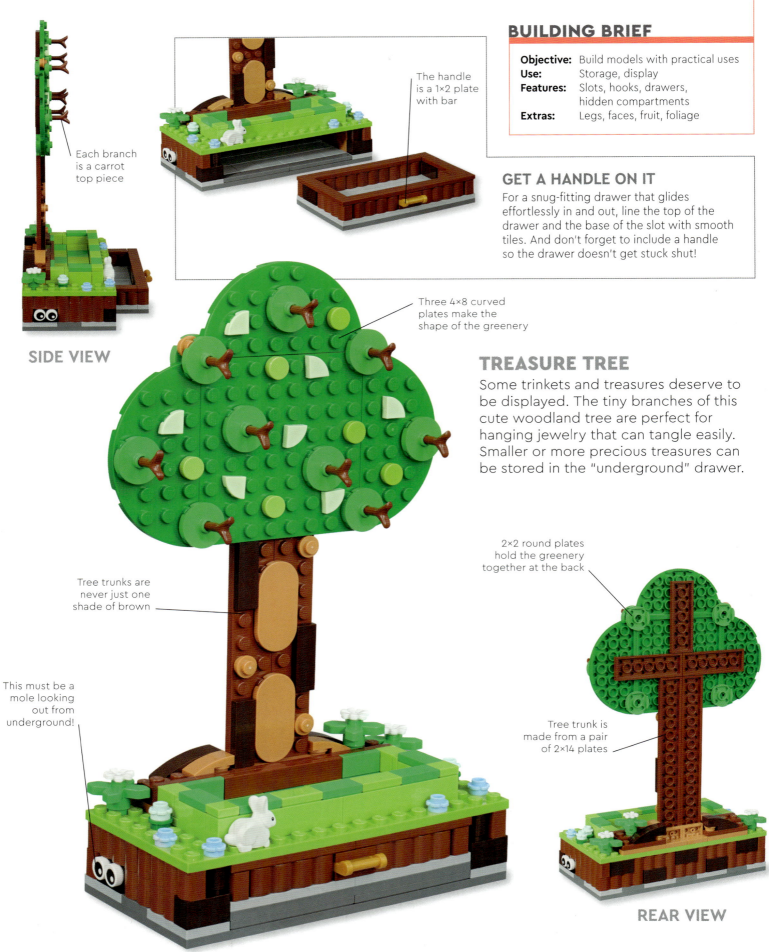

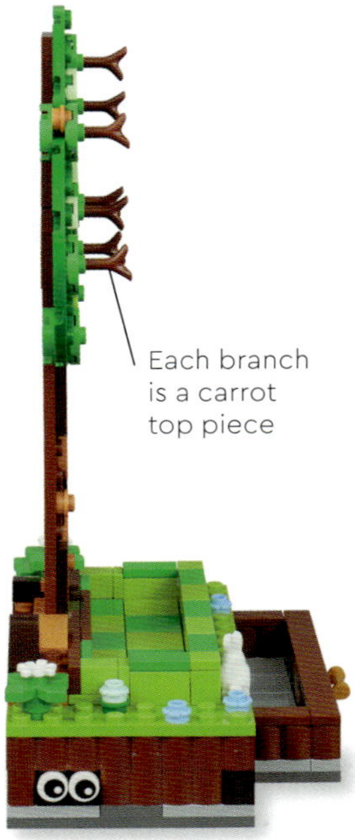
Each branch is a carrot top piece

SIDE VIEW

The handle is a 1×2 plate with bar

BUILDING BRIEF

Objective: Build models with practical uses
Use: Storage, display
Features: Slots, hooks, drawers, hidden compartments
Extras: Legs, faces, fruit, foliage

GET A HANDLE ON IT

For a snug-fitting drawer that glides effortlessly in and out, line the top of the drawer and the base of the slot with smooth tiles. And don't forget to include a handle so the drawer doesn't get stuck shut!

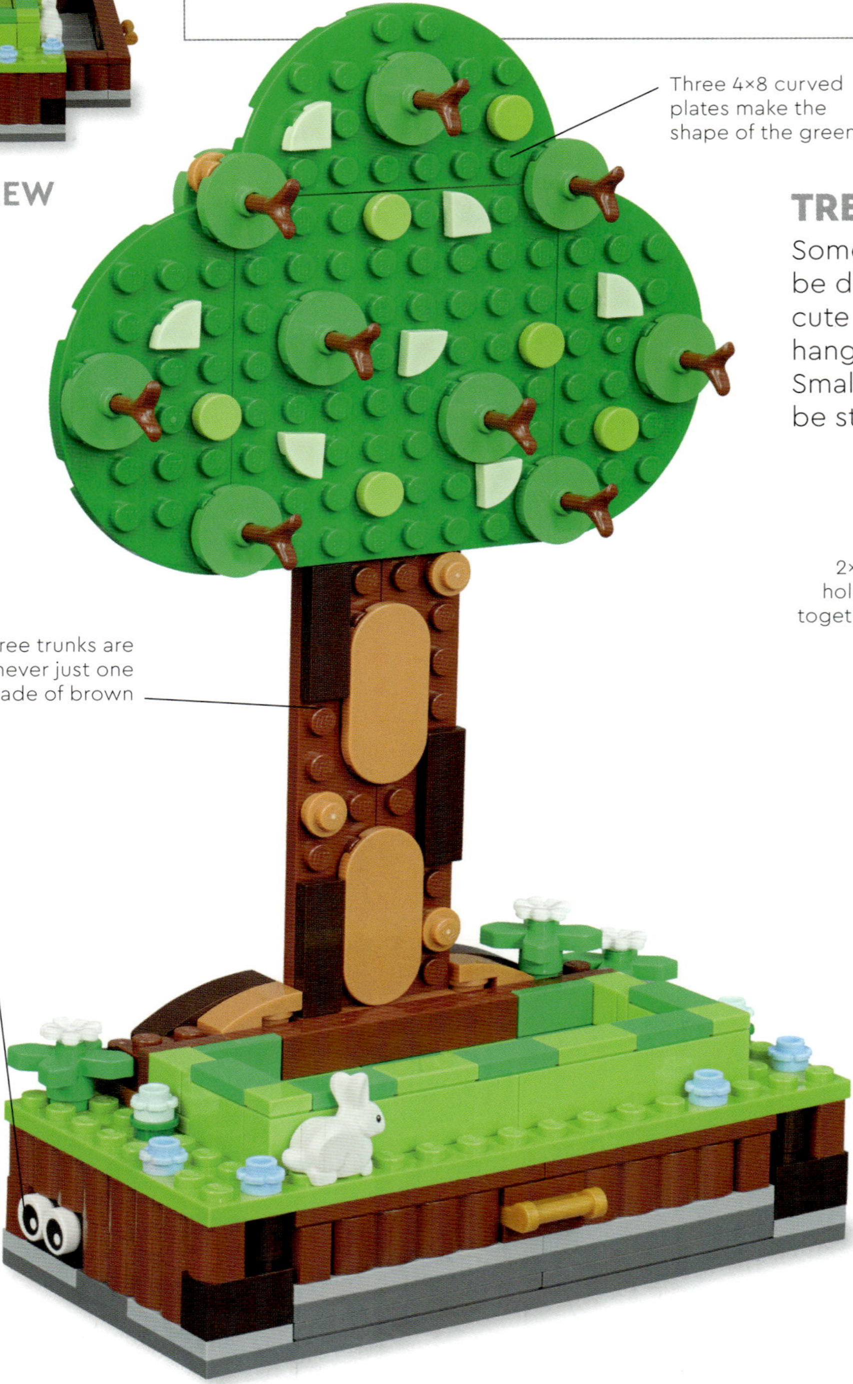
Three 4×8 curved plates make the shape of the greenery
Tree trunks are never just one shade of brown
This must be a mole looking out from underground!

TREASURE TREE

Some trinkets and treasures deserve to be displayed. The tiny branches of this cute woodland tree are perfect for hanging jewelry that can tangle easily. Smaller or more precious treasures can be stored in the "underground" drawer.

2×2 round plates hold the greenery together at the back
Tree trunk is made from a pair of 2×14 plates

REAR VIEW

TREASURE STORAGE

Do you have somewhere special to keep coins and other treasures? Create models for storing and displaying your most prized and petite possessions. These build ideas have a nature theme. You might choose to theme yours around monsters, rainbows, sea life—whatever inspires you!

TRY THIS

For your most precious items, why not build a model with a secret compartment? Ideally, it shouldn't look like it has any kind of opening at all!

BAA BAA BANK

Build a money bank for saving your pennies. Be sure to include a slot to slide your money through. When you've filled your bank, remove one of the sides to retrieve your coins. Or build a bigger bank and keep saving! You could also use this bank to store special stickers or notes.

FRONT VIEW

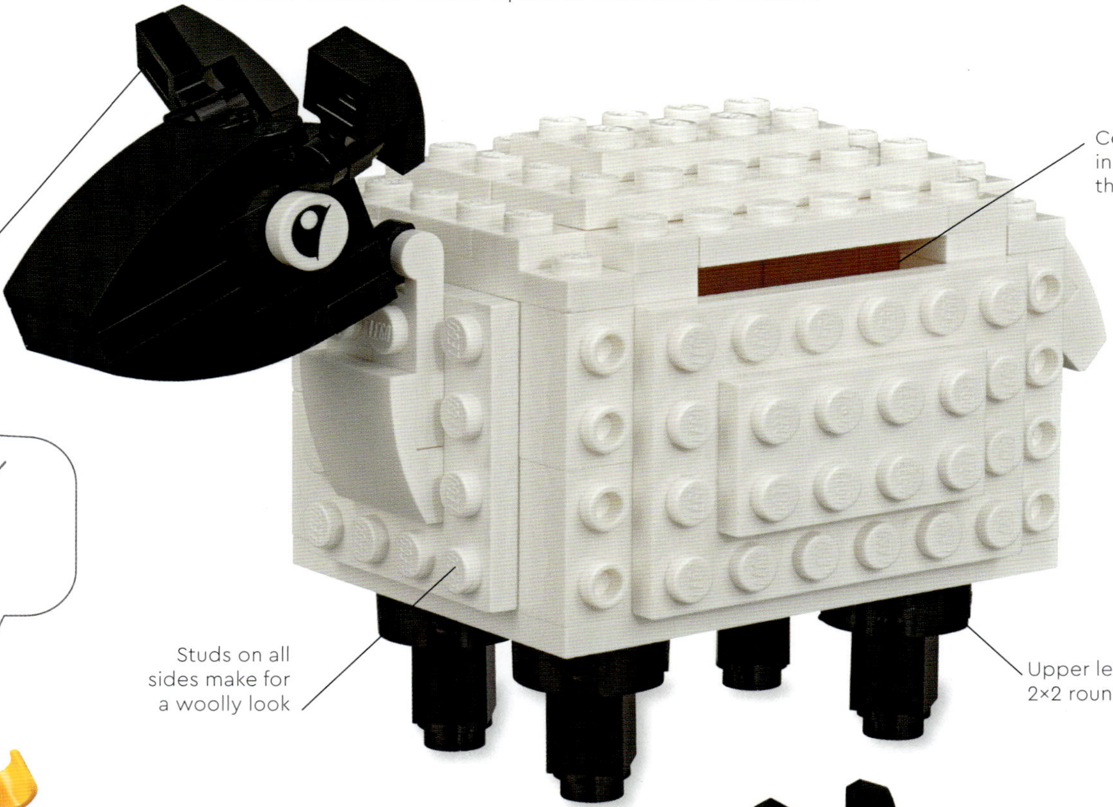

Angled ears are built using clips and bars
Coins go in through this slot
Studs on all sides make for a woolly look
Upper legs are 2×2 round plates

THAT'S WAY TOO CUTE TO BREAK INTO!

SHEEP SHAPE

The plates on each side are built onto walls of bricks with side studs. One wall is built with a large gap to create a slot for coins, and a way to get them out again by removing the plates.

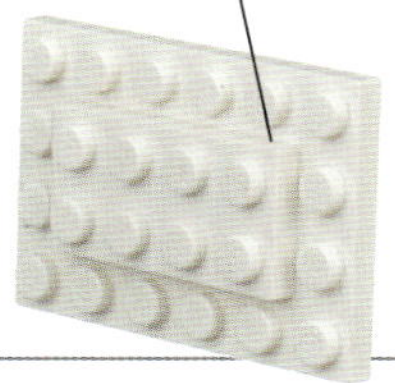

Removable side is a 2×4 plate on a 4×6 plate

DESK DECOR

Add some wow to your workspace with some colorful and functional LEGO models. You could build something to keep your stationery neat and tidy, or a beautiful ornament to bring you joy. You could even create a LEGO picture to complete your desk makeover.

BUILDING BRIEF

Objective:	Build useful models for your workspace or bedroom
Use:	Decoration, storage
Features:	Compartments, bright colors
Extras:	Windows, doors, flowers

HOW BEE-UTIFUL!

FLOWER HEAD

FLOWER VASE

Living plants and flowers need watering regularly, but LEGO flowers are very low maintenance! Try building a vase then fill it with LEGO versions of your favorite blooms. This would also make a great gift.

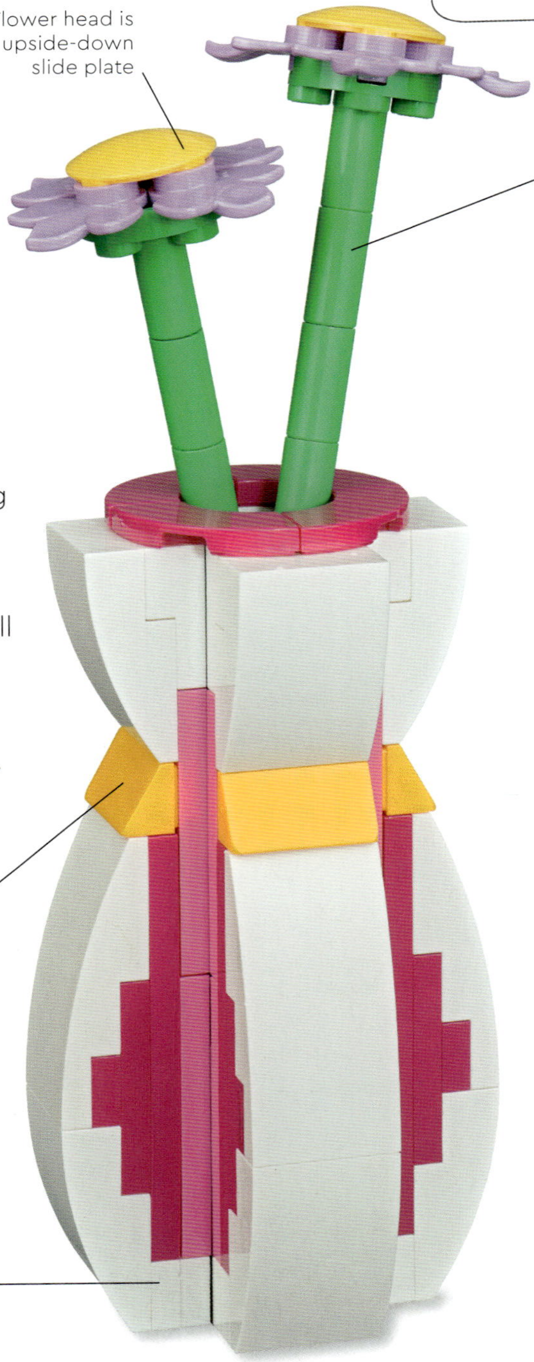
Flower head is an upside-down slide plate
The stems are stacked candle elements
Four sideways 1×2 slopes make this yellow stripe
The flowers are not attached inside the vase

SEPARATE SIDES

All four sides of the vase are identical, and each one starts out as a flat row of plates. They stand upright when attached to a base of bricks with side studs, creating a cavity for the flower stems.

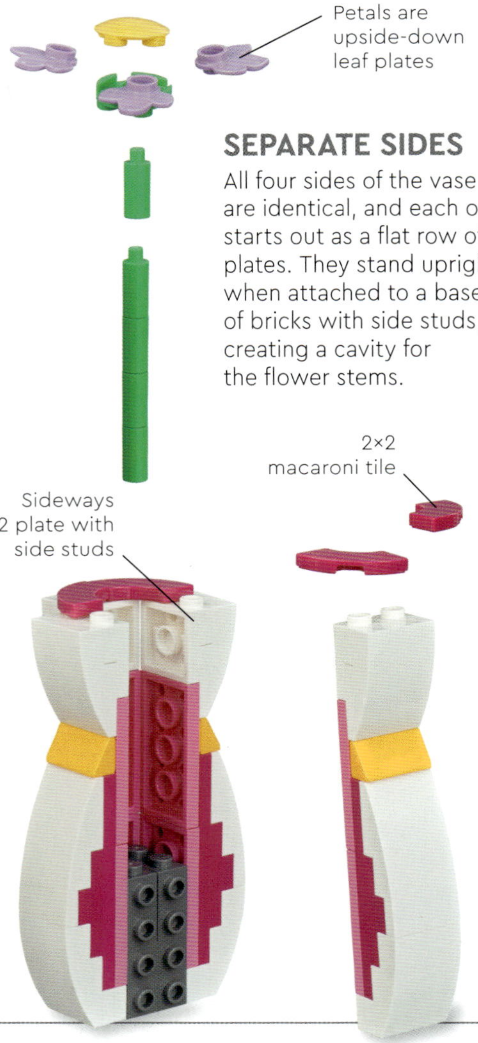
Petals are upside-down leaf plates
2×2 macaroni tile
Sideways 2×2 plate with side studs

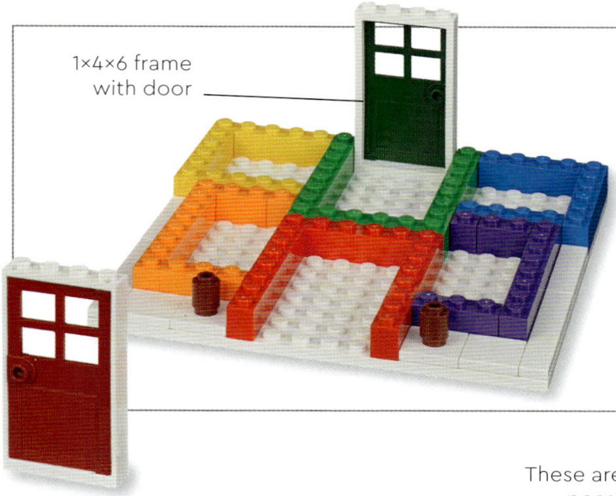
1×4×6 frame
with door

FLOOR PLAN

The base of the build is a 16×16 plate. A desk caddy with a smaller base could easily tip over when tall items are placed inside it. The doors make it easy to retrieve small items that drop into the tallest sections.

This window is
made from two
1×2×2 frames

SIDE VIEW

DESKTOP CADDY

This house-themed holder has lots of different rooms that make perfect compartments for pens, pencils, and other small items. You could build a desk caddy in the shape of a vehicle, an animal, or something awesomely abstract.

These are real
pens with
built-in
LEGO plates
Smooth tiles
give the tops a
finished look
The smaller
sections are handy
for erasers and
paper clips

CHANGE IT

Add a drawbridge, turrets, and maybe some royal residents to convert this house into a castle. You could even add a secret space for your most prized possessions.

NICE HOUSE . . . IF YOU DON'T MIND A GIANT PEN IN THE KITCHEN!

BUILDING BRIEF

Objective:	Build LEGO pets and their homes
Use:	To provide shelter, food, and fun things to do
Features:	Pet, foliage, food to eat, home comforts
Extras:	Soft furnishings, toys, unusual housemates

PET HOMES

Picture your perfect pet, then imagine its ideal place to live within your home. When building a house for a LEGO pet, you can let your imagination run wild. You don't have to build a solid structure with a roof or windows. What creature comforts does your pet need?

Greenery provides shade—or a snack!
Ears made from a plate with a clip
TIME FOR A "HOP" QUIZ. THE WINNER GETS THIS CARROT!
This rabbit's feet are made from 1×2 rounded plates

BUILD TIP

Because 1×1 rounded plates with bars have two curved corners, they can be angled to make connections outside the usual LEGO grid system.

FUNNY BUNNY

It takes just 11 pieces to build a brick bunny. Appropriately, a jumper plate makes the large back legs, with two plates attached for the big back feet. Conversely, a single plate serves as the smaller front paws.

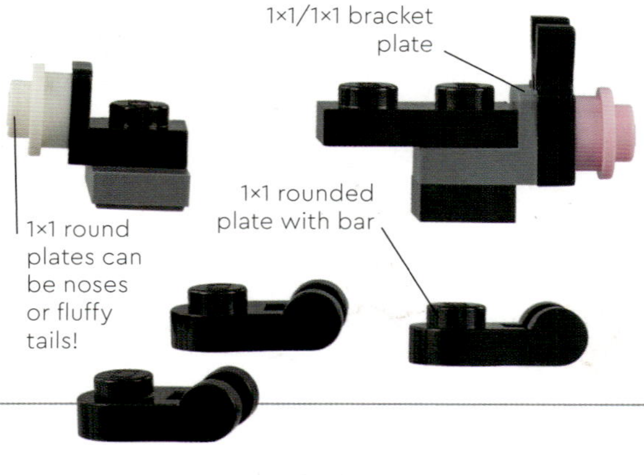

1×1/1×1 bracket plate
1×1 rounded plate with bar
1×1 round plates can be noses or fluffy tails!

BUNKING BUNNIES

These LEGO rabbits have plenty of space to hop around in this double-decker den. Experiment with building your own pet home on multiple levels, or build a long rabbit run with bunny-friendly obstacles and toys. Don't forget lots of leaves to nibble on!

Purple plate matches flower behind
Fly build clips onto the long, red tongue

LEAF ME ALONE

This chameleon cleverly blends right in with its leafy home. Add a twig for it to perch on and a fly for lunch, and this chameleon is sitting pretty! Can you think of other pets that camouflage with their habitats?

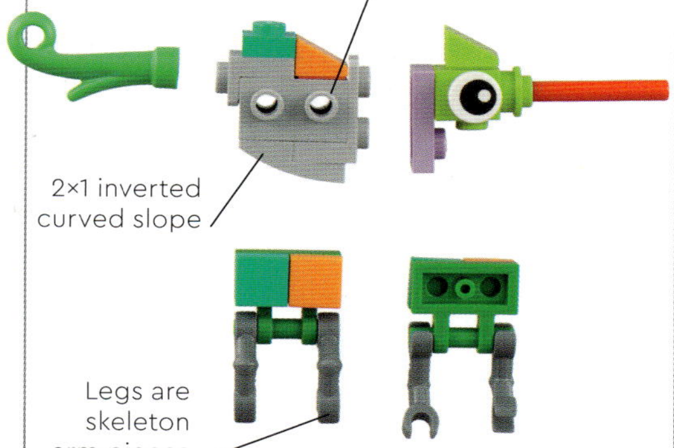
Start with a 1×2 brick with four side studs
2×1 inverted curved slope
Legs are skeleton arm pieces

ANY COLOR YOU LIKE

These shade-shifting creatures are masters of disguise. If you choose the colors for your chameleon based on the background you build behind it, it should be almost invisible.

ARE YOU HUNGRY? TAKE MY HOT DOG!

1×4×1⅓ curved slope backrest
This flower petal piece makes an ornate lampshade base

SNAPPY HOME

It takes a brave minifigure to have a pet crocodile and an even braver one to keep it in their own home! This croc seems comfortable on that soft-looking rug, or is it just waiting to pounce?

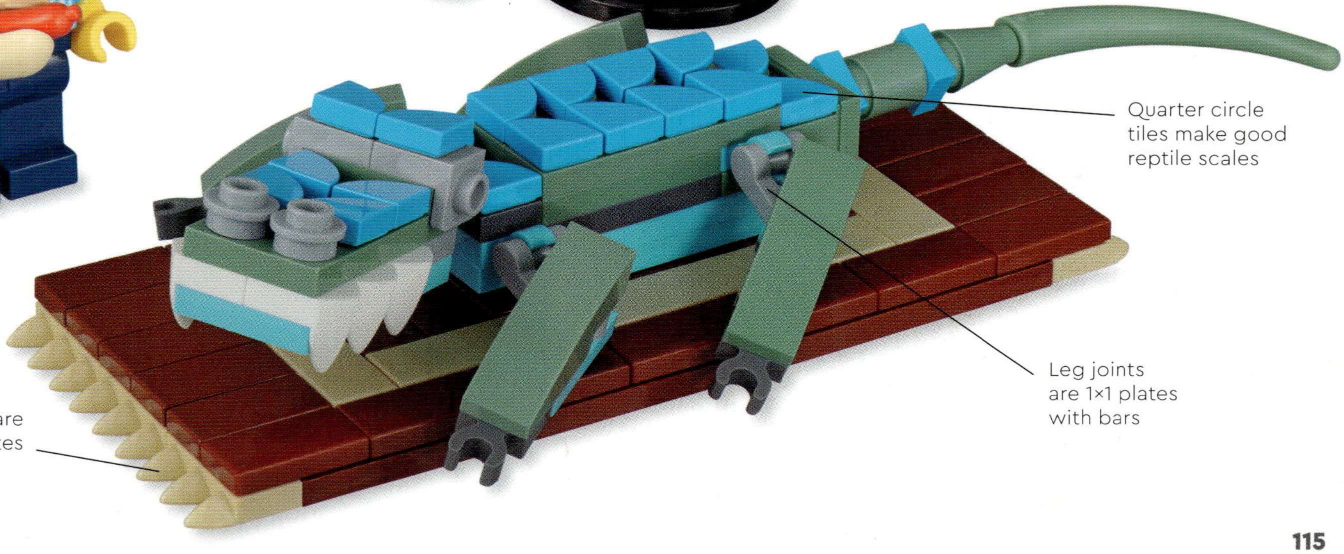
Quarter circle tiles make good reptile scales
Leg joints are 1×1 plates with bars
Rug tassels are tooth plates

GAMES

Have you played the board games you have hundreds of times by now? If so, maybe it's time for something different. You could build LEGO versions of classic games, or invent new ones of your own. Organize a game-building and playing session with friends and make a trophy for the winner!

BUILDING BRIEF

Objective: Build a game
Use: Having fun with your family and friends
Features: Boards, counters, spinners
Extras: 3-D elements, timer, dice, trophy

LEVEL UP

Unlike other board games, LEGO games don't need to fit inside a box! You can make yours as big and as challenging as you like.

COUNTER

You could use a standard die for your games, but this LEGO spinner is way more fun. Spin it to find out how many spaces you can move.

Numbers are made from a range of tile shapes

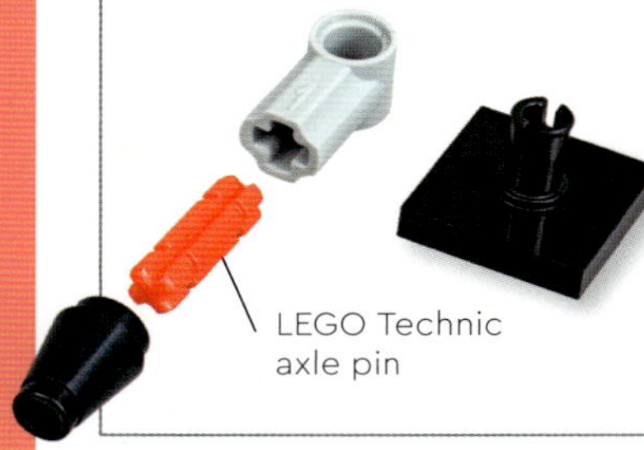

LEGO Technic axle pin

IN A SPIN

The spinner is built onto a 2×2 tile with a pin using a LEGO Technic connector.

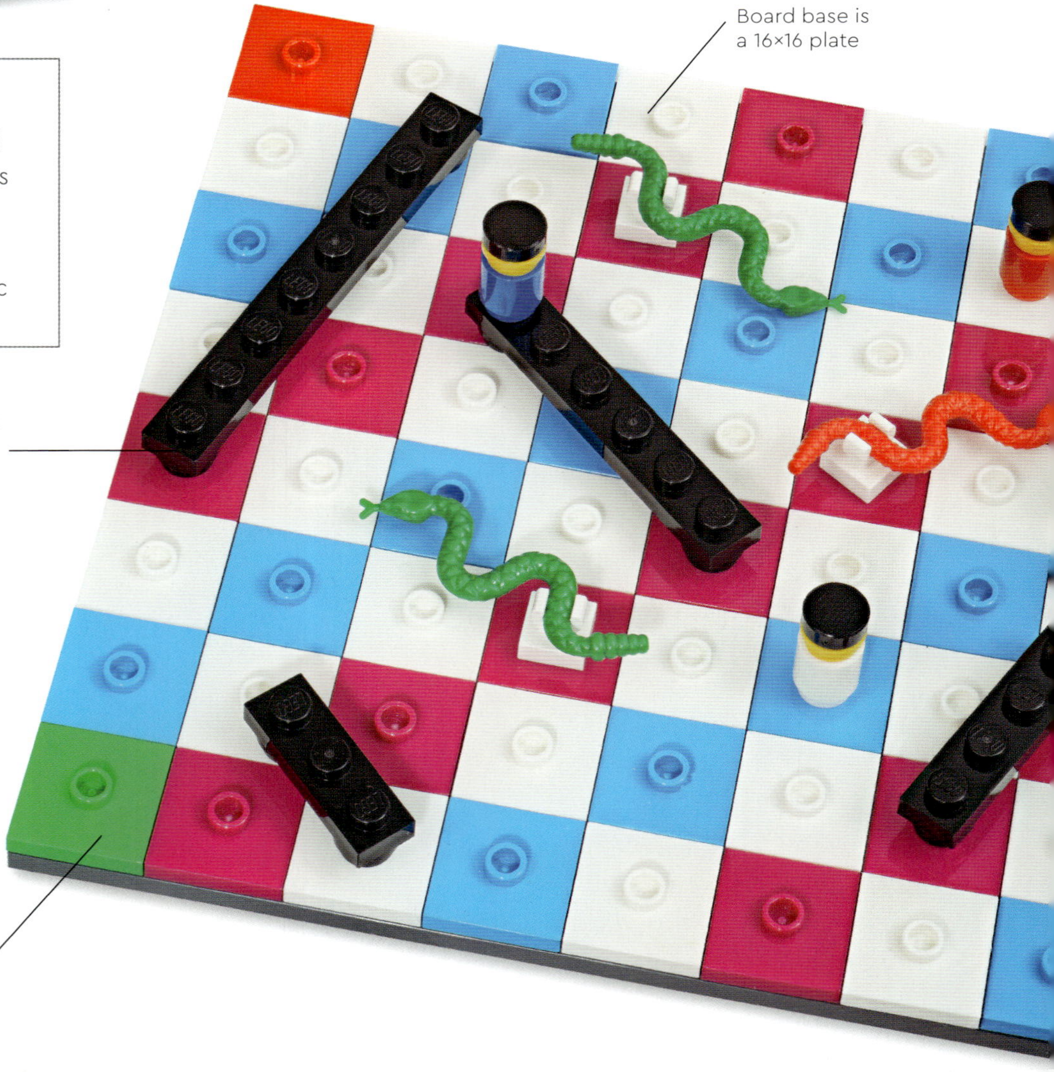

Board base is a 16×16 plate

Each ladder is attached to just one round plate

Green marks the starting point

SNAKES AND LADDERS

Adding long plates and some snakes to this checkered board turns it into a family favorite. Jumper plates are ideal for making a game board like this as they have one stud in the middle to place your pieces on.

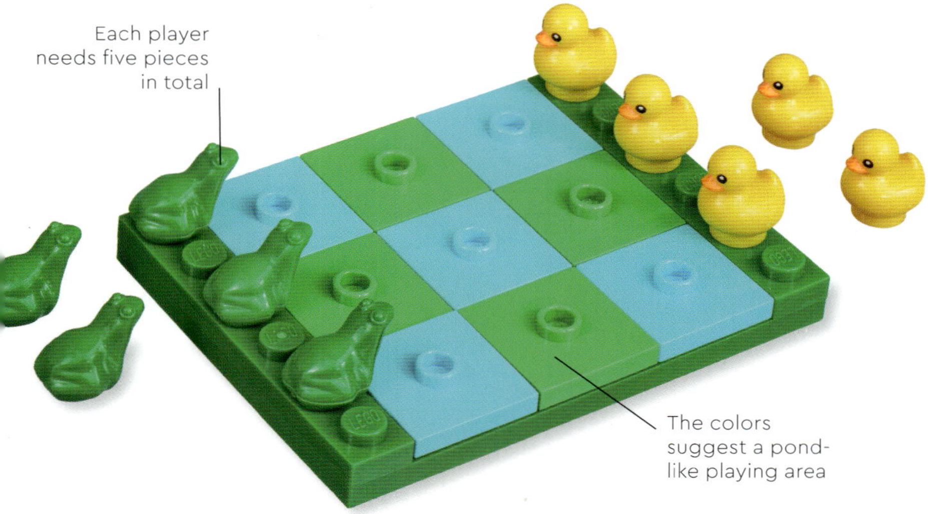
Each player needs five pieces in total
The colors suggest a pond-like playing area

THREE IN A ROW

The object of this game is to get three ducks or frogs in a row. It's an adorable version of tic-tac-toe. Do you have any other small animals or accessories you could use? Its small size makes it ideal to travel with.

2×2 tiles top both parts
2×8 base plate

MAKING SHAPES

Each stack attack shape is made from bricks sandwiched between plates and tiles. This cross shape is made in two parts that slot together. The bottom part has a 2×8 base plate, and the top shape is built around a 2×8 brick.

The middle layer is usually a brick
Shapes can be turned in any direction

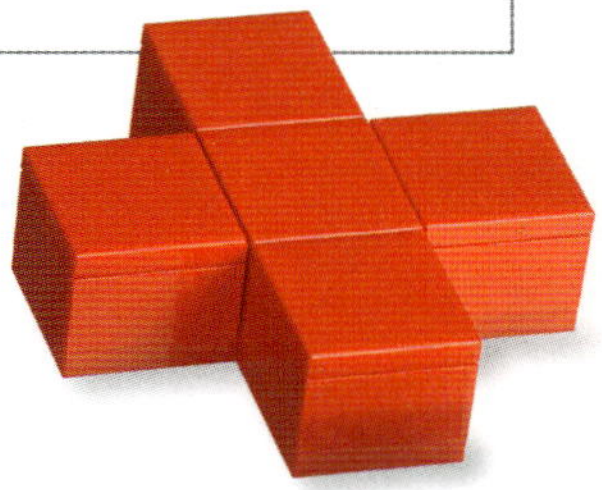

STACK ATTACK

Use bricks, plates, and tiles to make LEGO blocks in all shapes and sizes. Then start stacking them up, taking it in turns to add to the stack. If you make the stack fall over, you're out! If you add a time limit, it will test how well you can build under pressure.

BUILDING BRIEF

Objective: Build LEGO lunch ideas
Use: Display (do not eat!)
Features: Lunchbox, carrot, egg, yellow peppers, salad, tomatoes
Extras: Side dishes, condiments

BENTO LUNCHBOX

If you don't feel like chopping, slicing, and cooking with real food, you can experiment with creating a LEGO lunch to display instead. You could build your favorite meal, or experiment with some unusual food combinations. It's much less messy, but it's a shame that you can't actually eat it!

DUCK SALAD

This Japanese bento-inspired lunchbox not only looks tasty (and nutritious) but it's also a quacking piece of art. Can you spot the duck egg eye and yellow pepper beak? Build a shallow bento box using base plates, bricks, and tiles, and fill it with colorful LEGO snacks.

Two 3×1 curved slopes connected to a plate make pepper slices

4×4 round plates topped with a radar dish for the eye

BUILD TIP

Plan out the size of your main "food" item before you build the lunchbox. That way, you'll know how big your box needs to be to fit your main course.

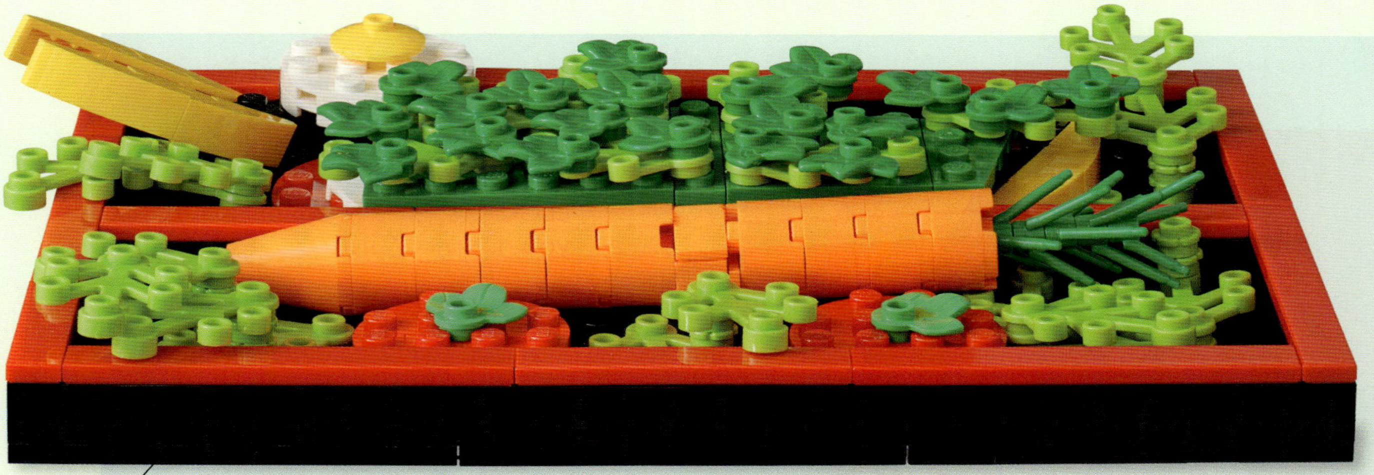

2×4 black bricks form the sides

SIDE VIEW

Stacked-up plant stems form the carrot top
Border of tiles for a smooth, authentic look

ROOTED TO THE SPOT

This carrot is mostly made from 2×2 round bricks on their sides, but right in the center of it are a plate and two headlight bricks. The 1×2 plate attaches to the base of the bento box to secure the carrot, so it doesn't roll around.

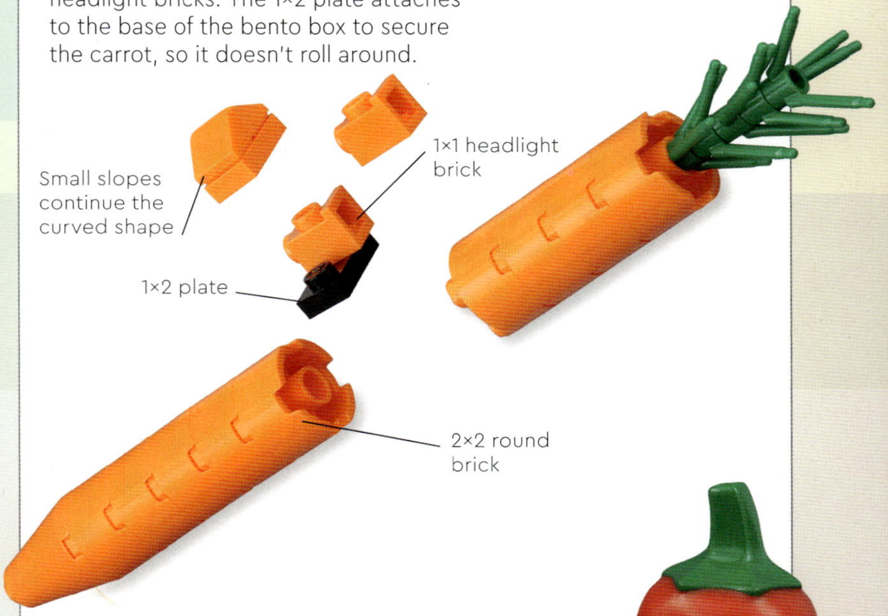

Small slopes continue the curved shape
1×1 headlight brick
1×2 plate
2×2 round brick

I LIKE MINE WITH EXTRA CHILI.

LIGHT AND BRIGHT

Build an eye-catching central feature, like this giant flower, or have a plethora of petite details. Have fun with your most colorful LEGO pieces and just build what makes you happy or fires your imagination.

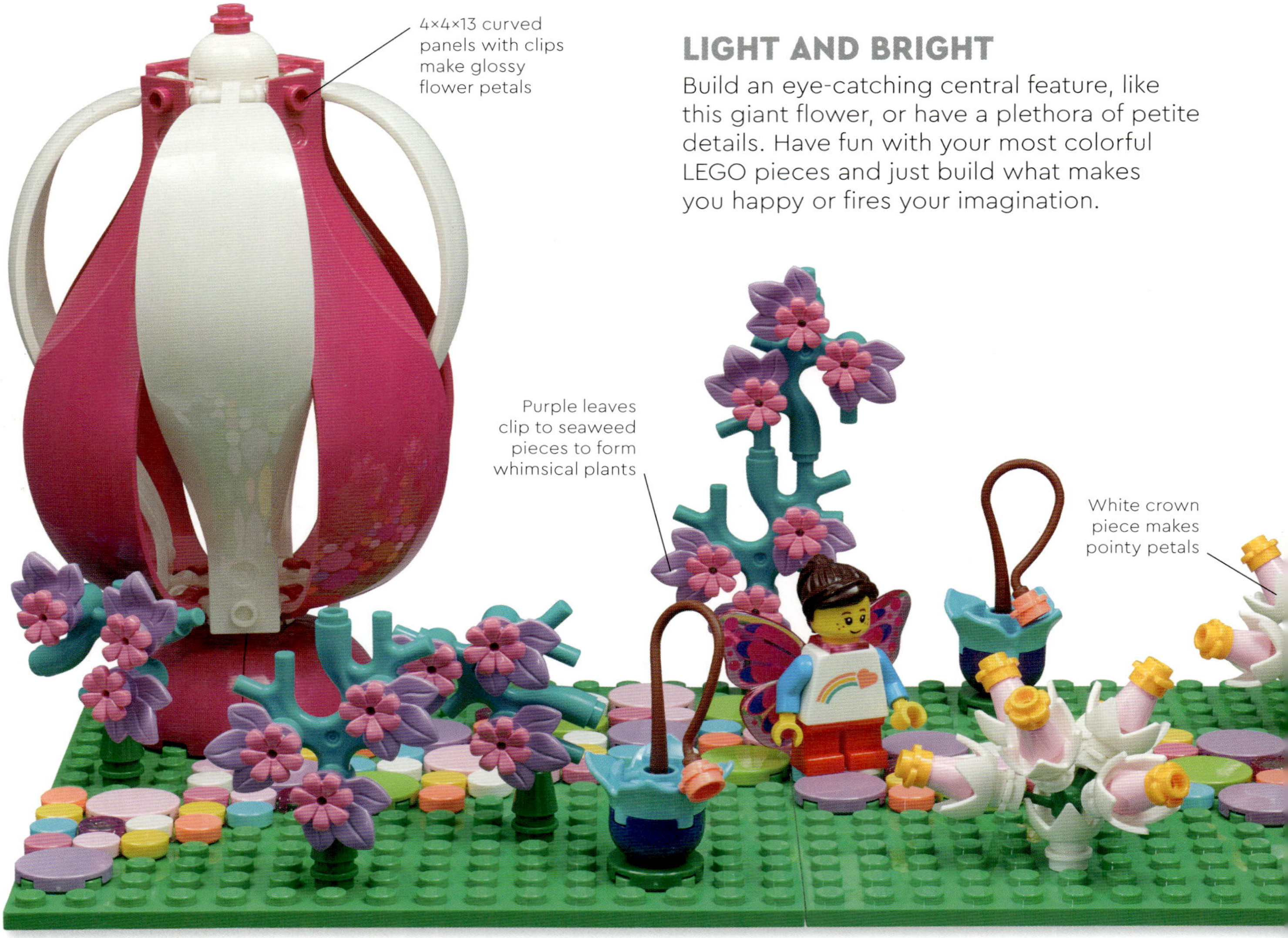

4×4×13 curved panels with clips make glossy flower petals

Purple leaves clip to seaweed pieces to form whimsical plants

White crown piece makes pointy petals

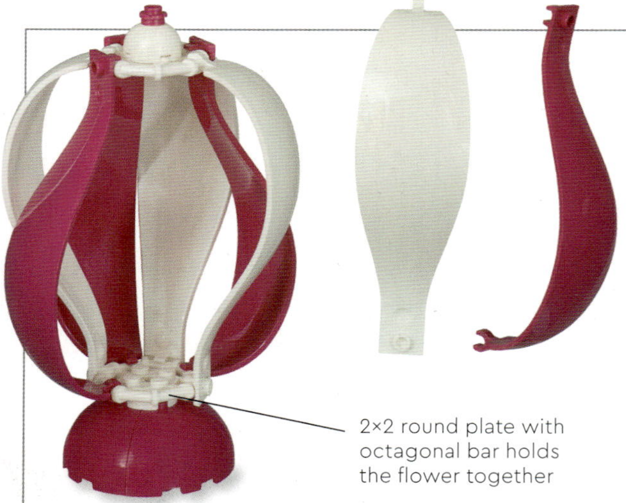

2×2 round plate with octagonal bar holds the flower together

BALLOON FLOWER

The bulb of this impressive flower is made by joining six 4×4×13 curved panels with clips to the bars of a round plate at both the top and the bottom of the build. Disconnect the plates at the top to let the flower open in full bloom.

CHANGE IT

Re-create your land with the same features but in different colors to give it a completely new feel. How would the "light and bright" land look in darker colors?

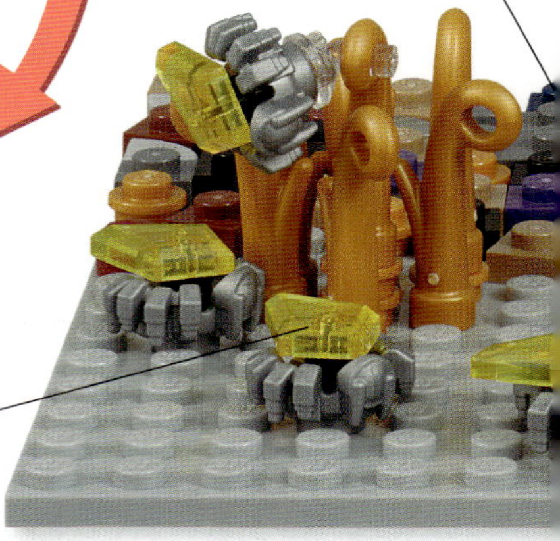

1×1 plates make a dangerous path—don't walk here!

Robot spider pieces topped with transparent tiles look like they have magical powers

FANTASY LAND

Build a make-believe land that's straight out of your imagination. This model idea shows two contrasting parts of a world—a bright and fun land, and an area that's much creepier. Go wild. There are no rules in your fantasy land, so things can be upside down, back to front, or just wonderfully weird!

BUILDING BRIEF

Objective: Build a fantasy world
Use: Anything you like!
Features: Out-of-this-world nature
Extras: Amazing creatures, jewels, rocks

BRANCH OUT

Each leaf is made by stacking a purple quarter circle tile and an orange leaf plate onto a gold flower element. Brown flower stems connect the poisonous leaves to a black 1×1 brick with side studs at the top of the trunk.

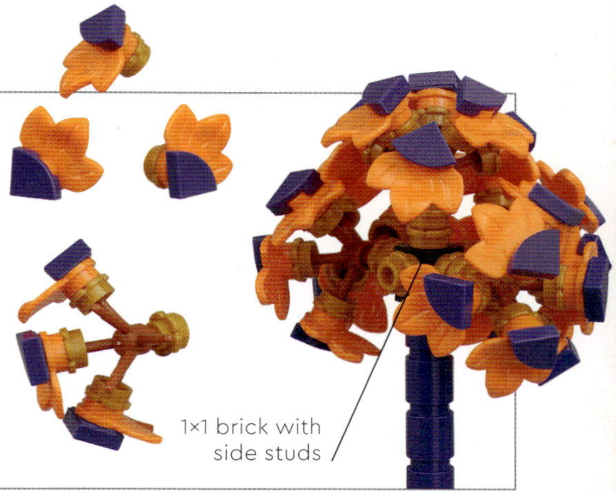
1×1 brick with side studs

DARK AND EERIE

Muted and metallic tones and spiky-shaped LEGO pieces are great if you want to create an eerie world. Build creepy critters, prickly plants, and toxic trees to set a very different mood. This could be a treasure cave or the lair of a magical creature.

WHY ARE THOSE ROCKS MOVING?
1×1 round bricks form the trunk

BUILDING BRIEF

Objective: Build your own movie set
Use: To make a minifigure movie
Features: Sets, actors, crew
Extras: Aliens, cameras, boom microphone

MAKE A MOVIE

Have you ever dreamed of being a movie director? Now's your chance! Build a LEGO movie set and shoot your own movie. What kind of movie will it be? A jolly comedy, an all-action superhero caper, or a startling science-fiction film? Build your set and all the filmmaking equipment, then assemble your minifigure cast and crew.

2×2×2 slope bricks make roof tiles
Two 1×6 plates at the back of each "house" gives them extra stability
Bar in a 1×1 cone is a camera stand

ALIEN INVASION

Movie sets use clever tricks. For exterior shots, you'll only need to build the fronts of any buildings because the interiors won't be seen. Think about ways you can make your movie look exciting with props and details. Those alien blobs look like they're multiplying!

1×1 brick with side stud

STICKY BUSINESS

Place a few bricks with side studs into the walls of the set houses so you can attach props or characters, like little alien invaders, onto them.

LEVEL UP

Get an adult's permission to film your mini movie on a camera or a smartphone. Then set up a screening in your home to show it to family and friends.

Lattice window for a cozy-looking home
Printed dome on a gear plate with teeth makes an alien
THE BLOBS ARE GETTING CLOSER!
L-shaped bar with a 1×1 round brick for a boom microphone
THE LEGO NEWS
The greatest hero ever!
IT'S A WRAP!
The legs of the director's chair are held by tiles with clips
Tiles on a 1×4 hinge plate make a clapboard

1×2 plate with bar in a 1×1 tile with clip holds the support plate at an angle

REAR VIEW

BEHIND THE SCENES

Can you assemble a minifigure who looks a bit like you? Build them a director's chair and a megaphone so they can tell the minifigure actors what to do next. Other members of the crew will need a clapboard, sound equipment, and, of course, a camera to film all the action.

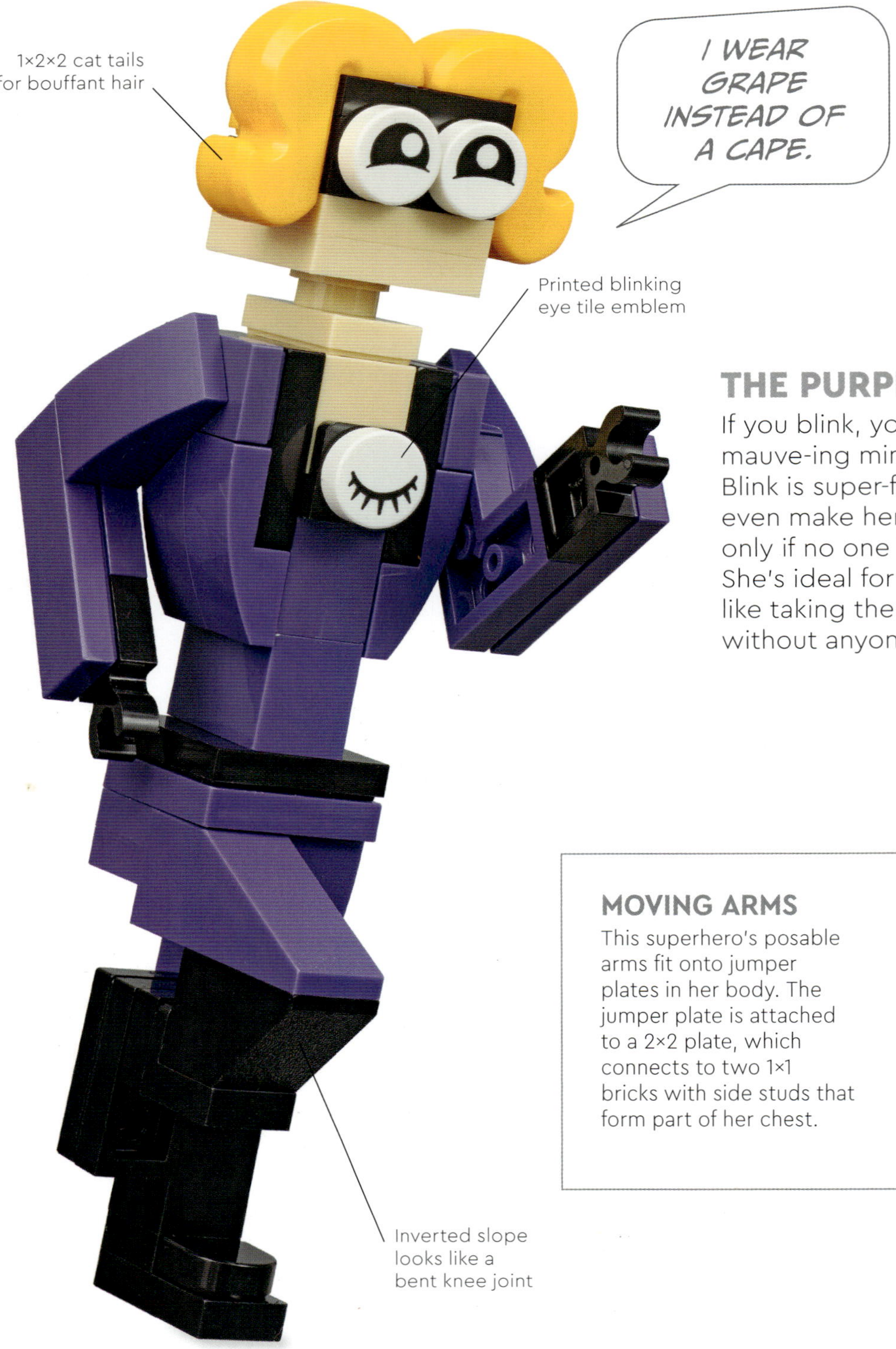
1×2×2 cat tails for bouffant hair
I WEAR GRAPE INSTEAD OF A CAPE.
Printed blinking eye tile emblem
Inverted slope looks like a bent knee joint

BUILDING BRIEF

Objective:	Build a LEGO superhero
Use:	Performing amazing feats
Features:	Suit, cape, accessories
Extras:	Vehicle, sidekick, nemesis

THE PURPLE BLINK

If you blink, you'll miss this fast mauve-ing minifigure! The Purple Blink is super-fast and she can even make herself invisible—but only if no one is looking at her. She's ideal for secret missions, like taking the last cookie without anyone noticing.

REAR VIEW

MOVING ARMS

This superhero's posable arms fit onto jumper plates in her body. The jumper plate is attached to a 2×2 plate, which connects to two 1×1 bricks with side studs that form part of her chest.

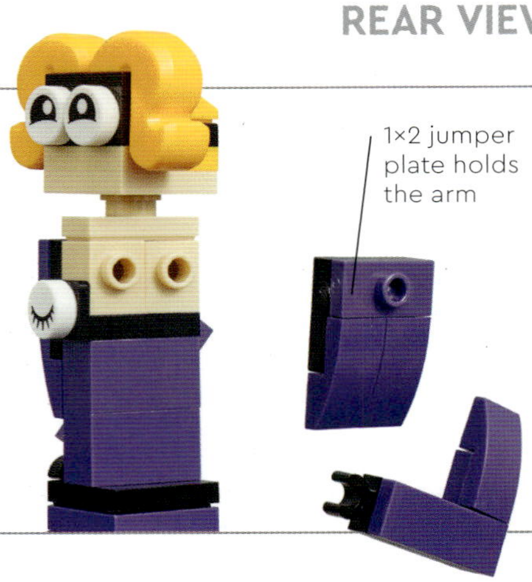
1×2 jumper plate holds the arm

SUPERHEROES

Have you ever imagined what it would be like to have superpowers? What powers would you choose? Well, until you develop your own super skills, why not build a LEGO superhero instead? Think about what powers they might have, and how they might help you in your daily life.

CHANGE IT

Do your heroes have a mean side? Think about how you could rebuild them as super villains. Would they have different superpowers?

BAT-TERRY

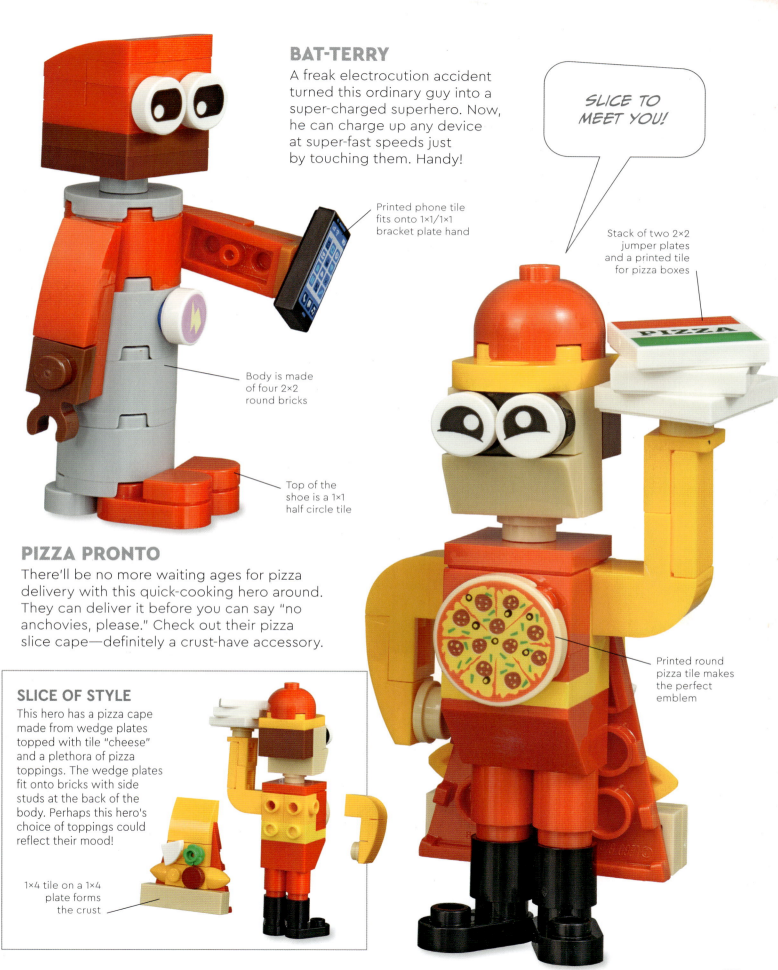

A freak electrocution accident turned this ordinary guy into a super-charged superhero. Now, he can charge up any device at super-fast speeds just by touching them. Handy!

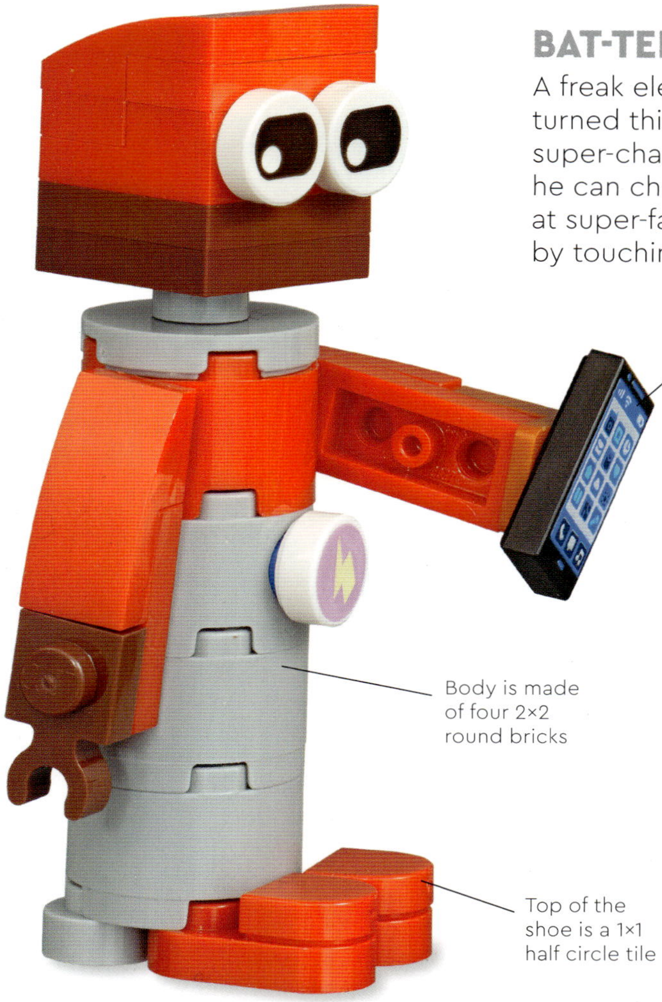

Printed phone tile fits onto 1×1/1×1 bracket plate hand

Body is made of four 2×2 round bricks

Top of the shoe is a 1×1 half circle tile

PIZZA PRONTO

There'll be no more waiting ages for pizza delivery with this quick-cooking hero around. They can deliver it before you can say "no anchovies, please." Check out their pizza slice cape—definitely a crust-have accessory.

SLICE TO MEET YOU!
PIZZA

Stack of two 2×2 jumper plates and a printed tile for pizza boxes

Printed round pizza tile makes the perfect emblem

SLICE OF STYLE

This hero has a pizza cape made from wedge plates topped with tile "cheese" and a plethora of pizza toppings. The wedge plates fit onto bricks with side studs at the back of the body. Perhaps this hero's choice of toppings could reflect their mood!

1×4 tile on a 1×4 plate forms the crust

TREASURE BOX

You can build simple LEGO boxes to store anything you like, but you need somewhere extraordinary to store your most special treasures. It could be fancy, with lots of impressive details, like this treasure box, or all about security with hidden compartments to make sure only you can find what's inside.

BUILDING BRIEF

Objective: Build a LEGO treasure box
Use: Keeping important objects safe
Features: Secret compartment, hinges, lid
Extras: Windows, gold detailing

CHANGE IT

Dress up your box for different occasions. Swap the gold pieces for pastels to celebrate spring or build a candle on the roof for your birthday.

ORNATE STORAGE

With latticed windows and ornate gold details, this looks more like a palace than a box. Lift the lid to find a small compartment. Take that out and there's a hidden section below to hide your most precious bits and pieces in.

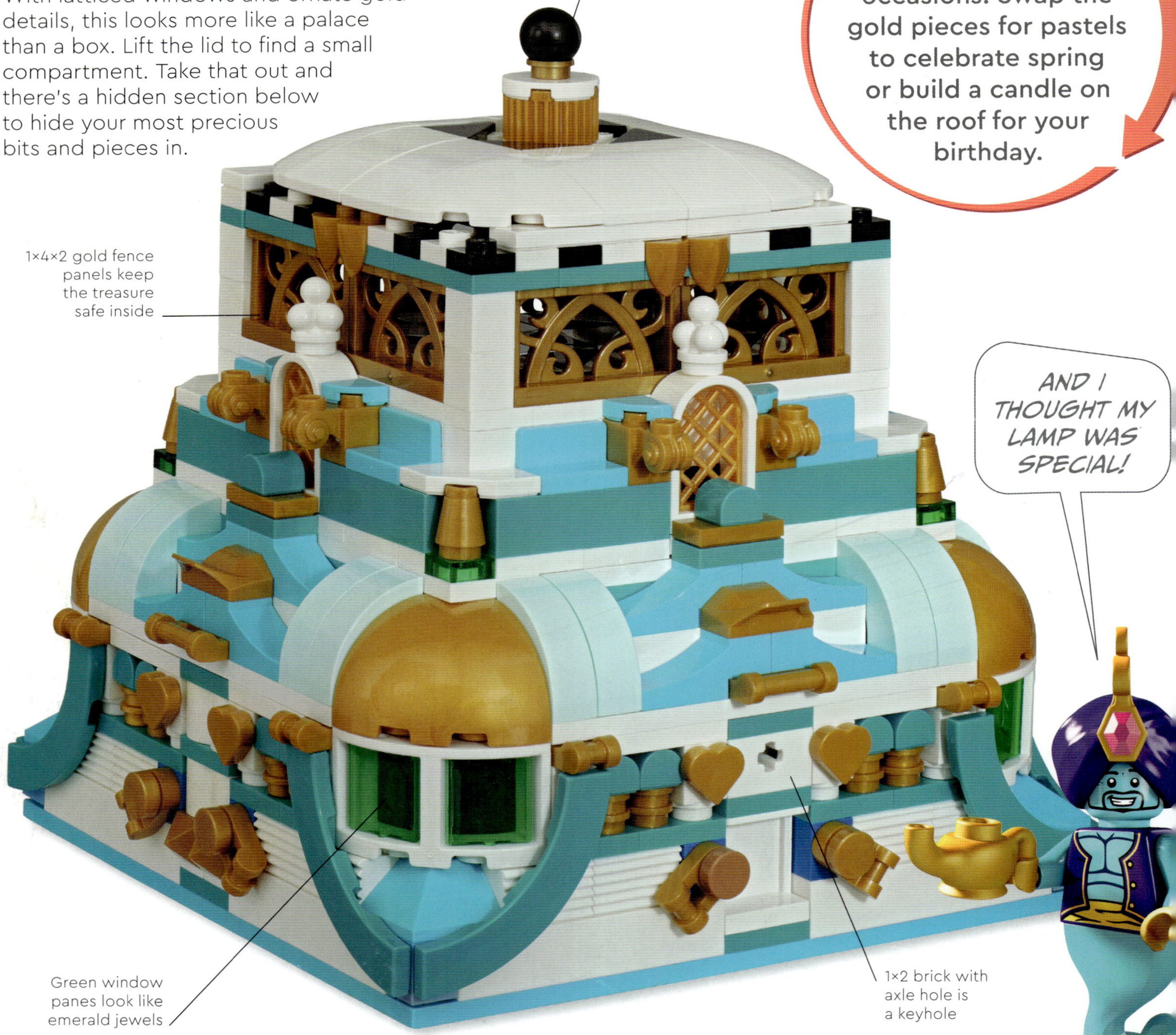
LEGO Technic ball joint crowns the top
1×4×2 gold fence panels keep the treasure safe inside
AND I THOUGHT MY LAMP WAS SPECIAL!
Green window panes look like emerald jewels
1×2 brick with axle hole is a keyhole

BUILT-IN VIEW

Give your box a palatial look and keep an eye on your treasure at the same time by adding arched windows. Arched window frames with gold lattice window panes slot between bricks in the center of each of the box's four walls.

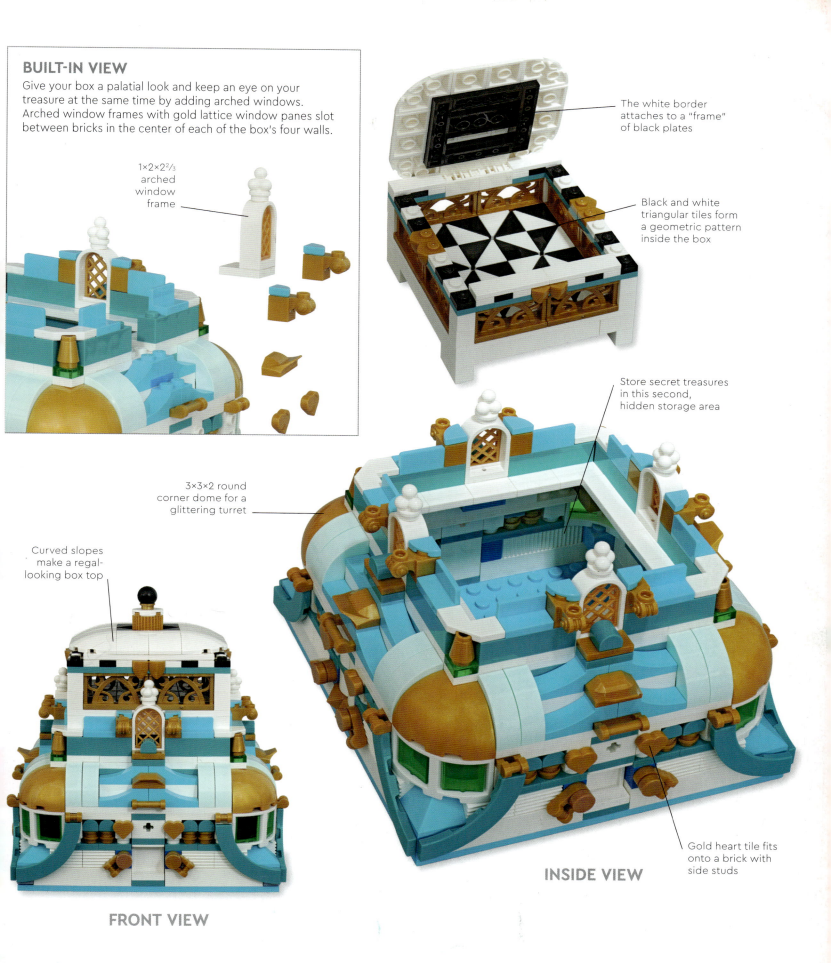

$1 \times 2 \times 2\frac{2}{3}$ arched window frame

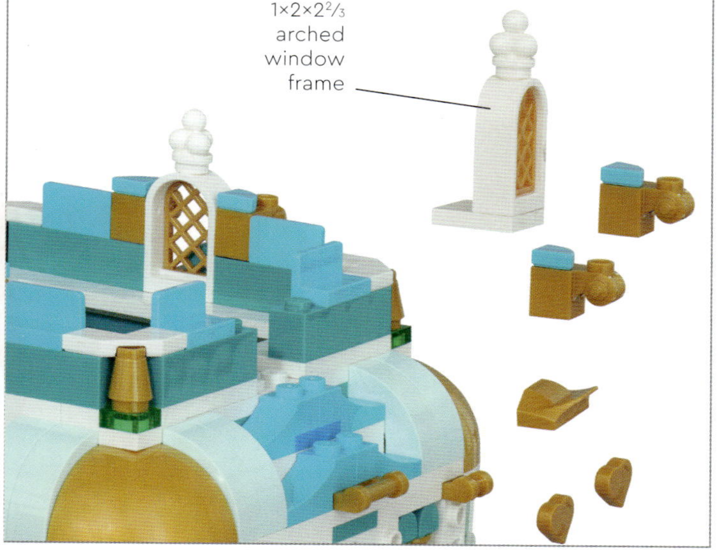

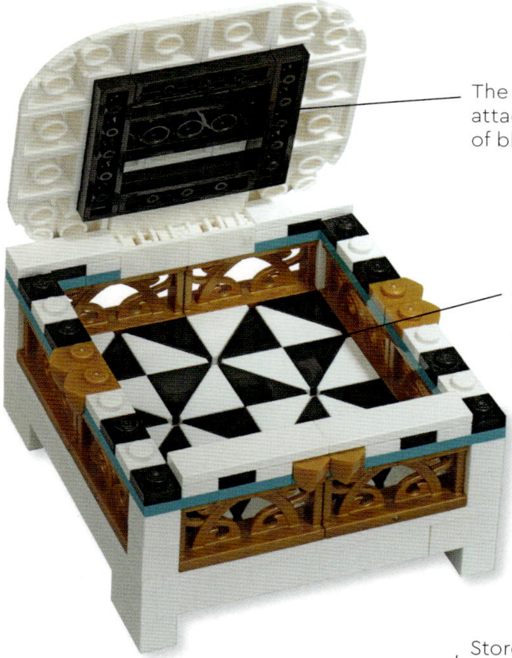

The white border attaches to a "frame" of black plates

Black and white triangular tiles form a geometric pattern inside the box

Store secret treasures in this second, hidden storage area

3×3×2 round corner dome for a glittering turret

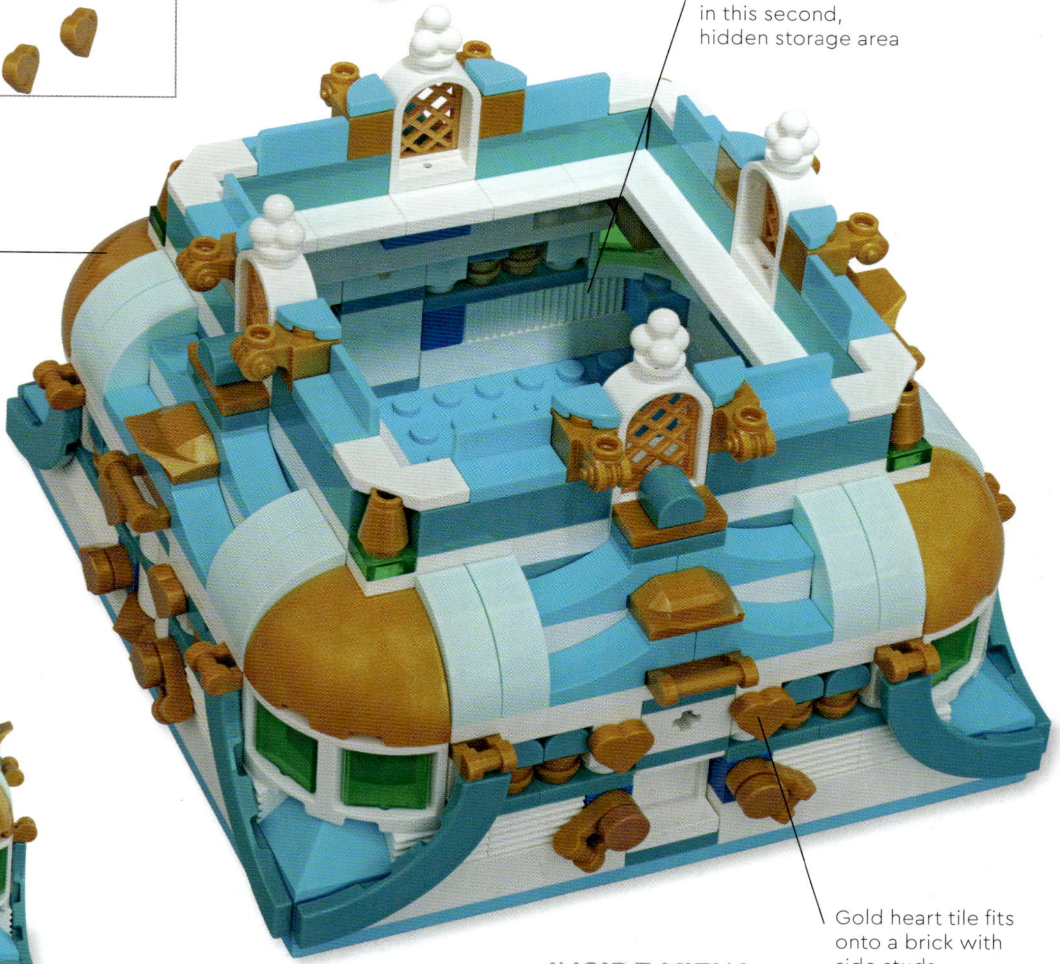

Gold heart tile fits onto a brick with side studs

INSIDE VIEW

Curved slopes make a regal-looking box top

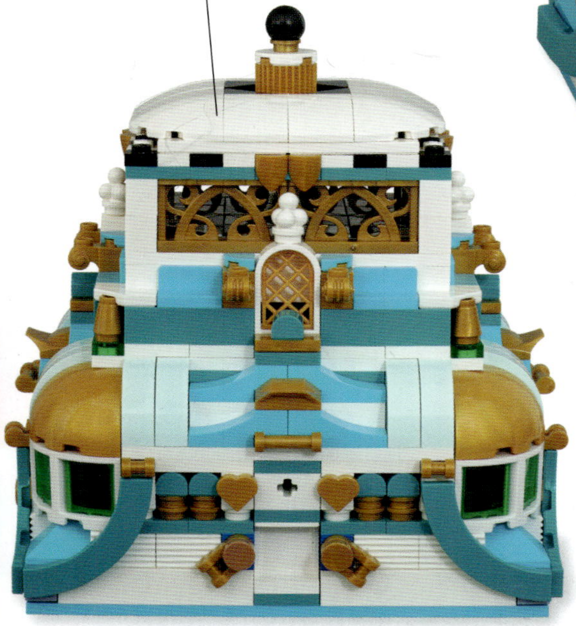

FRONT VIEW

LEGO® LETTERS

Can you make the letters of the Roman alphabet out of LEGO pieces? There are so many different alphabets and ways to build them. You can keep the corners and curves of your letters simple or get creative with some unusually shaped pieces. Use them to spell out your name, create a sign, or write a message.

BUILDING BRIEF

Objective:	Build alphabet letters
Use:	Making signs or messages
Features:	Corners, curved edges, angled pieces, patterns
Extras:	Decorations such as flowers, eyes, or tiny creatures

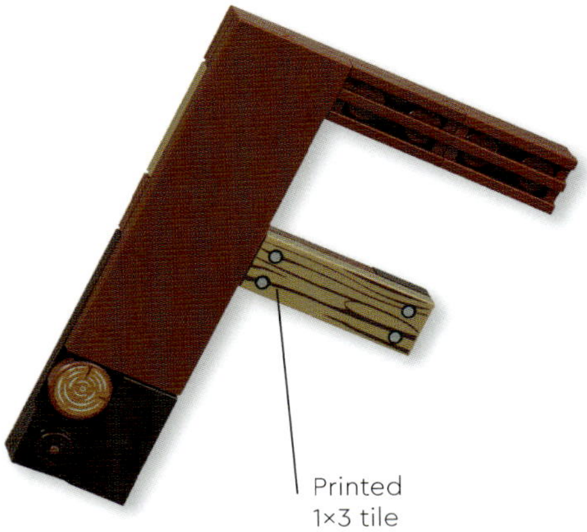

Printed 1×3 tile

CAPITAL IDEAS

Will you make all your letters the same color, or make each one completely different? You could also make patterns or a frame, and include little details such as flowers for a personal touch, or eyes to bring them to life.

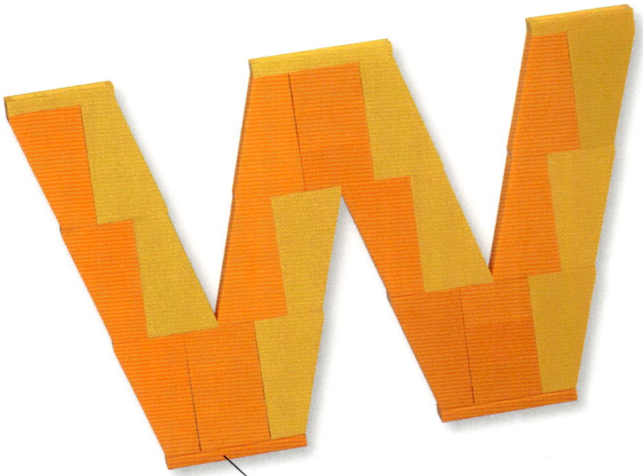

Both "feet" are 1×4 plates

Slopes and curved slopes combine to make this "G" shape

Letters can be themed and decorated, like this blossoming "B"

FLAT VOWEL

This letter is designed to lay flat, but could be positioned upright on a base using a bracket plate or a brick with side studs. Using round plates to connect the sections avoids any corners sticking out at the joins.

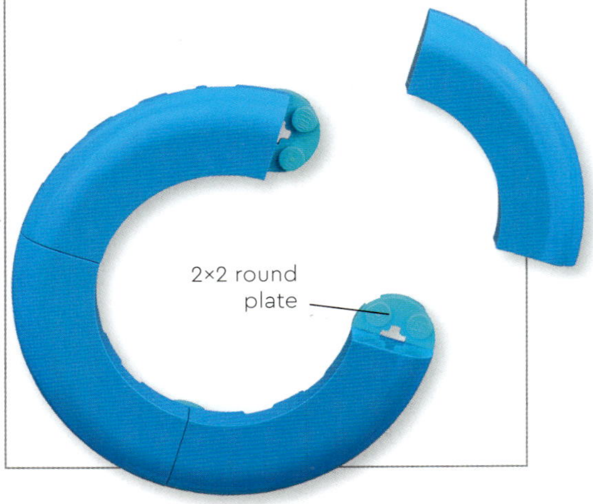

2×2 round plate

"O" is made from four 5×5×1 round corner bricks

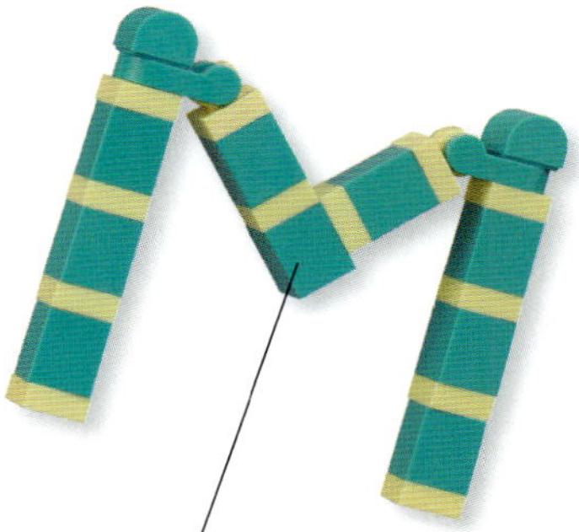

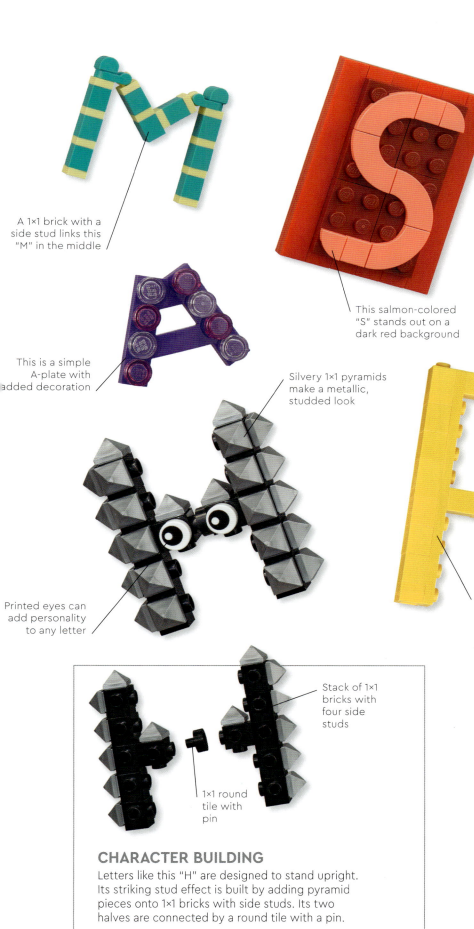

A 1×1 brick with a side stud links this "M" in the middle

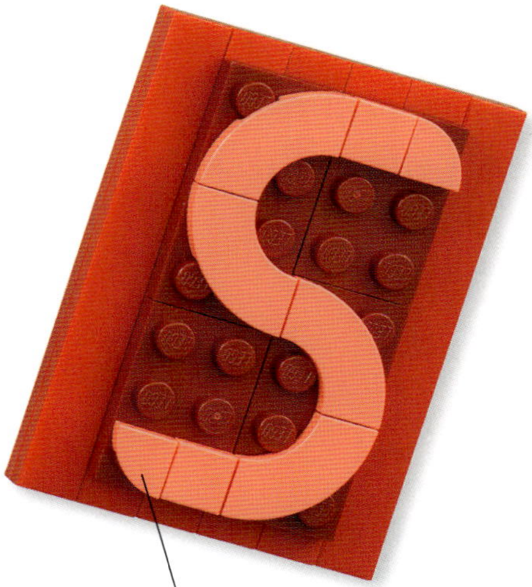

This salmon-colored "S" stands out on a dark red background

LEVEL UP

Use these building techniques to make your own code alphabet that only you and a friend can understand! Then write coded messages to each other.

This is a simple A-plate with added decoration

Silvery 1×1 pyramids make a metallic, studded look

Printed eyes can add personality to any letter

The loop is a sideways 1×6×2 curved arch

This 1×10 plate is built onto bricks with side studs

I WILL MAKE BEAUTIFUL WORDS WITH THESE LETTERS!

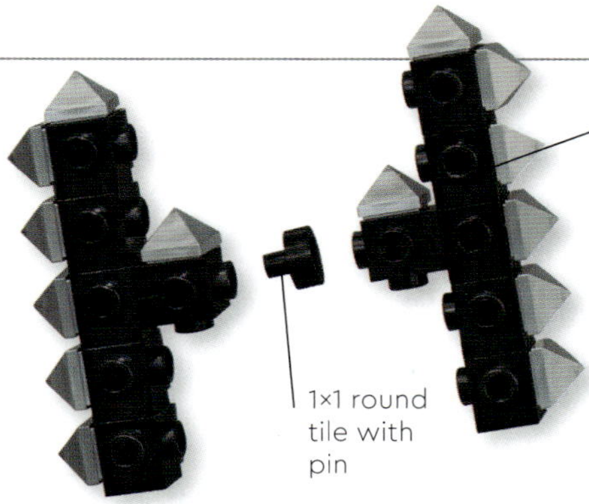

Stack of 1×1 bricks with four side studs

1×1 round tile with pin

CHARACTER BUILDING

Letters like this "H" are designed to stand upright. Its striking stud effect is built by adding pyramid pieces onto 1×1 bricks with side studs. Its two halves are connected by a round tile with a pin.

DREAM HOUSE

Everyone has a different idea of what their dream house might look like, so this would be a fun co-building project. Get together a group of family and friends, agree on the room size, who will build which room, and then each person can create something amazing. Fit your models together when you've all finished.

BUILDING BRIEF

Objective: Build a dream house
Use: Eating, sleeping, relaxing, playing
Features: Living room, bathroom
Extras: Furniture, knickknacks, pets, toys

You could use a printed tile to show the TV turned on!

TV CABINET

LEGO Technic plate with ring connects the screen and stand
Plate with rail forms a pelmet
Flowers in a 1×1 round brick vase brighten up the room

LIVING ROOM

You could build your own home, with a few modifications, or something completely different. This cozy room is all about comfort, with an armchair perfectly positioned for TV watching and tea drinking.

2×2 tile cushion

ARMCHAIR

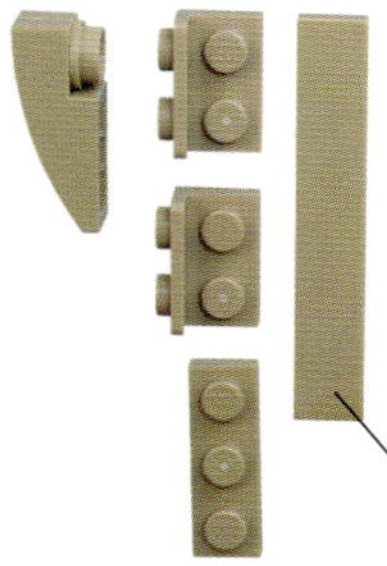

1×4 tile covers the studs

CURTAIN UP

This curtain build fits onto a brick with side studs in the wall. A 3×1 curved slope, connected sideways to 1×2/1×2 bracket plates, looks like a tied-back curtain.

BUILD TIP

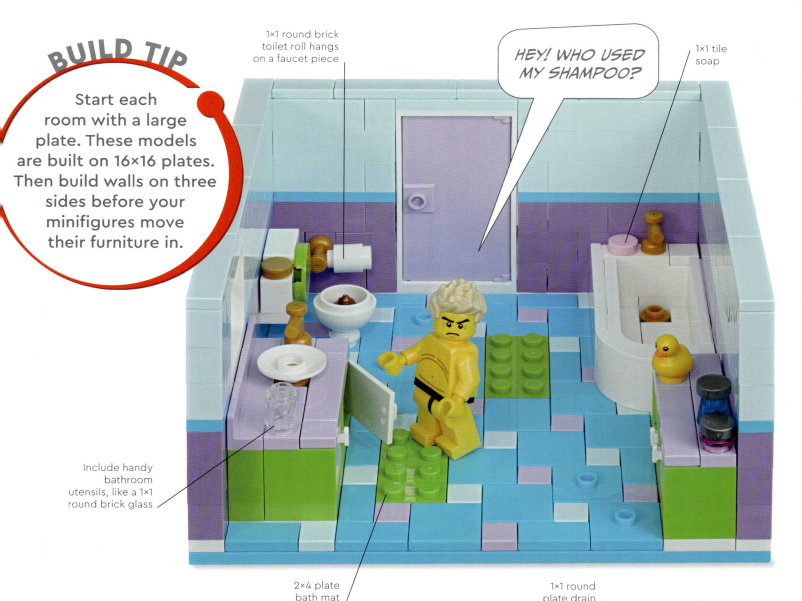

Start each room with a large plate. These models are built on 16×16 plates. Then build walls on three sides before your minifigures move their furniture in.

1×1 round brick toilet roll hangs on a faucet piece
HEY! WHO USED MY SHAMPOO?
1×1 tile soap
Include handy bathroom utensils, like a 1×1 round brick glass
2×4 plate bath mat

BATHROOM

Soft, pastel colors make this bathroom a calm space. Different sizes and color tiles laid in a pattern look great on the floor. Bath mats made from 2×4 plates ensure the minifigure doesn't slip and fall.

WAS IT YOU?

2×2 radar dish attached to a 1×1 tile with bar is a sink basin

SINK UNIT

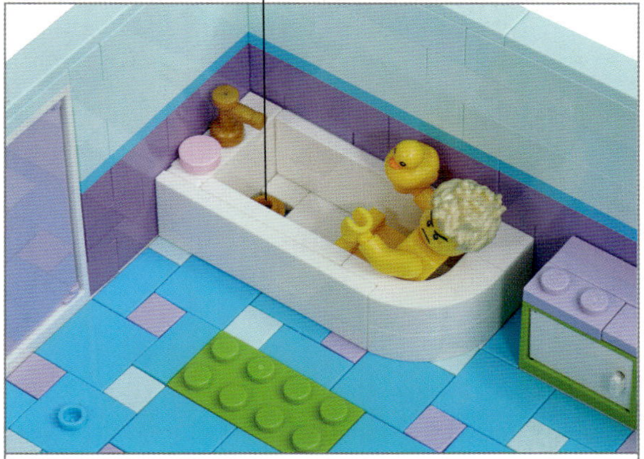
1×1 round plate drain

RUB-A-DUB-DUB

Two 1×3×2 curved arches turned on their sides form the rounded bathtub corner for this minifigure to rest his back on. The outer edge of the tub is a layer of plates covered by shiny white tiles.

BUILDING BRIEF

Objective: Extend your dream house
Use: Eating, sleeping, relaxing, playing
Features: Playroom, kitchen
Extras: Ball pit, armchair, oven, fridge, dining table

BUILDING THE DREAM

How many rooms might your dream house have? There are essential spaces, such as a kitchen, bathroom, and living room, but what other room ideas can you think of? How about a playroom, garage, home cinema, game room, swimming pool and spa, or you could make a room just for LEGO building? Now *that* would be awesome!

PLAYROOM

No grown-ups allowed—this room is for kids only! What would your dream playroom have? This lucky minifigure has a reading tent, lots of storybooks, and a ball pit filled with all the colors of the rainbow.

Each stripe is a row of 1×2 and 1×1 bricks
Two layers of jumper plates make a well-stocked bookshelf
Plates and curved slopes make the tent base
Curved slopes give the armcha its rounded shap
1×1 round plates fill the ball pit
I CAN'T WAIT TO DIVE IN!

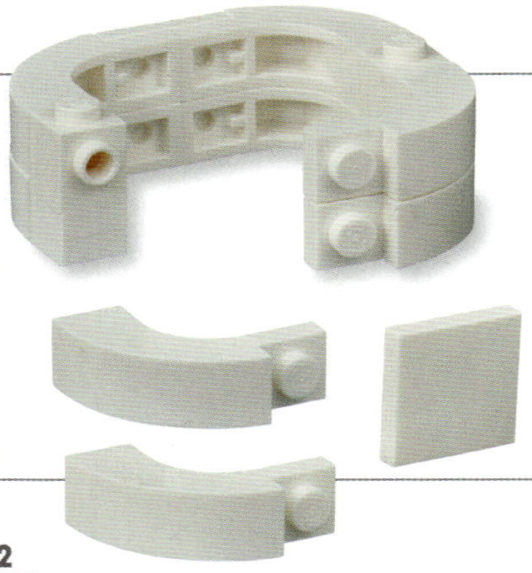

BALL PIT

Curved arches create the walls of the ball pit. The bottoms of the arches connect to bricks with side studs. The tops are held together with tiles.

ANOTHER ORDER . . . I'M GOING TO NEED A BIGGER TABLE!

Wall clock attaches to a bracket plate in the wall

Make a checkered floor by alternating black and white tiles

Stack up two round plates and a 1×1 brick for a table leg

KITCHEN

In your dream house, maybe a top chef bakes fresh cakes in the kitchen every day! A good cake-baking area needs a large oven, a well-stocked fridge, and a clock for timing your bakes so they don't burn.

Grille tiles make the stovetop

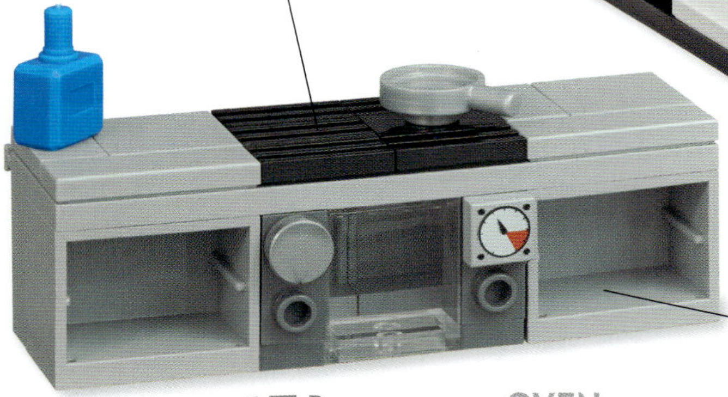

2×3×2 containers make great storage

OVEN

LEVEL UP

Once you've built all the rooms of your dream house, move outside and design your ideal yard. What will you fill it with? Go wild!

FRIDGE DOOR

Two 2×2 curved slopes and a small tile fit onto a 2×3 plate to form the fridge door. The slopes connect to two 1×2 bricks with side studs on the fridge to keep the door in place.

Back of a 2×2 curved slope

BUILD YOUR EMOTIONS

Sometimes it can be hard to explain your emotions. Why not try and build your mood and let your LEGO models do the talking for you? It will help others understand how you feel, and it may also help you work through some feelings. If you're not sure how you feel, just start building and see what happens!

BUILDING BRIEF

Objective:	Build to express your feelings
Use:	Working through your emotions, showing how you feel
Features:	Small scenes, abstract art
Extras:	Bigger scenes, moving parts, display stand

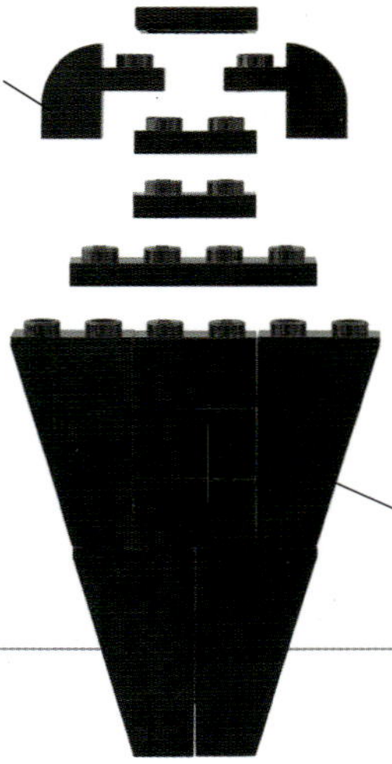
2×2×1 curved slope
1×2×3 inverted slope

DARKNESS RISING

With its suggestion of a head and shoulders, this build could be the looming shadow of sadness personified. It has a narrow base and grows outward.

Use dark pieces to represent a shadow
I'LL JUST SIT HERE FOR A LITTLE WHILE.

SADNESS

Sadness can be a shadowy feeling. What could you build to represent it? The process of building something and being creative may even make you feel a little less blue (or gray).

Transparent bricks suggest the heads are floating
The hats could represent academic or career options

CONFUSION

Life can be very confusing. This minifigure can't decide which hat to wear! Visualizing your choices or problems with your LEGO pieces can help you to find solutions. The wizard's hat it is!

ANGER

Using color creatively can really help express your feelings. This model is fiery red, and the minifigure looks pretty angry. It would be hard to stay mad after making this imaginative model!

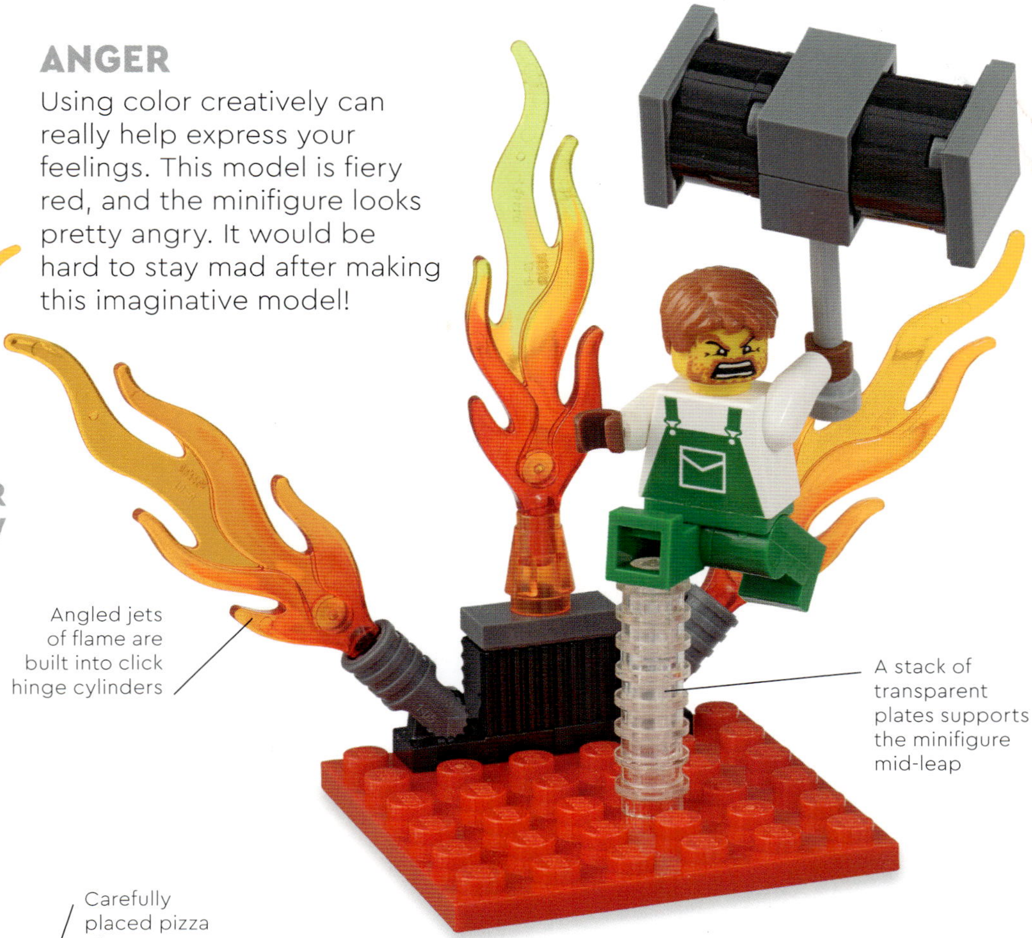

The hammer is built around a brick with a cross hole

REAR VIEW

Angled jets of flame are built into click hinge cylinders

A stack of transparent plates supports the minifigure mid-leap

CHANGE IT

What other ways can you think of to make parts look as though they are floating, apart from using transparent bricks and plates?

I NEED WHAT HE'S HAVING!

HAPPINESS

Build what makes you happy and keep it close to give your mood a boost whenever you look at it. This minifigure is on cloud nine with an endless supply of freshly baked pizza.

Carefully placed pizza tiles stay stacked

Stacked-up 3×5 cloud tiles

A broad base stops the build from falling over

REAR VIEW

FISH TANK

Be inspired by this fish tank and build yourself a LEGO pet like this goldfish. You can create any kind of fish you like and they're *really* low maintenance. You could even repurpose the tank to create a cozy home for a snake, lizard, spider, or another dream pet.

BUILDING BRIEF

Objective:	Build a pet and its tank
Use:	Companionship, relaxation, decoration
Features:	Tank, fish, rocks, aquatic plants
Extras:	Other fish or sea creatures, treasure chest, shipwreck

Curved slopes make realistic frond tops

AQUATIC PLANTS

Bars run through the middle of these plant builds

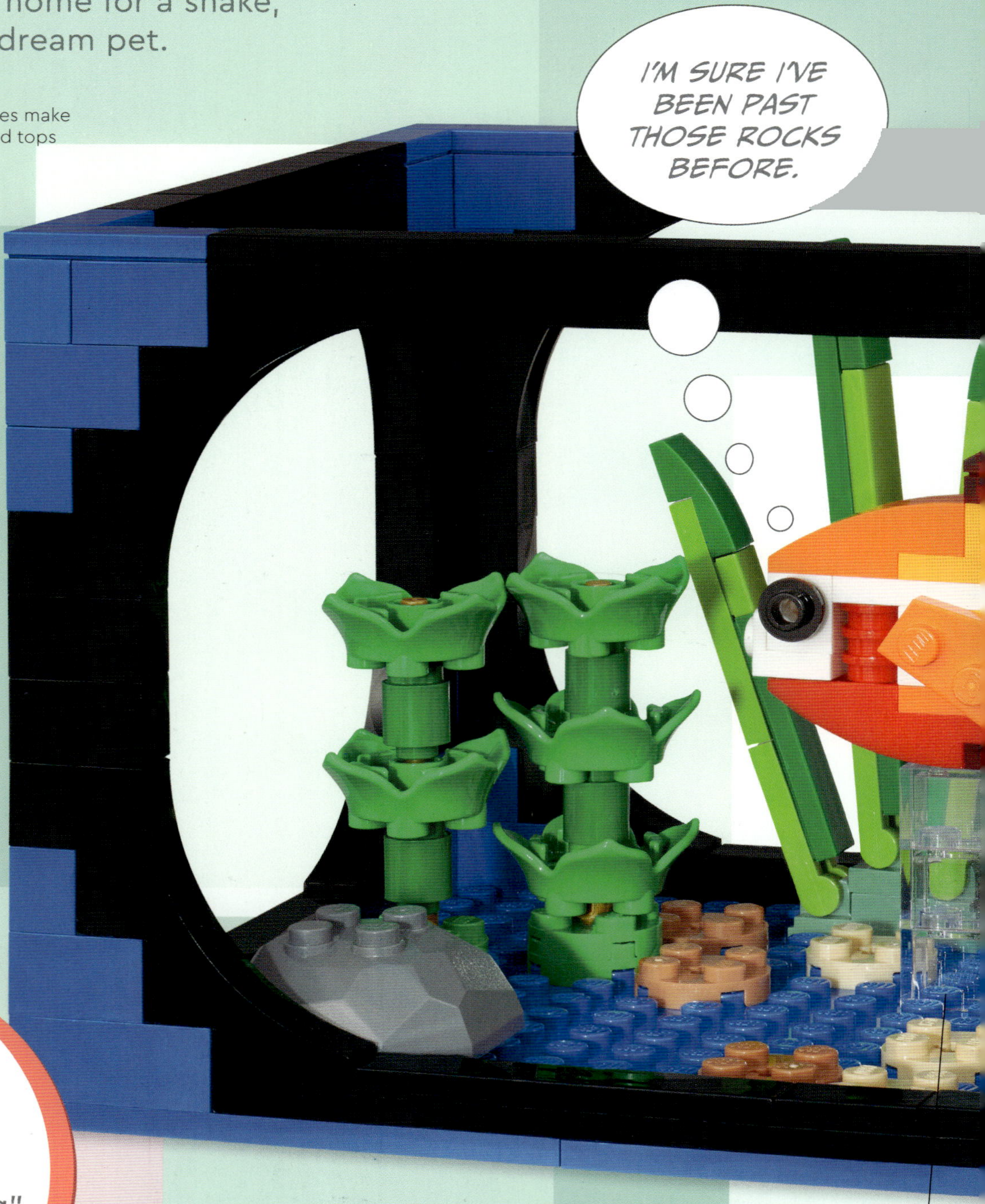
I'M SURE I'VE BEEN PAST THOSE ROCKS BEFORE.

Transparent bricks are used to make the fish "float"

CHANGE IT

Instead of building a tank, try turning your whole room into an aquarium by making lots of "floating" fish and standing them on every surface!

FEELING TANK-FUL

Whatever type of pet you build, it needs space to swim, run, or hop about. This fish tank has rocks for the fish to explore, and plants to hide behind or nibble on. You could add a treasure chest or a shipwreck.

Mouth made from a 1×1 /1×1 bracket plate
Transparent red 1×2 plate with slope
1×1 brick with two side studs

GOING FOR GOLDFISH

The fish's eyes and pectoral fins are built onto bricks with two side studs, while its gills are stacked 1×1 round plates. Its dorsal, pelvic, and tail fins are made from transparent red bricks for a realistic, shimmering look.

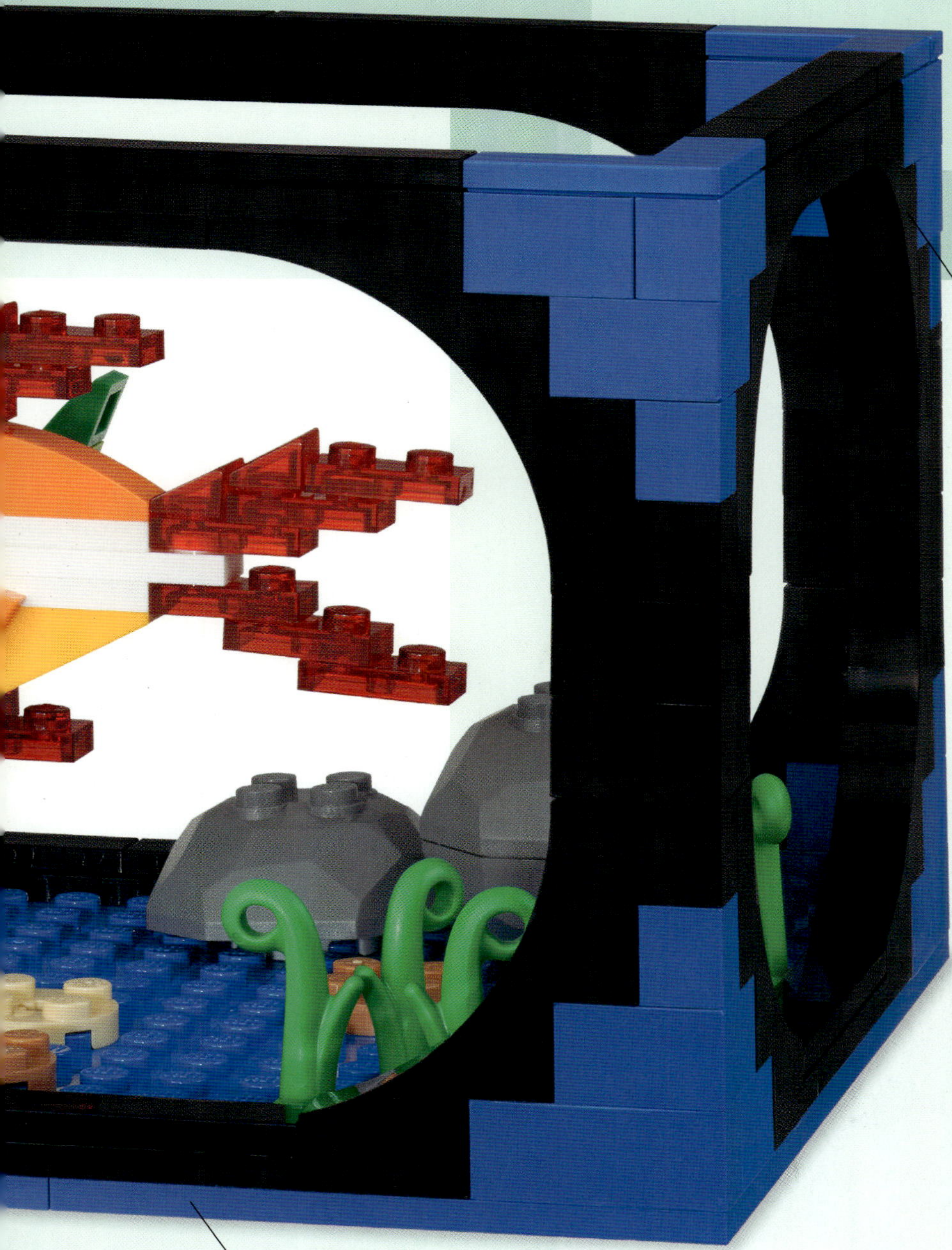
Half arch bricks support the top of the tank
The base is made from three 8×16 plates

Four open sides give good views from every angle

SIDE VIEW

BUILDING BRIEF

Objective:	Design your own robot
Use:	Help with specific tasks
Features:	Useful tools, sturdy body, buttons and controls
Extras:	Wheels or tracks, items to fix or take care of

HELPFUL BOTS

Have you ever dreamed of having a robot to help you with all the boring or time-consuming jobs you'd rather not do? Maybe your dream robot would be an expert in homework or just love cleaning up. What would your robot look like, and what tools would it need to carry out its duties?

Head is a transparent 2×2×2 dome

Watering can body and handle is a 1×1 brick with bar

The spout clips onto a plate with clip

LEVEL UP

Some LEGO sets build into real working robots. They're often used in computer programming classes, so ask your teacher if your school has one!

GARDEN-BOT

Going away on vacation, or don't have time to care for all your plants? Garden-bot is here to help! It has a sapling for a brain so it can truly understand what plants want. You could even build some leafy plants for it to tend to.

Plant is made from leaf plates and round plates

POTTED PLANT

GARDEN ROLLER

Garden-bot gets around on wheels rather than legs. These are made from 1×1 round plates slotted onto plates with handlebars. Its posable arms are made from bar holders with clips slotted onto bars. They attach to tiles with clips on the body.

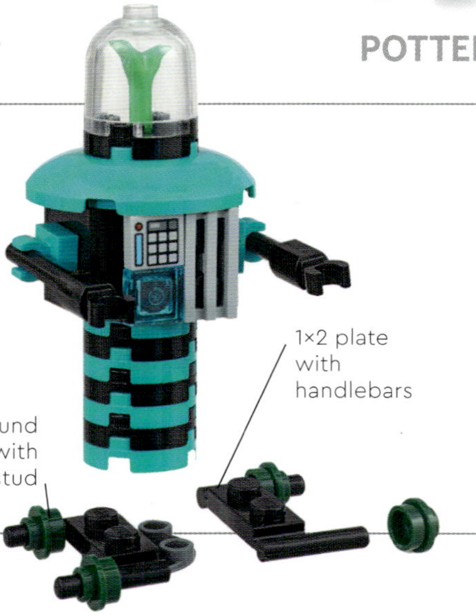

1×1 round plate with open stud

1×2 plate with handlebars

AHA, NOW I CAN TAKE OVER THE WORLD!

Control screen is a transparent book cover piece

ROBOT CONTROLLER

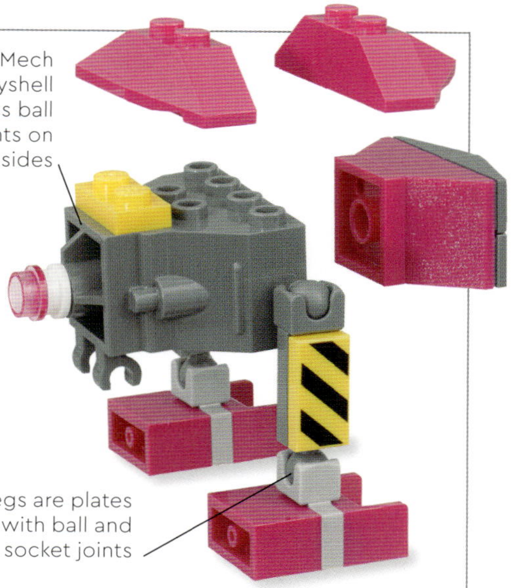
Mech bodyshell has ball joints on both sides
Legs are plates with ball and socket joints

A SIDEWAYS LOOK

This bot is built around a large, hollow bodyshell piece, more often used as the cockpit for minifigure battle mechs. Turn it sideways, and its undercarriage makes an ideal eye socket, while its clips become hanging claws for holding tools.

FIX-IT-BOT

This robot is a helpful mechanic. It can fix anything, from car engines to computers. Watch out, though: an evil alien is trying to recruit it. Fortunately, this robot prefers tinkering with machines to taking over the world.

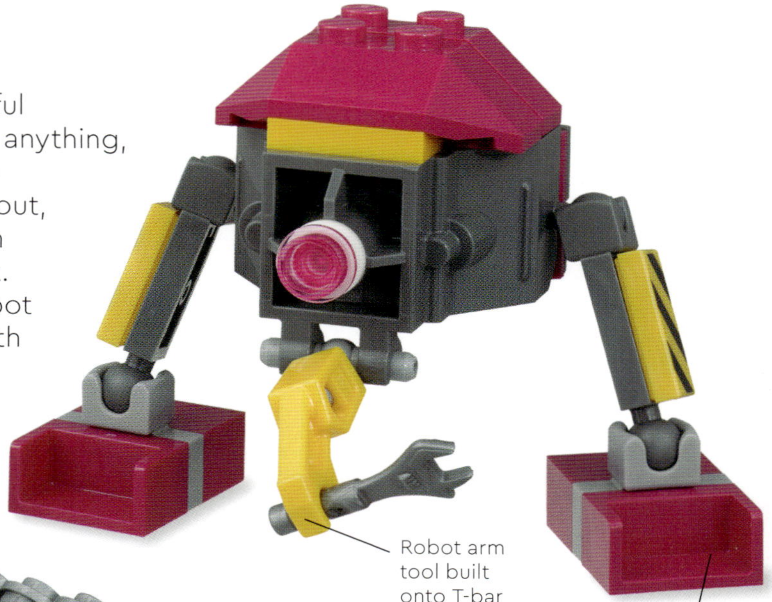
Robot arm tool built onto T-bar element
Sideways panel-piece feet can serve as shovels

Realistic eight-cylinder piston engine

ENGINE

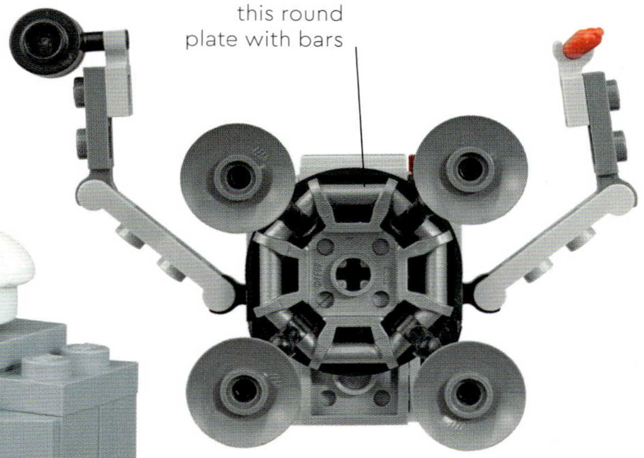
Legs clip onto this round plate with bars

UNDERNEATH VIEW

CHEF-BOT

This robot could be a family favorite. It loves to cook, and it never complains about washing the dishes! Its long arms can hold hot pans at a safe distance, and its control panel programs the oven to the perfect temperature.

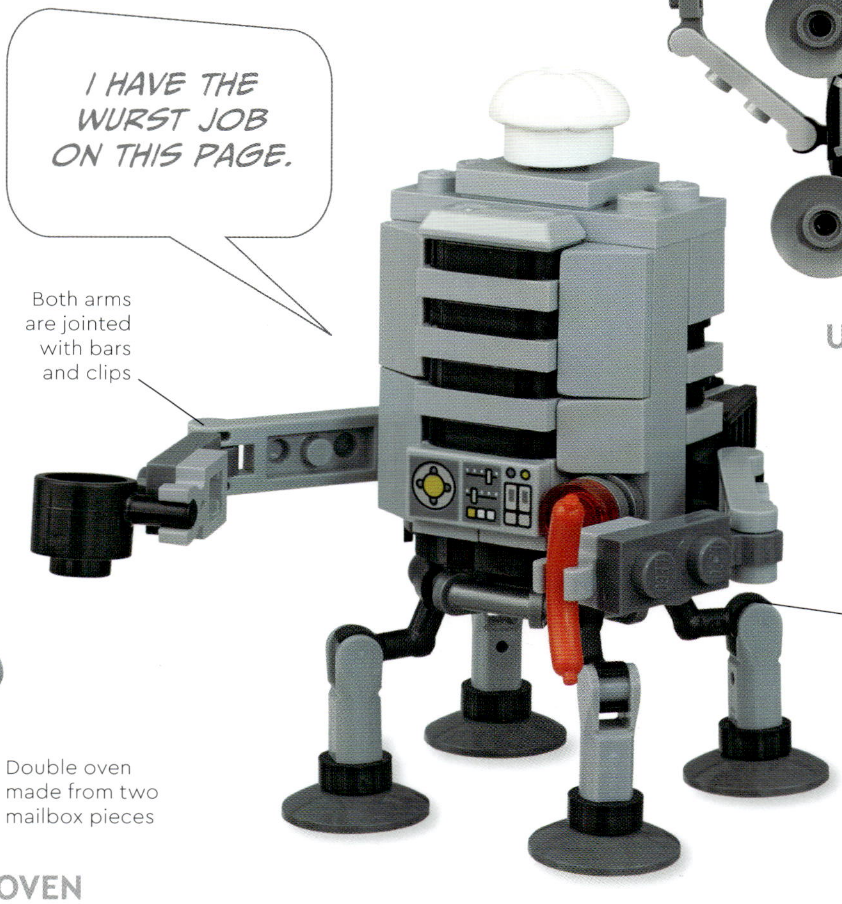
I HAVE THE WURST JOB ON THIS PAGE.
Both arms are jointed with bars and clips
Legs are skeleton arms clipped to bar holders with bars

Double oven made from two mailbox pieces

OVEN

Do you dream of racing planes? Steaming along in a steampunk vehicle? How about partying with itsy-bitsy insects? There are no limits to the adventures you can have with your LEGO® pieces. They can be historical, fantastical, or out of this world. Set your imagination free!

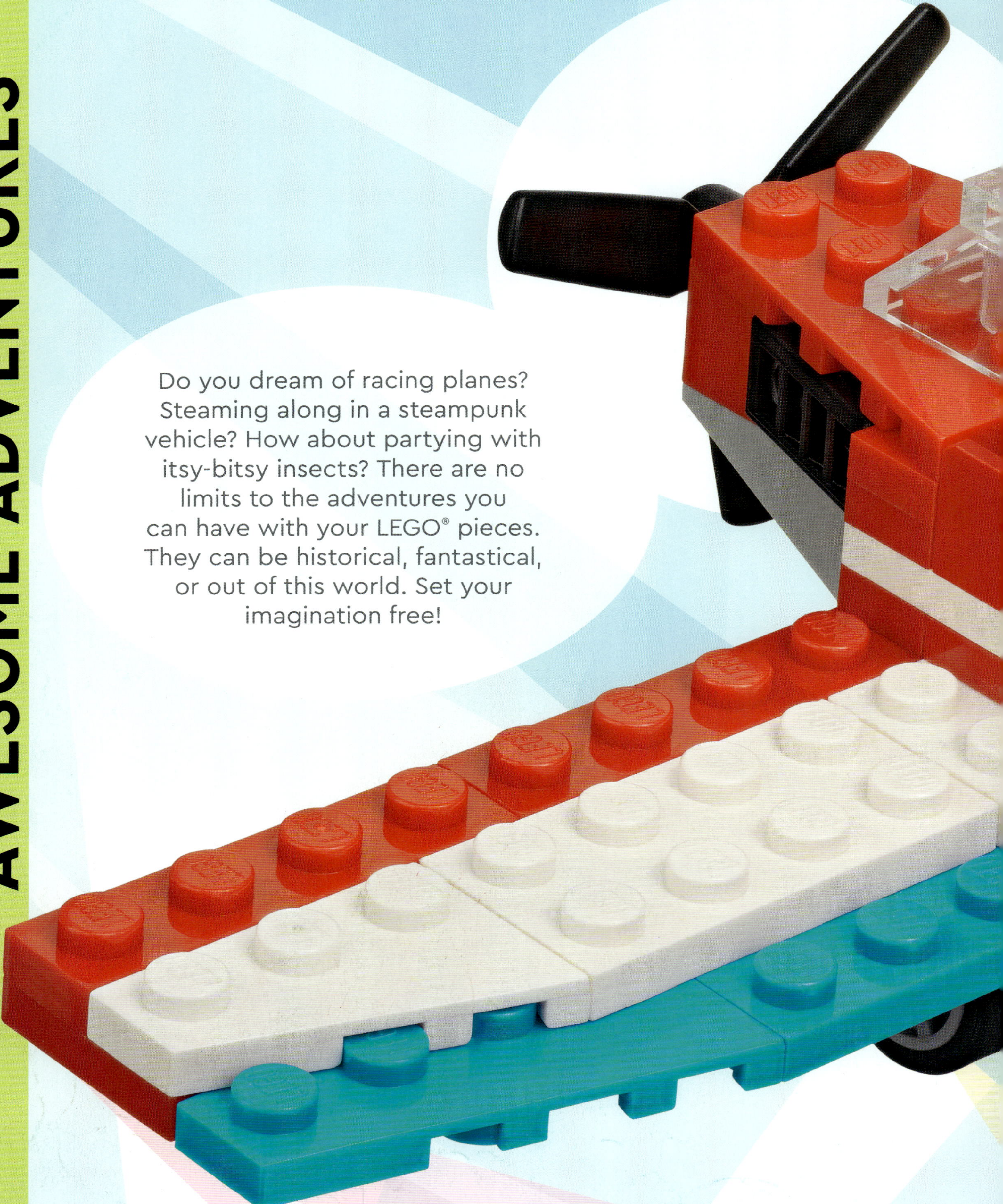

28

SKI LIFE

There's no fun like snow fun! Winter sports are a great outdoor activity, and this ski resort has everything a minifigure skier or snowboarder could possibly want. Just make sure your minifigures are bundled up nice and warm before they hit the slopes. It gets c-c-c-cold out on that mountain.

BUILDING BRIEF

Objective: Build ski-resort sights
Use: Fun, exercise, and fresh air for your minifigures
Features: Chairlift, ski rack, trees, refreshment stand
Extras: Lodge, ski jump, lockers

CHAIRLIFT

Skiing down a mountain is fast and fun. Trudging back up isn't. Save your minifigures a long, cold climb by building a ski lift to whisk them to the top. Then, you can build a beautiful view for them to admire while they are up there!

LEGO Technic axle connector and a bar hold the hose in place
Chairs can slide along this long hose piece
Blue transparent bar icicle
If you don't have 2×2×10 girders, stack up 2×2 bricks instead
You could add a 2×2 brick under the girder to make your lift slope

SKI RUN

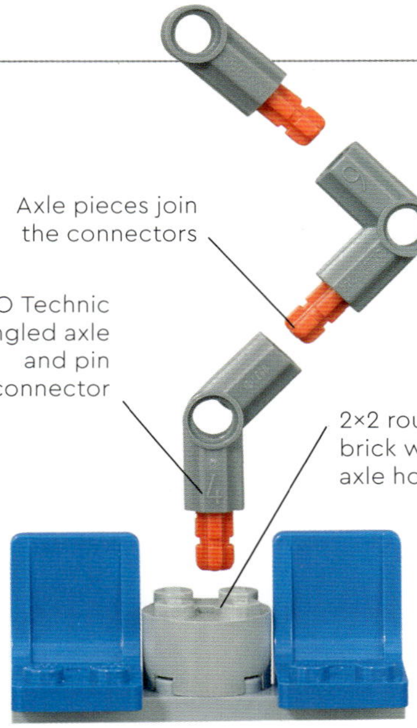
Axle pieces join the connectors
LEGO Technic angled axle and pin connector
2×2 round brick with axle hole

RIDE AND SLIDE

Thanks to LEGO® Technic axle and pin connectors, these little chairs can move along the hose piece on the chairlift model. If you don't have the same parts, try out other pieces with rings and holes instead.

LEVEL UP

Grab a friend or family member and build a little lodge or a sloping ski jump together for your minifigures to enjoy. You could even build a whole ski resort!

Printed 2×4 tile sign
1×2 log bricks form the stand's sides

White tooth plate looks like melting snow

REAR VIEW

SKIS AND TEAS

No skis? No problem. Build a ski stand so visitors can hire a pair for the day. You could create a refreshment stand as well.

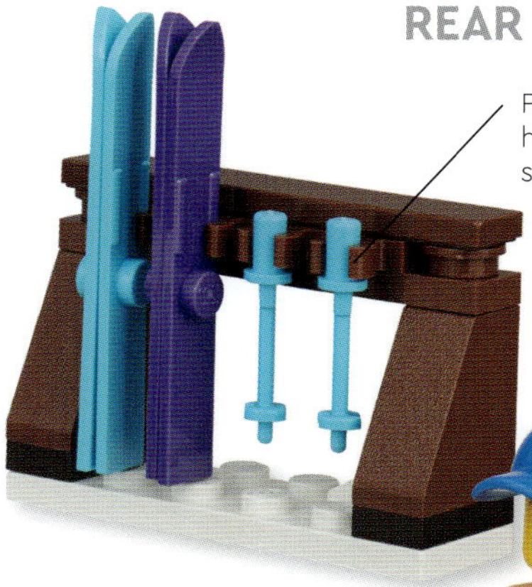

Plates with clips hold up the ski equipment

SKI RACK

IS THAT MAN YODELING?

ARRRGGHHH!!
Attach slope bricks at right angles for branches

TREES

To make your resort look picturesque, add some snowy scenery, such as pine trees. But be sure to leave the ski run clear!

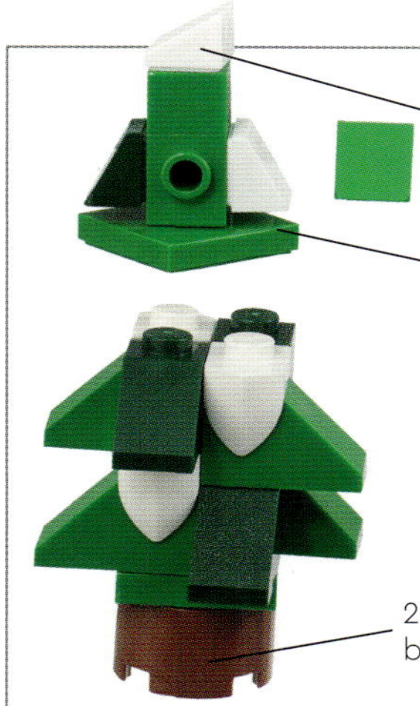

White 1×1 slope is a snowy treetop
2×2 jumper plate
2×2 round brick trunk

SKI JUMPER

Jumper plates allow you to center parts of your models. Attach a jumper plate to the final layer of branches to give your pine tree a conical shape.

BUILDING BRIEF

Objective: Build a pirate treasure hunt
Use: Seafaring, plundering
Features: Island, pirate ship
Extras: Treasure chest, treasure, small seagoing vessels

PIRATE ADVENTURE

Arrrr you and your minifigures ready to set sail for adventure? Think of everything your pirates need for an action-packed treasure hunt. Will you make a desert island? What about a ship that's fit for a captain? And don't forget the treasure—it could be gold coins, sparkling jewels, or even pizza!

One palm tree brings this island to life
I WISH THAT CUPCAKE WASN'T MADE OF GOLD. I'M SO HUNGRY!
Dark tan plates look like wet sand
4×4 plates with gear teeth look like splashy seawater

SAFE AND SOUND

Stack up treasure on a 1×3 plate and then pop it into the chest to keep your gold from falling out. It will make it harder for passing pirates to steal, too!

1×1 plate with swirl
1×1 round tiles make convincing coins

LEVEL UP

This small desert island is made with just a handful of pieces. You could create a bigger bit of land or even build a chain of small islands.

TREASURE ISLAND

Your pirates will definitely be on the hunt for treasure, but where will the chest be hidden? You could tuck it away on a tiny desert island made of tan plates that look like a sandy shore.

FISH AND SHIPS—MY FAVORITE!

A MAST, ME HEARTIES

Your pirates won't get far without a sturdy sail. Build the mast and then attach any large plate you like to create a sail for the ship.

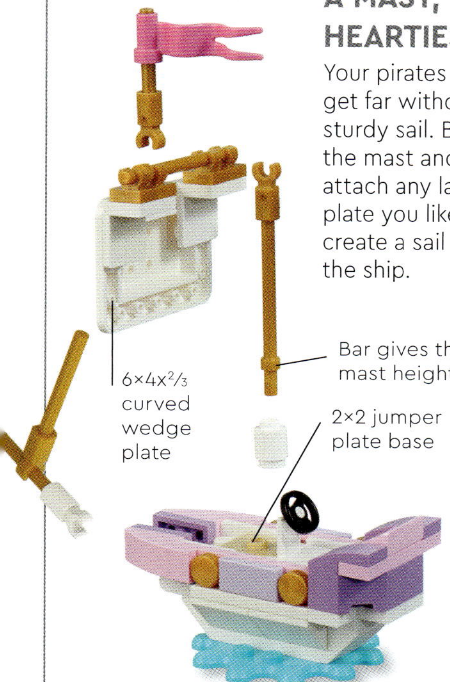
Bar gives the mast height
6×4×2/3 curved wedge plate
2×2 jumper plate base

PIRATE SHIP

Pirates can't search for treasure without a ship! Create a colorful vessel that's just the right size for the captain, or make it big enough to fit a whole band of buccaneers.

Bar looks like a bowsprit
Round tiles look like cannons

Bar holder with clip connects the flag pole to the mast

REAR VIEW

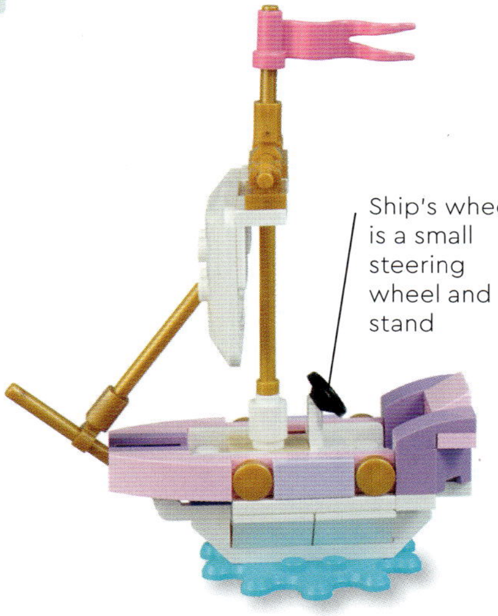
Ship's wheel is a small steering wheel and stand

SIDE VIEW

I SHOULD HAVE ADDED AN ENGINE!
Large barrel piece makes this little boat

TUB BOAT

If your captain wants their own ship, make smaller boats or rafts for the treasure-seeking crew. Be creative with the pieces you have.

BUILDING BRIEF

Objective: Build climbing activities
Use: Challenging your minifigures
Features: Walls, footholds, platforms, ropes, wires
Extras: River, hungry alligator

CLIMBING ACTIVITIES

Do your minifigures want to push themselves to their limits? Build them some LEGO® climbing activities to test their fitness and nerve—and to have fun! You could build a climbing wall, a zipline, cargo nets, super slides, swings, and more. Don't forget some safety gear, such as harnesses, ropes, and helmets.

Half arches hold the LEGO string safety ropes
DON'T LOOK DOWN! DON'T LOOK DOWN!
Use any small pieces you have to make footholds—even a minifigure wrench!

LEVEL UP

Expand these two builds into a big outdoor playground or obstacle course. It could even have a thrilling jungle or Australian outback adventure theme.

CLIMBING WALL

To build this gripping activity, simply stack up gray bricks to form a rectangular wall. Be sure to build in some bricks with side studs to attach hand- and footholds for your minifigures to grab as they climb.

Fence pieces will keep your minifigures safe
Long plates support the wall from behind

SIDE VIEW

ZIPPING TROLLEY

The minifigure can really zip along the wire thanks to a zipline handle piece. A bar holder with clip and a claw piece connect the pulley to the handlebars that the minifigure holds below.

Bar holder with clip

ZIPLINE

Build your own extreme zipline for your minifigures to whiz along. Make sure the starting end of the build is higher than the other so that gravity powers your minifigures downward. You can add an alligator-infested river below to increase the excitement or dream up some other perils!

Zip wire is a LEGO string with studs at each end
The steeper the slope, the faster your minifigure will travel
SEE YOU LATER, ALLIGATOR!
Small string with stud keeps the minifigure attached to the pulley
1×1×6 pillars give the starting side its height
Blue plate steadies the build and looks like a river

BUILDING BRIEF

Objective: Build flying apparatus
Use: Sports in the air
Features: Wings, handles, harnesses
Extras: Obstacles, trophy, parachute

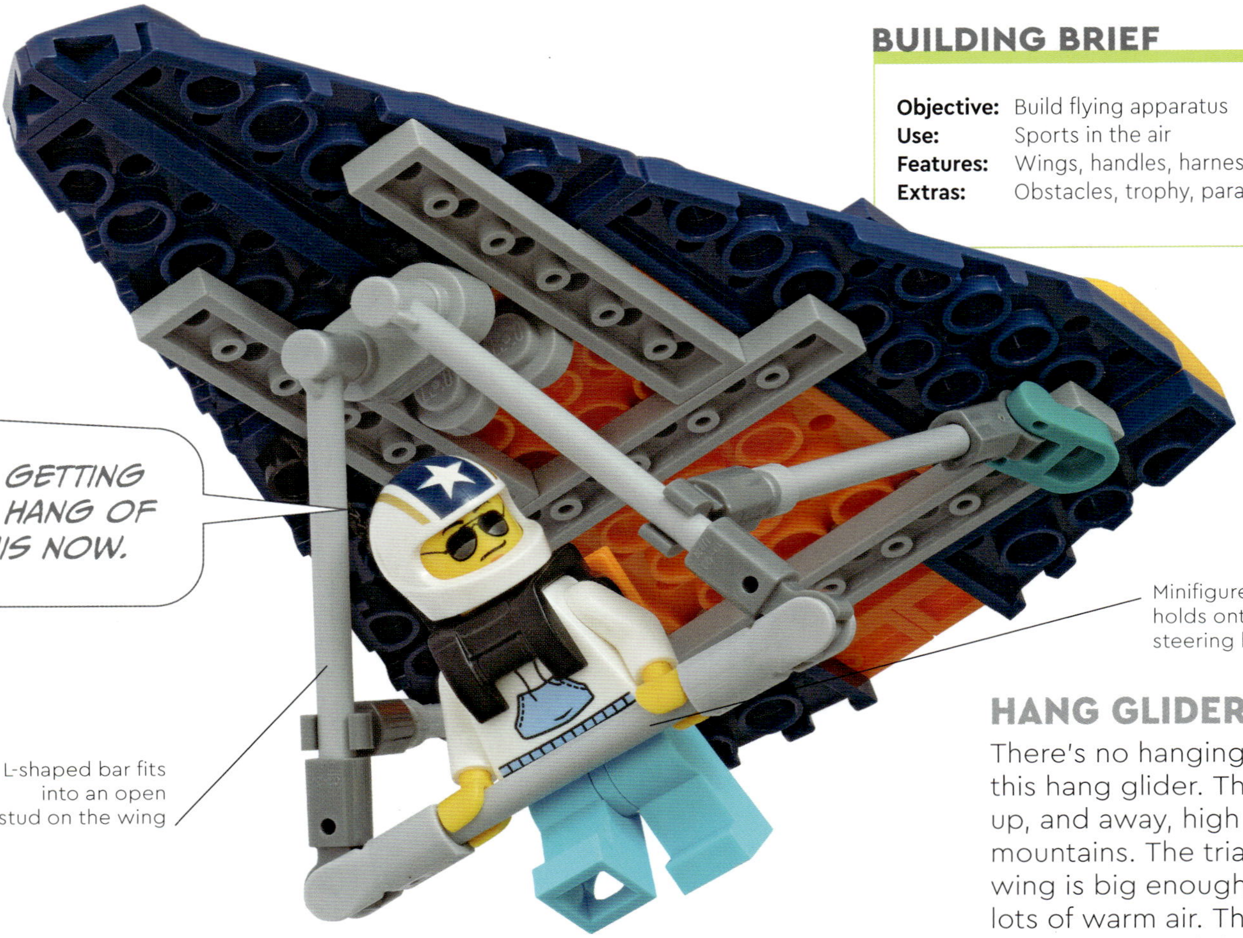
I'M GETTING THE HANG OF THIS NOW.

L-shaped bar fits into an open stud on the wing

Minifigure holds onto the steering bar

HANG GLIDER

There's no hanging about for this hang glider. They're up, up, and away, high over the mountains. The triangular wing is big enough to catch lots of warm air. That's what keeps a hang glider aloft.

AIRBORNE ADVENTURES

Time flies when you're having fun—especially when you're having fun flying. Turn your minifigures into high fliers by providing gear to get them airborne. How about a hang glider or a magical flying broomstick? These ideas are only a launching point. Build balloons, glider planes, or rideable birds—the sky's the limit!

Equip your minifigure with an ingot piece parachute

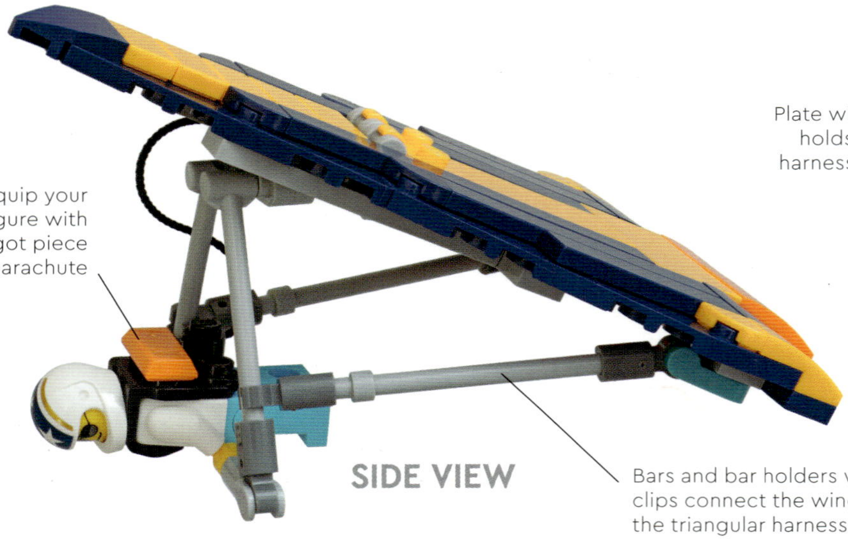

SIDE VIEW

Bars and bar holders with clips connect the wing to the triangular harness

Two 2×1 wedge slopes make this pointed shape

Plate with clips holds up the harness below

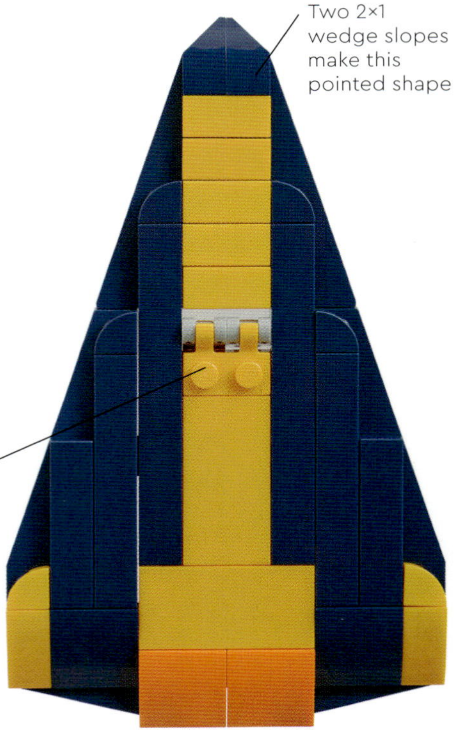

TOP VIEW

BROOMSTICK RACING

It's sorcerers' school sports day, and the broomstick race is on! Build a course for the racers, with hurdles to hover over and mini markers. Which witch (or wizard) will lift the winner's trophy?

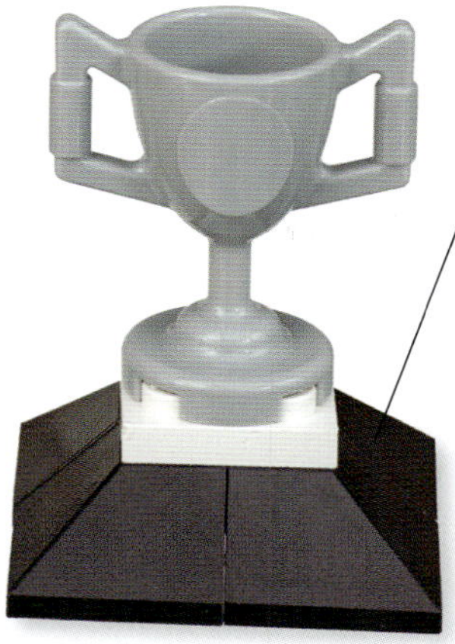
Four 2×2 corner slopes make a nice trophy stand

TROPHY

LEVEL UP

Put your flying and building skills to the test by making an entire broomstick racecourse. Build triple bar jumps, water ditches, brick walls, or hoops.

WHY FLY BROOMSTICKS? BECAUSE VACUUM CLEANERS ARE TOO HEAVY!

Use fence pieces or stack up bricks to build a wall

If you don't have a broomstick piece, try building your own using a bar and cone
Build a transparent stand to make your minifigure "fly"
Megaphone pieces hold up this jump
Light bulb pieces on top of the cones help riders to spot them

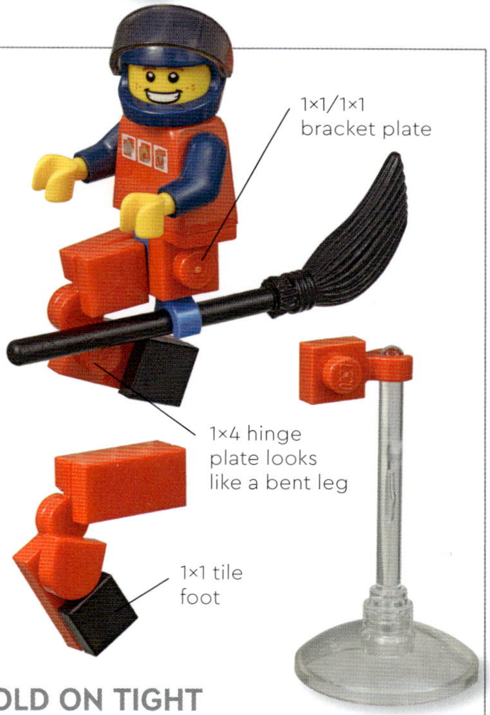
1×1/1×1 bracket plate
1×4 hinge plate looks like a bent leg
1×1 tile foot

HOLD ON TIGHT

This minigure's legs are specially built to make it look like the minifigure is sitting on the broomstick. A blue plate with a clip right in the middle of the legs fits onto the broomstick to keep the minifigure onboard.

BOARD SPORTS

Board sports are known as extreme sports, and you'll have extreme fun with these LEGO boarding builds. Pick a skatepark for an urban minifigure or a snow-covered slope for an outdoorsy one. Then grab some slope pieces and slide into action!

BUILDING BRIEF

Objective:	Build structures to board on
Use:	Boards sports, competitions
Features:	Ramps, slopes, ledges
Extras:	Fences, graffiti, scenery

BUILD TIP

Skaters and snowboarders need smooth slopes to slide down. Try to cover up any studs so that your minifigures don't have a bumpy ride.

I'M WHEELY ON A ROLL!
1×2 slopes for a ledge
1×3×2 inverted arches give the skate ramp its slopes

RAMP IT UP

A ramp built from inverted arches is perfect for a minifigure to practice their drop-ins. The taller the ramp, the faster the drop, and the more "air" your minifigure will get on the other side. Why not build a whole skatepark with pipes, benches, and rails?

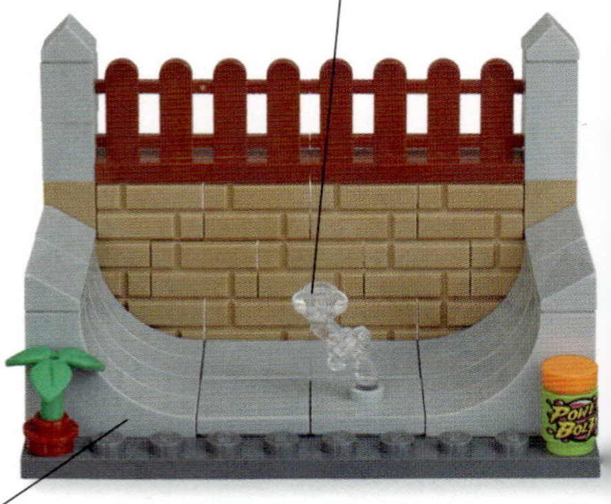
Transparent bar with angled stud holds the board at an angle
You could build some colored pieces into your ramp to look like graffiti

FRONT VIEW

Inverted arches also connect plates at the model's base

SNOWY ARCHES

Six white 1×3×2 inverted arches form the curve of this snow-packed quarter pipe. A stack of bricks and slopes behind the arches makes space for scenery and gives the snowboarder a place to start their snowy adventure.

Flower stems are spiky pine needles
What other bits of scenery could you add to your slopes?
THERE'S A TREE-MENDOUS VIEW FROM UP HERE.
Gray slopes are rocks in the snow
Large tile piece looks like the flat base of the slope
Curved slopes make a snowbank for soft landings

GO WITH THE SNOW

Who wants to come in from the cold? Not this snowboarder. It's way too much fun out here! Give their snowboard run a suitably wintry look with white bricks and green fir trees.

BUILDING BRIEF

Objective:	Build sports on water
Use:	Minifigure recreation, racing
Features:	Boards, boats, sails
Extras:	Rapids, scenery, animals

WATER SPORTS

Make a splash with some LEGO water sports builds. You could choose windsurfing, kayaking, or whatever floats your boat. Will it be smooth sailing? If your minifigures like a challenge, throw in some obstacles, rocks, dive-bombing birds, or even a shark to leave your minifigures all at sea.

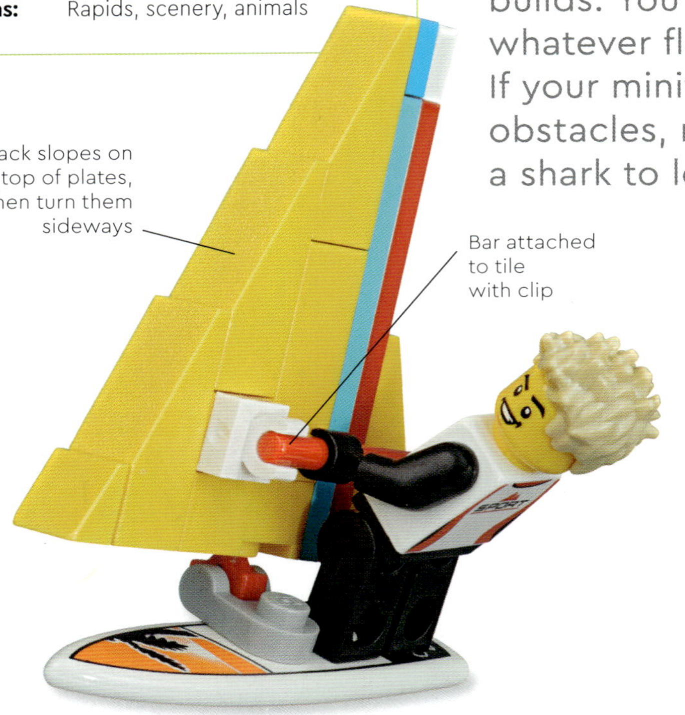

Stack slopes on top of plates, then turn them sideways
Bar attached to tile with clip
SPORT

WINDSURFING

Ah, a breezy day out on the water. Great! With the wind in their sail (and hair), the windsurfer whizzes over the sea's surface. Slope pieces give the sail its triangular shape.

CAN YOU ROW ANY FASTER?
LEGO string connects the wakeboarder to the boat

Don't forget to pack safety gear such as a life buoy
1×1 tile with clip holds the oar

ROW, ROW, ROW YOUR BOAT

Not exactly extreme sports! A slow tow from a rowing boat isn't much fun for this intrepid wakeboarder. They're starting to get that sinking feeling. Can you build a motor on the back?

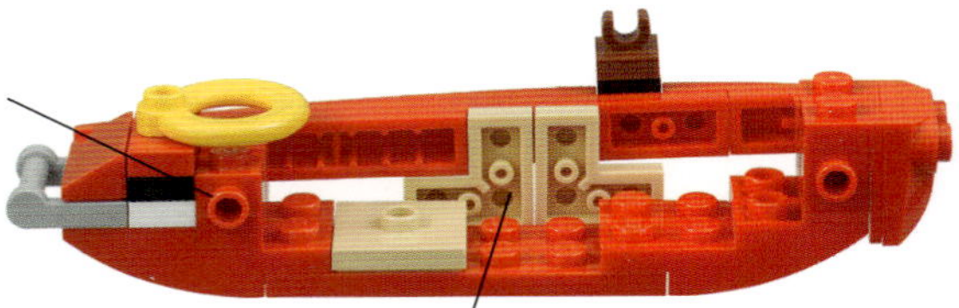

1×1 brick with side stud
2×2 corner plate

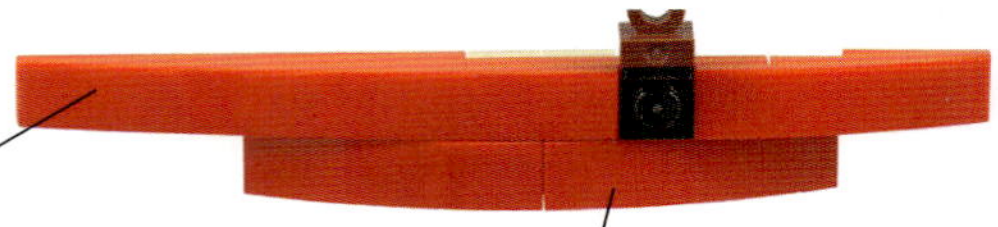

8×1 curved slope
Smaller curved slopes attach to corner plates

SHIPSHAPE

Curved slopes attach to bricks with side studs at either end of the rowing boat to form its sides. Two 2×2 corner plates placed in the center of the slopes add stability and allow you to attach slopes to the lower part of the hull to make it seaworthy.

1×1 bricks with side studs form this tree trunk
Slopes create a rocky backdrop
I'M GETTING NOWHERE FAST IN THESE "RAPIDS"!
1×1 slopes are water spilling over rocks
1×2 blue transparent tiles make a smooth river

WILD WATER KAYAKING

Can the kayaker guide their craft safely through these steep, bubbling rapids? To give your paddler an even harder time, extend this scene by adding more rocks and rapids farther downstream.

Use transparent plates to look like bubbling water
1×2 hinge plate holds the kayak at an angle

SIDE VIEW

RACING PLANES

These old-fashioned planes will never break the sound barrier, but they are fun to race. Build checkered posts to show the takeoff and landing points. Then chug-chug-chug . . . get those propellers whirling. Will your planes have to fly through or past obstacles? Chocks away!

BUILDING BRIEF

Objective: Build racing planes
Use: Airborne travel and races
Features: Wings, propellers, cockpit, tailfins
Extras: Finishing posts, course markers, obstacles, aircraft hanger

FLYING TIPS? MINE ARE THE BEST.
Curved slope for a streamlined tailfin
These hinge bricks let the wing tips raise and lower
Wheel trim piece connects the propeller blade to the nose

A flag helps your racers spot the finishing line from a distance

FINISHING POST

RACING PLANE

Look at the checkered wingtips on this classic plane. See how they tilt upward? The tips are called winglets, and they help improve air flow over the wing.

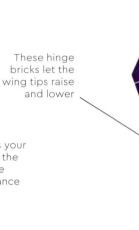

CHANGE IT

Get your friends on board! Build a plane each, then swap out one piece of your model (the wings or tail) for the same piece on a pal's build. Is your mashup plane a winner?

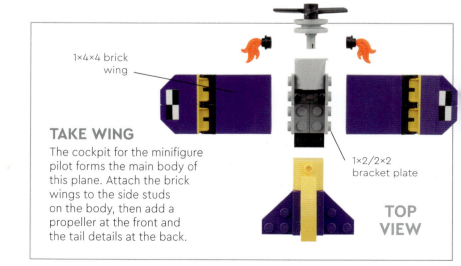

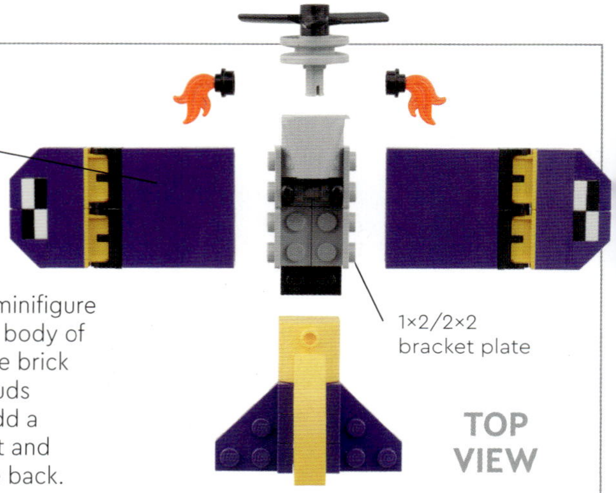
1×4×4 brick wing
1×2/2×2 bracket plate

TOP VIEW

TAKE WING

The cockpit for the minifigure pilot forms the main body of this plane. Attach the brick wings to the side studs on the body, then add a propeller at the front and the tail details at the back.

This stack of 1×2 log bricks supports the wing

1×1 transparent plate is a landing light

FRONT VIEW

STUNT PLANE

Since the 1920s, daring pilots have performed rolls, loops, and dives in their biplanes. This LEGO stunt plane has an extra move to show off. It can convert to a monoplane!

LOOK OUT! I'M HOT ON YOUR TAILFIN.

Slope bricks create the smooth angle of the tailfin

2×1 grille slope is an engine air vent

This post tells pilots where to go on the racecourse

COURSE MARKER

MINI PLANE

Big isn't always better when it comes to aircraft. This mini plane is light, speedy, and quick to build. Any drawbacks? Just one—there isn't much legroom for the minifigure pilot.

SORRY . . . NO PASSENGERS.

Just a plate and a $2\times4\times\frac{2}{3}$ curved slope form this wing

Propeller spins on a 2×2 tile with pin

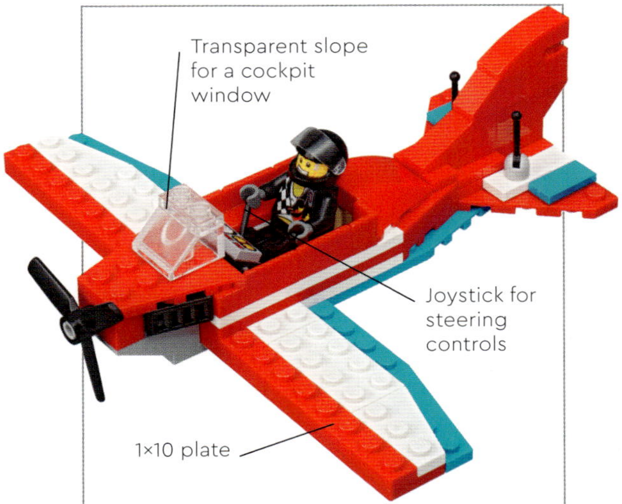

Transparent slope for a cockpit window

Joystick for steering controls

1×10 plate

SINGLE WINGS

The stunt plane is built from the bottom up, so the top level of wings is connected last. If you want to make a monoplane instead of a biplane, leave off the second wing layer. Or make a triplane by adding another set of wings on top of the biplane!

CUTE CRITTERS

These tiny LEGO critters are the same size as real ones. But look closely and you'll see they have big ambitions. What other adventures might a minibeast get up to when we're not looking? A tap-dancing centipede would cause a stir. So would a team of cricket-playing crickets. And a butterfly chef baking cupcakes would really take the cake.

BUILDING BRIEF

Objective: Build imaginative minibeasts in all shapes and sizes
Use: Creating critter pasttimes and scenes to play in
Features: Insects, arachnids, molluscs
Extras: Easel, pirate weapons, musical instruments, habitats

SCORPION ARTIST

Stay away from the scorpion painter! She might lash out with her stinger—or even her paint roller—if something disturbs her concentration. The tile with clip on her tail looks like a stinger but it's also a handy paintbrush holder.

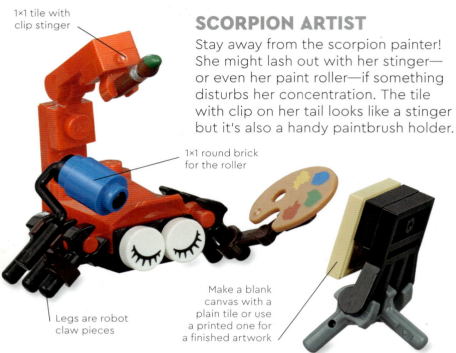

1×1 tile with clip stinger
1×1 round brick for the roller
Legs are robot claw pieces

Make a blank canvas with a plain tile or use a printed one for a finished artwork

LEVEL UP

You could combine your minibeast scenes into one wonderful world. Try building cozy homes, schools, playgrounds, and other sociable spaces for your critters.

SNAIL PIRATES

This motley mollusc crew sail the seven vegetable patches looking for treasure to steal. All three have a signature snail look thanks to their radar dish shell, but they're put together in different ways and with a variety of pieces.

This 1×1 round plate connects to the shell
Tooth plate tail

SPE-SHELL SNAILS

Each snail is built from the inside out using small bricks, plates, and slopes to make a sturdy body. Their shells, which attach sideways, are added last.

Clip holds the pirate's weapon

1×2 plate with bar forms the face

This bigger shell is a 4×4 radar dish
Handlebar mustache

Two radar dishes make the speaker surround
Claw piece is a sharp stinger
AND NOW FOR OUR FAVORITE SLOW TUNE!
Use a wide base plate to hold your bouncing band build steady
Dangling robot-arm legs

This 2×1 tile with bar holds the flower onto the stalk

REAR VIEW

BOOMING BLOOM

Do you like pop music? How about poppy music? A critter band has turned a flower's stem and leaves into a stage. There's even a giant speaker system in the flower head! What other minibeast band members could you add?

DISCO DECKS

The fly creates a buzzing atmosphere on these dazzling decks! Round plates with bars spin the record-printed 2×2 round tiles. The disco lights are sandwiched between two half round plates.

4×8 half round plate
1×1 round plate with bar

BUILDING BRIEF

Objective:	Build a throwing game
Use:	Playing with friends and family
Features:	Monster heads, projectiles
Extras:	Catapult, snapping jaws

MUNCHING MONSTERS

If you're aiming for models that double as fun games, then snap to it and build some hungry monsters. Once you have built your monster models, come up with a jaw-dropping game to play with friends. Make a catapult to see who can fling the most treats into the models' mouths, or invent your own challenge.

IS HE TRYING TO DISTRACT ME FROM MY SHOT?

CATAPULT

This catapult uses a digger bucket to launch 2×2 round tiles into the monsters' mouths, but you could use any open LEGO container. Try a crate, a round barrel, or use bricks to build a box.

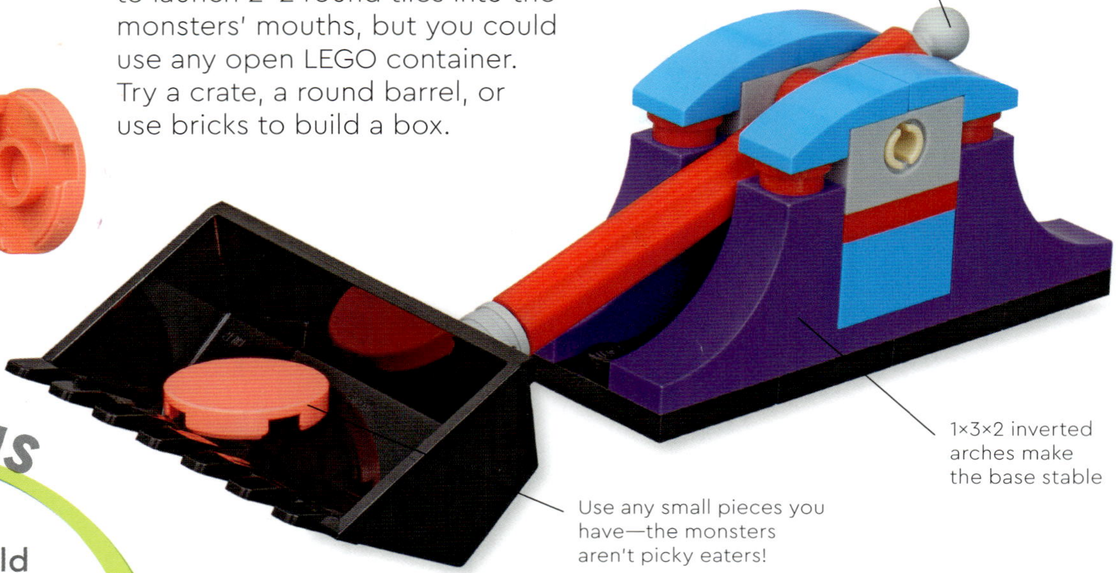
Press here to launch tiles
1×3×2 inverted arches make the base stable
Use any small pieces you have—the monsters aren't picky eaters!

TRY THIS

Instead of monsters, build boats to catch "cannonball" pieces for a pirate themed throwing game, or go medieval and make castles with open roofs.

LEGO Technic axle with tow ball
LEGO Technic axles and connectors make a strong arm
LEGO Technic pin
Pin fits into this 1×2 brick with hole

This digger bucket has two click hinge "fingers" on its base

ARMED AND READY

Build the catapult base first, then make the launching arm. This lies in the center of the base and attaches to it at one end with LEGO Technic pins. The pin connections allow the arm to move up and down like a seesaw.

JUST CHECKING THE SCORES OVER HERE!
Plate with ring nostril
Top teeth are 1×1 vertical tooth plates
Pyramid slopes make sharp bottom teeth
4×4 macaroni bricks shape the lower jaw

MONSTER FEATURES

A monster can look like anything you can imagine. With their long snouts and snapping jaws, these monsters look a bit like alligators with a fantastical twist. They have the same jaw shape but they have different features on the tops of their heads, including horns, eyelashes, and nostrils.

Add cones in different sizes for unusual horns
This plate with gear teeth looks like eyelashes

CLOSED JAWS

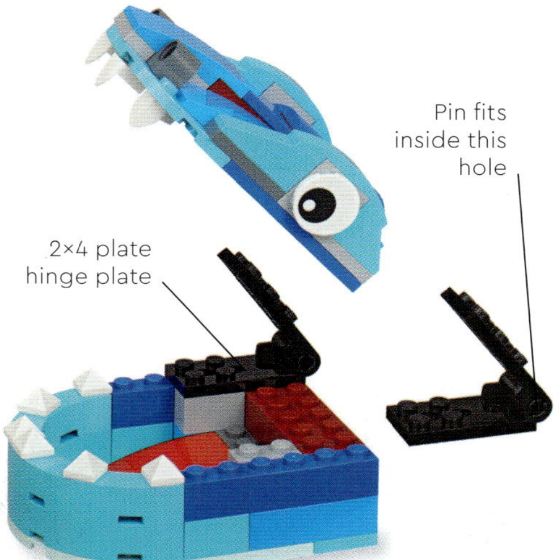
Pin fits inside this hole
2×4 plate hinge plate

OPEN WIDE

The top of the monster's jaw connects to two LEGO Technic 2×4 hinge plates with pin holes. These plates can attach to two more hinge plates on the bottom jaw. This connection allows your monster's mouth to open and snap shut.

SEA CREATURES

Splash! Build some briny buddies and dive in for an undersea adventure. Watch where you put your flippers, though. Stepping on a sea urchin might bring your story to a painful end. What other LEGO sea creatures could you build? How about clams, jellyfish, shrimp, or wiggly marine worms?

BUILDING BRIEF

Objective: To build underwater animals
Use: Creating an undersea scene, learning about nature
Features: Tails, arms, spines, claws, eyes
Extras: Coral reef, seabed, sea plants

LOBSTER

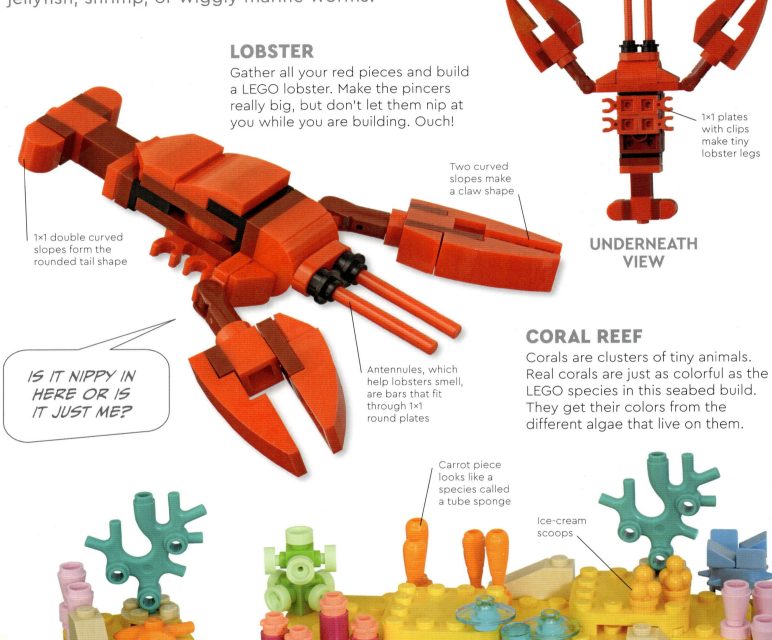

Gather all your red pieces and build a LEGO lobster. Make the pincers really big, but don't let them nip at you while you are building. Ouch!

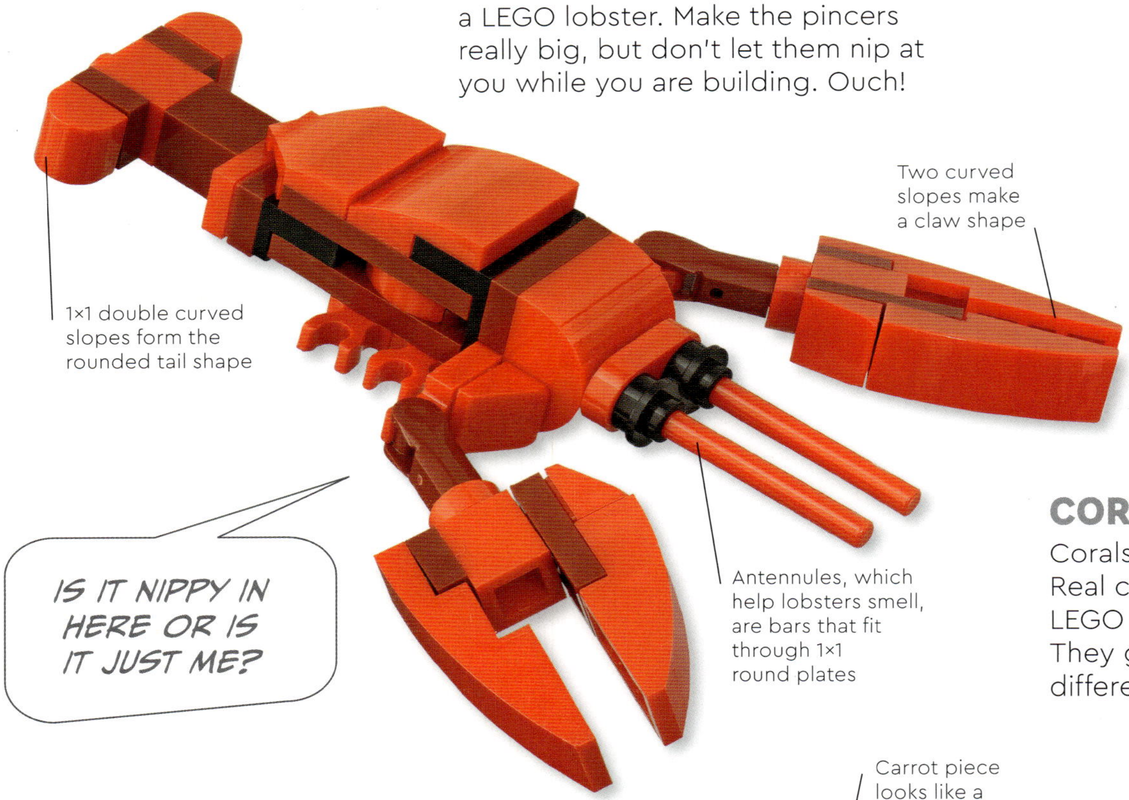

1×1 double curved slopes form the rounded tail shape
Two curved slopes make a claw shape
Antennules, which help lobsters smell, are bars that fit through 1×1 round plates
IS IT NIPPY IN HERE OR IS IT JUST ME?

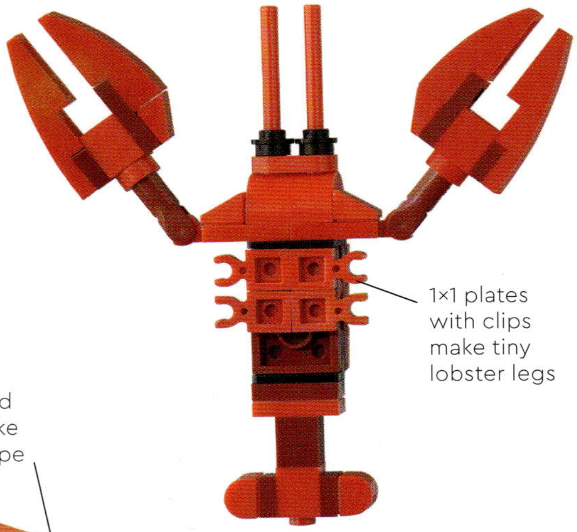

1×1 plates with clips make tiny lobster legs

UNDERNEATH VIEW

CORAL REEF

Corals are clusters of tiny animals. Real corals are just as colorful as the LEGO species in this seabed build. They get their colors from the different algae that live on them.

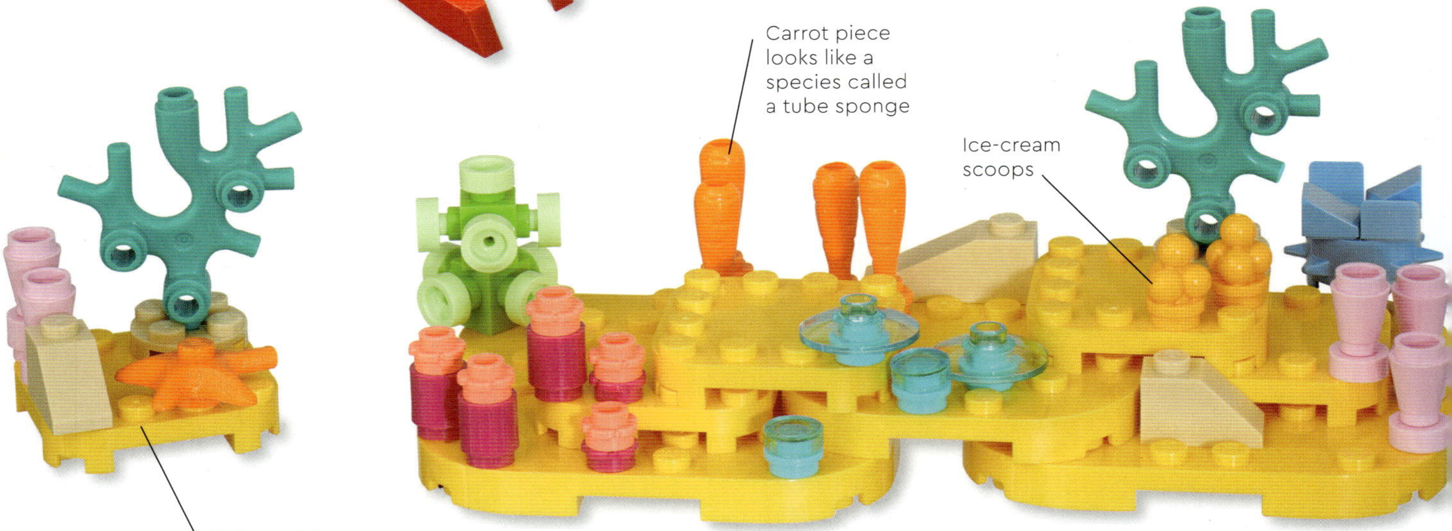

Carrot piece looks like a species called a tube sponge
Ice-cream scoops
Yellow plates form the seabed

ANGELFISH

These beautiful fish are not as serene as they look. They're always quarreling with each other! If you build a school of angelfish, get ready for some brick-busting fish fights. Most of this little fish's body is built sideways from the tail fin.

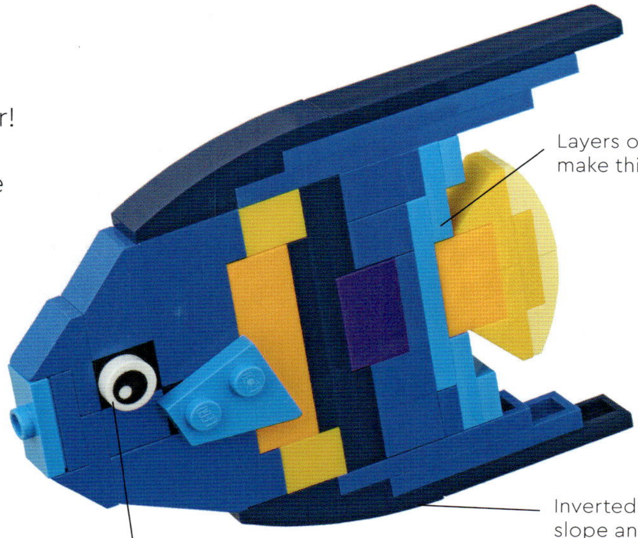
I HAVE TO ADMIT, I'M NO ANGEL!
Layers of plates make thin stripes
Inverted curved slope and 1×4 tile form a long fin
Attach eyes to bricks with side studs

URCHIN

What's tiny, crawls along, and can't swim? A sleepy-looking sea urchin. But don't try to push it around. Its sharp spikes give a nasty sting.

Urchins don't really have visible eyes but yours can!

IN A PRICKLE

Two 2×2 bricks with side studs turned on their sides form the middle of the urchin's body. With studs all around, you can add pieces on every surface to make a spiny sea creature.

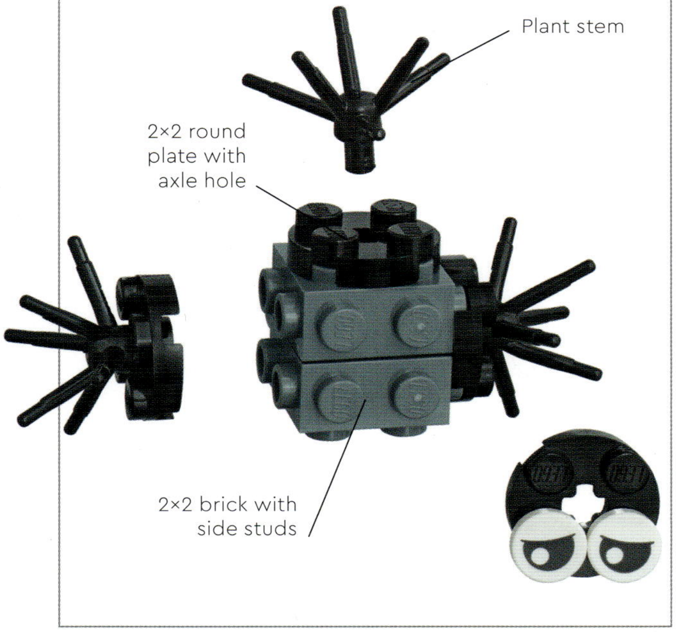
Plant stem
2×2 round plate with axle hole
2×2 brick with side studs

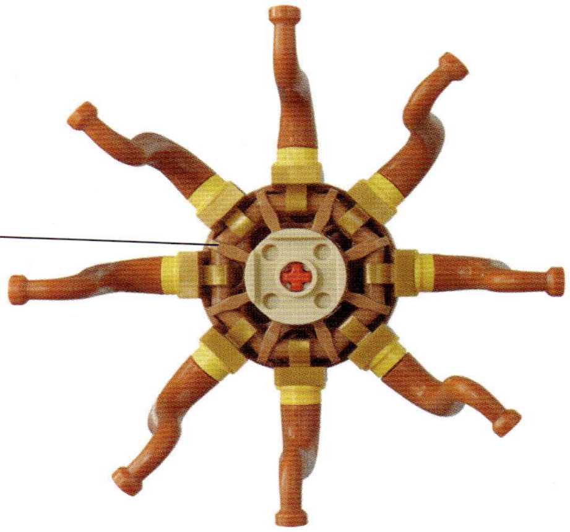
This 2×2 round plate with octagonal bar is the perfect base for an octopus body

UNDERNEATH VIEW

OCTOPUS

The big-brained octopus is very curious. It wants to know why people call its arms "tentacles." It has eight, so they should be "eightacles." Right?

4×4 dome is the head or "mantle"
Tentacles are elephant trunk pieces!
1×1 tiles with clips connect the tentacles to the body

BUILDING BRIEF

Objective:	Build an underwater scene
Use:	Creating undersea adventures
Features:	Coral reef, mermaid palace, underwater vehicle
Extras:	Undersea plants, seabed, camera

UNDERWATER WORLD

This LEGO submersible is here to check on the seabed environment. Good news! The plants and coral are flourishing. The fish are healthy. And the mermaid's palace is clean and tidy. But wait—what if the mermaid thinks this strange robotic-looking "fish" with arms is a threat? She might find a trident. Let's hope this submersible is reversible!

Layers of radar dishes in different sizes form the roof

SIDE VIEW

MERMAID PALACE

The mermaid clearly lives in harmony with her environment. She's letting seaweeds thrive in her garden, and all fishy visitors are welcome in her elegant sea-green palace.

If you don't have arch pieces, you could make rectangular windows instead

Clips hold fish to make it look like they are swimming by

Transparent minifigure heads look like towers of bubbles

WISHES UPON A STARFISH DO COME TRUE!

DEEP-SEA SUBMERSIBLE

Geologists use small craft called submersibles to survey the ocean depths. Build yours with a big front windshield for a good view, and movable arms to collect samples. Maybe even add a camera to your vehicle.

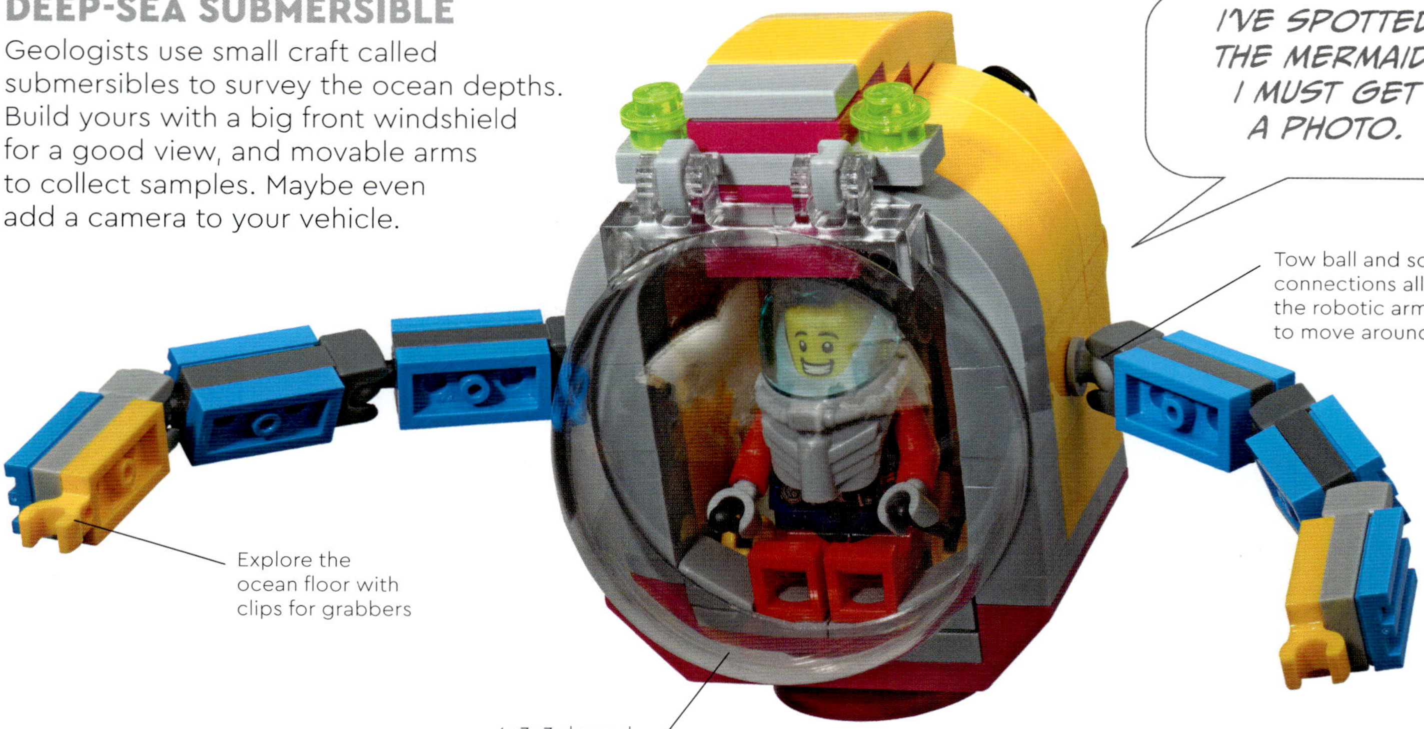
I'VE SPOTTED THE MERMAID! I MUST GET A PHOTO.
Tow ball and socket connections allow the robotic arms to move around
Explore the ocean floor with clips for grabbers
6×3×3 domed windshield

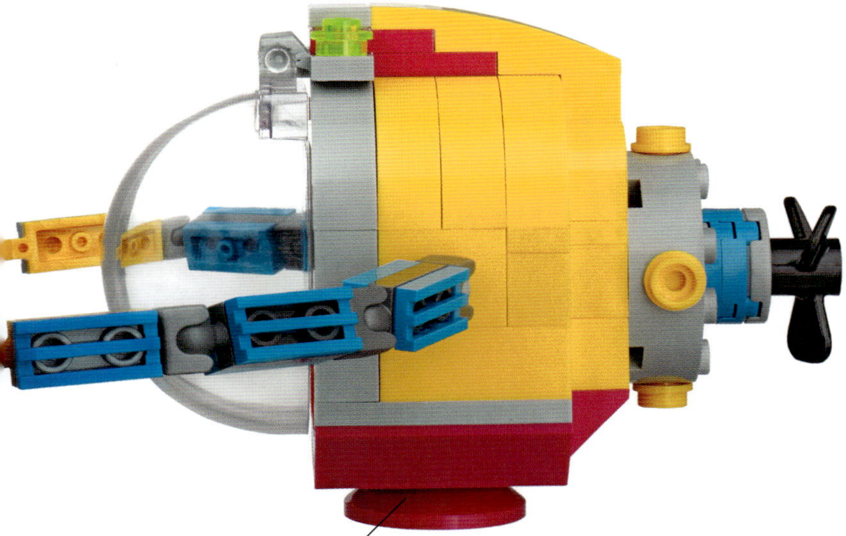
Radar dish for a soft landing on the sea floor

Could this tunnel lead to a secret underwater garden?

DEEP SEAT

Make sure you build the walls of your submersible taller than three bricks high—the height of a seated minifigure. Bricks with curved tops form the roof and make sure the pilot has plenty of headspace.

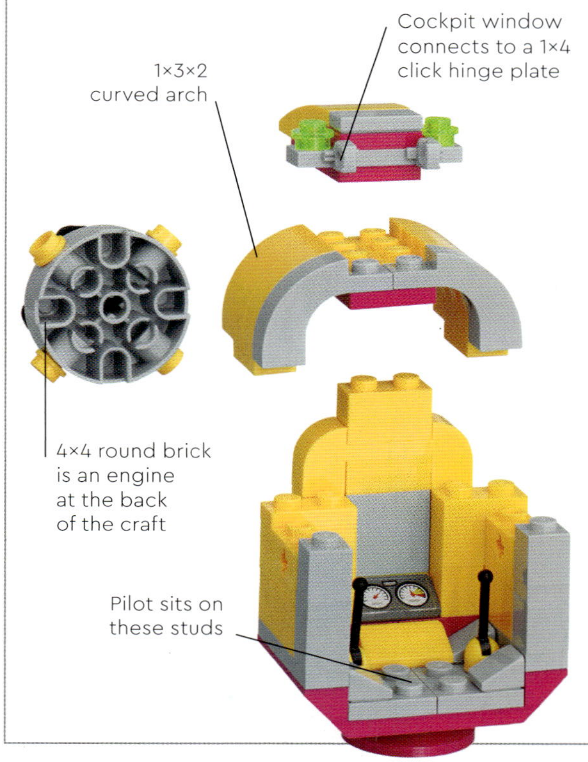
Cockpit window connects to a 1×4 click hinge plate
1×3×2 curved arch
4×4 round brick is an engine at the back of the craft
Pilot sits on these studs

LEVEL UP

The mermaid isn't the only one living under the sea! Build a neighborhood for merfolk. They'll need homes and places to meet, such as stores and restaurants.

BUILDING BRIEF

Objective: Build an enchanting garden
Use: A calming place for fairy folk
Features: Trees, pond, plants
Extras: Water fountain, walls, archway

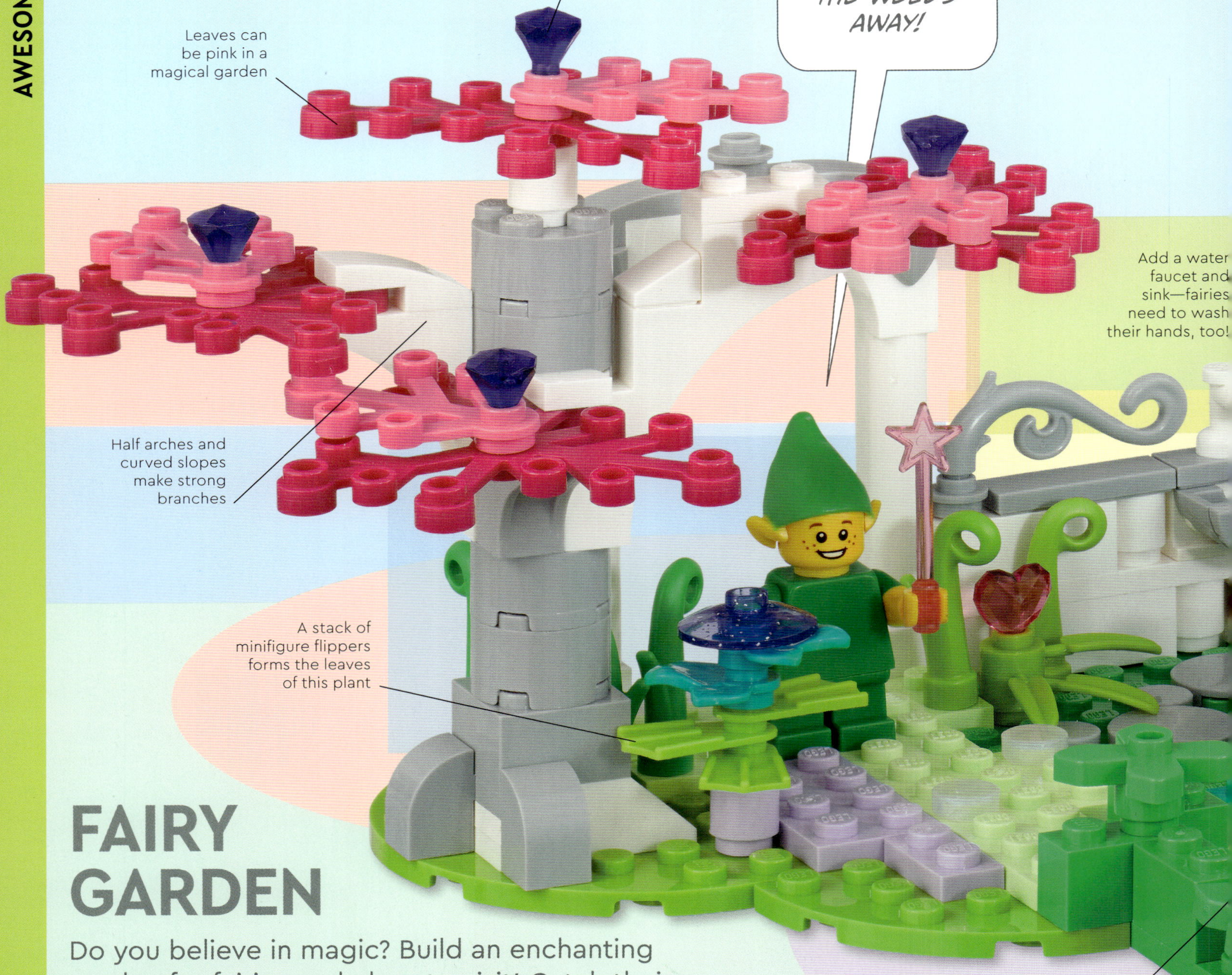

Jewel pieces for fairy fruit
I JUST MAGIC THE WEEDS AWAY!
Leaves can be pink in a magical garden
Add a water faucet and sink—fairies need to wash their hands, too!
Half arches and curved slopes make strong branches
A stack of minifigure flippers forms the leaves of this plant
Transparent blue plates make a tranquil pond

FAIRY GARDEN

Do you believe in magic? Build an enchanting garden for fairies and elves to visit! Catch their eyes with lots of color, shimmering jewels, and sparkly pieces. Don't forget to add inviting plants and flowers and even a splashy fountain. Then leave your model out and see if you get any tiny, magical visitors . . .

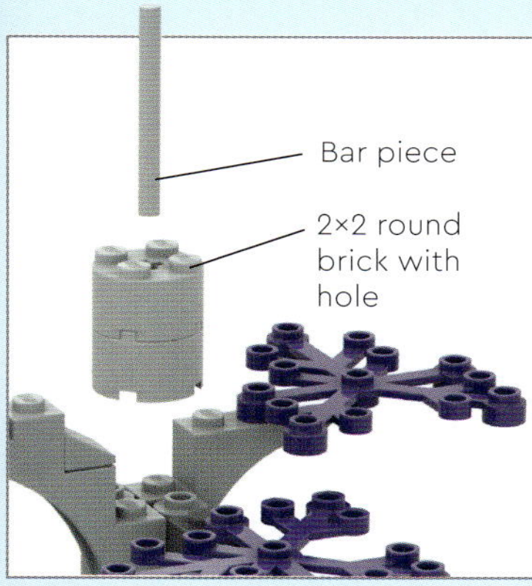
Bar piece
2×2 round brick with hole

FAIRY STURDY

Stack up 2×2 round bricks with axle holes to make the trunk of this charming tree. Then slide a bar through the bricks' holes. The bar adds extra stability—just like magic—making it tricky for these trees to topple over.

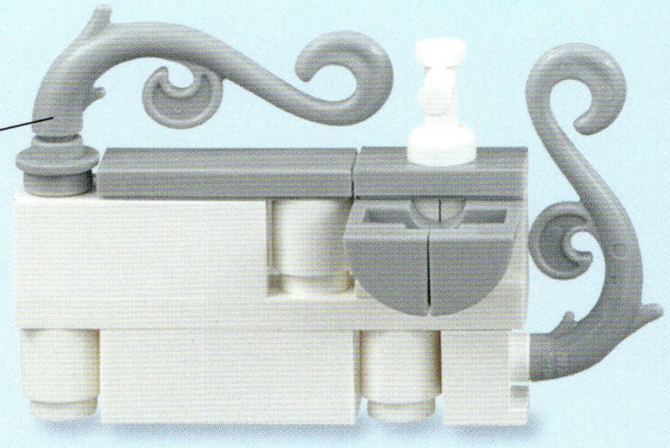
Gray plant stems look like carved stone

FAIRY SINK

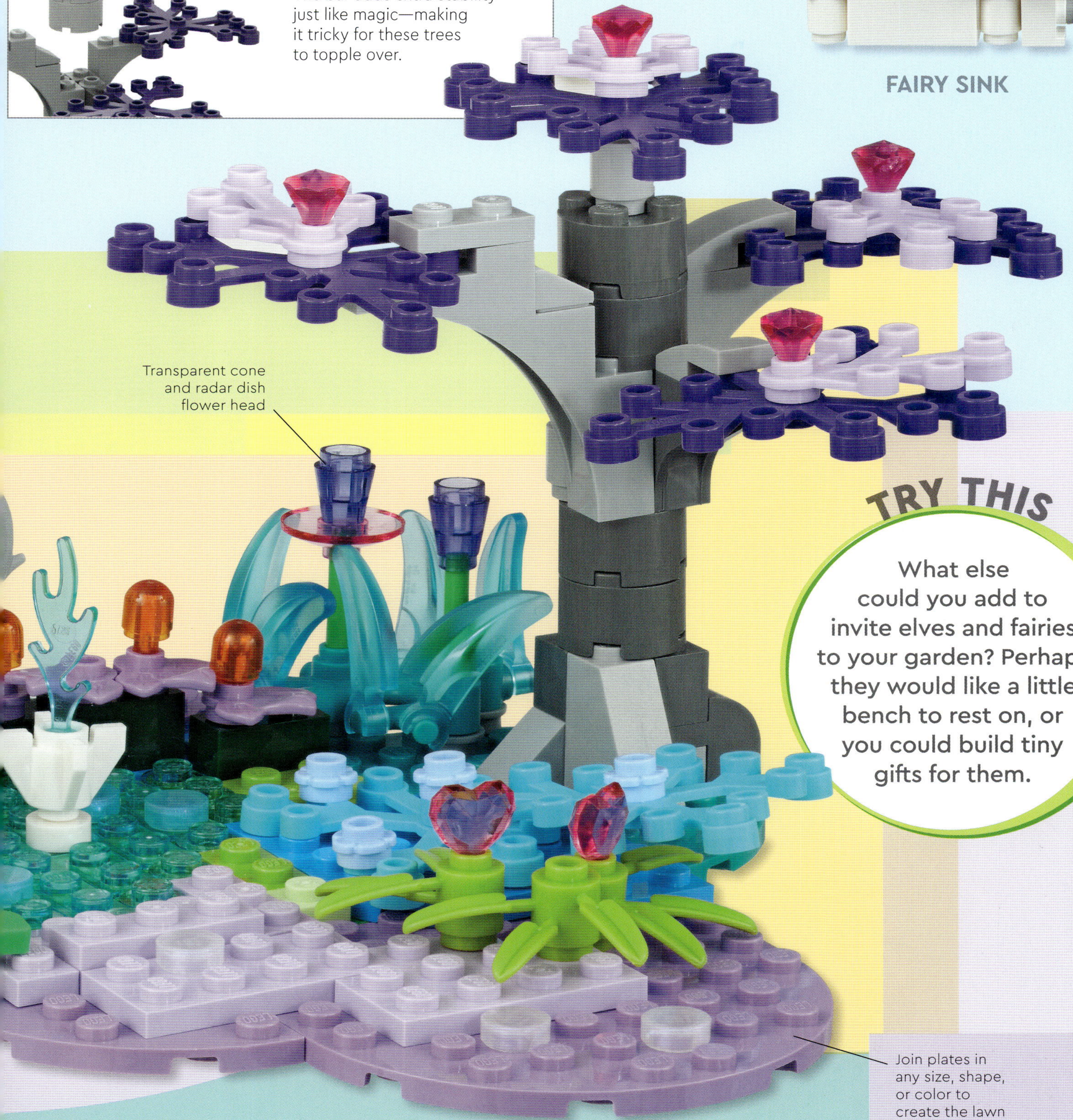
Transparent cone and radar dish flower head
Join plates in any size, shape, or color to create the lawn

TRY THIS

What else could you add to invite elves and fairies to your garden? Perhaps they would like a little bench to rest on, or you could build tiny gifts for them.

BUILDING BRIEF

Objective: Build steampunk vehicles
Use: Fantastical adventures
Features: Pipes, wheels, valves, steam engines
Extras: Propellers, legs, flags, horns

STEAMPUNK VEHICLES

Imagine a world where the technology of the past is still being used. A hissing, clanging world of contraptions powered only by steam. That's the fantastical world of steampunk. Give your vehicles a steampunk look by adding valves, joints, and pipes for the steam to travel through. Then get your goggles on—we're off!

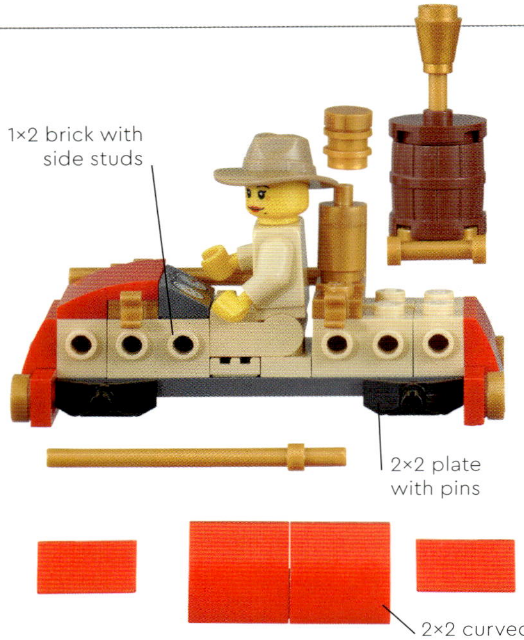
1×2 brick with side studs
2×2 plate with pins
2×2 curved slope

STEAM-POWERED SIDES

The base of this vehicle is one long 2×8 plate. Plates with pins attach beneath the base plate for the large wheels to connect to. Above the plate are bricks with side studs, which hold the smooth side panels of the car.

STEAM CAR

The big, spoked wheels on this car look like they come from a horse-drawn carriage. The boiler that powers it is at the back, and there's an exhaust pipe for the steam to escape.

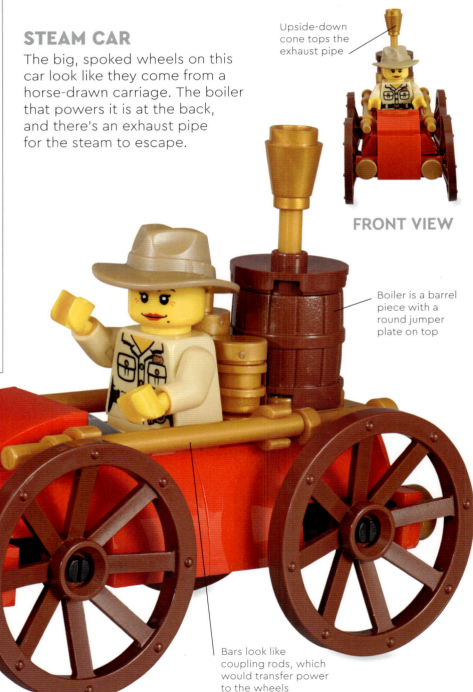

Upside-down cone tops the exhaust pipe

FRONT VIEW

Boiler is a barrel piece with a round jumper plate on top
Curved slopes shape the hood
1×1 round tiles are glittering headlights
Cart wheel for a vintage look
Bars look like coupling rods, which would transfer power to the wheels

THIS PLANE IS CHOCK-FULL OF FUN!
This faucet piece's nozzle fits into a ring on a plate to form an exhaust pipe
Telescope pieces are steam pipes
3×1×2 curved slope wing attaches sideways
Propeller spins on a 2×2 tile with pin

1×1 tile and plates make tail stripes

REAR VIEW

PETITE PLANE

This goggle-wearing pilot is stoked to be flying this mini steampunk plane. Let's hope the plane's engine is well stoked, too. Running out of steam would really bring her down.

LEVEL UP

Once you've mastered a few steampunk vehicles, try out other types of transportation or even locations. Aim to create a whole steampunk city!

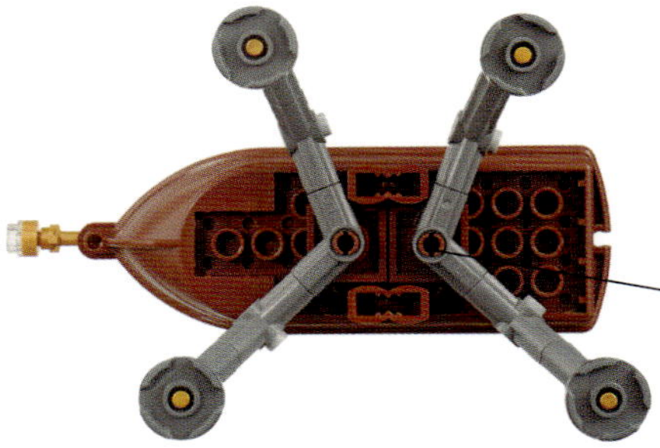
Pin attaches to a tile with hole under the boat

UNDERNEATH VIEW

FEET OF ENGINEERING

These steampunk daytrippers are walking their boat to the beach on its long, jointed legs. The legs connect to the underside of the boat with LEGO Technic pins. Is that the pier coming up? Duck!

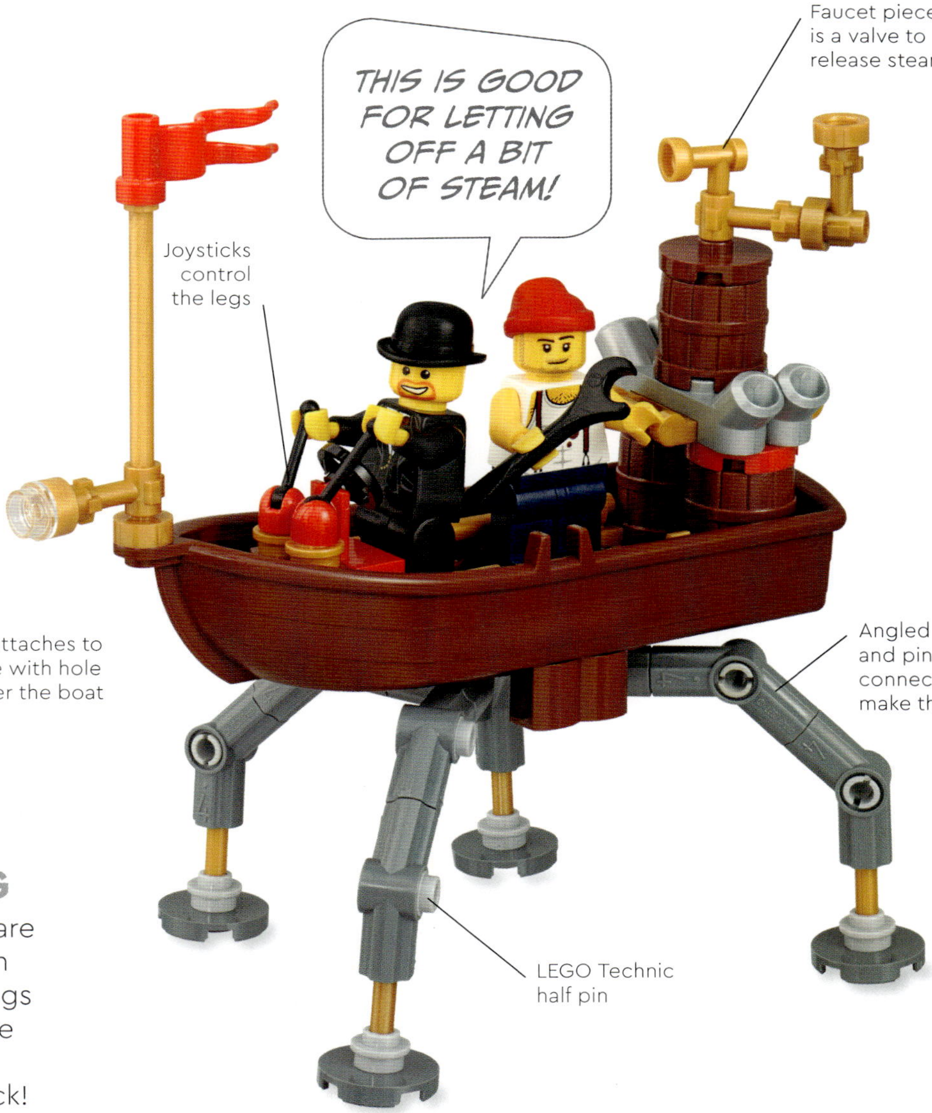
THIS IS GOOD FOR LETTING OFF A BIT OF STEAM!
Faucet piece is a valve to release steam
Joysticks control the legs
Angled axle and pin connectors make the legs
LEGO Technic half pin

BUILDING BRIEF

Objective: Create your own legend-inspired adventure
Use: Telling stories, unusual adventures
Features: Hero, animals, transportation
Extras: Magical fruit, mountaintop

BRICK TALES

Use your LEGO® pieces to illustrate a favorite tale or legend, or better still write your own. Creating the hero of a story is a great way to start. This hero is half human, half apple. When her career as a giant tortoise racer loses its a-peel, she flies off to the mountains. Why not take a seed of an idea and see how it grows?

1×1 brick stalk
Top of the apple is a 1×6×2 arch
The lower arches are inverted

APPLE BIRTH

Who's bursting out of this apple? It's our hero, Rosy! She's been growing inside, nourished only by fruit juice. Sweet! The apple is made from arches, their curves forming a hole.

I DON'T THINK MY TORTOISE IS HUNGRY.
Use a long bar to hold tempting snacks in front of the tortoises
Slope bricks for the side of the shell

TOODLE-PIP! SEE YOU AT THE FINISH.
Dome holds together a bunch of bananas
Hinge cylinder attaches to a click hinge plate

TORTOISE RACING

In Rosy Apple's world, tortoise racing is an old tradition. Riders urge their tortoises on with a fruity lure. Different colors and saddles show whose tortoise is whose.

UNDERNEATH VIEW

Each tortorise is built up from a 4×4 round plate

BUILD TIP

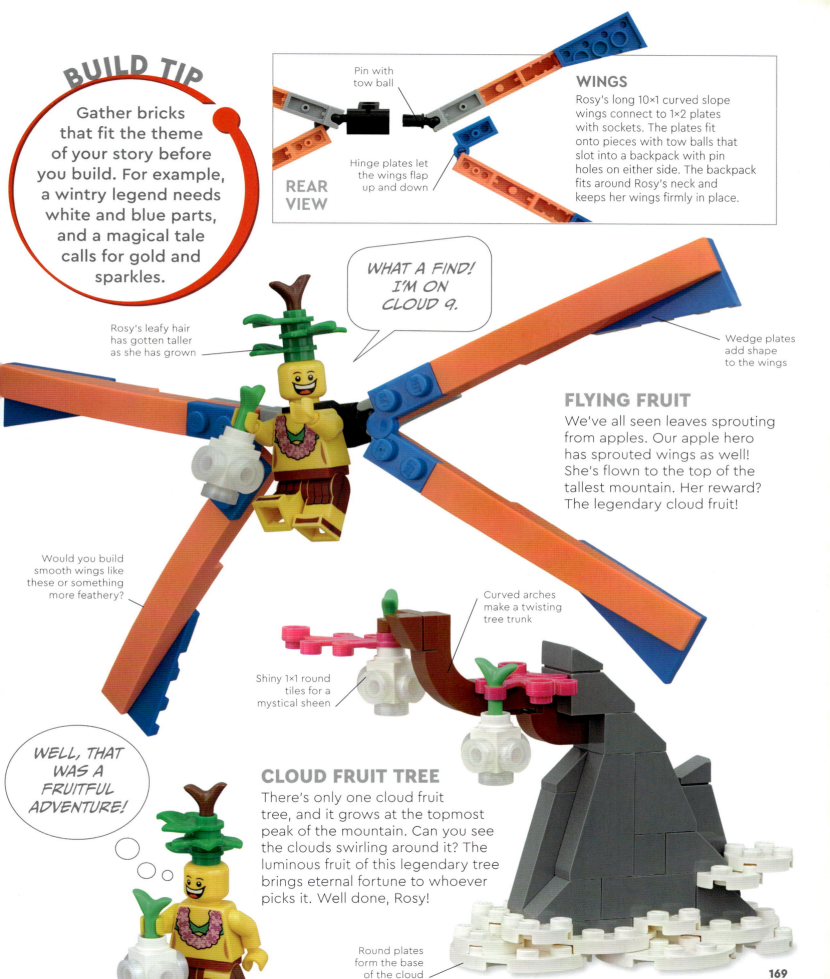

Gather bricks that fit the theme of your story before you build. For example, a wintry legend needs white and blue parts, and a magical tale calls for gold and sparkles.

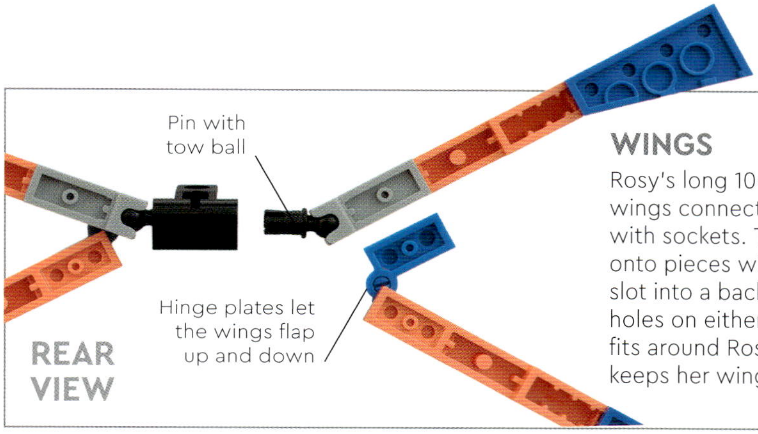

Pin with tow ball
Hinge plates let the wings flap up and down
REAR VIEW

WINGS

Rosy's long 10×1 curved slope wings connect to 1×2 plates with sockets. The plates fit onto pieces with tow balls that slot into a backpack with pin holes on either side. The backpack fits around Rosy's neck and keeps her wings firmly in place.

WHAT A FIND! I'M ON CLOUD 9.
Rosy's leafy hair has gotten taller as she has grown
Wedge plates add shape to the wings
Would you build smooth wings like these or something more feathery?

FLYING FRUIT

We've all seen leaves sprouting from apples. Our apple hero has sprouted wings as well! She's flown to the top of the tallest mountain. Her reward? The legendary cloud fruit!

Curved arches make a twisting tree trunk
Shiny 1×1 round tiles for a mystical sheen
Round plates form the base of the cloud

CLOUD FRUIT TREE

There's only one cloud fruit tree, and it grows at the topmost peak of the mountain. Can you see the clouds swirling around it? The luminous fruit of this legendary tree brings eternal fortune to whoever picks it. Well done, Rosy!

WELL, THAT WAS A FRUITFUL ADVENTURE!

BUILDING BRIEF

Objective:	Build a majestic dragon
Use:	Magical adventures, storytelling
Features:	Large wings, horns, tail, teeth
Extras:	Rider and saddle, movable limbs, shimmering features

A friend could build the body while you make the head

SIDE VIEW

BUILD TIP

Small plates and tiles look like scaly dragon skin. Features like this make a model look detailed and realistic, even if the build is a mythical creature!

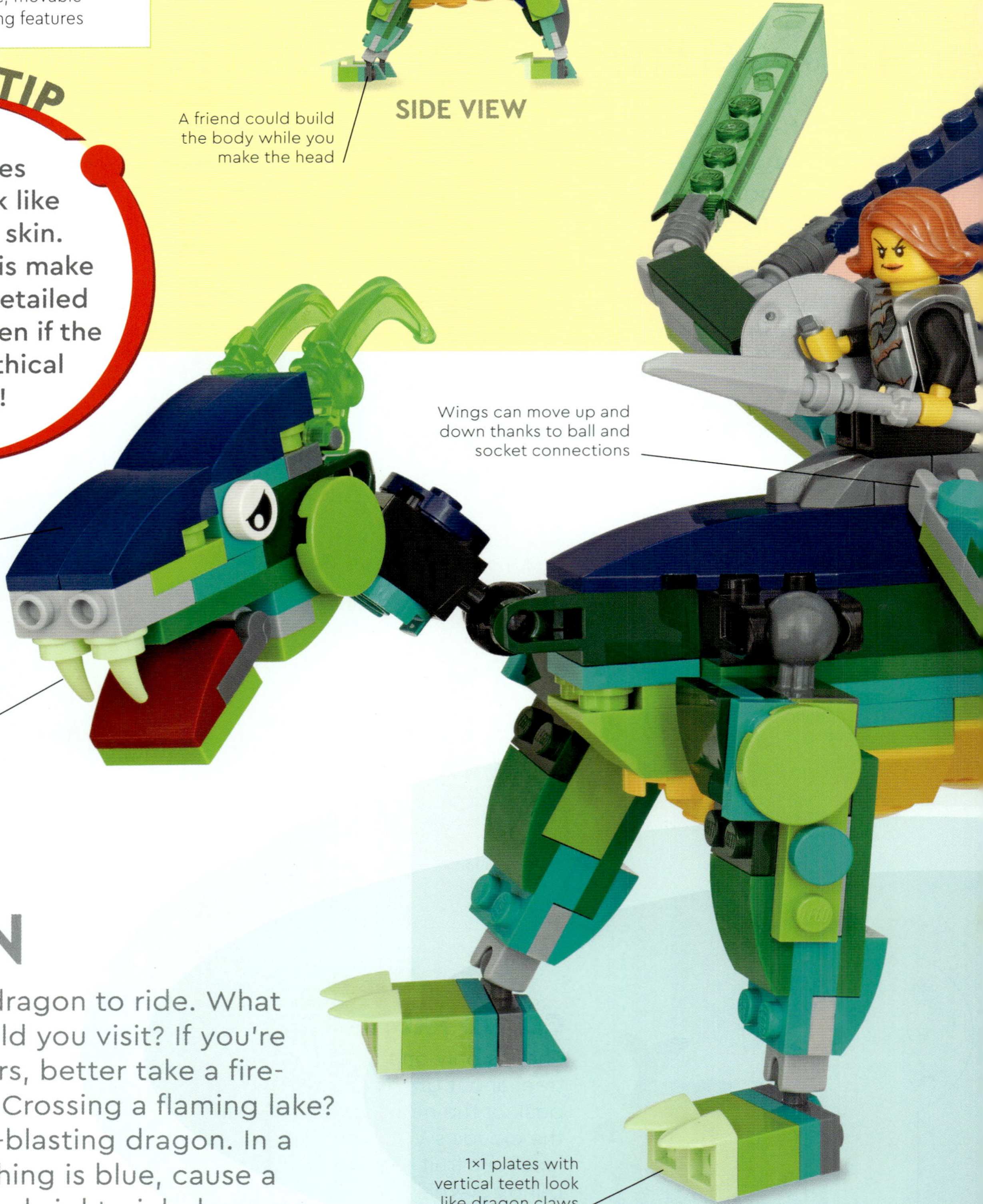
Wings can move up and down thanks to ball and socket connections
Curved slopes give the head a smooth shape
Sharp teeth are neon green horn pieces
1×1 plates with vertical teeth look like dragon claws

DRAGON

Imagine having a dragon to ride. What magical lands would you visit? If you're battling ice warriors, better take a fire-breathing dragon. Crossing a flaming lake? Then go for an ice-blasting dragon. In a land where everything is blue, cause a stir by flying in on a bright pink dragon. Remember, the wilder your story, the wilder your dragon might look.

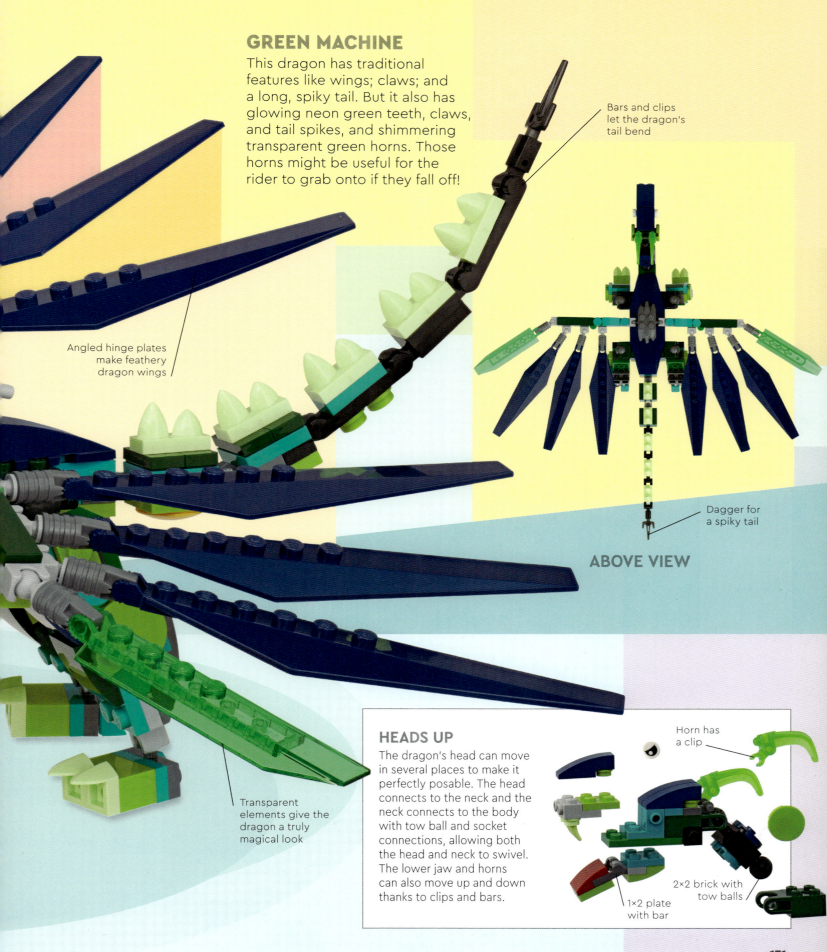

GREEN MACHINE

This dragon has traditional features like wings; claws; and a long, spiky tail. But it also has glowing neon green teeth, claws, and tail spikes, and shimmering transparent green horns. Those horns might be useful for the rider to grab onto if they fall off!

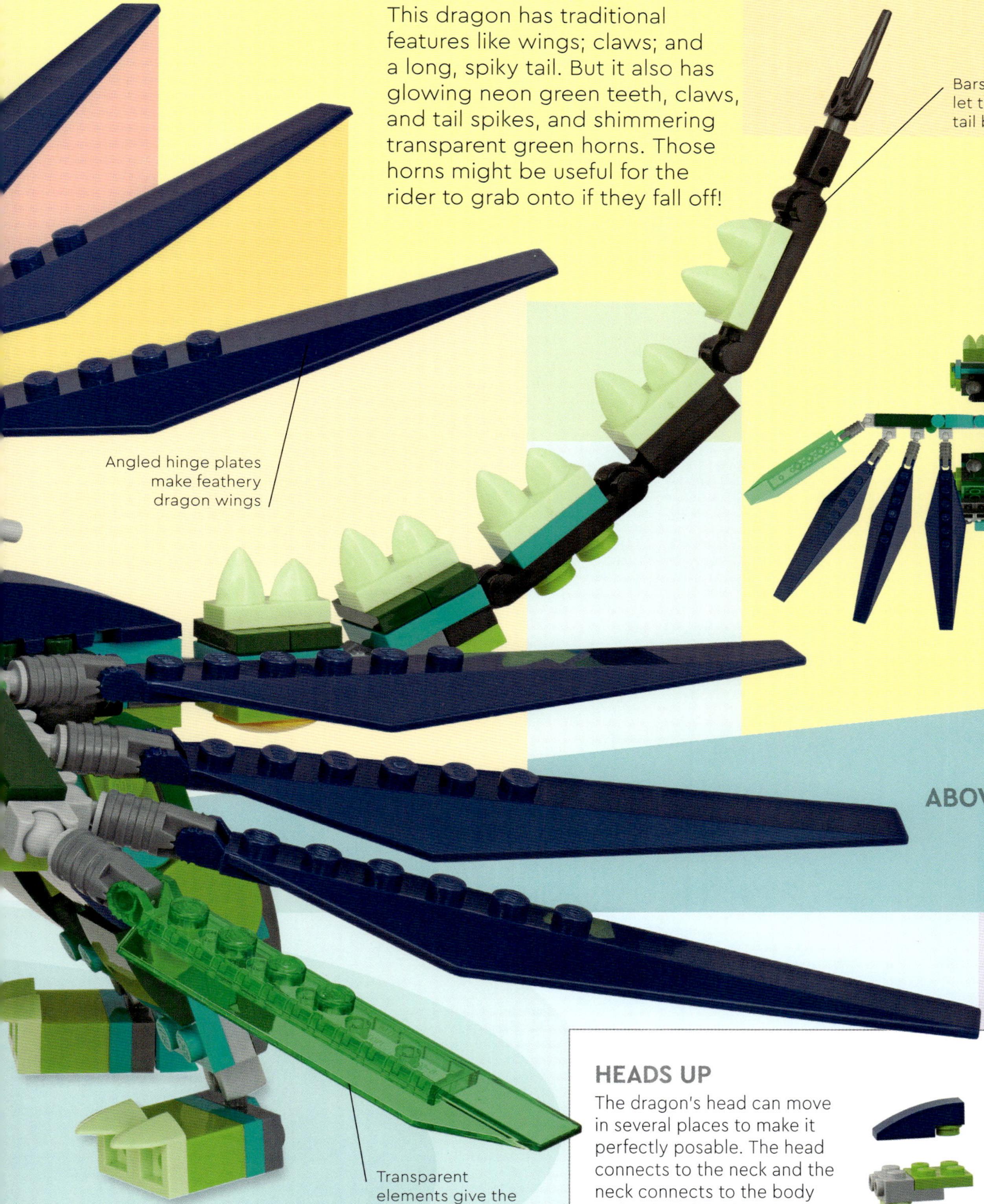
Bars and clips let the dragon's tail bend
Angled hinge plates make feathery dragon wings
Transparent elements give the dragon a truly magical look

Dagger for a spiky tail

ABOVE VIEW

HEADS UP

The dragon's head can move in several places to make it perfectly posable. The head connects to the neck and the neck connects to the body with tow ball and socket connections, allowing both the head and neck to swivel. The lower jaw and horns can also move up and down thanks to clips and bars.

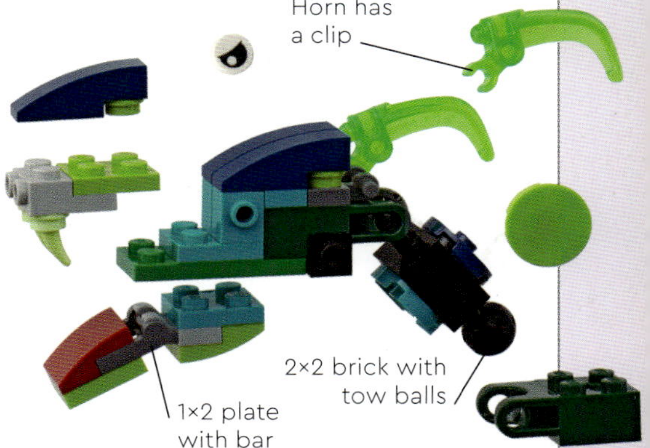
Horn has a clip
2×2 brick with tow balls
1×2 plate with bar

DOORWAY TO ANOTHER WORLD

What's through this bedroom door? A landing? A hallway? No, it's a magical world of wonder. Every day, the minifigure skips through the door to go sailing with her fantasy friends. Sometimes Teddy goes, too! Build a doorway to a magical land so your minifigures can go on their own adventure.

BUILDING BRIEF

Objective: Make a doorway that leads to an unexpected place
Use: Magical adventures
Features: Room, door, fantasy land
Extras: Furniture, magical friends

CONTRASTING WORLDS

First, build a perfectly ordinary bedroom. Nothing too exciting or unusual to see here! The tan, brown, and white tones used in this room contrast with the vibrant colors of the fantasy land through the bedroom door.

TOP DRAWER

This tall set of drawers has a core of standard 1×2 bricks and 1×1 headlight bricks. Jumper plates attach sideways at the front to form the drawer handles. There's also a 2×2 jumper plate on top for Teddy to stand on.

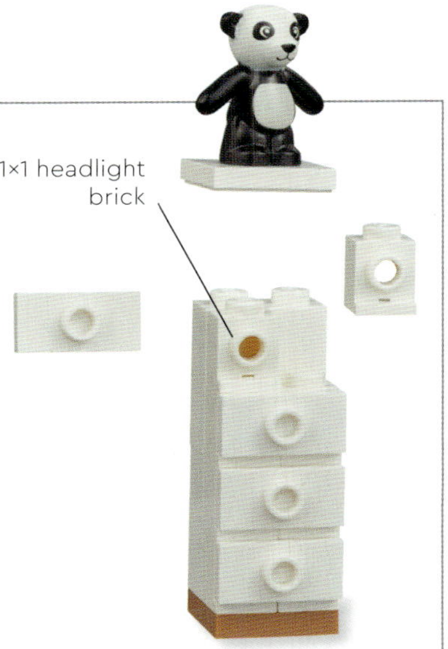
1×1 headlight brick

Rounded window with spokes makes a traditional headboard
Bedside lamp made from cones
1×1 tiles and slopes in a pattern form a patchwork quilt
If you don't have a door piece, simply leave the entryway open

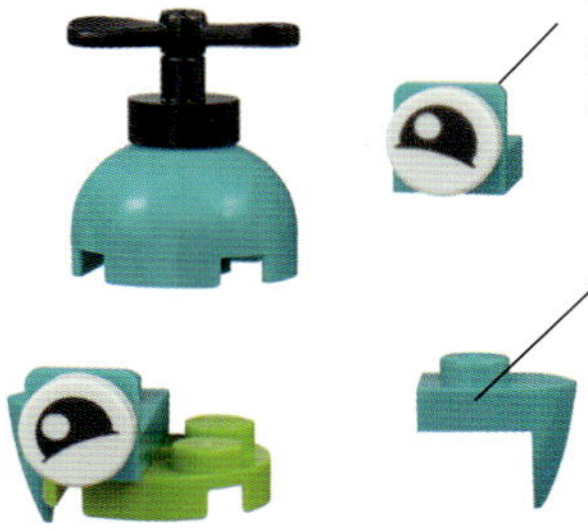
1×1/1×1 inverted bracket plate
1×1 tooth plates make cute ears

BUBBLE BUDDY

This adorable creature is made from mostly round plates and domes. The printed eye tiles attach to the heads via 1×1/1×1 inverted bracket plates.

CHANGE IT

Each time your minifigure returns home and closes the door, take your "new world" model apart and create another land for them to visit next time.

Trees here are shades of purple instead of green

SIDE VIEW

Include growing trees to show that this world is flourishing
Propeller helps this creature get around
Striped 2×2 round brick trunk
Barrel boat bobs along on bubbling blue water
This merry-go-round spins on a turntable piece

RAINFOREST HABITAT

Rainforests are vital to our planet. They're home to more than half of its plant and animal species. Imagine walking through a dark, steamy rainforest. What's that rustling sound? Who's that peeping through the leaves? Set the scene for a tropical adventure by building a LEGO rainforest.

BUILDING BRIEF

Objective: Make a tropical rainforest
Use: Exploring nature, animal habitats
Features: Tropical plants, trees, waterfall
Extras: Rainforest-dwelling creatures, rocks, fungi, flowers

TRY THIS

Other forests, including temperate rainforests, are home to different plants and animal life. Do your research and build another type of forest.

2×2 ridged round bricks are tree trunks
The dark forest floor teems with plant life, such as fungi and colorful flowers
Real-life surfaces have small bumps and hills

I WONDER WHAT YOU'RE THINKING ABOUT.

RAINFOREST LAYERS

You'll need four layers: The emergent layer at the top is formed of really tall trees. Below that, the canopy is a dense layer of trees that blocks out the sunlight. Lower still is the leafy understory. Then, the forest floor.

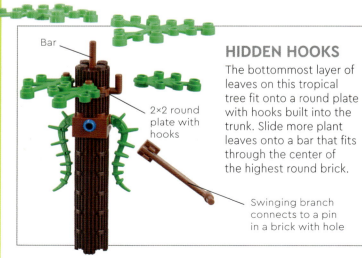

Bar
2×2 round plate with hooks
Swinging branch connects to a pin in a brick with hole

HIDDEN HOOKS

The bottommost layer of leaves on this tropical tree fit onto a round plate with hooks built into the trunk. Slide more plant leaves onto a bar that fits through the center of the highest round brick.

I WANT SOME BINOCULARS.

Add plant pieces between layers of rock for a tropical look
2×1 green slope for a mossy rock
WHERE HAS THAT MONKEY GONE?
1×1 round tile for churning water

LUSH WATERFALL

Tropical vegetation surrounds this bubbling waterfall in the rainforest. You could build a taller waterfall if you like, with two or even three tiers. Why not include some animals or minifigure swimmers in your scene?

CURTAIN OF WATER

The flowing waterfall is made from one piece. If you don't have it, use any blue pieces to build the same shape. Curved slopes can also make a convincing cascade. You could add some secret treasure for explorers to find behind the fall!

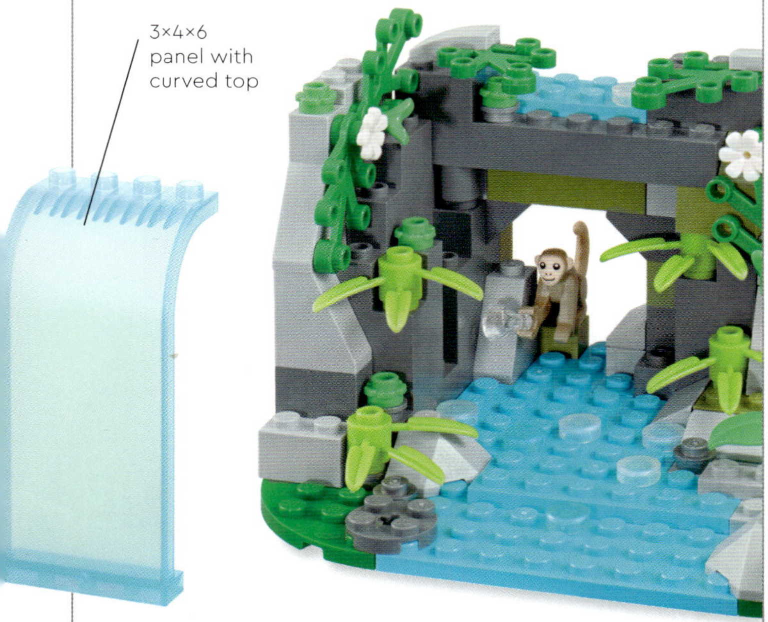
3×4×6 panel with curved top

2×2 round plates look like worn-away rocks

SIDE VIEW

BUILDING BRIEF

Objective: Build rainforest flora and fauna
Use: Observing animals and plants, rainforest adventures
Features: Legs, tails, beaks, eyes, stems
Extras: Moving body parts

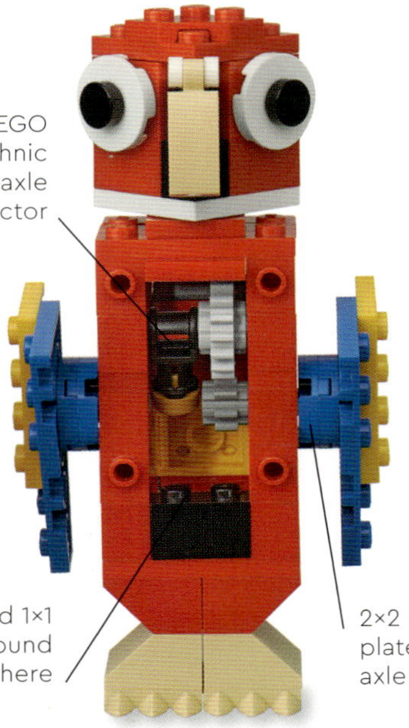
LEGO Technic axle connector
Load 1×1 round bricks here
2×2 round plate with axle hole

SURPRISE-WING MOVE

This parrot's left wing fits onto two 2×2 round plates with an axle through their holes. Pulling the wing forward moves the axle, which turns two gears inside the parrot's body. The gears force a LEGO Technic axle connector backward so it knocks into a tail-feather trapdoor at the rear—and out comes the parrot poop!

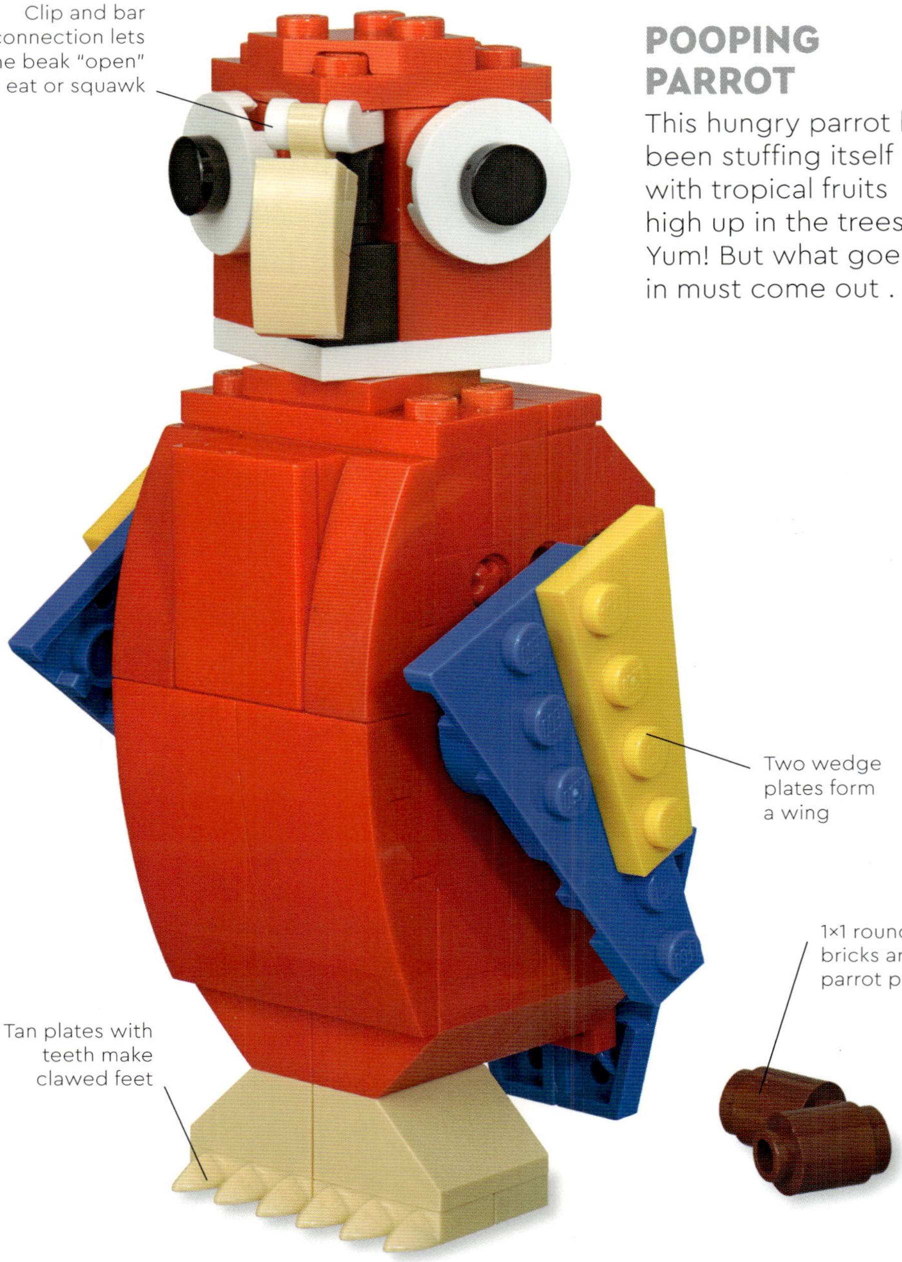
Clip and bar connection lets the beak "open" to eat or squawk
Two wedge plates form a wing
1×1 round bricks are parrot poop
Tan plates with teeth make clawed feet

POOPING PARROT

This hungry parrot has been stuffing itself with tropical fruits high up in the trees. Yum! But what goes in must come out . . .

RAINFOREST LIFE

Build some rainforest-dwelling animals and plants and go on your own expedition. Will your animals get together and campaign to save the rainforest? What if a tiny insect made off with the juiciest fruit while a parrot posse and a monkey mob were fighting over it? If you'd rather stick to a real-life scene, you could study rainforest creatures and try to build accurate models.

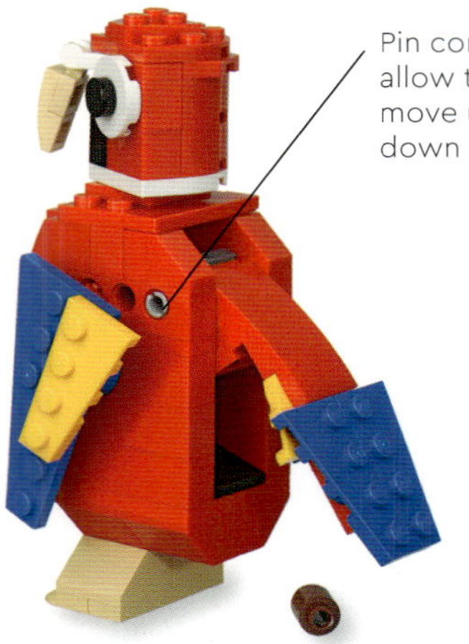
Pin connections allow the tail to move up and down

REAR VIEW IN ACTION

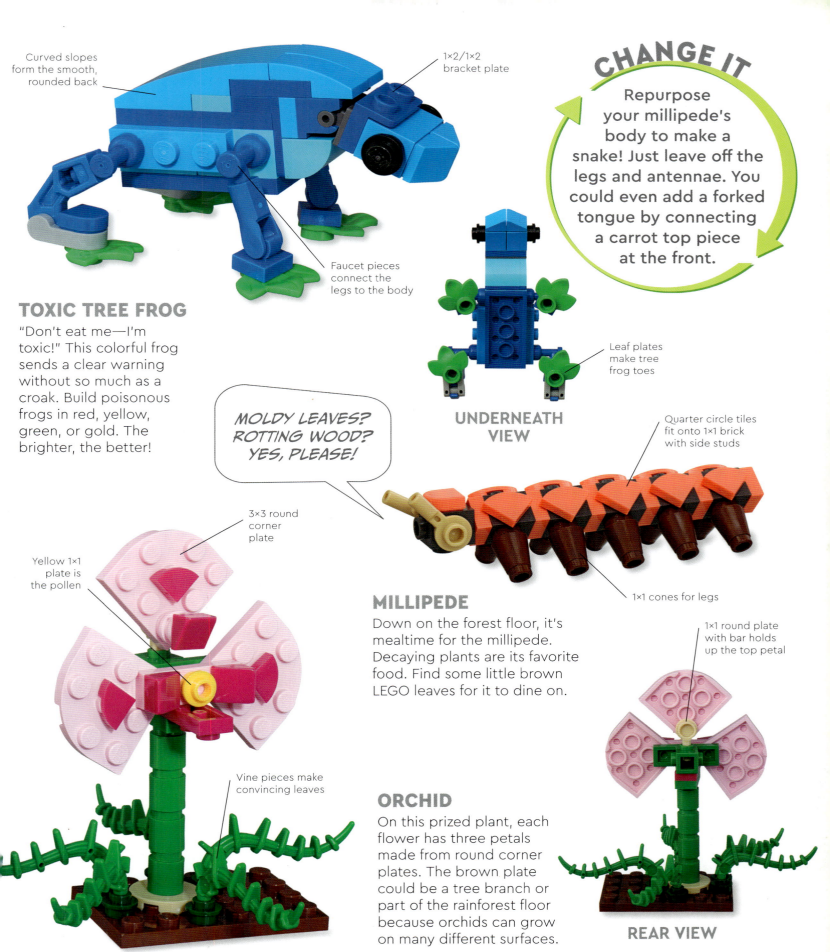

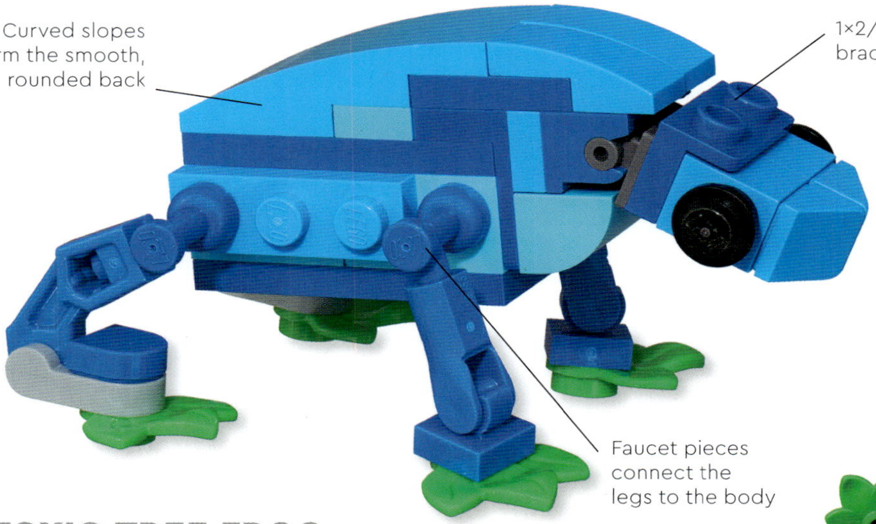
Curved slopes form the smooth, rounded back
1×2/1×2 bracket plate
Faucet pieces connect the legs to the body

TOXIC TREE FROG

"Don't eat me—I'm toxic!" This colorful frog sends a clear warning without so much as a croak. Build poisonous frogs in red, yellow, green, or gold. The brighter, the better!

Leaf plates make tree frog toes

UNDERNEATH VIEW

CHANGE IT

Repurpose your millipede's body to make a snake! Just leave off the legs and antennae. You could even add a forked tongue by connecting a carrot top piece at the front.

MOLDY LEAVES? ROTTING WOOD? YES, PLEASE!

Quarter circle tiles fit onto 1×1 brick with side studs
1×1 cones for legs

MILLIPEDE

Down on the forest floor, it's mealtime for the millipede. Decaying plants are its favorite food. Find some little brown LEGO leaves for it to dine on.

3×3 round corner plate
Yellow 1×1 plate is the pollen
Vine pieces make convincing leaves

ORCHID

On this prized plant, each flower has three petals made from round corner plates. The brown plate could be a tree branch or part of the rainforest floor because orchids can grow on many different surfaces.

1×1 round plate with bar holds up the top petal

REAR VIEW

BUILDING BRIEF

Objective: Add seasonal differences to the same scene
Use: Exploring nature, display
Features: Plants, fence, tree, treehouse
Extras: Sports equipment, snow, festive decorations, animals

THE FOUR SEASONS

One yard. Four seasons. Lots and lots of changes! Following the seasons in a year can feel like a big adventure. Try altering the details on a favorite model to make different versions for each season. Flowering window boxes, ducklings, swimming pools, fallen leaves, and snowballs all tell a season's tale.

Small slopes for treehouse roof tiles

Pale leaves for budding trees

This 1×2 brick with hole (with 1×1 slopes on top) makes a snug birdhouse

SPRING

In springtime, the garden bursts into life. Yellow daffodils bloom and baby bunnies are born. There's sure to be a family of newly hatched chicks in the birdhouse under the treehouse, too.

SUMMER

Time for a lazy summer picnic. Well, it's too hot for tennis! The tree's leaves are darker now, and give good shade. Look under the treehouse. Is that one of the chicks, all grown up?

Blanket made from 1×1 tiles

SIDE VIEW

Switch out light green pieces for darker green

End of the ladder flips up thanks to clips

Darker green plates make a lush summer lawn

FALL

Fall turns everything gold and brown. Spiders and toadstools appear, and leaves begin to drop. Raking them up is hard work, but it's nearly time for Halloween fun. Can you spot the creepy pumpkin in this scene?

LEVEL UP

Choose one season and build your treehouse as it would look in different years, decades, or even centuries. How would the design and decor change?

The two parts of the roof rest on each other
Orange, yellow, and brown leaf pieces make fall hues
2×2 radar dish on a 1×1 round brick makes a toadstool
Dark tan base plate looks like mulched leaves

WINTER

The chilly winter tree is bare, snow is everywhere, and icicles hang from the treehouse. Don't let your minifigures go inside and leave the snowman on his own. Warming up with a snowball fight is much more fun!

THIS YARD IS FUN IN EVERY SEASON!
Add a few white slopes for a dusting of snow
Unicorn horn pieces make spiky icicles
1×1 round plate snowball
Snowman body is a 1×1 brick with side studs

TREE ANGLE

A treehouse needs a sturdy cover whatever the season! Make a classic sloped roof by using 1×2 hinge bricks and 2×2 hinge plates to hold each side of the roof at an angle.

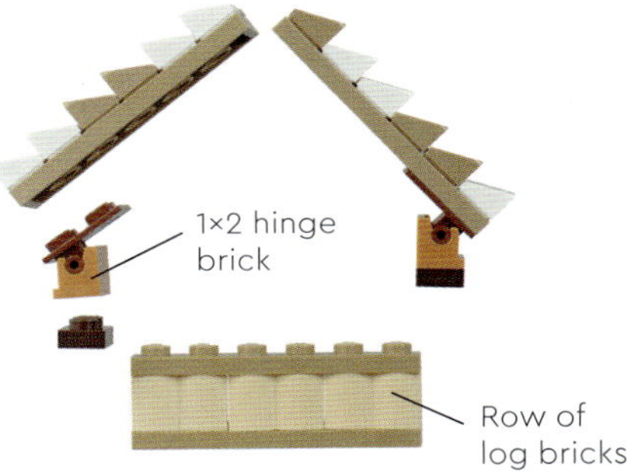
1×2 hinge brick
Row of log bricks

REAR VIEW

WITCH'S HOUSE

This cranky cottage is nestled so deep in the woods that tree roots are twisting around its walls. What other homes could you build for fantasy or fairy-tale characters? A vampire might like a house without windows, or a werewolf an apartment over a butcher's shop. Maybe build a new home for Rapunzel so she's not stuck in that tower forever.

BUILDING BRIEF

Objective:	Build an enchanted house
Use:	A home for a fairy-tale character
Features:	Door, windows, roof, magical details
Extras:	Vines, garden, trapdoor

COZY HOME

This house looks cozy enough, with its hat-shaped roof and lattice windows. But beware—the higgledy-piggledy steps are slippery with moss. And why are there bones by the path?

CHANGE IT

Build the base of the cottage, then add different details for whoever will live there. An elf might want a more colorful hat roof, and a fairy may enjoy some sparkles!

Brim made from four 6×6 round corner slopes
Change the color of the leaves with the seasons
Gold and silver pieces add a magical twist

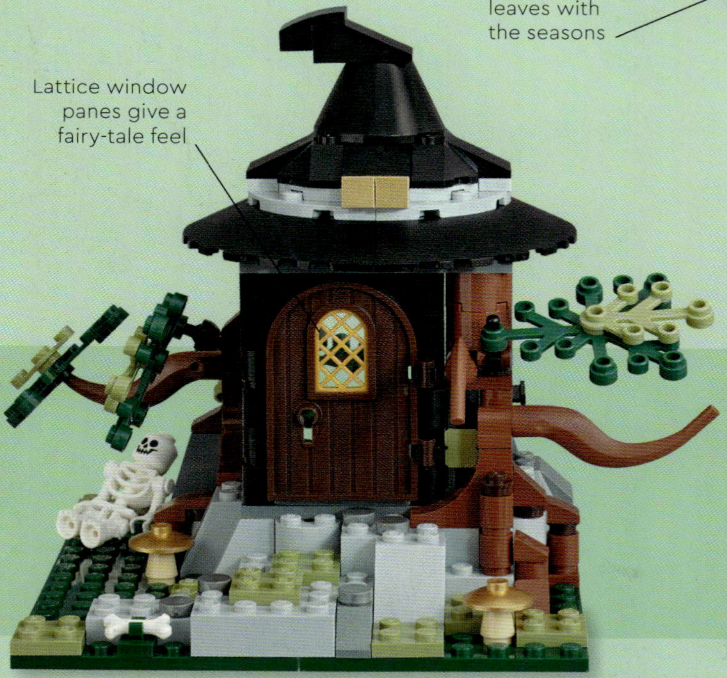
Lattice window panes give a fairy-tale feel

FRONT VIEW

The top of the hat doubles as a crooked chimney
6×5 plant leaf slots onto the end of a mechanical claw piece
Vine pieces fit into parts with pin holes
Sinister-looking bone held up by a tile with clip
YOU'RE IN LUCK. THE LAST GUEST JUST DEPARTED . . .

HATS OFF

Two 2×2 round bricks sandwiched between the layers of this hat help hold it together and keep the parts centered. The round brick on top of the 6×8 plate stabilizes the plates and slopes above it.

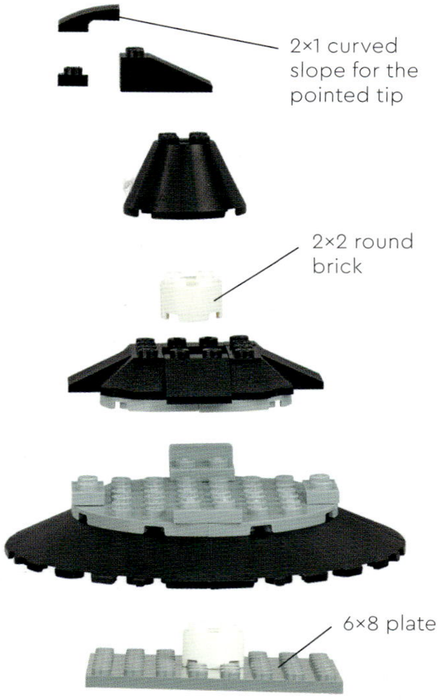
2×1 curved slope for the pointed tip
2×2 round brick
6×8 plate

RAINBOW BUS

This colorful school bus is heading over the rainbow. There's sure to be a LEGO school there, where students learn to build better and better models. You could make your bus longer than this one if you like, with even more colors, seats, and equipment inside.

BUILDING BRIEF

Objective: Build a unique vehicle
Use: Road trips, getting to and from school
Features: Wheels, seats, steering wheel, mirrors, door, windows
Extras: Bunk beds, kitchen, removable roof

HAPPY TRAVELS

The bus's color scheme may be unusual, but it still needs all the usual features for a safe and comfortable journey. This one has movable wing mirrors, big windows, chunky wheels, and a flip-out "bus stopping" signal.

2×2 tile stop sign tells cars to wait

REAR VIEW

A rainbow theme means you don't need to have lots of pieces in the same color

1×1×3 bricks for window frames

Bricks with wheel arches give the tires room to rotate so this bus can really roll

SIDE VIEW

SCHOOL'S OUT

Want a break from classes? Your bus can also be a vacation home on wheels. Just add beds, a sink, and cooking equipment. And give it a pop-off top so you can let the sunshine in.

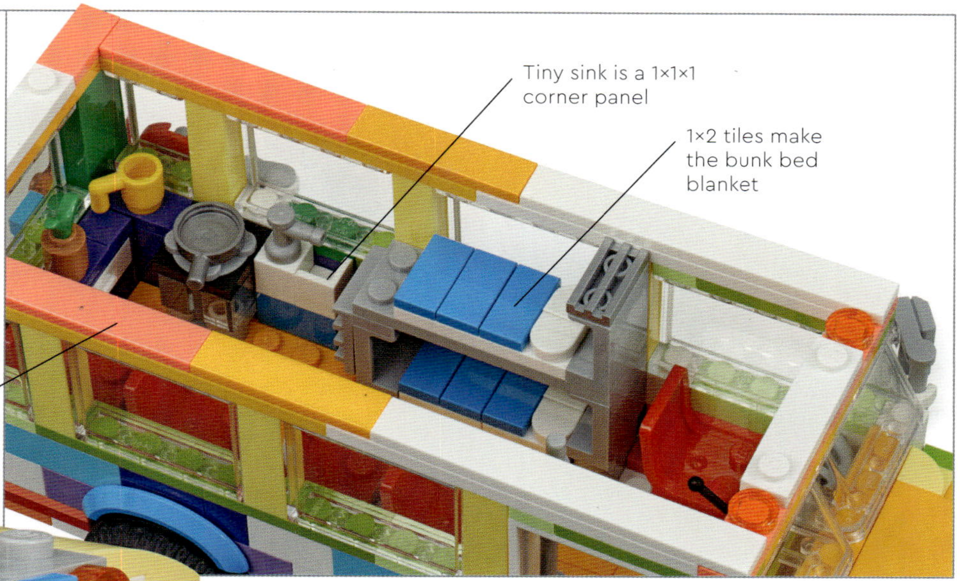

Tiny sink is a 1×1×1 corner panel

1×2 tiles make the bunk bed blanket

Tiles line the top of the bus so the roof can lift off easily

BUILD TIP

Most LEGO vehicles are built from the bottom up, starting with the chassis. The last parts you add should always be the wheels, otherwise your vehicle might roll away!

2×2 slide plate headlights

Transparent door can open outward

THIS BUS IS BASED ON AN IDEA BY LEGO FAN EMMETT L.

MEET THE BUILDERS

BARNEY MAIN

TIM GODDARD

PIECED TO MEET YOU!

MARIANN ASANUMA

JASON BRISCOE

ROD GILLIES

JESSICA FARRELL

FIND OUT WHAT MAKES US "BRICK"!

NATE DIAS

MARIANN ASANUMA

What is your favorite LEGO® element?

My favorite LEGO® element has to be the 1×1 "cheese" slope. It is so versatile and useful for so many things. It can be the curve of a car, the detail of a mosaic, or a part of a micro build.

BUILDER BIO

Location:
Salt Lake City, Utah, USA
Day job:
LEGO artist
LEGO speciality:
Mosaics and architectural models

A flower bouquet by Mariann, with a vase made from transparent plates and bricks.

What's the most challenging thing you've ever built?

That's a tricky question to answer as I worked at LEGOLAND® California for five years and worked on so many models there. Probably the hardest thing that I built was a 5 ft (1.5 m) cathedral with 50,000 LEGO pieces.

Where do you get your LEGO building ideas from?

From just about everywhere—movies, books, dreams. My tip is to look for inspiration in the world around you. There are ingenious designs and interesting details even in the smallest of things—just look and you will find it.

Do you plan out your builds?

It depends on what I am building. If it is a real thing, I do research—I usually pull up images online of the animal, person, or building from as many angles as possible. If I am building something from my imagination, sometimes I draw out my idea on paper.

Do you have a top LEGO building tip?

Practice, practice, practice! If you want to become a LEGO artist like me, the best way is to build as much as possible so you can learn lots of different techniques.

MARIANN'S BENTO LUNCHBOX, PAGES 118–119

BUILDER BIO

Location:
Norfolk, UK
Day job:
Electrical engineer
LEGO speciality:
Space and dystopian builds

JASON BRISCOE

What do you most love about building with LEGO pieces?

I like exploring new ways of using elements and looking at the way they can connect to other elements. Finishing a model always feels like a real a sense of achievement. It's a great feeling to create something unique in the world.

Do you have a top LEGO building tip?

People often say to me, "I could never build like that." But the truth is, they can. My tip is to experiment: play with the elements and create. Also, look at other people's models—the pieces they have used and how they use them. You can learn a lot by studying great-looking builds.

Do you plan out your builds?

No! I'm a "freebuilder." I usually have a vague idea of what I want to create but I never know how I'm going to do it. As I build, I try out all sorts of ideas and techniques and I find that that process generates other ideas.

This fire department creation by Jason is built at an unusual scale. The firefighter figures are slightly bigger than those in Miniland at the LEGOLAND® Parks, as is the fire engine.

What's your favorite building technique?

I use a lot of bricks on their sides and tiles to create smooth surfaces. Some people prefer to see LEGO studs on their builds but I like it when it's not immediately obvious that my models are made from LEGO pieces!

If you could design a new set for the LEGO Group, what would it be?

I really love building spaceships but there are a lot of space-themed sets and fan ideas around . . . I think a large-scale tram or Mississippi paddleboat would be cool!

JASON'S TIME MACHINE, PAGE 94

NATE DIAS

What's the most challenging thing you've ever built?

For the final of the LEGO® *Masters* TV series, I built a life-size human man, along with the contents of his office and his inner child (below right). I made the scene with my partner on the show—my friend Steve. It was a massive challenge as the scene was so big, and we had a very strict timescale, too.

BUILDER BIO

Location:
Nottingham, UK
Day job:
Science teacher
LEGO speciality:
Animals and people

What is your favorite LEGO element?

It may sound boring, but my favorite LEGO element is the 1×2 plate. It's the smallest element that you can build something with depth from, and you can make any "2x" brick with a bunch of them.

Do you plan out your builds?

For different projects, I take different approaches. Sometimes, I sketch out a build on paper, and other times I will design a model on the computer. Often I just sit down with a big pile of LEGO pieces and see what I can come up with.

What do you love most about building with LEGO pieces?

I love that you can build anything in the world (or in your mind) with just some small pieces of plastic. Whatever you can imagine, you can build it!

NATE'S SUPERHERO, THE PURPLE BLINK, PAGE 124

YOUR INNER CHILD

Nate's winning model for the first-ever LEGO® *Masters* TV series, which aired in 2017.

What are you building at the moment?

Some (almost) life-size LEGO pets. They are based on LEGO minifigure-scale animal elements, but a lot bigger. I am hoping to display them together at some LEGO shows as a sort of LEGO animal sanctuary.

BUILDER BIO

Location:
County Kildare, Ireland
Day job:
LEGO artist
LEGO speciality:
Architecture, art,
and organic forms

JESSICA FARRELL

Do you remember the first LEGO set you owned?

Yes, it was Basic Building Set (set 135). My mother gave it to me when I was four. It didn't come with instructions, just ideas on the box. I was frustrated in the beginning, as my buildings kept falling down, but it was so rewarding when I eventually figured them out! I still have the set today, in its original box.

Do you plan out your LEGO models?

When I start a new design, I rarely work out details on paper or a computer. Instead, I imagine shapes, colors, and connections. I have lots of mental images and mathematical calculations going on inside my head. Sometimes it feels like I've already finished the model before I even start building!

"Here There Be Dragons," one of Jessica's favorite models because of the vibrant color scheme and textured, churning water.

Which of your models in this book is your favorite?

It's a tie between the ancient castle (pages 70–71) and the fairy garden (pages 164–165). I'm really interested in old architecture, as seen on the castle, but I also love nature and I enjoy creating imaginary plants.

How often do you build?

Since creating things from LEGO pieces is my work as well as my hobby, I get to play almost every day! It's not all designing and creating, though. I also have to spend a lot of time organizing my pieces and tidying up after building!

Do you have a top building tip?

I'll pass on a tip that was given to me by a good friend, who is a LEGO set designer: Whenever you come across a new or interesting LEGO element, fiddle around with it, connect it to other parts in as many ways as you can, and then try to imagine lots of different ways the piece could be used.

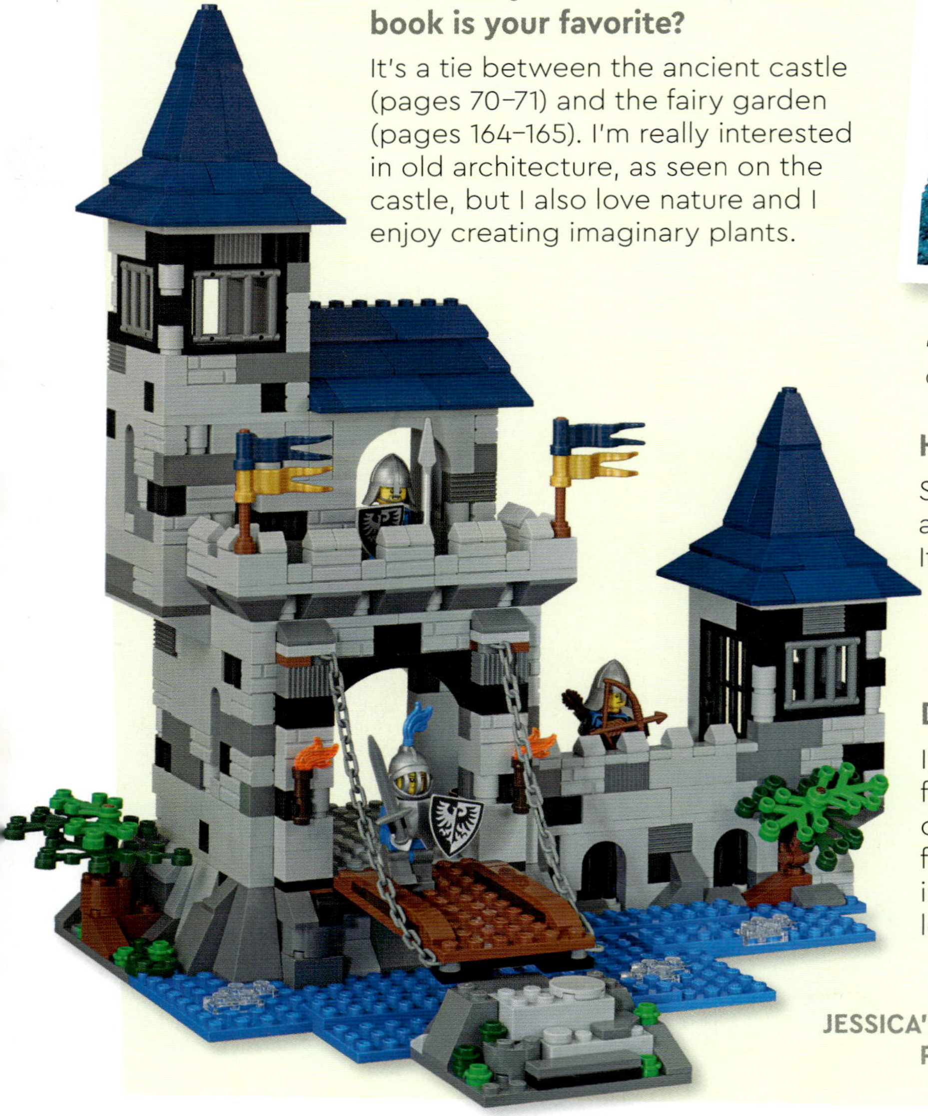

JESSICA'S ANCIENT CASTLE, PAGES 70–71

ROD GILLIES

BUILDER BIO

Location:
Edinburgh, Scotland
Day job:
Marketer and innovator
LEGO speciality:
Microscale and steampunk builds

Which of your models in this book is your favorite?

My microscale landmarks—particularly Sydney Harbour Bridge and the Opera House (far below). I love microscale building, but it can be a real challenge. I built those landmarks over and over again, stripping them back and simplifying them until they were just right.

The *Atlantica*—Rod's steampunk-style submarine inspired by the works of author Jules Verne.

How old were you when you started building with LEGO pieces?

I started LEGO building when I was seven or eight, then, like many people, I stopped building during my teens and 20s. However, I rediscovered my love of building when I had my own kids—they loved it, although probably not quite as much as I do!

What do you do when a build doesn't go according to plan?

I put it to one side for a while and build something else. Eventually inspiration will strike and you'll think of the technique you need or a way to make the model work, then you'll take another look at it. The important thing is not to get frustrated. Creativity is rarely a smooth path from inspiration to completion!

What do you love most about building with LEGO pieces?

I love having a creative medium for such a huge variety of subjects. And you can share all that creative variety within a friendly and welcoming online community of fans.

If you could design a new LEGO set for the LEGO Group, what would it be?

A large-scale set of the *Nautilus* submarine from Jules Verne's *Twenty Thousand Leagues Under the Sea*. It's one of my favorite books and films. Someday I might give it a try, but it would be an ambitious project—at minifigure scale, it could end up 6 ft (1.8 m) long!

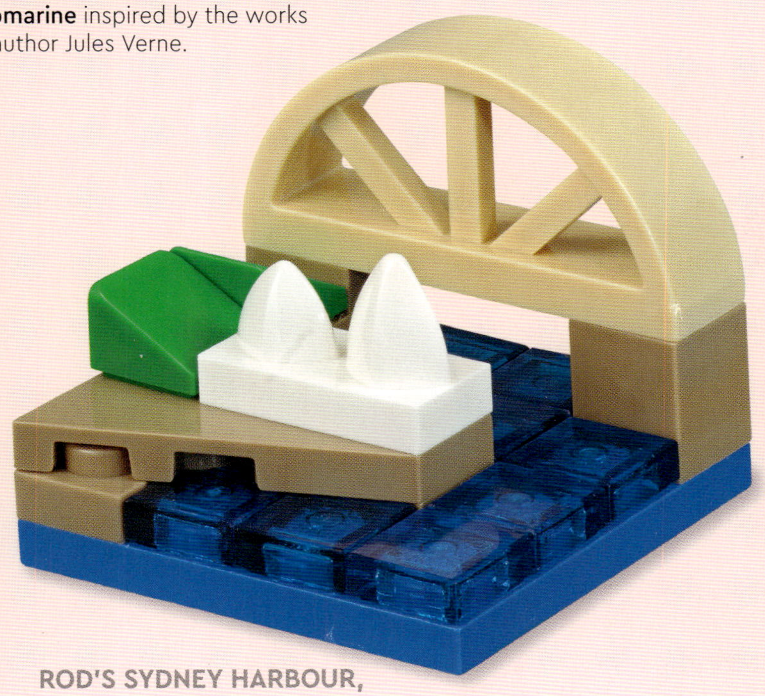

ROD'S SYDNEY HARBOUR, PAGE 54

BUILDER BIO

Location:
London, UK
Day job:
Manager of an analytical chemistry laboratory
LEGO speciality:
Robots, spaceships—anything futuristic

TIM GODDARD

Which of your models in this book is your favorite?

I really like the galactic gym (pages 78–81), which was the first thing I built for this book. It's an exciting mix of a real sports center on Earth with alien athletes thrown in! It has so many fun details like a working vending machine, a shower, and lots of exercise equipment to help the aliens keep fit.

What LEGO element is your favorite?

At the moment, it is the ingot element. That part originally only came in gold to represent a gold bar but it's now available in all sorts of colors. It can be used to make interesting walls, floor details, or roof tiles. It's also very useful for adding futuristic features to robots and spaceships, especially in white and gray.

TEAL (Technical Engineer Assistant Laborer)—one of Tim's awesome space mechs.

Where do you get your LEGO building ideas from?

Ideas come from all over the place. Sometimes a new part will inspire me to build something, and other times a film, art book, or computer game might spark my imagination.

What do you do when a build doesn't go according to plan?

That's an easy one: I just take off the bit that isn't working and try something else! That is what is great about LEGO building—you can easily remove something you don't like. Trial and error is all part of the building process.

What are you building at the moment?

A massive, six-wheeled space explorer rover! It will have a living area at the front and a spaceship landing pad at the back. It will take me a few weeks to finish. If at some points I'm not happy with how it looks, I'll stop building for a few days until a new idea comes to me, then I'll start building it again.

SHOWERING ALIEN AT TIM'S GALACTIC GYM, PAGE 80

BARNEY MAIN

BUILDER BIO

Location:
Swindon, UK
Day job:
Design engineer
LEGO speciality:
Remote-controlled battling robots!

Which of your models for this book is your favorite?

The hot-air balloon on page 61. I built a similar model for the original LEGO® *Ideas Book* (published in 2011) and I have seen lots of models inspired by it over the years. The new version is slightly smaller and more of a light bulb shape, and it has more adventure-themed details!

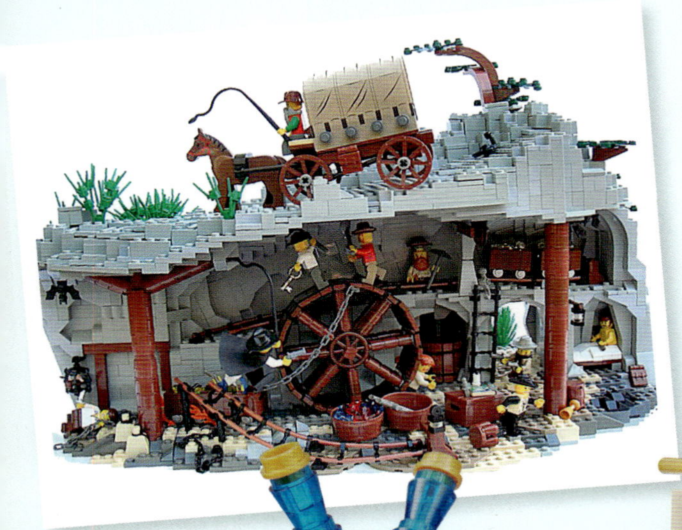

A rootin'-tootin' underground cowboy mine by Barney.

If you were a minifigure, which of your builds in this book would you most like to try out?

The judging panel mechanisms on the TV talent show model (pages 50–51) are so much fun to play with. I'd definitely get the fish!

Do you remember the first LEGO set you had?

Pirate's Treasure Surprise (set 1747, released in 1996)—it's a small island with a pirate and a rock that opens to reveal a stash of treasure. It's simple but wonderful!

BARNEY'S MEDIEVAL BAND, PAGES 74–75

What do you do when a build doesn't go according to plan?

I don't take it apart! It's handy to have a pile of half-finished models that can be mixed up into something new. The wizard's wand (left) was left over from another model, but it fitted so much better with the medieval band.

What are you building at the moment?

I've been building a life-size robotic Roman gladiator for a few years. I'm not sure it will ever be finished! It's full of motors and electronics to make it move, but the neck keeps getting stuck at strange angles and making grinding noises.

BRICK TYPES

By now, you probably know that there are lots of different kinds of LEGO® pieces. But do you know what they are called? It can be useful to know more about the LEGO pieces in your collection, but you don't need all of these parts to build great LEGO models. You can be creative with the pieces you do have.

Small parts and small balls can cause choking if swallowed. Not for children under 3 years.

MEASUREMENTS

The size of a LEGO® piece is described by the number of studs it has. For example, a brick that has two studs along and three studs up is called a 2×3 brick. Tall parts have a third number, which is the height of the piece in standard bricks.

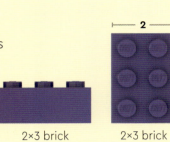

2×3 brick (side view)

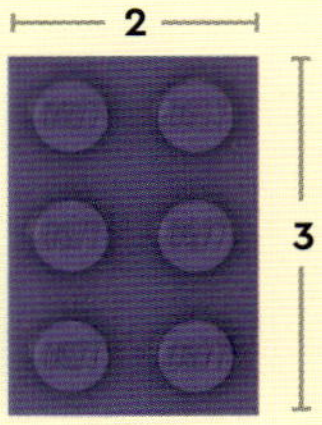
2
3

2×3 brick (top view)

1

1×1×3 brick

1×2 jumper plate

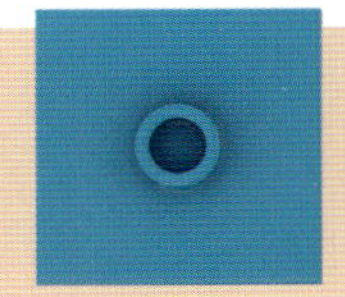

2×2 jumper plate

JUMPER PLATES

These plates have only one stud in the middle, but they follow the same measurement system as standard plates. Jumper plates let you "jump" the usual grid of LEGO studs. They are useful for centering things in your models.

BRICKS

Where would builders be without this essential element? Bricks are the basis of most builds. They come in many shapes, sizes, and colors.

2×2×3 brick

1×2 ridged brick

2×2 round brick

2×2 corner brick

1×2 textured (masonry) brick

TILES

Tiles have tubes on the bottom but no studs on top. They can give your builds a smooth finish, while printed tiles can add interesting details to your models.

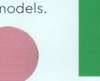

1×1 printed round tile

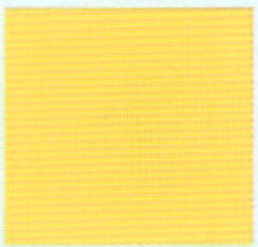

2×2 tile

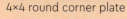

2×2 round tile

1×4 tile

PLATES

Plates are similar to bricks. They have studs on top and tubes on the bottom, but plates are thinner. Three stacked plates are the same height as one standard brick.

4×4 round corner plate

Three 1×2 plates

1×2 brick

2×3 curved plate with hole

THERE ARE MORE THAN 150 SHADES OF LEGO PIECES IN THE WORLD!

SIDE STUDS

If you want to build in multiple directions, choose a piece with studs on more than one side. These parts let you build upward as well as outward.

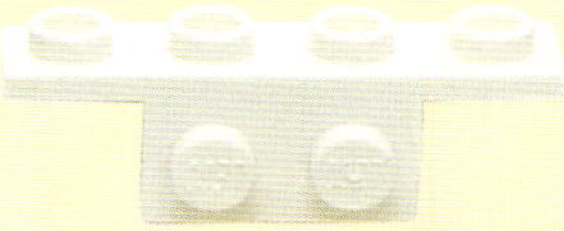

1×4/1×2 bracket plate

1×1 brick with one side stud

1×1 headlight brick

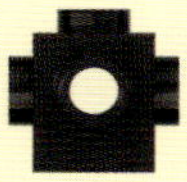

1×1 brick with four side studs

1×2/2×2 bracket plate (side view)

CLIPS

Pieces with clips can attach to other elements, such as bars.

1×2 plate with clip

1×1 plate with clip

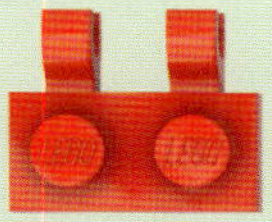

1×2 plate with two clips

1×1 tile with clip

2×3 tile with two clips

7×3 ladder with two clips

BARS

These long, thin pieces are just the right size to fit in a minifigure's hand. They can also be used with clips to add movement to your builds.

1×1 plate with bar

1×2 plate with bar

Bar with stopper

JOINTS

Plates and bricks with tow balls and sockets can make flexible, movable connections on your builds.

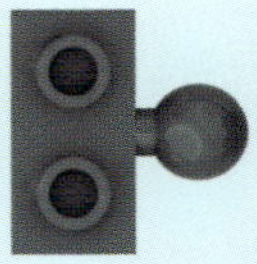

1×2 plate with tow ball

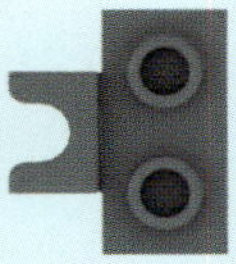

1×2 plate with tow ball socket

2×2 brick with two tow balls

SLOPES

Slope bricks have diagonal angles. They come in many sizes and they can be curved or inverted (upside down).

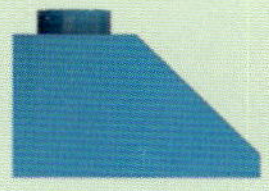

2×1 slope brick

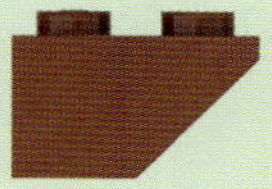

2×1 inverted slope brick

3×1 curved slope

HINGES

You can add different types of motion to your builds with hinge pieces. Adding hinge plates and hinge bricks to your models will allow them to move from side to side or to tilt up and down.

1×4 hinge plate

1×2 hinge brick with 2×2 hinge plate

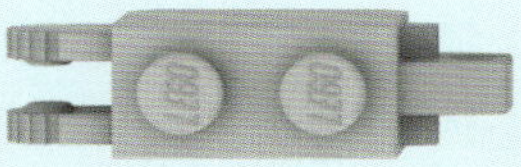

1×2 click hinge brick (top view)

1×2 hinge brick with 1×2 hinge plate (top view)

LEGO® TECHNIC

These eclectic elements expand the range of functions you can build into your models. They are particularly useful for builds with lots of moving parts or technical details.

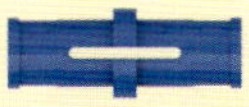

friction pin

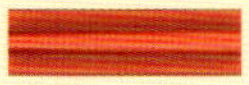

axle

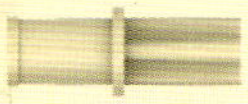

axle pin

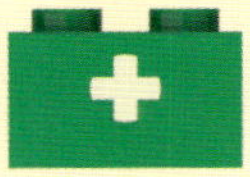

1×2 brick with axle hole

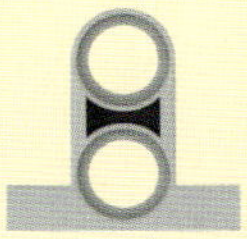

1×2×1²⁄₃ pin connector plate with two holes

axle connector

axle with ball joint

1×3 beam

axle and pin connector

angled axle and pin connector

USEFUL PIECES

All LEGO® pieces are helpful when it comes to making models, but there are some parts that are extra handy to have when you're making something specific, such as a vehicle or an animal. These particularly useful parts are grouped by model type. Do you have any in your collection?

VEHICLES

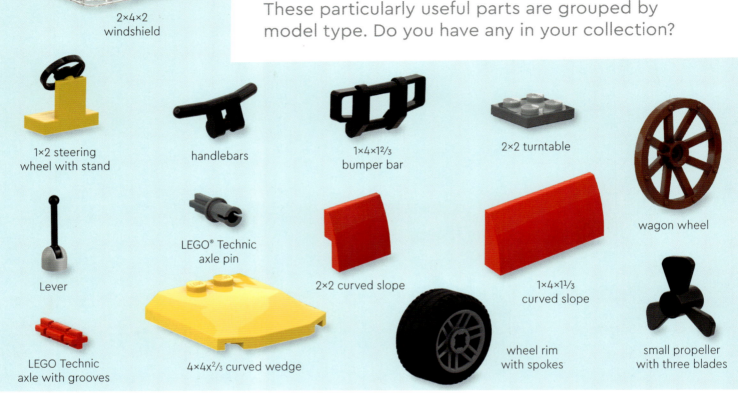

2×4×2 windshield

1×2 steering wheel with stand

handlebars

1×4×1⅔ bumper bar

2×2 turntable

wagon wheel

Lever

LEGO® Technic axle pin

2×2 curved slope

1×4×1⅓ curved slope

small propeller with three blades

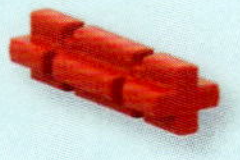

LEGO Technic axle with grooves

4×4x⅔ curved wedge

wheel rim with spokes

ANIMALS

medium horn

small horn

angled axle connector

angled axle and pin connector

printed LEGO Technic ball

1×1 printed round tile

1×2 plate with three teeth

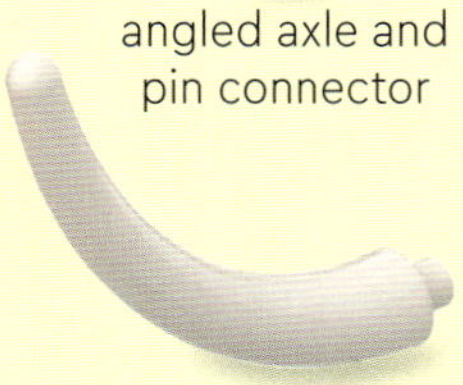

dinosaur tail end

unicorn horn

1×1 plate with vertical tooth

1×1 slope

1×1 plate with horizontal tooth

2×2 round plate with octagonal bar

2×2 brick with click hinge finger

click hinge cylinder with axle hole

1×2 rounded plate

mechanical claw

BUILDINGS

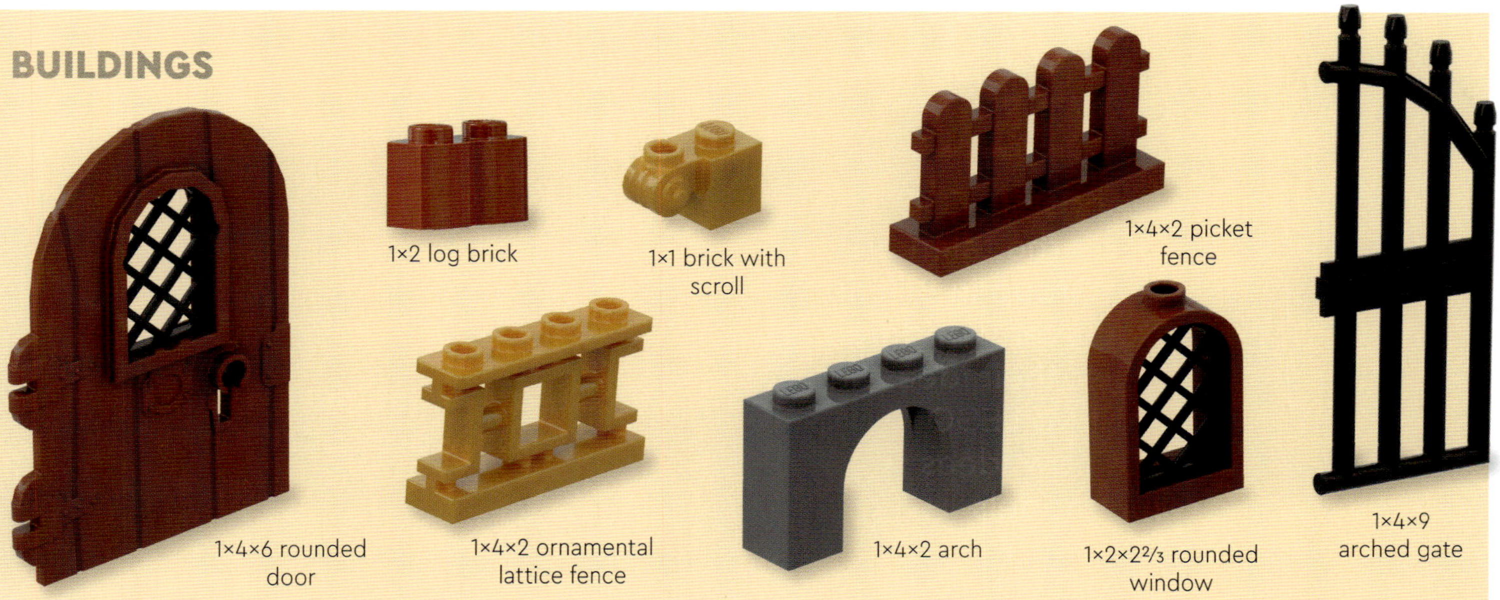

1×4×6 rounded door
1×2 log brick
1×1 brick with scroll
1×4×2 picket fence
1×4×2 ornamental lattice fence
1×4×2 arch
1×2×2⅔ rounded window
1×4×9 arched gate

PLANTS AND TREES

2×2×4 prickly bush
palm-tree top
6×5 swordleaf plant
seaweed
plant stem with three leaves
2×2 ridged round brick
1×5×4 arch
four-scoop ice cream
curly plant stem
1×1 round plate with three leaves
flower stem with six stems
coral

DECORATIONS

4×1 wave flag
whip
1×1 round plate with petals
2×2 round tile
plume
SQUAWK!
1×1 round plate with swirl
parrot
1×1 jewel
bulb with bar
2×2 round plate with gear teeth
ski pole

FROM IDEAS TO LEGO® MODELS

Over the years, thousands of LEGO® sets have been made by the talented designers at the LEGO Group in Billund, Denmark. But have you ever wondered where the designers get their ideas and inspiration from? Meet two LEGO designers and find out how ideas become the awesome models you get to play with!

Lauren Cullen King, Senior Graphic Designer

George Gilliatt, Designer

How did you become a LEGO® designer?

Lauren: After graduating from college in the US, I kept in touch with many of my professors. One day, one of them posted a link to an ad for a graphic design job at the LEGO Group on social media. I decided to take a chance and apply for it, and here I am!

George: While I was studying product design in college in the UK, I became an intern at the LEGO Group. I started off designing new LEGO elements and play experiences as part of the Creative Play Lab, before moving to a second internship in the Creator 3-in-1 team. After that, I went back to college for one more year to finish off my degree before being offered a job as a LEGO product designer.

What is the best part of your job? What's the worst part? Why?

Lauren: The best part of my job is that I get to work with an amazing group of creative people from all over the world. Plus, drawing every day is a big perk for me personally. I would say the most challenging thing is to be living far away from my friends and family back in the US. Thankfully, we are able to keep in touch over the phone and through social media.

George: The best part is reading people's feedback on the products I've helped to design, and hearing from fans of all ages who have been inspired by them. Hopefully, the LEGO products we're producing now will inspire the builders of tomorrow. I also hope that something like the LEGO® Creator Space Shuttle Adventure (set 31117) will make children believe that one day they can be astronauts!

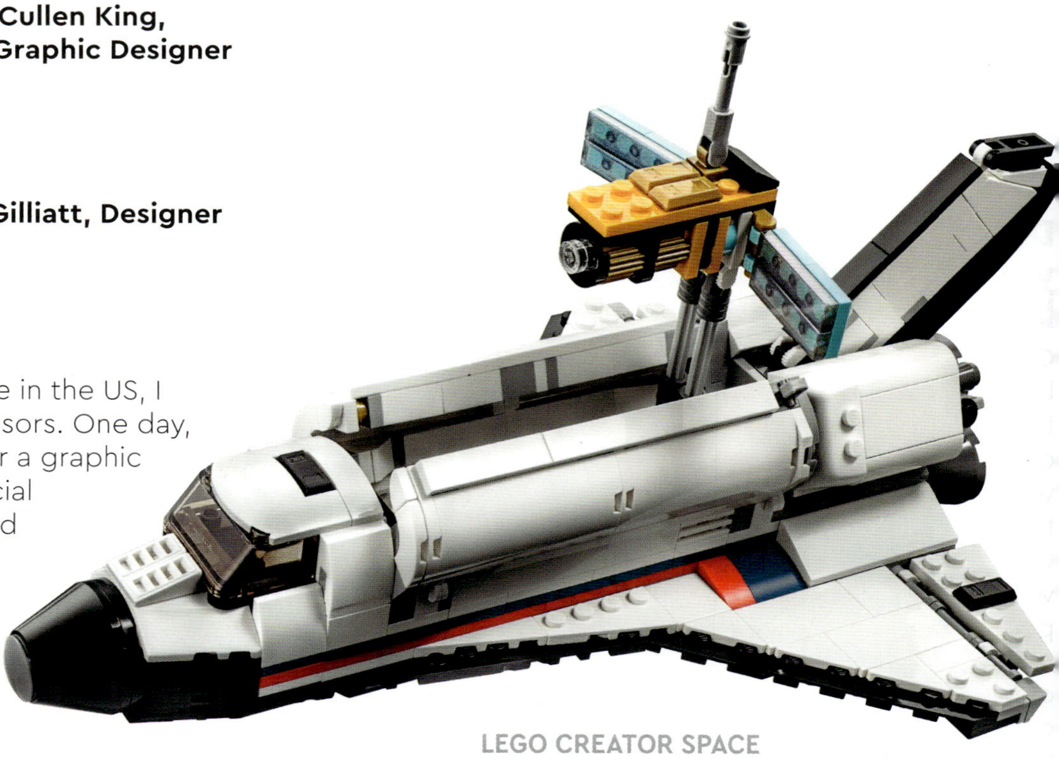

LEGO CREATOR SPACE SHUTTLE ADVENTURE

TECHNIC

LEGO BIONICLE KOPAKA

When did you start building with LEGO pieces?

George: The first-ever LEGO set I owned was the LEGO® BIONICLE® Kopaka (set 8536) from 2001. It got me hooked on construction toys, and I haven't stopped building them since then!

George's UFO pyramid, which made it to the quarter-finals of a 2011 building contest when he was a teenager.

Do you have a favorite model you made using LEGO pieces before becoming a designer?

George: When I was 13, I started entering online building competitions (with my parent's permission) that allowed some of the world's best LEGO designers to show off their skills. My favorite creation was a model that combined two existing LEGO themes: LEGO® Alien Conquest and LEGO® Pharaoh's Quest. I created a giant UFO pyramid! This model was so special to me because the picture I posted of it online included me in it—and it was only at that point that everyone else in the contest (who were all adults) realized that they were competing against a teenager! It made me realize that you can achieve anything you want, regardless of age, if you dedicate yourself to it and work hard.

What was the first model you designed or helped to design? What lessons have you learned about building sets since then?

Lauren: The first set I created graphics for was the LEGO® Juniors Family House (set 10686). Most of the decorated minifigure parts I designed are still used in other sets today!

George: The first LEGO product I got to be a part of the development of was LEGO Riverside Houseboat (set 31093), designed by Gemma Anderson. Gemma taught me so much about designing an official LEGO product, and I had so much fun coming up with what the alternate models could be and discovering how to design a fun, strong, buildable model.

LEGO JUNIORS FAMILY HOUSE

LEGO RIVERSIDE
HOUSEBOAT

How many people does it take to make one idea into a LEGO set?

George: It takes a lot of talented people to make one idea into a LEGO set. Besides the designer(s) of the set, a graphic designer, like Lauren, will be involved if the product has any decorations. In addition, project managers and product leads make sure the products are produced on time and to budget. There are also packaging designers and marketers, and, of course, the people who run the factories that produce all the LEGO elements. It's a real team effort!

Where do the ideas for LEGO sets come from?

George: Lots of different places. Sometimes our managers will give us a brief, other times fans will submit ideas to us, and now and then we might just come up with a cool idea ourselves!

Are you sometimes inspired by models built by fans?

Lauren: Yes, our engaged and creative fans create such amazing models, and that is inspiring! I like to look for the little details that the fans notice. Sometimes they capture something that I might have missed.

Do LEGO fans ever get involved in LEGO set design? For example, do LEGO fans ever test out new set designs?

George: Every new LEGO set is tested out by some of the best fans of all—children! We always put the models in the hands of the children because they will usually be the ones building and playing with the sets at the end of the process, and they will always spot things to improve that we as adults miss.

Lauren: Through the LEGO® Ideas website, fans can submit set ideas. If 10,000 other fans like it and it is approved by LEGO judges, we get to work with the fan designer to bring their concept to life!

Can you walk us through the process of transforming an idea into a LEGO set?

George: I always begin a new LEGO set by doing my own research on what I need to build so that I can become an expert on that subject. For example, when designing the LEGO Creator Majestic Tiger (set 31129), I watched a lot of video footage of tigers and learned all about where and how they live. The next step is to build a concept model, to get a rough idea of what the model will look like. The model will then be refined over several months before it's in its final form.

What are some of the challenges along the way?

George: Sometimes it's tricky to replicate a shape with LEGO pieces, or things fall apart because they are not strong enough. In most cases, somebody else will have faced the same challenge as you, so it always helps to talk about any issues and ask for help. That way, we can deal with them together as a team.

Do LEGO designers have to follow lots of building rules?

Lauren: As a graphic designer at the LEGO Group, I have lots of LEGO guidelines and rules to follow when creating characters, decorations, and stickers. Then, of course, we also have production, quality, and safety standards that need to be adhered to.

George: Yes! We have to ensure that every LEGO set experience complies with our brand's ethos and meets the abilities of the builders of particular sets or themes. LEGO sets can be passed down through generations of family members, so we need to make sure they have longevity, they're safe, and they're the best product they can be.

What tips do you have for budding LEGO set creators?

George: Build, unbuild, rebuild . . . My favorite thing to do as a child was to rebuild my sets into as many other things as I could. The natural limitations that come with using a restricted selection of pieces really inspires creativity and forces you to use the bricks and elements in interesting ways. Challenge yourself to come up with something completely new!

LEGO
CREATOR
9+
31129
3 IN 1
CREATOR

LEGO CREATOR MAJESTIC TIGER

DK Penguin Random House

Senior Editor Tori Kosara
Project Editor Beth Davies
Senior Designer Anna Formanek
Production Editor Siu Yin Chan
Senior Production Controller Lloyd Robertson
Managing Editor Paula Regan
Managing Art Editor Jo Connor
Publishing Director Mark Searle

Packaged for DK by Plum Jam
Editor Hannah Dolan **Designer** Guy Harvey

Inspirational models built by
Jessica Farrell, Tim Goddard, Jason Briscoe, Rod Gillies, Barney Main, Mariann Asanuma, and Nate Dias
Rainbow bus model based on a design by
Emmett L., built by Jessica Farrell

Photography by Gary Ombler

Cover design by Mark Penfound

Dorling Kindersley and Plum Jam would like to thank:
Randi Sørensen, Heidi K. Jensen, Lydia Barram, Paul Hansford, Amy Jarashow, Martin Leighton Lindhart, and Nina Koopman at the LEGO Group; Victoria Taylor for additional writing and editorial assistance; Lisa Robb, Karan Chaudhary, Tom Bletso, and James McKeag for design assistance; Laura Gilbert for proofreading; and Megan Douglass for Americanizing.

First American Edition, 2022
Published in the United States by DK Publishing
1745 Broadway, 20th Floor, New York, NY 10019

22 23 24 25 26 10 9 8 7 6 5 4 3 2 1
001-321878-Sep/2022

Manufactured by Dorling Kindersley, One Embassy Gardens, 8 Viaduct Gardens, London SW11 7BW, UK under license from the LEGO Group.

A catalog record for this book is available from the Library of Congress.

ISBN 978-0-7440-6093-5

Printed and bound in China

For the curious

www.dk.com
www.LEGO.com

MIX
Paper | Supporting responsible forestry
FSC™ C018179